Listening

Second Edition

Andrew D. Wolvin
University of Maryland—College Park
and University College

Carolyn Gwynn Coakley
High Point High School
University of Maryland—University College

wcb
Wm. C. Brown Publishers
Dubuque, Iowa

Library of Congress Catalog Card Number: 84–72661

ISBN 0–697–00286–1

Printed in the United States of America
10 9 8 7 6 5 4 3 2 1

Contents

An Instructor's Manual to accompany *Listening,* second edition, is available upon request. It can be obtained by writing the Speech Editor, Wm. C. Brown Company Publishers, 2460 Kerper Boulevard, Dubuque, IA 52001.

Preface

This text is intended for those who want to understand the nature of listening in the process of human communication. It is designed for students who wish to understand (and improve) their own behaviors as receivers in many dimensions.

As communication scholars and educators focus on interpersonal communication and reading behaviors of students, the responsibilities of the receiver as an equal partner in the communication process become clear. Yet most of the literature and research in this field stress the source and disregard the role of the listener. Analysis of communication time supports the idea that most people spend more time listening than speaking, reading, and writing. Thus, listening is significant.

Interest in listening is evident in college and university courses, in units in basic speech communication courses, and in a wide variety of programs developing in language arts and reading in elementary and secondary schools. Many corporate and industrial organizations have added listening training to their programs for employees.

Communication scholars recognize the difficulty in identifying precisely what is involved in the skills of listening behavior.[1] Much of this difficulty lies in the problem of testing these skills. An emphasis on comprehension in such tests makes one wonder if we are pinpointing *listening* skills or testing *thinking* (and memory) skills.

While it is difficult to determine precisely the difference between listening and thinking, instruction in listening skills can yield benefits. We once assumed that knowing how to organize a speech would enable a person to prepare and present it and to listen with comprehension to the speeches of others. Such an assumption about transferring skills may be hasty. Students testify that learning about listening skills in their academic lives is useful in undoing old habits and replacing them with improved listening practices.

The principles in this book are drawn from research in the field of listening behavior as well as from a variety of disciplines: speech communication, reading, psychology, education, and sociology. The research provides the foundation for both the theoretical and the practical aspects which are incorporated into the book.

This book is designed to provide students with a foundation in the theory and research concerning the process of listening as the basis for knowing about listening behavior and, then, applying that knowledge to development of their own skills. To that end, our consideration begins with a view of listening as a *communication* skill within the context of the entire human communication process. The reader is introduced in chapters 1–4 to the specific functions essential to our understanding of listening behavior.

In addition, the reader is introduced to decisions which the responsible listener must make, strategies that the skilled listener must utilize, and factors which the knowledgeable listener must consider in order to assume—along with the speaker—equal participation in and equal responsibility for effective communication transactions. These chapters are followed with chapters which treat different listening purposes—discriminative, comprehensive, therapeutic, critical, and appreciative. These chapters are designed to provide readers with an understanding about their listening responses to these different objectives and with some ideas as to enhancing their own skills within these areas.

While an understanding about listening is critical to improving one's own listening behavior, we also think it is useful to know about the primary role of listening in human communication (as treated in our first chapter) and to reflect on individual listening skills as we function in different roles at various communication levels. To that end, we have developed Chapter 10 to furnish the reader with an understanding of how listeners function in a variety of listening roles (in conversation, interviewing, teleconferencing, etc.) at the intrapersonal, interpersonal, and public levels of communication.

In this second edition of our book, we have provided the reader with significant recent contributions to the research and theory in listening behavior. The communication field is a very dynamic area; every day scholars provide us with new information and new insights. As a result, our comprehension of listening as a communication behavior has been revised and has become more sophisticated as the study of listening itself has developed. Much of this new insight is the result of efforts of the International Listening Association, which has drawn attention to the need for research and training in listening and has provided an important network for teachers and scholars of listening to join together and share their interests and understanding.

The second edition of this book, then, incorporates a more detailed discussion of discriminative listening through nonverbal communication channels. We also have furnished additional data concerning techniques for recall of information, including memory development and notetaking. Likewise, our discussion of therapeutic listening, reflecting current insights into this special type of behavior, has been revised. The reader will note, too, that we have restructured the book so that the first type of audition to be treated is discriminative listening. Since auditory and visual discrimination forms the foundation for effective listening at the other levels, we feel it is essential that the reader first understand the principles of listening discriminately. Furthermore, throughout the book, we have presented updated information, new examples, and a reordering of much of the material. Finally, at the end of each chapter, we have included additional activities designed to enable the reader to apply to his or her listening behavior the principles of effective listening described. These activities can be used by individual readers or by groups in classroom settings. We hope that you will agree that these revisions produce a more effective book which reflects the field of listening as it has developed since our first edition in 1982.

The reader also should note that the authors have designed an *Instructor's Resource Manual* to accompany this text. This manual, which is available from William C. Brown Company Publishers to instructors adopting this book as a classroom text, in itself represents a detailed work dealing with listening pedagogy. The manual includes syllabi, objectives, test questions, many additional activities designed for classroom use, as well as descriptions of recommended films, published listening tests, and the International Listening Association.

We are encouraged by the great interest in listening behavior which we encounter both in academic institutions and in the corporate world. The dedication to improved listening is a commitment which can improve communication in all aspects of our personal and professional lives. We are pleased to have the opportunity to contribute to the improvement of communication in the lives of our readers with *Listening,* which is one of the first revised editions of a book on this subject.

Both *Listening* and the *Instructor's Resource Manual* have been designed for all who have the desire to grow; for through listening, we can grow as individuals and in our relationships with others.

NOTES

1. For a review of this issue, see Robert N. Bostrom and Carol L. Bryant, "Factors in the Retention of Information Presented Orally: The Role of Short-term Listening," *Western Journal of Speech Communication,* 44 (Spring, 1980): 137–145.

Acknowledgments

Preparing a book requires the assistance and support of many people. We are especially grateful to Jim Coakley and Darlyn Wolvin for their patience, understanding, and empathic listening throughout the process. We express our appreciation to Brad and Brooke Wolvin, nine-year-old twins pictured on page 124, who consistently demonstrate that skills in good listening *can* be developed at an early age. We likewise are indebted to our listening students at High Point High School, the University of Maryland at College Park and at University College, and at the U.S. Department of State Foreign Service Institute. Their ideas, interests, and responses have helped to shape our thoughts about listening and have given us the framework for these ideas. We appreciate the support and encouragement we have received from our colleagues in the newly formed International Listening Association. Interaction in this professional association provides us with a stimulating forum of listening scholars, teachers, and practitioners.

Readers familiar with our earlier work, *Listening Instruction* issued by the ERIC Clearinghouse on Reading and Communication Skills, will recognize some of our ideas about the process of listening. We appreciate the support of William Work, Director of the ERIC Speech Communication Association Module, in the development of this text.

We are grateful to all who have used this book, throughout the country and, indeed, throughout the world, for the substantial amount of constructive feedback that you have given to us on this project. We appreciate knowing the strengths of this book, and we have exerted considerable effort to adapt those areas of the book which our readers believed should be changed. We hope that you will continue to provide us with feedback, an essential component of true communication, whether oral or written.

Additionally, we are grateful to our photographer, Bob Tocha, and our illustrators, Ted Metzger, president of Visual Technics, Inc., and Neal Ashby, recipient of the Maryland Distinguished Scholar in Visual Arts award. All three willingly shared with us their time and creativity.

No book can be produced without the unfailing editorial support we have received from William C. Brown Company Publishers. Our editor, Judith A. Clayton, and our reviewers have played a major role in putting this book in final form.

Finally, we want to thank you, our readers, for your interest in listening and for your dedication to improving your own listening skills. We think that effective listening should be a major communication objective for everyone.

Concepts You Will Encounter

Hearing without Listening
Tuning Out
Listening with Understanding
Basic Language Skill
Verbal Communication Time
Listening's Role
Mass Media Demands
Listening's Influence
Two-Step Flow of Communication
Diffusion of Innovation
Multistep Flow of Communication
Rewards of Effective Listening
Listening Instruction
Costliness of Poor Listening

The Need for Effective Listening 1

"Is anyone *really* listening?" is a question that is too frequently asked in an age when so much of our communication is done orally. Unfortunately, many people fail to realize that *meaningful* oral communication is a result of *both* the sending *and* the receiving of messages. If only our ears were as actively involved as our mouths, our failure to listen would not be such a vital concern to so many individuals.

Our Failure to Listen

Daily, individuals, ranging from singers and cartoonists to business executives and counselors, are calling attention to our failure to listen. Let us examine what some of these individuals are saying about this problem which is so prevalent in our society.

In the song, "The Sounds of Silence," Paul Simon has written

> And in the naked light I saw
> Ten thousand people, maybe more—
> People talking without speaking,
> People hearing without listening. . . .[1]

Who is hearing without listening? Nation to nation? The young to the old? The old to the young? Child to parent? Parent to child? Employer to employee? Employee to employer? Husband to wife? Wife to husband? We cannot say that these people are not listening to each other merely because they do not agree with one another on various issues, for listening does not mean agreeing.[2] Listening means engaging in three separate but interrelated steps: hearing; attending to the speaker; and making a sincere effort to understand what the speaker is saying.

Too frequently we do not engage in the total listening process; instead, we mechanically or mentally tune out the speaker. The practice of mechanically tuning out the speaker can be seen in the person who, rejecting all "handouts," changes the television channel when a welfare agent begins to speak. A much more common practice, mentally tuning out the speaker or "closing our earlids",

Listening—truly listening—involves more than just hearing.
Photo by Robert Tocha.

is illustrated in this cartoon caption: A husband, looking at his wife, says "Go ahead. Keep talking, Martha; I've tuned you out."[3] Mentally tuning out the speaker also is demonstrated in the following human interest article:

> Communication . . . requires . . . listening carefully and trying to understand the message of others.
>
> We need to do less talking and more listening.
>
> One schoolboy said to another, "My teacher talks to herself."
>
> His friend replied, "That's nothing. So does our principal, but he doesn't know it. He thinks everybody's listening."[4]

Many scholars who investigate listening believe that our failure to listen too often stems from a lack of "model" listening behavior from those whom we tend to imitate. If those in the positions to be role models, for example, parents and teachers, do not demonstrate effective listening behavior, it is unlikely that children and students will develop effective listening behavior. The following impressive public service announcement illustrates a type of listening behavior that far too many children encounter:

> A father is reading a newspaper when his son enters the room and says, "Hey, Pop? Can I talk to you?"
>
> The father, never looking up from the paper, says, "Sure, what is it?"
>
> First, the son discusses school; he says, "I'm gonna be short some credits for graduation, and I'm going to need to go to summer school."

> Dad, who is obviously not listening, responds by saying, "That's good."
> The son then makes a second attempt to gain his father's attention. He says, "You know, I think I'll drop out of school, Pop. I'm not going anywhere."
> Dad, still reading his paper, mutters, "Well, whattaya know?"
> Finally, the son says, "Say, I took my first trip today. That acid. Man, was it groovy."
> Dad replies, "Okay. Whatever you think's best."
> The son leaves, and the mother enters the room. She asks what the son had said. Dad replies, "Oh, it wasn't important."[5]

But, it was important—important to the son, who did not want his father to be one of those people who hear but do not listen. Likewise, having parents who listen was important to another child who, finding no listeners at home, left this note to his parents before he packed up his problems and ran away: "If anyone asks you where I am, tell them I've gone looking for someone with time because I've got a lot of things I want to talk about."[6] In this note, this child calls attention to another important listening factor that "role models" too frequently are unwilling to give: their time. When we consider, for example, that research shows that the average family with teenagers spends only about 14½ minutes a day engaging in parent-child communication—with 12½ of these minutes devoted to the discussion of such topics as "What's for dinner?", "Where's the *TV Guide?*", and "Who's using the car tonight?"—we quickly realize that the remaining 2 minutes spent in communicating openly and forming relationships are hardly adequate.[7]

Just as parents are in a position to be "models" of effective listeners, so are teachers. The importance of teachers presenting themselves as models of desirable listening attitudes, behaviors, and skills is, indeed, emphasized in John Stammer's four-step MAPP (representing Model, Assess, Prepare, and Practice) listening plan, in which he places modeling as the first step that teachers should take in order to help students improve their listening effectiveness.[8] Unfortunately, like some parents, certain teachers do not demonstrate "model" listening behavior. In his popular book, *Love,* Leo Buscaglia presents this poignant example of a teacher who hears but does not listen:

> I used to love the idea of "share and tell" in the classroom. I thought this was a time when people would listen. But, you see, someone told the teachers that they had to have their enrollment slips in by 9:05 so they used this time for share and tell. Little kids went up and said, "Last night my daddy hit my mommy with the rolling pin and knocked out two front teeth, and the ambulance came and took her away, and she's in the hospital." And the teacher looked up and said, "All right, who's next?" Or the little kid came up and showed teacher a rock, "I found a rock on the way to school today." She said, "Fine, Johnny, put it on the science table." I wonder what would happen if she picked up the rock and said, "Let me see the rock. Look at that. Kids, look at the color of that rock. Feel it. Who made a rock? Where does a rock come from? What's a rock? What kind of rock is this?"[9]

We wonder, too. We wonder whether Johnny will react in the same way that his teacher did when Johnny is an adult and his child or his student shares a rock with him. Without role models of effective listening behavior, he just might react in the same way.

Executives of major corporations also are recognizing an almost universal failure to listen. They are beginning to realize that inefficient listening is costly to corporations—costly in wasted money, misused time, deflated morale, reduced productivity, and alienated relationships. Moreover, inefficient listening in business is costly to consumers, as J. Paul Lyet, chairman and chief executive of the Sperry Corporation, notes: "Poor listening is one of the most significant problems facing business today. Business relies on its communications system, and when it breaks down, mistakes can be very costly. Corporations pay for their mistakes in lower profits, while consumers pay in higher prices."[10] Recognizing the costliness of poor listening, both within and outside the corporation, Sperry made listening a part of its management philosophy, adopted the corporate advertising theme, "We understand how important it is to listen,"[11] and then introduced its theme to the public on September 11, 1979, when it launched a new advertising campaign. The first series of advertisements, stressing the costliness of ineffective listening, began with an ad headlined by "It's about time we learned how to listen."[12] At the bottom of each printed ad and at the end of each televised release, the corporate theme appeared. Besides this, in small print at the bottom of many of the printed ads, the reader was invited to write to Sperry for a listening quiz or booklet. Then, on March 31, 1981, a second series of advertisements, which stresed the rewards of effective listening, began with an ad headlined by "The risks and rewards of listening well."[13] Since 1979 when Sperry's commitment to effective listening was first made known to the general public, the corporation has spent $10 million on its listening research and advertising campaign.[14] The results of this costly campaign, according to Kenneth F. Thompson, Sperry's group executive vice president, have been "far greater than any of us anticipated—very, very positive all the way through."[15] Outside the corporation, Sperry's name has become more widely known in a positive way, as the campaign has generated much interest in listening. For example, during the first series of ads, more than 25,000 individuals contacted Sperry to inquire about speakers and program ideas on listening;[16] and from 1979 through 1983, Sperry distributed over half a million listening quizzes and booklets to those who requested them.[17] In addition, many company presidents and business groups have contacted Sperry to request information on listening.[18] Indeed, the vast response to Sperry's advertising campaign indicates that, as Sperry's Director of International Communications, J. Peter Hynes, has declared, there is a "tremendous thirst for listening."[19]

For years, psychotherapists, religious leaders, and counselors have emphasized that many of our relationships deteriorate because we do not listen. Rogers, a psychotherapist, believes that the major barrier to communication is our tendency to react to a statement by forming an evaluation of it from our own point of view. Rogers believes that this barrier can be avoided if we listen to one another with understanding. Listening with understanding requires that the listener make a sincere attempt "to see the expressed idea and attitude from the other person's point of view, to sense how it feels to him, to achieve his frame of reference in regard to the thing he is talking about."[20] The need to listen with understanding is also being communicated by the clergy and by counselors. In the midst of a wedding ceremony we attended, the priest advised the young couple always to keep the channels of communication open, always to listen to one another, and never to build a wall between them. He further stressed that marriage counselors have found that the inability to listen ranks high on the list of qualities that make a marriage fail.[21] A recent study by Holman and Burr of Brigham Young University further confirms the previous findings of marriage counselors. The 57 married couples surveyed reported that communication—covering the ability to talk out problems without defensiveness or emotional outbursts and the willingness to listen to another point of view—is the most important factor in marriage.[22]

The importance of listening, however, extends beyond listening to spouses. According to Sherod Miller, co-author of *Straight Talk,* listening is important in all relationships: "The ability to send clear messages, to be heard and understood, is central to any ongoing relationship—husband and wife, parent and child, employer and employee, friends, siblings, you name it."[23] Miller's clause, "you name it," can refer to many individuals outside of our family, professional, and social lives. It can refer to our clergy, lawyers, political representatives, members of civic organizations to which we belong, insurance agents—in fact, all those with whom we have the need to share vital concerns. It certainly includes physicians, who quite frequently play very significant roles in our lives. Unfortunately, according to the results of a study conducted at the Presbyterian Medical Center in Denver, many physicians do not listen carefully to their patients.[24] Yet, in the view of psychiatrist Dr. Walt Menninger, many people who need someone to listen to them desperately turn to physicians, who are not always the sensitive listeners whom the patients need:

> In my work as a psychiatrist, I sense again and again the desperate feelings of people who feel no one respects what they have to say. . . . Often, people's physical ills are a disguised message, a "ticket of admission" to see someone who will listen to a complaint. Regrettably, many doctors don't want to be bothered by anything other than a clear physical problem. Yet, a sensitive doctor realizes some time spent in careful listening will point to a hidden agenda of a patient's concern. And that act of listening can give more relief to a patient than any 10 prescriptions of a tranquilizer.[25]

Indeed, our failure to listen in significant relationships can be quite destructive to the relationships as well as to the individuals in need of effective listeners.

Furthermore, there is evidence that we Americans do not even do well that which we spend so much time doing: listening to and viewing television. In a study sponsored by the Educational Foundation of the American Association of Advertising Agencies, 2,700 subjects viewed two of the sixty 30-second segments of various television broadcasts (news shows, situation comedies, adventure series, mystery shows, public service announcements, and advertisements) that were used in the study. Immediately after viewing, each subject answered six true-false questions relating to information in the segment. The researchers found that the standard range of misunderstanding of all sixty communications tested was between 23 percent and 36 percent and that, overall, viewers answered 29.6 percent of the 32,400 questions incorrectly.[26] Thus, it appears that we even fail to listen effectively to messages that are aired on the medium which we personally choose to listen to during much of our leisure time.

Finally, the most tragic effect that our failure to listen effectively can have is the loss of life. A frequently-cited, yet graphic, example of how poor listening can lead to the deaths of many is the 1977 ground collision of two Boeing 747 jumbo jets in Tenerife, the largest of the Canary Islands. Preparing for takeoff at Tenerife's Los Rodeos Airport, the KLM pilot was told by the tower controllers to taxi eastward up the full length of the runway, make a 180 degree turn, and hold until the plane was given takeoff clearance. Meanwhile, the tower controllers told the Pan American pilot, who also was preparing for takeoff, to follow (about three minutes behind) up the same runway, turn off at the "third intersection" (Ramp C-3), and then to report when his plane had cleared the runway. Taxiing eastward, the Pan Am pilot did not count Ramp C-1 because the crew considered it to be inactive since it was blocked by aircraft; thus, the pilot headed on toward Ramp C-4, which he assumed to be the "third intersection." At the same time, the KLM pilot—rather than holding after he had made his 180 degree turn at the east end of the runway and waiting for takeoff clearance as he had been told to do—rolled westward on the runway for takeoff. Just as the Pan Am plane was approaching Ramp C-4, the KLM plane—at a speed of 186 miles per hour—reached Ramp C-4. The two planes collided in the fog and exploded in flames; 576 lives were lost. Investigators of the accident—the worst, to date, in aviation history—note what would have happened if there had not been listening errors: "If both pilots and the tower controllers had fully heard—and understood—one another, the KLM pilot would never have sent his craft hurtling toward takeoff before the Pam Am plane was off the runway."[27] We might add that if the Pan Am pilot had not assumed that he was not to count Ramp C-1 as one of the intersections and had, instead, asked for clarification from the tower controllers, his plane might have been clear of the runway before the KLM plane reached the "third intersection" (Ramp C-3). Truly, a failure to listen effectively can have devastating effects.

The examples and individuals we have cited have stressed that people frequently do not listen. Do people not listen because listening is unimportant in our society? Because listening proficiency is insignificant in our language development? Because we devote little time to listening in our daily lives? Because the role of listening in our lives is minor? Because listening has little effect or influence on us? Because listening as a skill has not received instructional emphasis in the schools? Let us look at these possibilities.

The Importance of Listening

How important is listening in contemporary society? How do we assess the importance of listening? One way is to examine the position that listening has in our language development. A second way is to determine the amount of time we devote to listening every day. Another approach is to explore the role of listening in our lives. Still another way is to discover the effects or influence that listening has on us. These criteria will be used as we investigate the importance of listening.

Listening's Position in Our Language Development

Of the four major areas of language development, listening is the most basic. Listening is the first language skill which we develop; as children, we listen before we speak, speak before we read, and read before we write.[28] Thus, our ability to speak, read, and write (as well as to master complex cognitive skills, such as reasoning) is directly and indirectly dependent upon our ability to listen. If we are not proficient in any one of these skills, we are handicapped in the processes of learning and communicating, two activities that are necessary in order for us to participate productively in modern life.

Listening's Demands on Our Time

Throughout all levels of our educational development, listening is the main channel of classroom instruction. This can be seen readily, from "Show and Tell" periods at the kindergarten level to two-hour lecture sessions at the graduate level. This also can be substantiated by the amount of time students are expected to listen in the classroom. Wilt found that elementary students are supposed to listen 57.5 percent of their classroom activity time. She also found that of the children's time spent in listening, 54 percent is spent listening to the teacher.[29] Markgraf found that high school students are expected to devote 46 percent of their classroom time to listening, and that 66 percent of this listening time is spent listening to the teacher.[30] At the college level, Bird discovered that college women spend 42 percent of their daily communication time listening. He also found that 82 percent of his subjects considered listening to be equal to or more important than reading as a factor contributing to academic success in college.[31] The results of these studies demonstrate that listening is a major vehicle for learning in the classroom.

The importance of listening in learning and communicating is also apparent in our daily lives. Not only do we spend more time listening than we spend in any other form of verbal communication, but also, thanks to modern technological advancements, we engage in considerable interpersonal communication and mass communication.

In a landmark study dating back to 1926, Rankin—investigating the frequency of use of listening in the ordinary lives of adults—found that listening is the most frequently used form of verbal communication. Adults spend 29.5 percent of their waking hours listening and 42.1 percent of their total verbal communication time listening, while they spend 31.9 percent, 15 percent, and 11 percent of their verbal communication time speaking, reading, and writing.[32] Four more recent investigations have supported Rankin's finding that listening is the most important form of verbal communication in daily life. In 1957 Brieter investigated the frequency of use of listening in the lives of housewives; she found that they spend 48 percent of their verbal communication time listening (followed by speaking, reading, and writing—in that order).[33] In 1974 Weinrauch and Swanda expanded on Rankin's study; they investigated the amount of time that 46 business personnel (including those with top, middle, and lower managerial responsibilities and those with no managerial responsibilities) spend in direct communication (reading, writing, speaking, and listening) during a typical work week. They found that the business participants spend 32.7 percent of their total direct verbal communication time listening, 25.8 percent speaking, 22.6 percent writing, and 18.8 percent reading. Although the percentage of time spent listening is lower in this study than it is in the other cited studies, it must be noted that this study does not include the amount of time the business participants spend listening beyond their working hours.[34] In 1975, Werner conducted an update study of the 1926 Rankin study. Utilizing 166 subjects (including high school and college students, housewives, and employees in a variety of occupations), she found that they spend 54.93 percent of their verbal communication time listening while they spend 23.19 percent, 13.27 percent, and 8.40 percent of their verbal communication time speaking, reading, and writing.[35] In 1977 Barker et al found that college students spend 52.5 percent of their total verbal communication time listening, while they spend 17.3 percent reading, 16.3 percent speaking, and 13.9 percent writing.[36]

In addition to Weinrauch and Swanda, others have investigated the amount of time business personnel spend engaged in listening. For example, Brown reports that most employees of major corporations in North America spend about 60 percent of their day listening,[37] and Keefe reports that executives spend as much as 63 percent of their workday engaged in listening.[38] Considering that business personnel may thus spend up to 63 percent of their time on the job listening, one can see that they are being paid up to 63 percent of their salaries for listening.

Studies investigating the frequency of the function of listening, in and out of the classroom, conclude that listening consumes more of our daily communication time than does any other form of verbal communication. Hence, quantitatively, the most important form of verbal communication is listening, a skill that does not automatically improve with use.

Listening's Role in Our Lives

Because modern technological advances in modes of transportation enable us to gather together as groups with greater ease, the role of listening in interpersonal, as well as in group and public, communicative situations has become more significant in the economic, political, social, mental, and spiritual phases of our lives. Whether the purpose of our coming together is to settle differences between nations (such as the balance of trade talks between the Japanese and the Americans), to investigate a country's affairs (such as the Senate Watergate Hearings), to advance a cause (such as "speak-outs" regarding the MX missile system), to introduce a new product (such as the home computer), to search for or strengthen social ties (such as Parents without Partners' meetings or block parties), listening plays a vital role in our efforts to attain our goals.

Moreover, technological advancements in the miniaturization of electronic circuits have contributed to listening's growing importance in our lives. Miniaturization has played a major role in providing many communication vehicles, among them, cassette tapes/recorders and teleconferences. Small, relatively inexpensive cassette tapes/recorders can now be easily transported (carried or worn, as the Sony Walkman is), installed in vehicles, or included in home entertainment centers. Although we primarily rely on cassette tapes/recorders for listening to music, we also use them for recording lectures, interviews, speeches, as well as other communication forms which we wish to listen to later while we study, review, transcribe, analyze, or engage in some other listening behavior. A more recent use of the cassette tape/recorder is to listen to audio "magazines." Geared toward the person who is interested in business but does not have time to read such magazines as *Dun's Business Month, U.S. News and World Report, Forbes, Fortune,* and *International Management,* these audio tapes provide the listener with current business, economic, and legislative information, special reports and interviews, or readings from a variety of business publications. Several companies, for example, Manufacturers Hanover and Citibanks, produce their own audio "magazines" for their employees, while other companies prepare audio "magazines" which can be purchased by the general public.[39] Still another innovative use of the cassette tape/recorder is to listen to books on tape; recorded books include current and classic selections, such as Herman Wouk's *The Winds of War* and Erma Bombeck's *At Wit's End* (to be discussed in the chapter on appreciative listening), as well as self-improvement books like Peter Drucker's *The Effective Executive* and Thomas A. Harris's *I'm Okay—You're Okay.*

Another means of communication which miniaturization has helped to create is teleconferencing, a communications system that allows participants who are "tied in" through the system to interact with one another. Teleconferencing is very advantageous to groups of individuals who cannot afford to travel to meetings but find it necessary to communicate as a group. For example, the participation of your authors in a number of teleconferences illustrates the use of the technique. In one of our graduate seminars we arranged for John Murphy, former Director of Training for New England Bell Telephone, to speak about his listening program to our students on the University of Maryland campus via audio teleconferencing. The students, interacting with Mr. Murphy, were able to ask questions and offer comments about his program. Likewise, the executive committee of the International Listening Association conducts meetings to discuss the business of the organization through telephone teleconference hook-ups to all of our offices throughout the country. Videophone technology may also result in further advances. The Walt Disney EPCOT Center utilizes an interactive video system enabling visitors to make dining reservations through videophone as they communicate with a reservation clerk in a central office. Quantum Science Corporation estimates that by 1986, businesses, using some 4,855 public and private video conference rooms, will hold 1.8 million meetings by teleconference.[40]

The importance of listening has also been accented by advances in the mass media. With the arrival of radio, motion pictures, and television, we have come to rely more and more on the spoken word for information about local, state, national, and international affairs, as well as for enjoyment. The mass media advancements, as well as the quickened pace of life, have helped to effect a shift from the eye and the printed page to the ear and the word of mouth. The demands that the mass media presently make on our ears appear to be only in the initial stages; the predictions of what is to come in the mass communications field indicate that listening will occupy an increasing amount of our time in the future.

In this mass communication revolution the increasing importance of the spoken word can be gauged by the amount of time that Americans spend in radio listening and television viewing. According to 1982 statistics compiled by the Arbitron Ratings Company, there are more than 9,100 radio stations on the air today, and 95 percent of all Americans age 12 and over listen to the radio an average of 22 hours per week. Arbitron also estimates that more than half of all radio listeners tune to both AM and FM stations and that most listeners are tuned in at 7 o'clock every weekday morning and between 10 and 11 o'clock on weekend mornings.[41] Data compiled by the A. C. Nielson Company in 1983 reveal that as of January, 1983, an estimated 83.3 million (or 98 percent) of American households owned at least one television set, more than half of these homes owned more than one set, and 89 percent owned color television sets. Nielson's 1983 report also reveals that there are 1,079 commercial and public television stations on the air, that the viewing levels are highest during the prime time hours (particularly between 8:30 and 9:30 on Sunday night), and that the average television household views an estimated 6 hours and 48 minutes of television per day.

The estimated weekly viewing time of specific age groups was determined to be as follows:

Women ages 55 and over	37 hours and 14 minutes
Women ages 35 to 54	33 hours and 23 minutes
Men ages 55 and over	32 hours and 59 minutes
Men ages 35 to 54	26 hours and 56 minutes
Women ages 18 to 34	26 hours and 56 minutes
Children ages 2 to 5	25 hours and 29 minutes
Men ages 18 to 34	24 hours and 39 minutes
Children ages 5 to 11	24 hours and 0 minutes
Male teens	23 hours and 40 minutes
Female teens	21 hours and 20 minutes[42]

Based on these findings, we can infer that young people, from ages 2 to 18, spend more than 20,000 hours before television sets, which is over 7,000 hours more than they spend in school from kindergarten through twelfth grade. Moreover, with their advance in age, there is an increase in television viewing time.

Listening's Influence on Our Personal Development

Recognizing that listening is the most basic skill in our language development, that it is the most frequently used form of verbal communication, and that it plays a significant role in our daily lives (both in and out of the classroom), we then attempt to determine the influence which listening has on our personal development. The Commission on the English Curriculum of the National Council of Teachers of English believes that people's "economic concepts, political ideals, and ethical standards are influenced, if not largely determined, by their listening."[43] Since much of our listening time is spent listening to the media, we should examine how the media affects us. According to McLuhan and Fiore, the electric media "far surpasses any possible influence mom and dad can now bring to bear. . . . Now, all the world's a sage."[44] They further stress the impact that media has on us:

> All media work us over completely. They are so persuasive in their personal, political, economic, aesthetic, psychological, moral, ethical, and social consequences that they leave no part of us untouched, unaffected, unaltered. The medium is the massage."[45]

The Commission on the English Curriculum also recognizes the impact which the media have on us; the commission has emphasized that many of our attitudes, principles, understandings, and ideas are being increasingly "left to the tutelage of the radio, talking pictures, and television."[46]

Additional sources have noted the impact which one particular medium, television, has on us. Testifying before the Commission on Violence, Gerbner commented on the influence of television:

> In only two decades of massive national existence television has transformed the political life of a nation, has changed the daily habits of our people, has moulded the style of the generation, . . . redirected the flow of information and values from traditional channels into centralized networks reaching into every home . . . it has profoundly affected what we call the process of socialization, the process by which members of our species become human.[47]

Further emphasizing the effects of television, the Interim Report of the Dodd Committee in 1965 concluded "that television, whose impact on the public mind is equal to or greater than that of any other medium, is a factor in molding the character, attitudes, and behavior patterns of America's young people. . . ."[48] According to Charles D. Ferris, former chairman of the Federal Communication Commission, "television has influenced our national and international affairs—from civil rights, Vietnam, and Watergate to Afghanistan and Iran. . . . It makes viewers participants in these events, and viewer reactions add another dimension to the events themselves."[49]

Although studies of the mass media have demonstrated that the spoken word is influential in the formation of habits and attitudes, they have also revealed that the mass media do not have as much direct influence on us as do our interpersonal contacts.[50] Results of several early experiments led Katz to hypothesize that any effect of the mass media on the general public normally operates through a "two-step flow of communication"; that is, ideas flow from the mass media to "opinion leaders" (friends, co-workers, family members, or any "significant others"), and from them to the rest of the community. Thus, personal contact serves to influence us more than the mass media (although many of the ideas we discuss with others originate in the mass media).[51] Later research studies by Rogers and Haven, leading scholars to identify the diffusion of innovation (the process by which a new idea spreads in a social system), suggest that impersonal information sources (who originate nearly always from the mass media) "are most important [to a potential adopter of a new idea] at the awareness stage"[52] (the first stage of the adoption process), while personal information sources (interpersonal contacts) increase in significance during the next two stages (interest and evaluation) and then decline in importance at the fourth or trial stage. After the fifth stage, adoption, the adoptor may again turn to the media for assurance that he or she has made the proper decision.[53] A more recent view, presented by Schramm, is that the flow of information—rather than being a two-step flow involving the mass media, opinion leaders, and others—is a multistep process, with the mass media greatly influencing what information flows and with "all people, at some time or other, in some relationship or other, on some subject or other, . . . probably influenc[ing] the flow."[54] The positions of these scholars illustrate the critical role of listening as an influential force in our lives as we function as receivers of both interpersonal and mass communication messages.

Further emphasizing the effect that the mass media has on us, media specialist Tony Schwartz, in his book with the descriptive title *Media the Second God,* argues that the advances of radio, television, and telephone have taken Americans into a postliterate society in which the "shift in the communication of non-face-to-face information from the written word to the electronic media is now dominant and has a deep and fundamental significance. It is restructuring much of the world."[55] Because information about events can be transmitted instantaneously, "today there is a much greater assumption among people that others share their knowledge,"[56] a sharing of information which affects all aspects of our lives. This combination of technology and instant information led futurist John Naisbitt to describe America as shifting from an industrial society to an information society.[57] Such a shift requires the development of new communication strategies, including effective listening skills, to cope with the vast amount of information which we must process.

How important is listening in this contemporary information society? It is the most basic skill in our language development; it is the most frequently used language skill; it plays an integral part in our everyday lives; and it appears to have a profound effect on the formation of our attitudes, skills, behavioral patterns, and understandings. The importance of listening has received ample endorsement:

> Listening can make the difference between knowledge and ignorance, information and misinformation, involvement and detachment, enjoyment and boredom.[58]
>
> The art of listening holds for us the desperate hope of withstanding the spreading ravages of commercial, nationalistic, and ideological persuasion.[59]
>
> What this country needs is not a good five-cent cigar. What this country needs is more good listeners![60]

The Rewards of Effective Listening

In 1983, Lordly and Dame, a Boston agency which markets public speakers, announced that the following individuals are in the $6,000 and above category for each public speaking engagement: Ann Landers, David Brinkley, Fran Tarkenton, Walter Cronkite, and the Reverend Robert Schuller.[61] Unlike effective speakers, effective listeners have no such monetary value placed on them. However, effective listeners can reap many rewards, one of which is monetary in nature. For example, the salesperson who first asks the customer about his or her needs and then listens to the customer's verbal and nonverbal responses is better able to determine how a product will meet the customer's needs than the salesperson who believes that selling chiefly involves assuming the role of speaker. In a televised advertisement that was aired in 1983, State Farm illustrated its awareness of the value of listening in selling (fig. 1.1).

Figure 1.1. Advertisement by State Farm Insurance Companies.
Reprinted by permission of State Farm Insurance Companies.

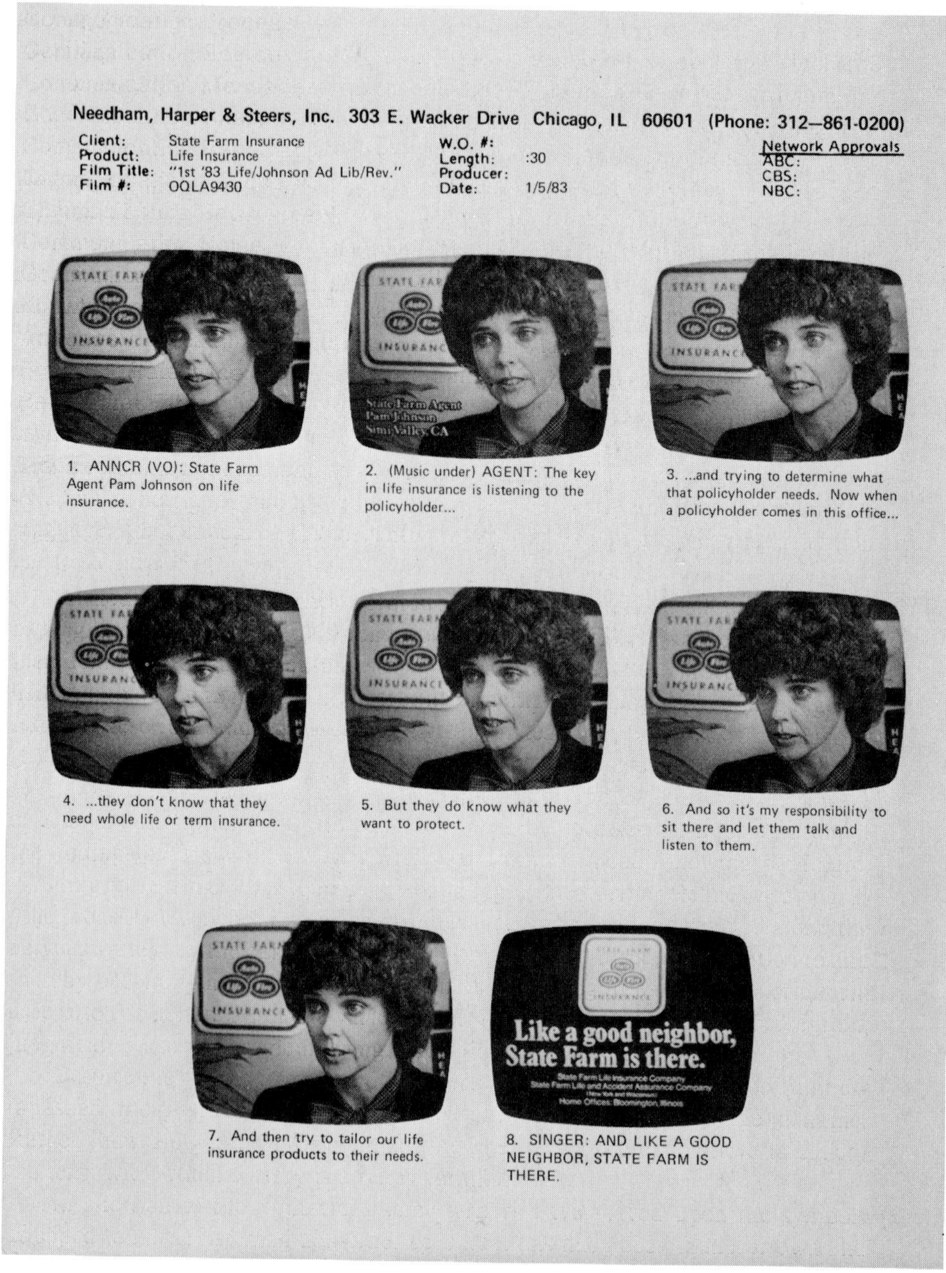
Needham, Harper & Steers, Inc. 303 E. Wacker Drive Chicago, IL 60601 (Phone: 312—861-0200)
Client: State Farm Insurance
Product: Life Insurance
Film Title: "1st '83 Life/Johnson Ad Lib/Rev."
Film #: OQLA9430
W.O. #:
Length: :30
Producer:
Date: 1/5/83
Network Approvals
ABC:
CBS:
NBC:
State Farm Agent
Pam Johnson
Simi Valley, CA
1. ANNCR (VO): State Farm Agent Pam Johnson on life insurance.
2. (Music under) AGENT: The key in life insurance is listening to the policyholder...
3. ...and trying to determine what that policyholder needs. Now when a policyholder comes in this office...
4. ...they don't know that they need whole life or term insurance.
5. But they do know what they want to protect.
6. And so it's my responsibility to sit there and let them talk and listen to them.
7. And then try to tailor our life insurance products to their needs.
Like a good neighbor,
State Farm is there.
8. SINGER: AND LIKE A GOOD NEIGHBOR, STATE FARM IS THERE.

Businesses with effective listeners are rewarded not only with more satisfied customers and increased sales but also with more satisfied personnel and increased productivity, both of which will often lead to increased profits. Through effective listening, we gain more information, up-grade decision-making, reduce the number of mistakes, spend time more productively (in conducting meetings, performing job tasks which are more clearly understood, avoiding misunderstandings, etc.), share more viewpoints, and improve management/employee relations. Indeed, businesses with effective listeners are more likely to prosper.

Effective listeners can also be rewarded by acquiring more information. Although many people prefer talking when they engage in communication situations, learning comes not from talking but rather from listening, an idea that is aptly expressed in one of Sperry's advertisements: "Nothing new ever entered the mind through an open mouth."[62] Largely through listening, one can become a more informed student, citizen, worker, consumer, spouse, parent, and any of the numerous other roles in which one serves. Having a broader information base, one is then better equipped to perform such activities as fulfilling assignments, making sound decisions, completing work-related tasks, purchasing items, resolving conflicts, solving problems, and engaging in conversations involving a wide variety of topics.

Furthermore, the effective listener is rewarded socially by being well-liked. In a study in which college students listened to three taped conversations between a man and a woman who varied the amount of time each talked and each listened, psychologist Chris Kleinke found that the person who talked 80 percent of the time but listened only 20 percent of the time was the least liked.[63] A friend who truly listens rather than just waits for an opening to express his or her ideas not only is sought after but also, when found, is usually retained as a friend. Psychologist Julie Rogers notes the binding effect which the act of listening can have: "[T]he most vital activity of any friend . . . interested in building good interpersonal relationships is listening, and listening and listening and listening. If you want a friend for life, listen, truly listen to each other, for nothing so permanently binds two people together."[64]

Another reward is improved family relations. Woelfle, quoting prominent psychologist Lee Salk, notes that "a happy home, the source of a happy child, is simply a place 'where people talk to one another, listen to one another, where they're important in one another's lives. . . .' "[65] Numerous books, such as Thomas Gordon's *Parent-Effectiveness Training* and Adele Faber and Elaine Mazlish's *How to Talk So Kids Will Listen and Listen So Kids Will Talk*,[66] as well as many family relations seminars conducted throughout the country, stress the values of effective listening within the family. When a family member is truly listened to, he or she feels recognized, accepted, understood, valued, and—as is expressed in the following impressive public service announcement—loved:

Opening song:	Take the time to listen—listen; Take the time to care. If I know you understand me, Then my mind is yours to share. Listen with your heart—listen; Listen with your mind. When you really listen, Love is what you find.
Dialogue:	*Older son*—Hey, Dad, can you help me figure this out? *Dad*—Later, I'm busy. (Here begins a telephone busy signal that continues throughout the remainder of the dialogue.) *Mom*—Honey, I'm worried about Robby. Let's talk. *Younger son*—Daddy, do you know what happens to bears in the winter time?
Announcer:	If all they hear is your busy signal, some very important people might stop calling; and there are messages you can't afford to miss.
Closing song:	When you really listen—really listen, love is what you find.[67]

Still another reward is increased enjoyment. Effective listening can heighten one's enjoyment of presentations such as plays, films, lectures, television or radio programs, and songs. For example, one of the authors increased her appreciation of Ronnie Milsap's song, "What a Difference You've Made in My Life," when she listened to the country musician explain what had inspired him to write the song. Learning that he had written it to let his fans know how they have changed his life has increased this author's understanding and appreciation of the song. Enjoyment is not limited, however, to creative presentations; any sound, such as a cat's purr or a grandson's Texas drawl, can bring delight to a particular listener.

Any discussion of the rewards of effective listening, which are far more numerous than those mentioned here, should include the reward of knowing that you have contributed to the growth of another person, an individual who needs to understand him or herself and to be understood. Many, many individuals are pleading to be understood. Their pleas often express or imply such questions as "Do you see where I'm coming from?", "Can you see my point of view?", "Can you relate to how I feel?", "Will you see it my way?", and "Will you put yourself in my place?" The best way that you can answer their pleas is to listen as they share their fears, hurts, doubts, views, whatever their concern may be. When they find someone who truly listens—listens to their verbal and nonverbal messages and their thought and feeling messages—and then communicates his or her understanding to them, they understand themselves better, they feel understood, and they perceive themselves as individuals possessing self-worth. Indeed, an effective listener can enrich the life of another as well as his or her own life by helping the other person fulfill, according to Ralph G. Nichols, the most fundamental need: *"The most basic of all human needs is to understand and to be understood."*[68]

The Schools' Instructional Emphasis on Listening

In spite of the importance of listening and the rewards of effective listening, instructional emphasis on the development of adequate listening ability in American schools has been slight. Although an accepted principle of curriculum making is that students "ought to be taught to do well those things which current living demands of them,"[69] America's educational system has, quantitatively, nearly placed an inverted emphasis on the four major language art skills.

In 1929, Rankin found that the schools' instructional emphasis on reading and writing was 52 percent and 30 percent respectively, while the schools' instructional emphasis on speaking and listening was 10 percent and 8 percent respectively.[70] Even today, the two oral language arts skills are receiving less instructional attention. This neglect on the part of the schools has been recognized by the Speech Communication Association (formerly known as the Speech Association of America): "For years the skills of oral communication have been neglected, or have been taught only incidentally or sporadically in most of our elementary and secondary schools."[71]

The most neglected langauge art skill at all educational levels, however, is listening. As we reflect upon our own early school days, how many of us can recall any structured listening training? Most of us can remember the numerous times that we, as "Blue Birds" (or, depending on our reading readiness, the "Red Birds" or "Yellow Birds"), were called to the reading circle where we became more and more proficient at reading about the activities of Jim, Judy, Tags, and Twinkle (or of people and animals with other names). Most of us can also remember the many hours when we, being closely watched by our teachers, sat at our desks and practiced drawing ovals and straight (very straight) lines on that wide-spaced yellow paper; we remember practicing and practicing until we had mastered printing, and how then we began practicing many more hours until we had perfected cursive writing. We also may remember the many times our teachers corrected our incorrect word choice and grammatical errors and our own special moments in front of the class when we showed and told. Can any of us, though, remember receiving structured, meaningful listening training? Too frequently, the only "instruction" in listening that we received was requests and commands to pay attention and/or a few lists of listening dos and don'ts. As we reflect upon our later school days (from junior high through higher education), we recall that we continued to receive little or no training in developing our proficiency in listening, the skill we use most frequently.

The fact that listening still remains the "orphan" of the language arts can be readily substantiated by the reports of several listening scholars who have investigated the status of the teaching of listening. In 1948, only one school in the United States, Stephens College, was teaching listening. Anderson, having corresponded with hundreds of teachers throughout the country, found that listening was being taught in very few schools in 1952.[72] Five years later, Letton reported that evidence demonstrating that listening was being taught in the schools was scarce.[73] In 1962, Brown and Keller noted that although there were approximately 50 thousand speech courses taught in institutions of higher learning, there was "only a handful of courses in listening." They believed that these findings demonstrate that Americans "have conceived the dual act of speaking and listening almost entirely from the speaker's point of view."[74] The almost exclusive focus on the transmission of messages has contributed to the neglect of the receptive aspect of the oral communication process. Markgraf, having surveyed 406 teacher-training institutions in 1962, reported that only three institutions offered specialized courses in listening and that 134 institutions taught listening as a separate unit.[75]

These findings indicate that the schools have neglected providing instruction in listening, the basic language skill. Apparently, many educators have not realized what the omission of listening in the language arts instructional program means as much as one sixth-grade girl has. After listening to Brown speak of the importance of *auding* (listening), she inquired, "Then leaving out auding in language would be like leaving out home plate in baseball, huh?"[76] A portion of one of Sperry's advertisements summarizes the schools' emphasis on listening: ". . . listening is the one communication skill we're never really taught. We're taught how to read, to write, to speak—but not to listen."[77]

Why has instruction in listening received such slight emphasis in the American schools? Scholars in the field have suggested many reasons why the teaching of listening has been neglected. Anderson has indicated two possible reasons: the first is that the eye still holds dominance over the ear in the thinking of many school administrators and teachers who received their education in a day when the spoken word was of relatively less importance, and, thus, many educators fail to acknowledge the importance of listening now. A second explanation is that deficiencies in listening are not easily detected.[78] Nichols reported that nonprofessionals attribute the neglect to their belief that "listening is probably determined by hearing acuity and intelligence, and that the schools can do comparatively little about either one" and that university staff members believed that the neglect was probably due to the "widespread assumption that *practice* and intelligence are the only significant components of efficient listening."[79] Still another reason may be that the school curriculum is already overcrowded.

Spearritt, as well as other listening scholars, has advanced the argument that listening has received so little attention because of the assumption that growth in listening skills is automatic and, therefore, instruction is unnecessary.[80] Since many children who come to first grade appear to have acquired—without systematic training—relatively adequate oral communication skills, many educators assume that through normal classroom activities at the various educational levels, students will develop listening skills sufficient to meet their needs.

Does experimental evidence support this assumption? Although they were measuring students' listening habits (rather than their capacity to listen), Nichols and Stevens conducted a study in which they investigated the percentage of students who could tell what their teachers were talking about when the teachers stopped in the middle of their lectures. The investigators found that 90 percent of the first graders, 80 percent of the second graders, 43.7 percent of the junior high students, and 28 percent of the senior high students could correctly answer the question.[81] Studies by Jones and Nichols, among others, have reported that, without direct listening training, college subjects correctly answer 50 percent of the items on an immediate recall test (covering the material in a ten-minute lecture) and 25 percent of the items on a delayed recall test.[82]

Lundsteen has speculated that the schools' neglect of the teaching of listening may be due to the fact that teachers have had little if any listening training and/or instruction in methods in teaching listening.[83] When Markgraf surveyed 406 teacher-training institutions in 1962, he found that less than half of the institutions (44 percent) included units on methods of teaching listening in their methods courses.[84] Fifteen years later when Wolff surveyed 70 colleges and universities, she found that only 14 percent offered listening courses.[85]

Still another reason why listening training has been neglected in the schools may be that there is a scarcity of instructional materials pertaining to listening. The findings of Heilman, Lynch and Evans, and Brown demonstrate that most instructional materials are sparse and lacking in substance. Heilman examined textbooks on teaching and curriculum guides to ascertain their treatment, if any, of listening. He found that 11 out of 15 textbooks published between 1946 and 1954 did not mention listening. Heilman also found that although many curriculum guides appeared to respect the role of listening in the educational process, they included few concrete suggestions for developing skill in listening.[86] In 1963, Lynch and Evans analyzed the content of 14 series of high school English textbooks to discover the number of pages devoted to listening. They found that of a total of 26,141 pages, 424 were concerned with listening.[87] In 1967, Brown analyzed the content of 54 language arts textbooks (published between 1959 and 1964) for grades 3 through 6. He found that listening was emphasized in only .63 percent of the lessons and on .57 percent of the pages.[88] The presence or absence of listening material in textbooks and curriculum guides does not necessarily indicate the presence or absence of listening instruction in the classroom; however, it seems reasonable to assume that teachers do utilize textbooks and courses of study as guides for what subject matter will be covered in the classroom. The fact that the first full-length book on listening, *Are You Listening?*, was not published until 1957 further emphasizes the lag that exists in the area of listening.[89]

The negligence of schools in providing listening training may be due to incorrect perception of the skills in which our students are, indeed, deficient. The findings of a recent study conducted by New York's Center for Public Resources illustrate differences between business and union officials' and school officials' perceptions of the skills possessed by persons entering the work force in the United States. Union and business officials identified mathematics and science skills as deficient, but they also noted a decline in speaking and listening skills. Likewise, these officials noted that speaking and listening skills were essential in all job categories at all job levels. Although business and union officials considered communication skills to be essential and in need of further development, school officials in this same survey assessed their graduates as being "adequately prepared" for entry-level employment.[90] It would seem that there is a gap between what skills a person needs to enter the work force, especially skills in speaking and listening, and what the schools are providing to our future workers, our students.

Not until 1978 did the federal government join those who believe that listening should be taught. In the 1978 Primary and Secondary Education Act, the government added listening and speaking to reading, writing, and arithmetic, as measures of literacy and as needed basic competencies.

The addition of listening as a basic skill has led to many positive results, such as the identification of listening skills and the development of curriculum materials for teaching these skills in ten states, and the identification of listening skills, the development of curriculum materials for teaching these skills, and of procedures for assessing these skills in three states,[91] as well as the addition, in 1983, of a listening proficiency test to the National Teacher Examination. Other positive results, although not direct consequences of the 1978 Primary and Secondary Education Act but possibly prompted by it, include the following: the incorporation of listening competencies in the "Basic Skills and Competencies for Productive Employment" in a 1983 report entitled *Action for Excellence,* developed by the Task Force on Education for Economic Growth of the Education Commission of the States (consisting of corporate executives, representatives of labor and education, and state legislators);[92] the recommendation for listening skill development by college and university systems such as the Coordinating Board of the Texas College and University system (in their pamphlet entitled "Goals for College Success: A Practical Reference for College Preparation");[93] a recommendation of the National Commission of Excellence in Education that high school graduates be equipped to "listen effectively";[94] the inclusion of learning outcomes for listening in the College Entrance Examination Board's report entitled *Academic Preparation for College: What Students Need to Know and Be Able to Do;*[95] the urging of Ernest Boyer, President of the Carnegie Foundation for the Advancement of Teaching and former United States Commissioner of Education, that all high school students be required to take a one-semester course in speaking and listening;[96] and the National Council of Teachers of English's placement of speaking and listening as part of their "Essentials to English" statement.[97] Perhaps the 1978 Primary and Secondary Education Act will prove to be the impetus which the educational system has needed to remedy the neglect of teaching the basic communication skill, listening.

The Business World's Reaction to Ineffective Listening

As a result of the educational lag in developing the listening efficiency of students, many leading corporations are recognizing that untrained listeners who were once students are now employees and that inefficient listening in business is costly. Lyman K. Steil, president of Communication Development, Inc., estimates that poor listening costs American businesses billions of dollars:

> With more than 100 million workers in this country, a simple $10 mistake by each of them, as a result of poor listening, would add up to a cost of a billion dollars. And most people make numerous listening mistakes every week.
>
> Because of listening mistakes, letters have to be retyped, appointments rescheduled, shipments rerouted. Productivity is affected and profits suffer.[98]

Many executives are not only becoming more aware of but also believing more in Nichols's finding that the average white-collar worker demonstrates only about 25 percent listening efficiency.[99] They also are beginning to agree that one of the greatest and most common weaknesses of most marketers, especially those in selling, is the failure to recognize that listening is equal in importance to talking.[100] Furthermore, they are beginning to adopt the following view:

> The most important factor for successful communication is not only the ability to use language well or to speak well or to present one's own point of view; it is rather the ability to listen well to the other person's point of view.[101]

Numerous research studies document the essential role of listening in organizations. Surveying 457 members of the Academy of Certified Administrative Managers to determine the 20 competencies critical to their jobs, Smith found that executives ranked active listening as the most critical managerial competency.[102] Examining Smith's study as well as 24 other studies conducted between 1972 and 1980, DiSalvo discovered that effective listening was identified as the most important communication skill necessary for entry level positions in various organizational contexts.[103] The results of another study, conducted by Sanford in 1980, reveal that presidents of Fortune 1000 companies identified failure of subordinates to accept or carry out responsibilities and their failure to obtain critical information as the two work situations which produce most anxiety in top management. According to Sanford, these deficiencies imply listening problems.[104] In an inventory of learning goals for managers in management education programs, Harvard's Institute for the Management of Lifelong Education found that the development of effective listening skills was ranked high by the respondents (consisting of directors of managerial training programs in over 50 corporations) and was preceded only by the abilities to (a) interact, (b) think critically about ideas received, and (c) balance conflicting viewpoints, all of these involving abilities which relate directly to the listening process.[105] In still another study, a Speech Communication Association task force surveyed 194 community college Career Advisory Board members (representing a wide range of occupations) to determine the members' perceptions as to the relative importance of 49 selected communication skills in the performance of career duties; survey results show that listening skills were consistently ranked as the most important communication skills for career competence.[106] The results of Downs and Conrad's survey of 700 middle managers from private industry and government agencies also revealed the importance of listening within organizations. Among the most necessary communication skills which effective supervisors and subordinates need to possess, listening was ranked fifth for supervisors and first for subordinates; moreover, failure to listen was ranked as the second most critical problem that distinguishes ineffective from effective subordinates.[107] Hunt and Cusella, surveying Fortune 500 organizations, found that training managers considered poor listening to be "'*one of the most important* problems facing' them, and that ineffective listening leads to ineffective performance or low productivity."[108] Finally, the results of Harris and Thomlison's 1983 survey of communication training needs in business organizations indicated that 185 business and organizational personnel ranked listening and motivating people as the two major areas most in need of additional training.[109]

Drawing upon research as well as experiential findings, executives are beginning to perceive listening as "the key not only to getting the job done but to peaceful growth and economic success as well."[110] Indeed, they are recognizing the importance of effective listening, as does John L. DiGaetani, writing about "The Business of Listening":

> The effects of really good listening can be dramatic. These effects include the satisfied customer who will come back, the contented employee who will stay with the company, the manager who has the trust of his staff, and the salesman who tops his quota. Good listeners are valued highly by the people they work with. . . .[111]

Recognizing the costliness of poor listening and the need for effective listening from the executive suite to the shop floor, executives in many leading corporations are providing listening training for their employees. For example, in 1979 Sperry retained as a consultant and trainer, Lyman K. Steil, who, together with Sperry's own management development specialists, developed a listening training program modeled in many respects after the pioneering work of Ralph G. Nichols. As of August, 1983, 20,000 of Sperry's 90,000 employees (beginning with top management) had taken the six-to-eight hour course which is tailored to meet the professional as well as the personal listening needs of the various participants, depending on whether they be salespersons, receptionists, systems analysts, customer engineers, or top executives.[112] Although many other corporations, such as Xerox, Pfizer, 3M, American Telephone and Telegraph, General Electric, Dun and Bradstreet, and Pitney Bowes, had included listening in their training programs before 1979, Sperry's well-received, in-house listening training program and advertising campaign generated much interest in listening among numerous other businesses. Thus, listening seminars are now being offered by such additional corporations as Ford, Honeywell, Control Data, IBM, Pacific

Telephone, Pillsbury Company, Bank of America, and Tektronix.[113] All of these companies are doing more than merely acknowledging the importance of effective listening; they are working toward eliminating the question, "Is anyone *really* listening?"

SUMMARY

In this chapter, we have called attention to the costly communication barriers that often result when we do not engage in the total listening process, which includes hearing, attending to, and understanding the sender's message. Also, we have shown that listening is the most basic of the four major areas of language development; that listening is the most frequently used form of verbal communication, and thus plays a significant role in our educational, personal, and professional lives; that listening appears to have a profound effect on the formations of our attitudes, skills, behaviors, and understandings. Furthermore, we have pointed out many of the beneficial effects of effective listening, such as increased profits, knowledge, and enjoyment, improved family and social relations, as well as enrichment of personal lives. Lastly, we have stressed that in spite of the importance of listening, America's schools—at all educational levels—have been negligent in providing instruction in listening; this neglect is attributable to numerous reasons, ranging from the failure of educators to recognize the importance of listening to the scarcity of instructional material pertaining to listening. As a result of the schools' insufficient emphasis on the development of adequate listening skills, many leading corporations are recognizing the need to provide listening training for their employees so that costly communication barriers resulting from poor listening will be minimized or completely eliminated.

SUGGESTED ACTIVITIES

1. Collect articles, cartoons, lines from songs and commercials, quotes, etc., which call attention to ineffective listening, and then share them orally with the class.
2. Compile a list of listening skills that you should improve or develop in order to be an effective listener in your *personal* life. Share this list orally with the class.
3. Maintain a listening log for a period of a week. Construct daily time charts divided into fifteen-minute intervals. Using S (for speaking), W (for writing), R (for reading), L (for listening), and N (for nonverbal communication or no communication), code your communication time during each waking hour. Use the code which represents the type of communication in which you engage during the major portion of each fifteen-minute interval. Then tabulate the following:
   a. The total number of fifteen-minute intervals you were awake.
   b. The total number of fifteen-minute intervals you engaged in no (or nonverbal) communication.
   c. The total number of fifteen-minute intervals you engaged in *each* type of verbal communication: speaking, writing, reading, and listening.

d. The total number of fifteen-minute intervals you engaged in verbal communication (a sum of the four totals calculated in c.)
e. The pecentage of waking hours you spent engaged in no (or nonverbal) communication, verbal communication, writing, reading, listening, and speaking.

Finally, compare your findings with those of Rankin, which are as follows:

No (or nonverbal) communication	30 percent
Verbal communication	70 percent
Listening	42.1 percent
Speaking	31.9 percent
Reading	15 percent
Writing	11 percent[114]

4. From your listening logs, determine the percentage of time you are expected to listen in your classes.
5. From your listening logs, determine the percentage of time you are expected to listen on your jobs. Then, compare your findings with those of Weinrauch and Swanda.
6. Maintain a seven-day listening log of time you spend listening to television. Then, calculate the average number of hours you listen to television per day and compare your personal television viewing habits with those reported in the *1983 Nielson Report on Television.*
7. Explore the importance of good listening in your planned or chosen profession/vocation. Interview, in person or over the telephone, at least one person working in your field of interest. Among the questions you should ask are the following:

   Specifically, what is your occupation?

   During a typical work day, what percentage of the day do you spend in verbally communicating with others?

   Rank the four means of verbal communication in which you engage (reading, writing, listening, and speaking), ranging from the one you use most to the one you use the least.

   List specific situations in which you engage in listening.

   In your area of specialization, how important is listening?

   What specific listening skills does a person holding your position need to possess?

   Do you consider yourself a good listener? Why or why not?

   Does your company provide any direct listening training? If so, what kind of training?

   After conducting the interview(s), discuss your findings on paper.

   Submit a copy of your findings to all other students and to the instructor.[115]
8. Contact educators at the elementary, secondary, and college levels and investigate what, if any, direct listening instruction they provide and why they do or do not provide it. Then, share your findings with the class.

9. Contact several local companies and find out whether any of them provide direct listening training for their employees. If they do, you are to inquire about the type of trainng that is provided. Then, share your findings with the class.
10. List any listening behavior that you find irritating; then examine your own listening behavior to see whether you engage in any of these annoying behaviors.

NOTES

1. © 1964, 1965 Paul Simon Used by permission.
2. Carl H. Weaver, *Human Listening: Processes and Behavior* (Bobbs-Merrill Company, 1972), p. 22.
3. *Washington Star,* 19 October 1971, p. A-12. Used with permission of Universal Press.
4. "Communicating: Not Easy Job," *Grit* 5 November 1972, p. 32.
5. Franciscan Communications, Public Service Announcement, WJZ-TV, Summer, 1972. Reprinted by permission of the publisher.
6. Doug Hooper, "Spend Time Helping Youth to Build Self-Image," *Grit* 16 August 1981, p. 15.
7. Suzanne Fornaciari, "How to Talk to Kids about Drugs," cited by John Barbour, "Lines of Communication," *The Evening Sun* 18 March 1981, p. B-1.
8. John D. Stammer, "MAPPing Out a Plan for Better Listening," *Teacher* 98 (March 1981): 37–38.
9. Leo Buscaglia, *Love* (New York: Fawcett Crest Books, 1972), pp. 44–45.
10. Sylvia Porter, "Poor Listening Is Big Problem for Businesses," *The Washington Star* 14 November 1979, p. F-B.
11. Advertisement by Sperry. Reprinted by permission of Sperry Corporation.
12. Advertisement by Sperry. Reprinted by permission of Sperry Corporation.
13. Advertisement by Sperry. Reprinted by permission of Sperry Corporation.
14. Stacey Lucas, "Skills: Listening Is a Learned Art," *Working Woman,* August 1983, p. 45.
15. John L. DiGaetani, "The Sperry Corporation and Listening: An Interview," *Business Horizons* 25 (March/April 1982): 35.
16. Lyman K. Steil, Del Kennedy, Diana Whitney, J. Peter Hynes, and Fred Taylor, "The Sperry Story" (Presentation delivered at the Second Annual International Listening Association Convention, Denver, Colorado, March 4, 1981).
17. Lucas, "Skills: Listening Is a Learned Art."
18. DiGaetani, "The Sperry Corporation and Listening: An Interview"; David Clutterbuck, "How Sperry Made People Listen," *Interpersonal Management* 36 (February 1981): 23.
19. Steil, Kennedy, Whitney, Hynes, and Taylor, "The Sperry Story."
20. Carl R. Rogers and F. J. Roethlisberger, "Barriers and Gateways to Communication," *Harvard Business Review* 30 (July 1952):47.
21. Father Walter Norris, nuptial message presented at the University of Maryland Chapel, University of Maryland, August 11, 1973.
22. "Communication Vital, Marriage Study Finds," *Grit* 18 April 1982, p. 2.
23. Jane E. Brody, "Communicating: How We Form, Maintain and Destroy Our Relationships," *The Evening Sun* 3 September 1981, p. C-1.

24. David D. Burns, "The All-Hits, No-Misses Way to Get What You Want," *Self,* April, 1981, pp. 69–70.
25. Dr. Walt Menninger's column "What We All Need Is a Good Listener" Copyright, 1979, Universal Press Syndicate. All rights reserved.
26. Educational Foundation of the American Association of Advertising Agencies, "The Miscomprehension of Televised Communications," mimeographed (New York: The AAAA Educational Foundation, Inc., May, 1980), pp. 2, 4.
27. " 'What's He Doing? He'll Kill Us All!' " *Time* 109 (April 11, 1977), p. 22.
28. Sara W. Lundsteen, *Listening: Its Impact on Reading and the Other Language Arts* (Illinois: NCTE/ERIC, 1971), p. 3.
29. Miriam E. Wilt, "A Study of Teacher Awareness of Listening as a Factor in Elementary Education," *Journal of Educational Research* 43 (April 1950): 631.
30. Bruce Markgraf, "An Observational Study Determining the Amount of Time That Students in the Tenth and Twelfth Grades Are Expected to Listen in the Classroom," in *Listening: Readings,* ed. Sam Duker (New York: Scarecrow Press, 1966), pp. 90–94.
31. Donald E. Bird, "Teaching Listening Comprehension," *Journal of Communication* 3 (November 1953): 127–128.
32. Paul Tory Rankin, "The Measurement of the Ability to Understand Spoken Language" (unpublished Ph.D. dissertation, University of Michigan, 1926), *Dissertation Abstracts* 12 (1952): 847–848.
33. Lila R. Brieter, "Research in Listening and Its Importance to Literature," cited by Larry L. Barker, *Listening Behavior* (Englewood Cliffs, New Jersey: Prentice-Hall, 1971), p. 4.
34. J. Donald Weinrauch and John R. Swanda, Jr., "Examining the Significance of Listening: An Exploratory Study of Contemporary Management," *The Journal of Business Communication* 13 (February 1975): 25–32.
35. Elyse K. Werner, "A Study of Communication Time" (M.A. thesis, University of Maryland—College Park, 1975), p. 26.
36. Larry Barker et al., "An Investigation of Proportional Time Spent in Various Communication Activities by College Students," *Journal of Applied Communications Research* 8 (November 1980): 101–109.
37. Leland Brown, *Communicating Facts and Ideas in Business* (Englewood Cliffs, New Jersey: Prentice-Hall, 1982), p. 380.
38. William F. Keefe, *Listen, Management!* (New York: McGraw Hill, 1971), p. 10.
39. David Hubler, "Wheels: Mind over Machine," *The Washington Post* 19 October 1981, p. D-5. Included in this article are the names, addresses, and phone numbers of three companies that sell "magazine" tapes: Newstrack, Executive Tape Service, Box 1178, Englewood, Colorado 80150 (800) 525–8389; "Sound of Business" Harris Trust and Savings Bank, 6 East P.O. 755, Chicago, Illinois 60690 (312) 461–7631; and Washington Audio Journal, Broadcast Center, U.S. Chamber of Commerce, 1615 H Street NW, Washington, D.C. 20062 (201) 659–6238.
40. Mary Mackintosh, "Tele-Execs Predict Reduction, Not Elimination of Biz Travel," *Meeting News,* November 1983, p. 143. For a description of how to use teleconferencing, see Martin C. J. Elton, *Teleconferencing New Media for Business Meetings* (New York: American Management Associations, 1982) and Leonard Lewin, ed., *Telecommunications in the United States: Trends and Policies* (Dedham, Massachusetts: Artech House, 1982).

41. Arbitron Ratings Company, *Radio Today* (Beltsville, Maryland, 1982).
42. A. C. Nielson Company, *1983 Nielson Report on Television* (New York: A. C. Nielson Company, 1983).
43. Commission on the English Curriculum of the National Council of Teachers of English, *The English Language Arts* (New York: Appleton-Century-Crofts, 1952), pp. 329–330.
44. From *The Medium Is the Massage* by Marshall McLuhan and Quentin Fiore. Coordinated by Jerome Agel. Copyright © 1967 by Bantam Books, Inc. Reprinted by permission of the publisher. All rights reserved.
45. *Ibid.*
46. Commission on the English Curriculum of the National Council of Teachers of English, *The English Language Arts,* pp. 329–330.
47. Dean George Gerbner, quoted in Nicholas Johnson, *How to Talk Back to Your TV Set* (Boston: Little, Brown and Company, 1970), p. 24.
48. The Interim Report of the Dodd Committee, quoted in Nicholas Johnson, *How to Talk Back to Your TV Set,* p. 37.
49. Charles D. Ferris, "The FCC Takes a Hard Look at Television," *Today's Education* 69 (September/October 1980): 66GS.
50. Daryl J. Bem, *Beliefs, Attitudes, and Human Affairs* (Belmont, California: Brooks/Cole Publishing Company, 1970), pp. 75–77.
51. Elihu Katz, "The Two-Step Flow of Communication: An Up-to-Date Report on a Hypothesis," *Public Opinion Quarterly* 1 (1957): 61–78.
52. Everett M. Rogers, *Diffusion of Innovations* (New York: The Free Press of Glencoe, 1962), p. 99.
53. *Ibid.,* pp. 99, 101.
54. Wilbur Schramm, *Men, Messages, and Media* (New York: Harper and Row, Publishers, 1973), p. 124.
55. Tony Schwartz, *Media the Second God* (New York: Random House, 1981), p. 14.
56. *Ibid.,* p. 15.
57. John Naisbitt, *Megatrends* (New York: Warner Books, 1982).
58. Commission on the English Curriculum of the National Council of Teachers of English, *The English Language Arts in the Secondary School* (New York: Appleton-Century-Croft, 1956), p. 251.
59. Wendell Johnson, "Do We Know How to Listen?" *ETC* 7 (Autumn 1949): 3.
60. Dr. Walt Menninger's column "What We All Need Is a Good Listener" Copyright, 1979, Universal Press Syndicate. All rights reserved.
61. "Talk Is Cheap?" *Spectra,* May, 1983, p. 1.
62. Advertisement by Sperry. Reprinted by permission of Sperry Corporation.
63. Chris Benton, "Listen—You'll Make a Good First Impression," *National Enquirer,* February 2, 1982, p. 37.
64. Dr. Walt Menninger's column "What We All Need Is a Good Listener" Copyright, 1979, Universal Press Syndicate. All Rights Reserved.
65. Gretchen Woelfle, "Family Man," *Texas Flyer,* April, 1981.
66. Thomas Gordon, *Parent Effectiveness Training* (New York: Peter H. Wyden, 1970); Adele Faber and Elaine Mazlish, *How to Talk So Kids Will Listen and Listen So Kids Will Talk* (New York: Rawson, Wade Publishers, 1980).
67. The Church of Jesus Christ of Latter-Day Saints, Public Service Announcement. Used with permission of The Church of Jesus Christ of Latter-Day Saints.

68. Ralph G. Nichols, "The Struggle to Be Human" (Address delivered at the First Annual International Listening Association Convention, Atlanta, Georgia, February 17, 1980), p. 4.
69. Harold A. Anderson, "Needed Research in Listening," *Elementary English* 29 (April 1954): 216.
70. Paul Tory Rankin, "Listening Ability: Its Improvement, Measurement, and Development," *Chicago Schools Journal* 12 (January, June 1930): 177–179, 417–420.
71. Speech Association of America, "Speech Education in the Public Schools," *Speech Teacher* 16 (January 1967): 79.
72. Anderson, "Needed Research in Listening," 221.
73. Mildred C. Letton, "The Status of the Teaching of Listening," *Elementary School Journal* 57 (January 1957): 181.
74. Charles T. Brown and Paul W. Keller, "A Modest Proposal for Listening Training," *Quarterly Journal of Speech* 48 (December 1962): 395.
75. Bruce Markgraf, "Listening Pedagogy in Teacher-Training Institutions," *Journal of Communication* 12 (March 1962): 34.
76. Donald P. Brown, "What Is the Basic Language Skill?" *ETC* 14 (Winter 1956–1957): 118.
77. Advertisement by Sperry. Reprinted by permission of the Sperry Corporation.
78. Harold Anderson, "Teaching the Art of Listening," *School Review* 57 (February 1949): 66.
79. Ralph G. Nichols, "Listening Instruction in the Secondary School," in *Listening: Readings,* ed. Sam Duker, pp. 242–243.
80. Donald Spearritt, *Listening Comprehension—A Factorial Analysis* (Melbourne, Australia: G. W. and Sons, 1962), p. 3.
81. Ralph G. Nichols and Leonard A. Stevens, *Are You Listening?* (New York: McGraw Hill Book Company, 1957), pp. 12–13.
82. Ralph G. Nichols, "Do We Know How to Listen? Practical Helps in a Modern Age," *Speech Teacher* 10 (March 1961): 119–120.
83. Lundsteen, *Listening: Its Impact on Reading and the Other Language Arts,* p. 8.
84. Markgraf, "Listening Pedagogy in Teacher-Training Institutions," pp. 33–35.
85. Florence I. Wolff, "A Pragmatic 'Sharing' Workshop in Listening Pedagogy: Who's Teaching Listening and How?" (Presentation delivered at the First Annual International Listening Association Convention, Atlanta, Georgia, February 19, 1980).
86. Arthur W. Heilman, "Listening and the Curriculum," *Education* 75 (January 1955): 285–286.
87. James J. Lynch and Betrand Evans, *High School English Textbooks: A Critical Examination* (Boston: Little Brown, 1963), pp. 495–496.
88. Kenneth L. Brown, "Speech and Listening in Language Arts Textbooks," *Elementary English* 44 (April 1967): 336–341.
89. Nichols and Stevens, *Are You Listening?*
90. James F. Henry and Susan Ueber Raymond, *Basic Skills in the U.S. Work Force* (New York: Center for Public Resources, 1982), pp. ii, iii, and 14.
91. Phil Backlund et al., "A National Survey of State Practices in Speaking and Listening Skill Assessment," *Communication Education* 31 (April 1982): 125–129.
92. Don M. Boileau, ed., "Education Research Notes Development," *Spectra* 19 (September 1983): 5.
93. Don Boileau, ed., "Education Research Notes Development," *Spectra* 19 (May 1983): 9.

94. The National Commission on Excellence in Education, *A Nation at Risk* (Washington, D.C.: United States Department of Education, April, 1983), p. 25.
95. Don Boileau, ed., "Education Research Notes Development," *Spectra* 19 (August 1983): 8.
96. Don Boileau, ed., "Education Research Notes Development," *Spectra* 20 (May 1984): 4.
97. *Ibid.*
98. Lyman K. Steil, "Secrets of Being a Better Listener," *U.S. News and World Report* 88 (May 26, 1980): 65.
99. Ralph G. Nichols, "Listening Is a 10–Part Skill," *Nation's Business* 45 (July 1957): 56.
100. Edward W. Wheatley, "Glimpses of Tomorrow," *Sales Management* 104 (May 1, 1970): 41.
101. Weinrauch and Swanda, "Examining the Significance of Listening: An Exploratory Study of Contemporary Management," p. 26.
102. "The 20% Activities that Bring 80% Payoff," *Training/HRD* 15 (June 1978): 6.
103. Vincent S. DiSalvo, "A Summary of Current Research Identifying Communication Skills in Various Organizational Contexts," *Communication Education* 29 (July 1980): 283–290.
104. Susan Mundale, "Why More CEOs Are Mandating Listening and Writing Training," *Training/HRD* 17 (October 1980): 37–41.
105. Arnold E. Keller, "The Quest for Professionalism," *Infosystems*, February, 1983, p. 94.
106. John Muchmore and Kathleen Galvin, "A Report of the Task Force on Career Competencies in Oral Communication Skills for Community College Students Seeking Immediate Entry into the Work Force," *Communication Education* 32 (April 1983): 207–220.
107. Cal W. Downs and Charles Conrad, "Effective Subordinancy," *The Journal of Business Communication* 19 (Spring 1982): 27–38.
108. Gary T. Hunt and Louis P. Cusella, "A Field Study of Listening Needs in Organizations," *Communication Education* 32 (October 1983): 399.
109. Thomas E. Harris and T. Dean Thomlison, "Career-Bound Communication Education: A Needs Analysis," *Central States Speech Journal* 34 (Winter, 1983): 260–267.
110. William F. Keefe, *Listen, Management!* (New York: McGraw Hill Book Company, 1971), p. 192.
111. John L. DiGaetani, "The Business of Listening," *Business Horizons* 23 (October 1980): 42.
112. DiGaetani, "The Sperry Corporation and Listening: An Interview"; Clutterbuck, "How Sperry Made People Listen"; Lucas, "Skills: Listening Is a Learned Art"; Steil, Kennedy, Whitney, Hynes, and Taylor, "The Sperry Story": Michael Kernan, "Listen . . . Now Hear This, You Aural Degenerates!" *The Washington Post*, 23 September 1980, pp. B-1 and B-7.
113. Clutterbuck, "How Sperry Made People Listen"; Lucas, "Skills: Listening Is a Learned Art," p. 45.
114. Andrew D. Wolvin and Carolyn Gwynn Coakley, *Listening Instruction* (Urbana, Illinois: ERIC Clearinghouse on Reading and Communication Skills, 1979), pp. 19–20.
115. *Ibid.*, p. 20.

Concepts You Will Encounter

Communication Process
Communication Source
Communication Messages
Communication Channel
Communication Receiver
Communication Feedback
Communication Environment
Communication Noise
Communication Skills
Knowledge
Attitudes
Frame of Reference
Perceptual Filter
Symbolic Language
Transactional Communication

The Process of Communication 2

As we study listening as a communication behavior, it is useful to view it from the overall perspective of communication as a *process*. Scholars in the communication field have come to recognize the *process* nature of human communication, viewing it as an ongoing, dynamic interaction of components. Communication, as a process, is thus never ending, in that one message may well influence yet another and serve as the stimulus for a continuation of the communication.

Components of Communication

As an ongoing human interaction, then, communication involves a number of components which make up the complex phenomena. There is a communication *source,* a speaker who originates a message. The process begins with an original stimulus (an event, object, person, idea) which the source wishes to communicate. The source encodes this idea, sorting and selecting symbols in order to translate the idea into a *message* to communicate by way of verbal and nonverbal language symbols.

The encoded message, then, is transcribed via a communication *channel.* In face-to-face communication, the five senses—sight, sound, touch, smell, and taste—serve as the major channels for this transmission. As Americans, we use the auditory and visual channels as our primary media in most communication, while in other cultures touch and smell may be utilized. In our society we also make extensive use of electronic channels in telecommunication (telephone, radio, television).

The verbal and nonverbal messages, transmitted via these channels, then are received and decoded (filtered and translated into a person's language code in order to assign meaning) by the communication *receiver.* The receiver, in turn, responds to the source, message, and channel by encoding and sending *feedback*—the response/reaction of the receiver as perceived by the source. This feedback creates the ongoing, dynamic nature of the communication process. The source decodes (interprets) the feedback and, ideally, adapts and adjusts the communication accordingly.

Figure 2.1.
Simple model of communication.

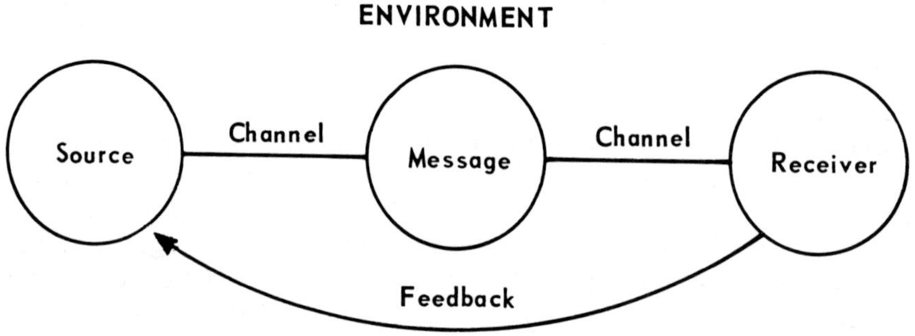

Throughout this process, the communication will be affected by two other important components. The *environment*—where the communication takes place—is one of these components. We communicate in specific settings, physical surroundings that will influence us as communicators. Temperatures, ventilation, lighting, room size all affect the outcome of our communication.

We also are affected by *noise*—internal and external interference—throughout the system. This interference can be internal, within the communicators themselves. A person may be preoccupied with personal concerns (worries, fatigue, hunger, illness, relationship with a supervisor) or may develop an emotional barrier in response to a word or idea presented in the message. This interference also can be external to the system: a loud sound in the room, other people talking, simultaneous messages being sent, static in the channel, or a lack of coherency in the message. Such interference can cause a person to lose track of the message which is being sent.

The communication components can be depicted in a simple model which illustrates the interaction of the various parts that make up the process (fig. 2.1).

Communication Variables

Critical to the effectiveness of communication as a human process are variables in the system, factors which facilitate or diminish the outcomes of the communication. These variables can affect the different components of the communication process.[1]

One key variable which affects the communication source and receiver is the communication *skill* which the communicators bring to the process. Skills in sending and receiving messages are learned by humans from early infancy; they include the ability to analyze and adapt to various communicators and communication situations. Abilities in encoding messages may incorporate verbal language facility, skill in structuring messages, and such nonverbal skills as vocal dynamics and physical expressiveness. Decoding skills, which will be the focus of much of this book, may include the individual's attention span, willingness to listen, vocabulary level, and listening effort.

These elements are essential not only to the sending of messages but also to the sending of feedback, responses to messages. Substantial training in speaking and listening skills can aid communicators in improving their effectiveness with these communication skills.

Communication skills combine with communicator *knowledge* to influence the entire process. Communicators, both source and receiver, should know about the subject matter under discussion, and they should share information about the verbal and nonverbal language code utilized to convey the messages. Communicators should know about message structure and about environmental control (how to regulate temperature, decrease noise, etc.) in order to communicate more precisely. It is helpful, also, for communicators to know about channel selection: how to choose the most appropriate medium to convey a message or feedback. The more extensive the knowledge about the communication itself and about the material to be communicated, the more effective the communicators should be.

Likewise, communicators share *attitudes,* predispositions to respond positively or negatively. These may be shared attitudes toward each other as communicators. For example, a speaker may not care for a group of union representatives he or she must address. Or a listener may be too supportive of a particular political candidate and hence overlook major flaws in the candidate's platform.

These positive and negative attitudes affect us as communicators in our orientations toward the message as well. As listeners, we may be so opposed to foreign aid programs, for instance, that we refuse to accept the basic thesis of a message by an official from the Agency for International Development. Or a manager may be asked to brief employees on a new company procedure which he or she does not believe is the most efficient method. This attitude, of course, will carry through in his or her presentation of the briefing.

Attitudes can affect us as communicators as well. Considerable research in the communication field indicates that a substantial number of people suffer communication apprehension, that is, anxiety about communicating with others. Speakers who experience stage fright may have negative attitudes toward their own abilities as communicators. Moreover, these negative attitudes certainly can influence our self-concepts as listeners. Many people feel they are not effective listeners, and, consequently, they are *not* effective listeners. But this negative self-concept may stem from the negative messages we hear as listeners throughout our formative years: "Be quiet and listen"; "You're not listening to me"; "Don't you ever listen?" We seldom hear positive, reinforcing messages about our listening behavior.

Positive and negative attitudes extend to other components of the communication process. We may dislike a particular classroom and thus have difficulty paying attention to instruction in that room. Or we may have negative attitudes toward certain communication channels. There are people, for instance, who cannot talk into telephone answering machines. They hang up to avoid the trauma of "At the sound of the tone, please leave your message!"

The attitudes, knowledge, and communication skills of communicators, both speakers and listeners, contribute to the *frame of reference* of the communicators. This frame of reference consists of the background, life experiences, social-cultural context of the person, as well as everything else which makes one a unique individual. All these elements create the *perceptual filter* through which we receive stimuli, send messages, and relate to the rest of the world around us. In short, the sum total of all that makes up our being as humans becomes part of our encoding and decoding as communicators.

The perceptual filter serves as our "screen" through which we process the stimulus we are receiving. Our *physical and psychological states* at any given time will affect our perceptions. A person who is depressed or who does not feel well, for example, undoubtedly perceives messages more negatively than an individual who is psychologically sound and physically well. Likewise, an individual's *sensory acuity* affects the perceptions. A person who has suffered sensory loss (such as eyesight) must rely more on the other senses in order to perceive the world. Furthermore, our *expectations* will shape our perceptions. Those who study perception stress the old adage, "We see and hear what we want to see and hear." If we are anticipating that a message will carry a specific point of view, then we tend to perceive that message to indeed have that viewpoint. As a result, each person's perceptual filter will lead him or her to perceive a message differently from others. McCroskey describes this influence of perception in communication: "People tend to perceive what they want to perceive or what they expect to perceive, whether or not such perceptions are in accord with what other people might consider reality."[2]

An episode of the television situation comedy, "Diff'rent Strokes," illustrates the principle. A burglar breaks into the luxurious apartment of the Drummond family to steal from the safe, but he winds up knocked out on the floor. Each family member then describes to the police what happened from his/her point of view. Mr. Drummond, Arnold's father, for example, describes to the police how he fought with the man and knocked him down, while Arnold's brother, Willis, relates how his karate expertise led to the man's undoing. Arnold's sister, Kimberly, has yet a different story, and even Arnold takes credit for foiling the robber's attempt. But Pearl, the family's housekeeper, has been watching the scene from the kitchen window, so she tells the police that the burglar had actually tripped on the rug and fallen down himself! Thus, each person's perception, stemming from his or her own frame of reference, led to an individual interpretation of the situation. We make these interpretations constantly throughout the communication process; it is these perceptual interpretations that lead to major difficulties in communicating and understanding messages.

Just as key factors relating to the source and the receiver will affect the outcome of the communication, so, too, will variables of the message itself have an influence on the communication.

The message is composed of the *content,* structured and presented by means of verbal and nonverbal language code. The content consists of the ideas and the point of view which the communicator wishes to express. As we have seen, those very ideas may or may not be consistent with the attitudes and the knowledge of the receiver. Consequently, it may be necessary for the source to adjust and adapt the message more satisfactorily to meet the needs of the listener. Norman Thomas, six times the Socialist candidate for the American Presidency, presented in his Socialist platform messages which were not consistent with basic democratic ideals of most Americans. As a result, Thomas's fundamental messages were never acceptable to the majority of the voters.

The *message structure* likewise influences the understanding of and acceptance of the ideas. Americans, brought up with a Western philosophical orientation, are accustomed to deductive structure, consisting of generalizations leading to a specific conclusion. (Good listeners pay attention to the material. You pay attention to the material. Therefore, you are a good listener.) Persons raised under the influence of Eastern philosophical thought, on the other hand, may not be so accustomed to a deductive structure of messages. While American communicators are trained to develop a message with an introduction, central point, body, and conclusion, Chinese may have a different structure to a message.

KI	(an introduction offering an observation of a concrete reality)
SHO	(tell a story)
TEN	(shift or change in which a new topic or aspect is brought into the message)
KETSU	(gathering of loose ends, a "nonconclusion")
YO-IN	(a last point to think about, which does not necessarily relate)

The audience, then, is allowed to draw its own conclusion; a central point is not presented in such a structure.

The message structure, stemming from the cognitive orientation of the person, extends to the *language code* itself. A key variable in effective communication, the language code (verbal and nonverbal) is central to the entire process.

Indispensable to the comprehension of the verbal message, of course, is the sharing of common language symbols. Through the course of time and accepted usage, we have come to associate certain meanings with words. But the words themselves are empty representations or symbols of the stimulus we have chosen to communicate.[3] Thus, the word *chair* is a collection of letters arbitrarily assigned to that piece of furniture on which we sit; the word itself represents the chair, much as a road map is used to represent the freeway on which we travel to work.

Because we use our verbal language to represent *symbolically* that which we intend to communicate, communicators are well advised to remember that it *is* a symbolic process, a process of representing our concepts and objects with words. It is foolish to react to a symbol, a word, as if it were the referent itself. Remembering that it is a symbolic process is particularly important for listeners responding to highly volatile messages, for instance to "hate" rhetoric. We need to set aside our biases and prejudices while decoding communications and to remember that speakers are using words to represent symbolically their ideas.

The study of semantics has been concerned with the human use of language as symbols in order to communicate meaning. It is clear that often we cannot simply "transfer" our intended meaning to another person through a carefully-worded message. The message must be one in which the other communicator can share some common elements in order to interpret the message and assign to it his or her own meaning. "The ability to use language," Condon reminds us, "means the ability to transfer something of experience into symbols and *through the symbolic medium to share experience.*"[4] And the famous semanticist, S. I. Hayakawa, cautions that "the habitual confusion of symbols with things symbolized, whether on the part of individuals or societies, is serious enough at all levels of culture to provide a perennial human problem."[5]

Messages are transmitted not only by symbolic verbal codes but also by nonverbal language, everything but the word itself. Communicators, then, ought to be sensitive to such nonverbal dimensions as vocal inflections and vocal quality; gestures and physical animation; eye contact; and even a person's physical appearance and dress. All these elements communicate messages about a speaker's emotional state, self-concept, and attitudes toward the communication itself.

The nonverbal and verbal messages are presented via the sensory channels: sound, sight, smell, touch, and taste. Our sensory acuity will greatly influence the effectiveness of these channels. A sensory block can, of course, eliminate the use of a particular conduit and perhaps require persons to compensate through other channels. A deaf or hearing-impaired person, for instance, must make extensive use of visual communication channels in order to lip read, utilize sign language, and "read" the nonverbal cues of the communicator.

The effectiveness of a particular conduit at a particular time is influenced not only by the communicator's sensory acuity but also by the *channel selection.* As we have noted, a sensitive communicator will consider carefully decisions as to when to place a phone call, when to conduct face-to-face interviews, when to send a memo. As listeners, we may respond consciously or unconsciously to these channels. Some individuals may have an aversion to the telephone, for example, as an invasion of privacy. Indeed, the telephone can be obtrusive. A person standing in line at a ticket window may have to wait longer while the clerk handles telephone calls, which take precedence when the callers interrupt the clerk.

As communicators, we probably are not very sophisticated when it comes to understanding the importance of channel selection. A manager should know when to send a memo, use a telephone call, conduct a person-to-person interview, or post a notice on a bulletin board, in order to reach employees most effectively. Parents should understand when the use of touch can be reinforcing to a child, when to put a note on the refrigerator door, or whether to discuss issues at the dinner table or in private. Likewise, relaying messages through another person requires special consideration.

The channels we select relate to the *environment* (physical setting) in which we communicate. Again, elements in the setting can enhance or can detract from

Within most communication transactions, we simultaneously serve as sources and receivers.
Photo by Robert Tocha.

the communication. We can exercise some control over the lighting, ventilation, seating arrangements, and even room colors. But a failure in electric power, for instance, could darken the room and end the communication.

It is clear, then, that communication is a complex process, made up of many interrelated factors which serve to facilitate or to impair the effectiveness of the process itself. All communicators within a particular situation should recognize what is operating within the process and should work to enhance participation. Too frequently, we tend to sit back and require the speaker to assume full responsibility for the communication. But effective communication is a *shared,* meaningful, active process which imposes upon speakers and listeners alike equal responsibilities for the outcome.

Communication as a Simultaneous Process

While all of these variables have an influence—positive or negative—on the outcome of the communication, we can work to maintain some control over them so as to facilitate the process. Throughout our communication efforts, it is helpful to us, as listeners, to keep in perspective that communication is *symbolic* and

Figure 2.2.
Transactional model of communication.

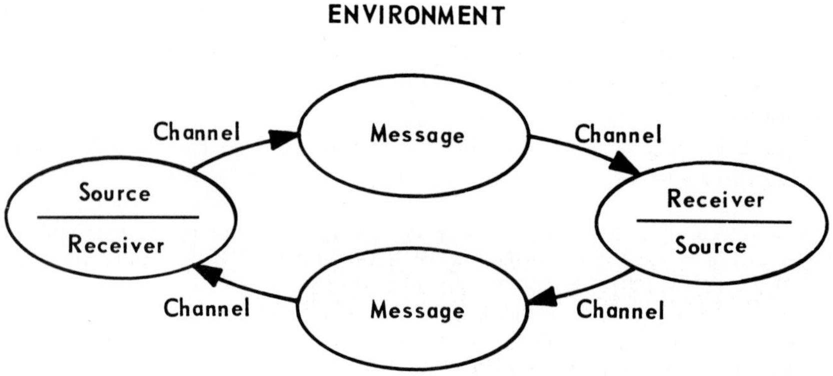

that it is a *process*. As we have noted, our language system comprises symbolic words and nonverbal dimensions which we utilize to *represent* the ideas we are expressing. We are constantly involved in a process of encoding and decoding messages in a fairly simultaneous sequence. We really function as source and receiver at one and the same time, sending messages and receiving/decoding feedback from the listener. And the listener, in turn, receives/decodes the message and, simultaneously, encodes/sends feedback messages.[6] This simultaneous process suggests that, ideally, we ought to view the source and the receiver as communicators rather than separating the two roles.[7] Thus, a model of the communication process might more realistically depict this simultaneous role-taking (fig. 2.2).[8]

This perspective of communication as the simultaneous interaction of the roles of source and receiver has come to be known as a *transactional* perspective. This view implies that communication is more than the interaction of a source and a receiver and that, indeed, we function as communicators in the process in encoding and decoding the messages. This simultaneous process, then, infers that we do not function as just a source or a receiver but, rather, that we perform both functions within most communication transactions. Smith and Williamson offer a description of the transactional model of communication:

> [B]oth persons in the communication situation are participating simultaneously. They are mutually perceiving each other; and both persons (not just the sender) are making adjustments to messages exchanged within the transaction. Both parties are simultaneously listening to each other; they are simultaneously and mutually engaged in the process of creating meaning in a relationship.[9]

The transactional model, therefore, offers a useful perspective to us as listeners. It is evident that the listener assumes the most important, involved role as a communicator in this transactional view. In the old linear model of communication, the speaker essentially pushed buttons to get a listener response, while the interactional view provides for the use of feedback from the receiver. The transactional approach, however, describes the listener as integral to the process, participating fully *throughout* the communication, not just as one who responds to messages.

John Stewart, a proponent of the transactional perspective in interpersonal communication, emphasizes the point:

> From a transactional perspective, human communicating is a process of meaning-creating rather than idea- or message-sending. When you're communicating, you're not transmitting your ideas to others but evoking their own ideas or meanings. . . . Consequently, although the words you use are important, your communication is also significantly affected by the other person's mood, needs, goals, attitudes, assumptions, past experiences, etc.[10]

Thus, as communicators, we constantly use our communciation skills, knowledge, attitudes, and frame of reference to function in the entire process of understanding verbal and nonverbal messages.

If you communicate with your professor in the classroom, for example, you may receive his or her lecture on intrapersonal communication and, at the same time, send him or her feedback through your nonverbal language that you agree, approve, support what the professor is telling the class about intrapersonal communication. As the professor develops the lecture, he or she should "read" the feedback he or she is receiving from you and your classmates and adapt the lecture accordingly.

Although such a view of the communication process is an important perspective for understanding the complexities of our roles as communicators, it is necessary to study the communication skills involved from a more distinct source and/or receiver perspective. And it is the focus of this book to examine the listening skills involved in the receiving process.

Implications for the Listener

The transactional perspective of the process of communication, then, is a useful perspective for the listener. It is helpful to remember that as a communicator, the listener is actively involved in receiving and sending (decoding and encoding) messages. While we listen to the verbal and the nonverbal messages of a speaker, we send verbal and nonverbal feedback messages back to our fellow communicators. And we send these messages through our perceptual filters: the frame of reference which comprises our background, experience, knowledge, attitudes, and communication skills. These variables affect our efficiency and our effectiveness in decoding and encoding the messages as we handle them simultaneously.

To be effective, the listener must develop a clear understanding of his or her frame of reference in order to know what perceptual filters are influencing his or her responses to messages. Moreover, the effective listener will develop the necessary listening skills in order to decode the messages and to encode feedback messages which will be appropriate to the communication. Effective feedback is probably as vital to true communication as is an effective message.

SUMMARY

In this chapter, we have examined the components of the communication process—source, message, channel, receiver, feedback, noise, and environment. These elements are affected by variables which facilitate or distort the communication process, depending largely on how effectively the communicators are able to control them. Such variables as communicator skills, attitudes, and knowledge combine with message structure, as well as with code and channel dimensions to complicate the communication process. Throughout, it is useful to retain the perspective that communication is symbolic (that we use verbal and nonverbal language to symbolically *represent* our ideas) and that it is an ongoing, transactional *process* in which source and receiver simultaneously encode and decode messages.

SUGGESTED ACTIVITIES

1. Design your own model of the communication process. Incorporate the components of communication and the variables which you think are essential to the process. Attempt to illustrate the simultaneous nature of the source and receiver functions within the process.
2. Illustrate the process of communication with a real-life situation involving a particular incident in which communication variables played a major role in the outcome of the communication.
3. Make a list of barriers to effective communication. Illustrate these obstacles with examples from your own communication experience.

NOTES

1. For a detailed discussion of variables influencing the communication process, you might like to read David K. Berlo, *The Process of Communication* (New York: Holt, Rinehart and Winston, 1960).
2. James C. McCroskey, "Human Information Processing and Diffusion," in *Speech Communication Behavior,* eds. Larry L. Barker and Robert J. Kibler (Englewood Cliffs, New Jersey: Prentice-Hall, 1971), p. 172.
3. This is the perspective held by semanticists, who argue that "words don't mean; people do." See, for instance, S. I. Hayakawa, *Language in Thought and Action* (New York: Harcourt, Brace and World, 1949).
4. John Condon, *Semantics and Communication* (New York: Macmillan Publishing Company, 1975), p. 9.

5. Hayakawa, *Language in Thought and Action,* p. 30.
6. An early proponent of this view was Wilbur Schramm in "How Communication Works," *The Process and Effects of Mass Communications* (Urbana: University of Illinois Press, 1955), pp. 3–26.
7. For a discussion of this perspective, see Roy M. Berko, Andrew D. Wolvin, and Darlyn R. Wolvin, *Communicating: A Social and Career Focus*, 2nd ed. (Boston: Houghton Mifflin Company, 1981), pp. 43–45.
8. One of the earliest communication scholars to develop a model of communication from a transactional perspective was Wilbur Schramm in "How Communication Works," *The Process and Effects of Mass Communication,* pp. 4–8.
9. Dennis Smith and Keith Williamson, *Interpersonal Communication* (Dubuque, Iowa: William C. Brown Company Publishers, 1981), p. 16.
10. John Stewart, *Bridges Not Walls* (Reading, Massachusetts: Addision-Wesley, 1973), p. 16.

Concepts You Will Encounter

Distinct Behavior
Listening Construct
Auding
Structural Approach
Aural Stimuli
Visual Stimuli
Components
Receiving
Otitis Media
Otosclerosis
Sensorineural Impairment
Presbycusis
Sociocusus
Binaural Hearing
Masking
Auditory Fatigue
Attending To
Selective Attention
Filter Theory
Analysis-by-Synthesis
Capacity Model
General Arousal
Energetic Attention
Scanning
Long-Term Memory System
Sensory Register
Short-Term Memory System
Rehearsal
Fluctuating Attention
Subliminal Perception
Assigning Meaning
Meaning as a Behavioral Disposition
Categorical System
Referent
Attributes
Criterial Attributes
Noncriterial Attributes
Single Attribute Category
Disjunctive Category
Relational Category
Conjunctive Category
Formal Attributes
Functional Attributes
Incorrect Categorization
Frame of Reference
Perceptual Filter
Emotional "Triggers"
Remembering
Responding
Overt Responses
Covert Responses
Agreement
Creative Listening
Purposeful Listening
Dynamic Process

The Process of Listening 3

Communication is an ongoing, transactional process involving both the sending and the receiving of messages. Although in this chapter we will focus only on the receptive aspect of the communication process, we must keep the perspective that even though listening is, in itself, a process, it is also an integral part of the total communication process.

The Nature of Listening as a Distinct Behavior

Basic to any attempt made to define listening is the answer to this question: Is listening a distinct behavior which is separate from other intellectual behaviors? Several factor studies—including those conducted by Caffrey, Caffrey and Smith, Karlin, and Hanley—have provided evidence that listening is indeed a distinct activity.[1] However, the factor analysis that has given decisive support that there is a separate listening factor was performed by Spearritt in Australia.[2] In his research Spearritt tested over four-hundred sixth graders in ten schools in Melbourne. He used thirty-four different tests to measure the reasoning, verbal comprehension, attention, auditory resistance, memory, and listening comprehension of these students. The factor analysis of the results of all of these tests isolated a disparate listening comprehension factor, distinct from the students' performance in reasoning, verbal comprehension, attention, auditory resistance, and memory.[3]

The studies which have isolated a listening component, particularly the study by Spearritt, illustrate that "listening is a kind of human behavior in itself, separate from reading, from memory, and from other intellectual behaviors, although dependent on them as they are probably dependent on it."[4] Since listening is a distinct function, it is useful to define this activity.

A Definition of Listening

The definition of listening is still in the developing process. Among the factors contributing to this delay are the following: listening is a complex, covert act difficult to investigate; much research in listening has not been coordinated or collated; and research in listening is in an exploratory state, with most of the research on listening having been conducted in the past four decades.

Despite these and other considerations, many of which current researchers and members of the established International Listening Association (ILA) are considering, a number of definitions have been proposed. The earliest of these cited in this chapter is dated 1925; the most recent is dated 1981. During the evolution of a listening definition, differences have emerged, involving the processes or elements encompassed, terms used, symbols included, and specifications made. These various definitions have often been based principally upon speculations, some more reasonable—in the light of present knowledge—than others. Nevertheless, they have all contributed to the framework of a listening construct, by raising questions, stimulating research, and/or adding ideas.

Proposed Definitions

Some of the proposed definitions of listening that have led to our current understanding of this complex act are the following:

> . . . an analysis of the impressions resulting from concentration where an effort of will is required—Tucker (1925)[5]

> . . . the ability to understand spoken language—Rankin(1926)[6]

> . . . the conscious, purposeful registration of sounds upon the mind [which] leads to further mental activity . . . all true listening is creative—Hook (1950)[7]

> . . . the ability to understand and respond effectively to oral communication—Johnson (1951)[8]

> . . . the process of reacting to, interpreting, and relating the spoken language in terms of past experiences and further courses of action—Barbe and Meyers (1954)[9]

> . . . the aural assimilation of spoken symbols in face-to-face speaker-audience situation, with both oral and visual cues present—Brown and Carlsen (1955)[10]

> . . . the capacity of an individual to understand spoken language in the presence of a speaker—Still (1955)[11]

> . . . a selective process by which sounds communicated by some source are received, critically interpreted, and acted upon by a purposeful listener—Jones (1956)[12]

> . . . a definite, usually voluntary, effort to apprehend accoustically—Barbara (1957)[13]

> . . . the act of giving attention to the spoken word, not only in hearing symbols, but in the reacting with understanding—Hampleman (1958)[14]

> . . . the process of hearing, identifying, understanding and interpreting spoken language—Lewis (1958)[15]

> . . . the composite process by which oral language communicated by some source is received, critically and purposefully attended to, recognized, and interpreted (or comprehended) in terms of past experiences and future expectancies—Petrie (1961)[16]

. . . the selective process of attending to, hearing, understanding, and remembering aural symbols—Barker (1971)[17]

. . . the process by which spoken language is converted to meaning in the mind—Lundsteen (1971)[18]

. . . a process that takes place when a human organism receives data aurally—Weaver (1972)[19]

. . . the process whereby the human ear receives sound stimuli from other people and through a series of steps interprets the sound stimuli in the brain and remembers it—Hirsch (1979)[20]

. . . the . . . act really consisting of four connected activities—sensing, interpreting, evaluating and responding—Steil (1981)[21]

Questions Crucial to the Construction of a Listening Definition

A quick glance at these definitions shows us that listening scholars do not agree on what listening is. A more careful study, however, will reveal to us that they raise many questions that are crucial for us to answer if we are to construct a definition of listening. Among the most critical questions are the following:

1. In the various definitions, what different terms are used? Which of these terms are synonymous?
2. Should both verbal and nonverbal symbols be included in a listening definition? Is there a visual factor involved in listening? Is the visual factor a necessary component of the listening act?
3. Can listening occur only in face-to-face situations?
4. What processes or elements are encompassed in the listening act?
5. Is hearing a component of listening, or is it only a necessary condition?
6. Is listening more than the mere perception of sound?
7. Does listening require conscious effort?
8. Is retention a necessary component of the listening act?
9. Is reacting and responding a necessary component of listening? Must the reaction be overt? Can it be only covert?
10. Is listening creative? If so, in what ways is it creative?
11. Is listening purposeful? If so, what are the purposes of listening?
12. Is listening a process?

In this chapter, we will answer these crucial questions.

Differences in Proposed Definitions

As we carefully study the proposed definitions, we find numerous differences in the authors' assignment of meaning to the term *listening*. One major difference is the elements or processes that are mentioned: analyzing, concentrating, understanding, registering, converting meaning to the mind, engaging in further mental activity, responding, reacting, interpreting, relating to past experiences and future expectancies, assimilating, acting upon, selecting, receiving, apprehending, attending, hearing, remembering, identifying, recognizing, comprehending, sensing, and evaluating. In naming the processes or elements involved in the listening act, it is also apparent that there are differences in the terms used. The fact that synonyms, such as *responding* and *reacting* and *understanding* and *comprehending,* are frequently used calls further attention to the need for a more specific definition.

Furthermore, writers differ concerning the types of symbols to which the listener attends. The majority of the authors have emphasized that listening involves attending to verbal sounds only as is indicated by again synonymous phrases such as "the spoken language," "spoken symbols," "oral communication," "oral language," "aural symbols," and "the spoken word." On the other hand, Tucker, Hook, Jones, Barbara, and Weaver include nonverbal stimuli as well.

Brown, observing such disagreements and verbal confusion, recognized the need for a more precise term to denote listening to verbal material. He proposed that the term *auding* be used to designate the comprehension of verbal sounds. A definition of reading—the other receptive language art skill—provided the key to the definition of auding; he defined auding as "the gross process of listening to, recognizing, and interpreting spoken symbols."[22] Brown, distinguishing between listening and auding, stated that "listening is a factor in auding precisely as looking is a factor in reading, that auding is confined to language whereas listening is not, and that listening, even when earnestly applied, to unfamiliar language is not enough."[23] Apparently, to Brown, listening is "paying attention to the sounds."[24]

Although Caffrey, Furness, Horrworth, and others have adopted the term *auding* and have limited their definitions to the inclusion of spoken words only, their definitions of auding differ. Caffrey defines auding as "the process of hearing, listening to, recognizing, and interpreting or comprehending spoken language."[25] Furness describes auding as consisting "of at least six processes: (a) hearing, (b) listening, (c) recognizing spoken language, (d) interpreting oral symbols, (e) supplementing meaning and knowledge of the symbols, and (f) being aware of facts or assumptions not uttered."[26] Horrworth expresses her interpretation of the findings of Brown, Caffrey, Furness, and others in the following paradigm: "Auding = Hearing + Listening + Cognizing." She further defines hearing as "the process by which sound waves are received, modified, and relayed along the nervous system by the ear"; listening as "the process of directing attention to and thereby becoming aware of sound sequences"; and cognition as "a generic term used often to denote all of the various aspects of knowing, including perception, judgment, reasoning, remembering; and thinking and imagining."[27]

Despite the frequent misuse of the term *listening,* the term is too fully established in our culture for listening researchers to attempt to change its name. Rather than using *auding* or coining a new term, we prefer to strive to clarify the term with which society is already familiar.

In addition to the limitations some writers have placed upon the symbols attended to in the listening act, other specifications have been made. Brown and

Listening Book

Chpt. 3, 4, 6, 7, 8

Gender

Chapt 1, 2, 4

Carlsen and Still stipulate that listening must be face-to-face. Brown and Carlsen also include visual cues as factors in listening. Furthermore, the viewpoint that listening requires purpose, creativity, and effort are expressed. And, beginning with the definition of Barbe and Meyers, the term *process* is frequently included.

New Directions toward a Unified Definition of Listening

It is apparent that researchers in the field of listening have employed varied definitions since 1925. Recent advancements, however, have been and are being made toward the elimination of the major factors that have contributed to the delay of a unified construct of listening.

The quantity of research in listening is steadily growing. This growth is evident in the amount of listening research cited in reviews, bibliographies, indexes and books. Although the quality of the research is sometimes suspect, new directions are being taken to improve the quality.

The coordination and collation of listening research appears to offer the most promise toward the improvement of the quality of investigation as well as the development of a listening construct. The newly formed International Listening Association (1979) has as one of its primary goals the establishing of a clearinghouse to allow the professional interchange of listening materials and research findings. Both the National Center for Educational Research and Development (NCERD) and the National Institute of Education (NIE) have already made contributions toward alleviating the problem of uncollated research. Both government agencies have directed the separate Educational Resources Information Center (ERIC) Clearinghouses to commission from recognized authorities information analysis papers in specific areas. Two ERIC Clearinghouses—the Clearinghouse on the Teaching of English and the Clearinghouse on Reading and Communication Skills—and the National Council of Teachers of English (NCTE) and the Speech Communication Association (SCA) have worked jointly with the government agencies and published works in the area of listening. Under the sponsorship of NCTE/ERIC, Lundsteen wrote a state-of-the-art monograph on listening in 1971. In this book, updated in 1979, she analyzes and synthesizes published and unpublished material on listening. Under the sponsorship of SCA/ERIC, Wolvin and Coakley co-authored a listening booklet in 1979; this booklet blends theory and research in listening with classroom practices for improving listening. In both works, the authors devote several pages to defining listening. Recognizing that not all of the questions are answerable as yet, Lundsteen prefaces her discussion of a definition of listening with the following remark: "Defining listening is a challenge. There are many unknowns in this problem calling for creativity and commitment to go beyond what is presented here."[28] Although, as Lundsteen has stated, many problems in defining listening still exist, progress is being made toward developing a concept of listening.

Aspects Encompassed in the Listening Process

Before we offer our own definition of the listening process, it may be useful for the reader to examine the process of listening structurally. In an attempt to answer the question, "What are the aspects which make up the listening process?", we have drawn on research in many fields, including listening, communication, psychology, and physiology.[29]

Stimuli

Various kinds of stimuli are involved in the act of listening.

Aural Stimuli. Although many definitions of listening have limited the symbols attended to in the listening act to spoken words, Weaver includes verbal data (words), vocal data (voice cues, such as inflections), and other kinds of sounds (nonlinguistic sounds) as types of aurally input data to which the listener attends and assigns meaning.[30] We support Weaver's view; the listener attends and assigns meaning to a shrilly screamed exclamation, "The house is on fire!", as well as to the sound of a smoke alarm.

Visual Stimuli. Must both the receiver and the sender be present in the face-to-face situation for listening to occur? We agree with those who believe that listening can occur without the listener seeing the message originator; one can engage in the listening act, for example, by way of television, public address system, intercom, and other communication media. However, we should point out that what we see (or "what we listen to with the third ear") can contribute to our listening effectiveness. When we consider Birdwhistell's findings that spoken words account for no more than 30 to 35 percent of all social interactions and Mehrabian's estimates that as much as 93 percent of a message's total meaning may stem from nonverbal cues, we realize that visual cues can assist us in assigning meaning.[31] Visual cues, however, are not necessary components of the listening act, as those who are blind can readily confirm.

Components

Various processes or elements are encompassed in the listening act.

Receiving. The first component, receiving, refers to the physiological process of hearing and/or seeing aural and/or visual stimuli (phonemes, words, vocal cues, nonlinguistic sounds, nonverbal cues).

The Seeing Process. The seeing process begins with light rays—reflected from an object—falling on the cornea in the front of the eye (fig. 3.1). The cornea is made up of tough, transparent tissue with no blood vessels. The rays then pass through the liquid *aqueous humor* contained in the anterior chamber directly behind the cornea. The rays proceed through the lens and the vitreous humor behind the lens. The cornea and the lens are separated by the iris which contains the pupil, an opening that can vary in diameter from approximately two to eight millimeters. The constriction of the pupil can improve the quality of the image formed and increase the depth of focus of the eye.

Figure 3.1. Anatomy of the human eye.
Drawing by Neal Ashby.

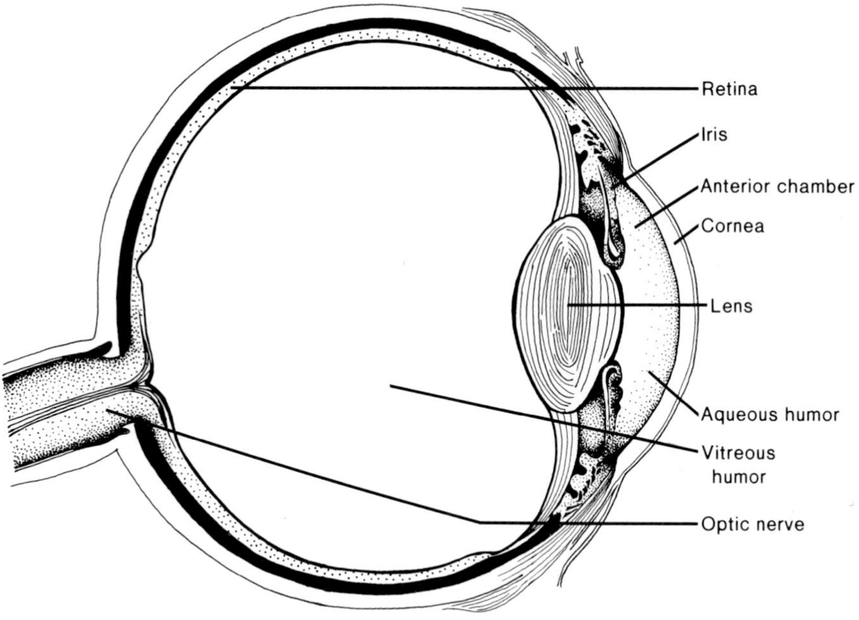

Once the light rays pass through the lens, they fall on the retina, the innermost part of the eyeball. The retina contains, at the back, the receptors which are sensitive to light. To reach these receptors, the rays pass back and forth across the surface of the retina, containing the optic nerve fibers.

The optic nerve fibers pass through the back of the eye to the optic thalamus (a station through which fibers pass) and on to the visual cortex, the visual center of the brain. These fibers are set into stimulation throughout the system by the light rays.[32]

The Hearing Process. The process of hearing is complicated by the intricacies of the hearing mechanism. Sound waves are received by the ear and transmitted to the brain. The outer ear (fig. 3.2), which consists of the pinna and the canal, serves to direct the sounds waves into the hearing mechanism. The pinna, the prominent part of the outer ear, serves only this purpose, while in other forms of animals the pinna—having the ability to move—can play a greater role in detecting and directing sounds. A dog, for instance, can move his ears to localize sounds. The external (auditory) canal of the outer ear is a passage which may be a bit over one inch in length. It contains hairs and wax to protect the tympanic membrane (eardrum) from penetration of dirt and objects.

Figure 3.2. Anatomy of the human ear.
Drawing by Neal Ashby.

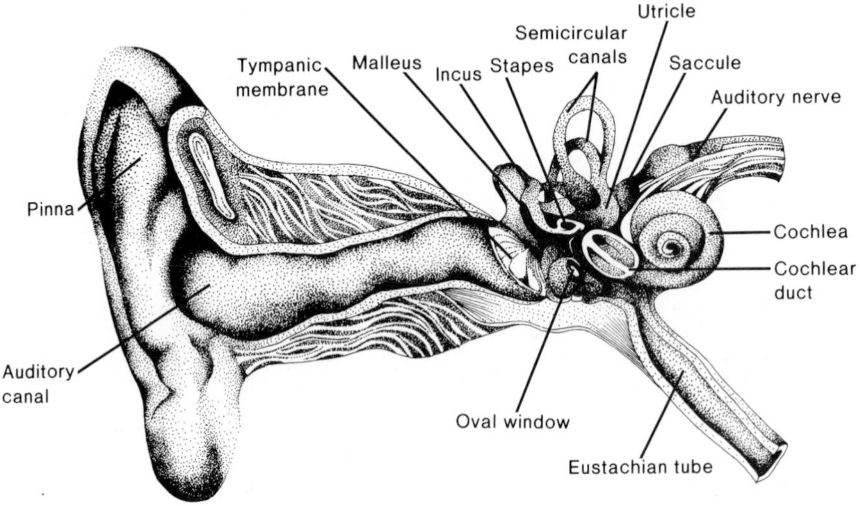

The middle ear connects the eardrum with the ossicular chain containing the smallest bones in the body—the malleus (hammer), the incus (anvil), and the stapes (stirrup). These bones connect the eardrum to the opening of the inner ear, the oval window. The middle ear also includes the Eustachian tube which serves as an equalizer of air pressure and thus enables the middle ear to compensate for external air pressure.

The inner ear serves as the final organ for hearing *and* as the sensory organ for balance. The balance results from the vestibular apparatus containing the utricle, saccule, and semicircular canals. The hearing part of the inner ear is the cochlea, which resembles a snail shell. The entire inner ear is filled with fluid. The cochlear duct, containing this fluid, includes the organ of corti, the end organ of hearing. This organ consists of four or five rows of hair cells which connect with nerve fibers which run into the center of the cochlea and form the cochlear branch of the VIIIth nerve (the auditory nerve). This branch joins the vestibular branch, and the VIIIth nerve proceeds to the brain stem and the cerebral cortex.

Normally we hear by air conduction since most sounds are air born and since the air conduction mechanism is more sensitive than the mechanism of bone conduction. The sound waves, channeled through the external canal, set the eardrum into vibration. The ossicular chain, connected by the hammer to the eardrum, is then set into vibration. The three tiny bones of the ossicular chain vibrate as a unit and produce a rocking motion of the stapes in the oval window, matching the sound waves of the air to that of the fluid. The fluid of the oval window then leads to a bulging outward of the round window, transmitted through the cochlear duct. The bulging leads to movement of the membrane, initiating nerve impulses carried to the cochlear portion of the VIIIth nerve and then to the cerebral cortex which hears the vibrations set in motion on the eardrum.

The vibrations in the cochlea are then converted to electrical impulses which lead to a release of a chemical which "fires" the fibers within the acoustic nerve and thus conveys the signal to the brain. The ear responds to a band of frequencies (measured by hertz, Hz) and to intensity (measured by decibels, dB). Normal speech is in the range of 400–4000 Hz and 60 dB.

Various theories of hearing attempt to explain how an individual, through this process, can discriminate pitches—the frequency (as measured by hertz, Hz) of sound. One theory, the Place theory, suggests that the cochlea resembles a spiral which is tuned to different pitch levels with the vibrations on this elastic membrane varying with the size of the diameter of the spiral. This idea, popularized by the German scientist Helmholz, holds that the base end of the cochlea, then, is sensitive to high frequencies, and the other end is stimulated by low frequencies.

An alternative theory of hearing explains pitch perception as the result of the frequency of occurrence of impulses in the auditory nerve. George von Bekesy, a Nobel prizewinning scientist who has spent years researching the hearing mechanism, speculates that the sound results from a wave traveling from the base to the apex of the cochlea.[33]

The complex process of hearing, which may never be fully understood by scientists, is made even more complicated by malfunctions *in* or *of* the hearing mechanism. The most common problem results from the blockage of the outer ear by an excessive accumulation of wax. The inner ear may become inflamed or infested (*otitis media*), often the result of a respiratory infection. At times, cases of otitis media may become chronic, particularly in younger children. Treating otitis media requires antibiotic drug therapy or a simple myringotomy, a surgical process of making an incision in the eardrum and inserting a small tube to allow the middle ear to drain. The inner ear also may be subject to what is known as "swimmer's ear," an infection which can result when water remains in the inner ear after one has been swimming, showering, or bathing. Persons prone to this condition must take special care (such as wearing ear plugs) to avoid permitting water to enter the ear.

Less common is a congenital condition known as *otosclerosis,* a progressive disease which turns the hard bone of the inner ear into spongy bone matter. For some unknown reason, the disease primarily affects Caucasian women. A new surgical technique, stapedectomy, consists of removing the stapes completely and creating a prosthetic link between the incus and the oval window. This technique has been found to restore hearing to within 10dB.

Some individuals suffer sensorineural impairment. In this condition, the sound is conducted properly to the fluid in the inner ear, but it cannot be perceived normally. The sensorineural impairment, in its extreme, leads to partial or com-

We can suffer hearing loss from exposure to occupational noise sources.

Photo by Robert Tocha.

plete deafness. Those individuals with a slight sensorineural loss may be prone to "shouting" in order to hear themselves as well as others. Other than attempting to arrest further sensory loss, most hearing specialists feel it is practically impossible to restore sensory loss once the nerve fibers in the cochlea or in the VIIIth nerve are destroyed.

Various mechanical devices are available, however, to restore the auditory acuity of persons who suffer hearing loss. A recent but expensive new technology is a cochlear implant. This consists of a small electrical coil implanted under the skin behind the ear on the mastoid bone (the part of the skull that forms the hump behind the ear). An electrical wire runs through the middle ear into the coils of the cochlea, and the device is powered by a small battery pack that the wearer carries in a pocket. More than 100 adults have received these implants, and the procedure is viewed as a significant breakthrough for overcoming the hearing loss for some profoundly deaf persons.[34]

The most common device is the hearing aid which can conduct the sound through amplification. Although hearing aids can help, "matching the aid to the ear and to the auditory problem of the wearer has never been easy," notes Denis Grady, "and until recently, it was impossible to amplify sound without distorting it."[35] Audiologists and engineers today are developing new electronic aids that can be adapted to specific kinds of hearing losses and provide excellent sound quality.

For decades Americans have perceived a stigma attached to hearing loss and have perpetuated the notion that we must hide our infirmities. As a result, many Americans who suffer hearing loss have been reluctant to wear hearing aids of any type. In 1983, President Ronald Reagan publicly wore a hearing aid to restore hearing which had been impaired by a film studio accident in the 1930's. His public acceptance of the hearing aid was hailed by many as an important step forward in changing American attitudes toward hearing aids. Even the *New York Times* observed that "President Reagan did himself a favor when he got a hearing aid. But he did an even greater favor for all Americans."[36]

Sensorineural impairment of the hearing function relates, in part, to the physical deterioration of the hearing mechanism through increased age. The progressive hearing loss is known as presbycusis. The process starts at about the age of twenty and becomes increasingly evident with each decade of an individual's life span.[37]

In addition to presbycusis, all persons are affected by sociocusis—hearing loss from exposure to occupational and nonoccupational noise sources such as tractors, riveting machines, rock'n'roll music, and jet plane flyovers. The influence of noise pollution continues to be a major environmental problem in the United States. The Public Health Service, for example, conducted a study of some of the common environmental sound levels (measured by decibels, dB, on the A-network of a sound level meter, abbreviated as dBA) of noises, and the findings are reported in table 3.1.[38]

This table reveals the high decibel level of rock music, a concern of many who study the damaging effects of noise. Ralph Naunton, a specialist on hearing hygiene with the National Institute of Health, estimates that some 13 million Americans (almost one out of every twenty) today suffer some type of hearing impairment, and he especially notes that loud music, particularly popular with teenagers and with joggers who use earphones, can damage the hearing mechanism.[39] Likewise, Cathleen Malatino, studying the noise level at indoor rock concerts, found that the decibel level ranges from 105 to 110 dB at all times. "When this level persists for two or three hours," she reports, "people are being subjected to an average of nearly 150 percent of the amount of noise the federal government considers safe for an entire day."[40]

The federal Environmental Protection Agency is charged with controlling noise pollution through the Noise Control Act of 1972. This legislation mandates

Table 3.1. 'A' weighted sound levels of some noises found in different environments

Sound Level, dBA	Industrial (and Military)	Community (or Outdoor)	Home (or Indoor)
—130—	Armored Personnel Carrier (123 dB)		
—120— Uncomfortably Loud	Oxygen Torch (121 dB)		
	Scraper-Loader (117 dB)		
—110—	Compactor (116 dB)		Rock'N'Roll Band (108–114 dB)
	Riveting Machine (110 dB)	Jet Flyover @ 100 ft. (103 dB)	
—100—Very Loud	Textile Loom (106 dB)	Power Mower (96 dB)	
— 90—	Electric Furnace Area (100 dB)	Compressor @ 20 ft. (94 dB)	Inside Subway Car-35 mph (95 dB)
— 80— Moderately Loud	Farm Tractor (98 dB)	Rock Drill @ 100 ft. (92 dB)	Cockpit-Light Aircraft (90 dB)
	Newspaper Press (97 dB)	Motorcycles @ 25 ft. (90 dB)	Food Blender (88 dB)
— 70—	Cockpit-Prop Aircraft (88 dB)	Propeller Aircraft Flyover @ 1000 ft. (88 dBA)	Garbage Disposal (80 dB)
— 60—	Milling Machine (85 dB)		Clothes Washer (78 dB)
— 50—Quiet	Cotton Spinning (83 dB)	Diesel Truck, 40 mph @ 50 ft. (84 dB)	Living Room Music (76 dB)
— 40—	Lathe (81 dB)	Diesel Train, 40–50 mph @ 100 ft. (83 dB)	Dishwasher (75 dB)
— 30—Very Quiet	Tabulating (80 dB)		TV-Audio (70 dB)
			Vacuum (70 dB)
		Passenger Car, 65 mph @ 25 ft. (77 dB)	Conversation (60 dB)
— 20—		Near Freeway-Auto Traffic (64 dB)	
— 10—Just Audible		Air-Conditioning Unit @ 20 ft. (60 dB)	
— 0—Threshold of Hearing (1000-4000 Hz)		Large Transformer @ 200 ft. (53 dB)	
		Light Traffic @ 100 ft. (50 dB)	

Note: Unless otherwise specified, listed sound levels are measured at typical operator-listener distances from source. Noise readings taken from general acoustical literature and observations by PHS.

the EPA to identify and regulate major sources of noise and to label noisy products. In addition, the agency attempts to coordinate noise control effects of state and local governments through the Quiet Communities Act of 1978.[41]

One local government that has been successful in noise control is the Seattle, Washington, government. In only one year, 1980, Seattle banished outdoor rock concerts from the Seattle Center, forced a large dairy to install quieter refrigeration units on its delivery trucks, required owners of heat pumps to enclose them in soundproof cases, and stopped the National Oceanographic and Atmospheric Administration from night dredging on Lake Washington. Curt Honrer,

Seattle's noise abatement coordinator, believes that the program has had a psychological spin-off: "The people themselves have more awareness of noise. They value their quiet."[42]

Despite these advances, enforcement of noise standards is difficult because few agencies can support the vast number of inspectors that would be required. Consequently, greater public awareness of the real problem of noise pollution and its effect on our physical and psychological system may be an important key to dealing with the situation.

Research on the effects of noise on humans is far from complete. In a review of this research, Sheldon Cohen concludes that we do know that noise can have a profound effect physically on the hearing mechanism and probably the functioning of other physical organs such as the heart. Public officials, however, are just beginning to accept the idea that noise can also result in psychological harm. In a recent landmark court case, several residents of the area surrounding the Los Angeles International Airport sued the city of Los Angeles for loss of property value and also for the mental and emotional distress they experienced as a result of the airport noise. "Not only were they granted compensation for loss of property value, but the California Supreme Court also affirmed their contention that jet noise interferes with daily life and causes 'a sense or feeling of annoyance, strain, worry, anger, frustration, nervousness, fear, and irritability.' "[43]

Hearing hygiene, it would seem, extends beyond care of the hearing mechanism through proper cleanliness and medical attention as necessary. Avoidance of exposure to noise sources is a further dimension of proper care of the hearing system. This proper care of the system, of course, supports effective listening behavior.

There are three additional factors that weaken the hearing process. One is binaural hearing problems—a lack of coordinated functioning of both ears and, consequently, the inability to discriminate the direction of the source of the sound. Another factor is masking—the existence of background noise or other types of interference (such as conflicting simultaneous messages) while the individual is attempting to hear the intended oral message. A third problem is that of auditory fatigue—fatigue from continuous exposure to sounds of certain frequency, such as a monotonous or droning voice, a ticking clock, a running appliance, and a dripping faucet. If any of these factors are operating, the process of hearing is weakened, and, thus, listening is impeded.

Is hearing an aspect or component of listening, or is hearing, like consciousness, only a necessary condition? A person who is totally deaf cannot listen because he or she cannot hear; therefore, hearing is a necessary condition. However, since *listening* and *hearing* are so frequently misused as synonyms, most listening scholars, including us, believe that hearing is an integral component of the listening process.

Attending to. The second component, attending to, refers to the focused perception on selected stimuli. This act embraces the moment before and during the reception of a potential stimulus.[44]

At any moment, numerous stimuli in our immediate environment are vying for our attention. These stimuli may be external, such as a speaker's words, a noise in the hall, a poster on the wall, or an attractive person in the room; or they may be internal, such as a headache, a distracting thought, or a numb foot. Suppose you are listening to a student speak in the classroom. The speaker's message is the stimulus you have selected to attend to. However, outside you hear a motor rev and shouts of other students; internally you feel hunger pains or have an itch. So what do you do? Can you divide your attention among several stimuli? If so, how many stimuli can you attend to at any given time?

Selective Attention. There are a number of stimuli to which we can attend at any one time.[45] However, there is no limit to the number of stimuli constantly competing for our attention. If all stimuli seeking our attention at any given instant were sent to the cortex, a neural overload would result. Thus, we must constantly engage in a process of selecting only those stimuli to which we will attend. It is believed that some discriminatory mechanism assists us in selecting the wanted from the unwanted aural stimuli.

Beginning with the first formal attention model proposed by Broadbent in 1958, many explanations of how this discriminatory process operates have been proposed. Like Broadbent's model, other early attention models (such as those proposed by Deutsch and Deutsch, Treisman, and Neisser) viewed information-processing as a series of steps with selective attention operating at a particular stage. A more recent attention model proposed by Kahneman also recognizes the limited capacity of attention energy; however, it treats attention as a resource that can be flexibly allocated (distributed) to different stages—rather than to one stage—of information-processing. The following brief explanations of five notable attention models illustrate theorists' varying views of the nature of selective attention.

According to Broadbent's 1958 model of attention, aural stimuli enter the nervous system through a number of sensory input channels. Broadbent posited that the various input lines converge onto a filter which functions as a selective mechanism. The filter selects stimuli not on the basis of analysis of meaning but rather on the basis of analysis of certain physical features (such as location in space, pitch, and intensity) toward which it is biased, and it then allows the selected stimuli to penetrate consciousness. Unselected stimuli are held in a short-term store for a brief period of time, after which they are attended to or lost.[46]

Deutsch and Deutsch found Broadbent's theory to be attractive when applied to simple and few discriminations. They questioned its application, however, to cases where numerous and complex discriminations are required. Thus, they proposed the following model:

> Another mechanism is proposed, which assumes the existence of a shifting reference standard, which takes up the level of the most important arriving signal. . . . Only the most important signals coming in will be acted on or remembered. On the other hand, more important signals than those present at an

immediately preceding time will be able to break in, for these will raise the height of the level and so displace the previously most important signals as the highest.[47]

Deutsch and Deutsch also discussed the role of general arousal in selective attention. They believed that some degree of general arousal is necessary for attention to operate. When aroused, an individual will attend to any incoming stimulus provided that it is not accompanied by a more important one. When asleep, however, an individual will respond to only very "important" messages (such as a person's own name or the cry of a mother's infant).[48] Experimental studies conducted by Moray, by Oswald, Taylor, and Treisman, and by Howarth and Ellis have indicated that some selective mechanism functions when a person recognizes his or her own name (an "important" word) during dichotic listening, during sleep, and during normal listening under noise.[49] Treisman has suggested that such "important" words and, perhaps, danger signals, "have permanently lower thresholds for activation or are more readily available than others . . . others would be lowered temporarily by incoming signals on some kind of conditional probability basis. . . ."[50]

The third model of attention was proposed by Treisman. She posited that messages, having arrived to some part of the nervous system over different input channels, are first analyzed for physical characteristics such as pitch, loudness, and location in space. A filter uses the information obtained by this analysis to identify the messages to be selected for attention. On other occasions, the filter bases its selection on more complex discriminations (such as the analysis of syllabic patterns, grammatical structure, or meaning). Treisman further postulated that the selective filter's tuning flexibility, determined by the perceived meanings in an individual's state of awareness, allows the filter to attenuate incoming information (that is, make the information more or less perceptible) rather than completely block it out.[51]

In 1967, Neisser proposed the two-process theory of analysis-by-synthesis. He postulated that incoming stimuli go through preattentive processing. During this processing, stored knowledge is actively used to analyze the stimuli's sensory and semantic features for important information. Viewing such focused attention as a result of all processing, Neisser theorized that attended and unattended stimuli differ only in the amount of processing given to them. Discounting the others' view that some incoming stimuli are never attended to because they have been blocked out or attenuated, Neisser theorized that they are not attended to merely because they have not been processed as fully as attended stimuli have been.[52]

More recently, Kahneman proposed a capacity model which views attention as a limited-capacity resource that can be flexibly allocated to various stages of information-processing. The way in which one distributes his or her attentional energy is governed by (1) automatic, unconscious rules (such as focusing on a speaker who states the listener's name), (2) conscious decisions (such as choosing to focus on the boss's message rather than on a co-worker's simultaneous message), and (3) the difficulty of the mental task (with more attentional energy being required and, therefore, being allocated to complex mental tasks). According to Kahneman, an individual can change his or her attentional distribution from moment to moment in order to meet the varying attentional requirements of conscious mental tasks (which demand considerable attentional energy) and automatic mental tasks (which demand little attentional energy and thus do not interfere with other ongoing information-processing tasks, such as rehearsal and elaborative mnemonic devices, which also require attentional energy).[53]

Although the dominant view of attention presently follows Kahneman's position, disagreements continue as to how selective attention operates, where discriminatory decisions are made, and what happens to unselected stimuli. However, there is experimental evidence, as has been cited previously, that attention is selective. As listeners, we base our selection of aural stimuli upon a priority system that exists within each of us. This priority system may stem from "the tendency for people to pay close attention to information that is consistent with their attitudes, beliefs, values, and behaviors, and little attention to stimuli which are inconsistent."[54] This need for consistency has led McCroskey to conclude that "selective attention is not so much the conscious 'tuning out' of inconsistent information as it is the unconscious 'tuning in' of consistent information."[55] This process of tuning in and tuning out has critical implication for our understanding of listening behavior. Bartlett summarizes the relationship of selective attention to listener perception: "Selective listening is determined mainly by the qualitative differences in stimuli in relation to predispositions—cognitive, affective, and motor—of the listener."[56]

Energetic Attention. Not only is attention selective, but also it is energetic. It requires both effort and desire. Although we can divide our attention, we can give complete attention to only one stimulus at a time. If we expend too much energy on too many stimuli, we will no longer be attending; instead, we will be scanning (that is, sweeping the perceptual field to discover that which should be attended to).[57] Thus, by concentrating our attention energy on one stimulus instead of on many, we can focus more sharply upon the selected stimulus.

Once we have selected a stimulus to which we will attend, it has our attention; that is, we become aware of it, and we further process it. In some cases, according to Hasher and Zacks, processing the stimulus will require minimal attentional energy, and thus it will not interfere with other ongoing information-processing operations. In other cases, the processing will require considerable attentional energy and thus will interfere with other cognitive operations. Whether the processing is automatic (as it appears to be when one is processing information such as spatial, temporal, and frequency-of-occurrence information) or effortful (as it appears to be when one is engaging in operations such as rehearsal and elaborative mnemonic devices), we must attend to the stimulus.[58] There is some evidence, however, that some stimuli which seem never to be attended to (or of which the individual seems never to be aware) enter and remain in the memory system.[59] Generally, however, only stimuli that have been attended to enter the memory system.

The memory system referred to in the previous paragraph is the long-term memory system (LTM). Presently, in experimental psychology there is no prevailing view of the structure of the human memory as there was in the 1960's and early 1970's when the multistore view prevailed. However, many notions incorporated in the multistore models (such as those conceived by Atkinson and Shiffrin and Norman and Rumelhart[60]) are still accepted. Thus, the multistore view is an important forerunner to current trends in memory research.

Adherents to the multistore view posit that the human memory consists of two or three (if the sensory register is included) separate and distinct structural components or stores: sensory register, short-term memory system (STM), and long-term memory system (LTM). The sensory register is the least permanent memory store; it is here that the stimuli in their raw form enter the memory system through various senses. Upon entering, or registering (without conscious effort on the part of the receiver), the stimulus is temporarily stored. The length of time the sensory stimulus can remain in the sensory register without the stimulus being lost (decaying with the passage of time or being erased by new sensory stimuli entering the sensory register) is quite limited; research shows that visual (iconic) sensory storage lasts only several hundred milliseconds,[61] while auditory (echoic) sensory storage lasts up to three or four seconds.[62] Thus, if the sensory stimulus is not immediately selected for attention (that is, transferred to the short-term memory store), it is lost.

The short-term memory store, or the working memory "where conscious mental processes are performed on information from both the sensory register and the long-term store,"[63] is also a temporary store. The selected incoming stimulus—having been converted from its raw, sensory form (for example, the separate sounds of o′ pĕn) to a meaningful form *open*—is stored only briefly because of two notable limitations on the STM. One limitation is the length of time that a stimulus may be stored in it. Research indicates that if the stimulus in the STM is not attended to, it will decay in a period ranging from twenty seconds to one minute.[64] However, the stimulus may be preserved as long as one desires if one gives it constant attention by engaging in the process of rehearsal (the silent or vocal repetition of the stimulus/stimuli or concentration on the stimulus/stimuli). In addition, rehearsal appears to increase the chances of a stimulus reaching the cortex for attention[65] and therefore being committed to the long-term memory system.[66] However, if a person, during rehearsal, is interrupted by another person's question or request, internal noise, or some other distraction which results in the rehearser's shift of attention, the disruption probably will cause the previously-rehearsed information to be lost within sixty seconds. In addition to this time limit, the STM has a limitation on the number of stimuli which it can hold simultaneously. Experimental evidence indicates that this limit is approximately seven units, or "the magical number seven, plus or minus two."[67]

Three examples will illustrate how a listener may use his or her STM or working memory. First, consider how the listener may process information that has entered the STM from the sensory register. Suppose Susan orally gives Steve a seven-digit number (with which he is unfamiliar) and asks him to dial it. Without rehearsing the number, Steve retains the seven-digit telephone number only until he has dialed it. Unfortunately, the line is busy. A few moments later, Steve must ask Susan to repeat the number since the unattended auditory stimuli no longer remain in Steve's STM. This time, Steve rehearses (silently or vocally repeats the number) from the time Susan gives the number to him until he reaches the party he is calling. Will Steve still remember the number after he has completed the conversation? He may have only used his STM to retain (through rehearsal) the number until he had completed his task (reaching the desired party) and then dismissed the number. Or he may have learned the number and transferred it to his long-term memory system from where he could retrieve it days, months, or years later. From this example, we can see that the STM provides a working memory in which one can temporarily maintain information that is immediately useful and then dismiss it or from which one can transfer information to the LTM and store it.

Also from the previous example, we can see, as Bostrom and Waldhart conclude, that retention of information may correlate with the communication purpose. They postulate that the short-term retention of a stimulus may in some interactions be more useful than long-term retention, particularly in interactions in which the relationships of the communicators may be more important than the details of the interactions.[68] For example, if Peter were having lunch with Judith, and he considered their relationship to be more important than the details of Judith's message, he may not find it necessary to retain—in his LTM—the details of her message, provided that he is able to respond appropriately to her message at the time it is communicated. Thus, in situations similar to this one, the listener's STM will adequately meet his or her needs.

A third example illustrates how a listener may use the STM to perform mental processes on the basis of information entering the STM from the long-term memory. If Daren, for instance, were to ask Tonya how many cabinet doors she has in her kitchen, she would probably be able to answer Daren's question correctly even though she has never stored the answer in her LTM. Since she cannot directly retreive the answer from her LTM, she will likely construct—by copying (*not* removing) vital information from the LTM to the STM for processing—a visual image of her kitchen and, while holding the image in the short-term memory store, count the doors. Thus, we also can see how information stored in the LTM is utilized in the working memory.

Unlike the STM, the long-term memory system is essentially a permanent storage system where all that one has previously learned is stored. While the STM consists of the current contents of a person's awareness (such as, in our examples, the telephone number that is remembered until it can be dialed, the present message that is remembered until it can be responded to, or the visual image of the kitchen that is remembered until the cabinet doors can be counted), the LTM consists of everything else in a person's memory system. A principal difference between the two memory systems is that the "STM has a fixed capacity that is subject to overload and consequently loss of elements in it . . . while LTM is, in effect, infinitely expansible."[69] To exemplify the functions of these two systems, suppose you are attending a party where you know very few of the other guests. If you are introduced (by names only) to several people in succession, your STM is presented with the names of Sheryl, Ray, Stacia, and Matt before you have learned the names of Michelle, Lenora, Eric, and John. The new names tend to push the former names out of your STM. Unless you quickly transfer each name to the LTM, you most likely will lose the name. However, as we have learned, the stimuli in the STM may be preserved longer and, thus, move to the LTM if they go through rehearsal. Thus, if you concentrate while you rehearse each name as you meet each person, the chances are greater that each name will reach the LTM. In this instance, however, we are limited by a lack of time to rehearse; thus, remembering all the names presented in rapid succession is nearly impossible. However, for listening to occur when there is not such a time limitation, the listener must attend to and rehearse, if possible, the aural stimuli in order to transfer the stimuli to the LTM for further processing and storage.

As we noted in the beginning of our discussion of memory, the multistore view of memory is no longer the prevailing view in experimental psychology. According to Lachman, Lachman, and Butterfield, the multistore models have been discarded by many cognitive psychologists for three principal reasons:

> One is that those models emphasized cognitive structure at the expense of flexible processing. Second, the models did not give sufficient due to people's knowledge—that is, to the contents of the long-term store. Finally, the models applied to a narrow range of laboratory phenomena rather than to many of people's cognitive skills.[70]

They further note that the discovery of critical weaknesses in the multistore theory has led to the emergence of three research trends: some individuals (such as Ellis and Warren and Warren[71]) are conducting memory research that is based on no general theory; others (such as Norman and Bobrow and Craik and Lockhart[72]) are working toward developing alternative theories; and still others (such as Atkinson and Juola and Shiffrin and Schneider[73]) are working toward correcting and extending the multistore theory.[74]

Even though the multistore approach to memory no longer prevails, many notions incorporated in the theory are still being used. For example, concepts which are still generally accepted are that stimuli enter the memory system through some sensory register (or buffer), that the short-term memory store has limited capacity, and that there are short-term and long-term memory stores. While some notions have been retained, other notions are being replaced. Perhaps the most notable of the new views is that the STM is an activated portion of the LTM rather than a separate store. In general, the emerging pattern in memory research is a shift from emphasis on fixed structure to emphasis on flexible processing.[75]

Fluctuating Attention. Relevant also to the listening act is an understanding of the waning of attention. We cannot pay attention to the selected stimulus for as long as we desire. Attention fluctuates. The fading of attention is sometimes not caused by distraction; instead, attention fades because of a succession of lapses that Haider has termed "microsleep." Thus, periodically, our attention energy will wane because we are "alseep."[76] At other times, though, when our attention wanes, it is not due to "sleep"; instead, it is due to our short attention spans or our lack of effort. The fluctuation of attention relates directly to the degree of effort that an individual can exert or has the capacity to exert at any given time in processing information. It becomes a process, therefore, of allocating our attention to those stimuli that we perceive most in need of our attention at any given time. "Different mental activities," as Kahneman has noted, "impose different demands on the limited capacity. An easy task demands little effort, and a difficult task demands much. When the supply of attention does not meet the demands, performance falters, or fails entirely."[77] Although the attention capacity has decided limits, we can increase the length of our attention span through "concentration, practice, and self-discipline."[78]

Unfortunately, no amount of concentration, practice, and self-discipline can assist us when we are being exposed to subliminal messages, messages which are presented below the threshold of consciousness. The classic demonstration of this technique was part of a movie showing at a theatre in Ft. Lee, New Jersey, in 1957. "Eat Popcorn" and "Drink Coca-Cola" were flashed—below the level of consciousness—on the screen during the Kim Novak film, "Picnic." Patrons reportedly were subconsciously persuaded to buy popcorn and Coke during the intermission. Such a technique has tremendous power, of course, because listeners are not able to counter the message since we are not even aware that we are receiving it. Although the use of subliminal techniques has been designated as contrary to the public interest by the Federal Trade Commission and the Federal Communication Commission, these techniques are used even today. For example, Hal Becker of the Behavioral Engineering Corporation has developed subliminal audio tapes to program the Muzak system in department stores in order to subliminally persuade people not to shoplift. Wilson Bryan Key, in *Media Sexploitation, Subliminal Seduction,* and *Clam Plate Orgy,* describes how sex appeals at the subliminal level are being used in advertising.[79]

While the development of subliminal techniques appears to be entering a sophisticated computer era, we should recognize that the research on the use of these techniques is far from conclusive. Indeed, experimentation has indicated that some of the early claims in the 1950's were unjustified.[80] Although the use of such subliminal techniques is justified by their users as means to legitimate ends, we can understand the dangers to us as receivers if the messages should be programmed to encourage us to act against our will. What is to stop a department store chain, for example, from programming customers with subliminal messages to buy products we do not even want or need or a political party from inducing us to vote for a particular political candidate? As listeners, we should have the right always to be aware of the messages to which we attend.

From this explanation of the process of attending to, it would seem that if we have a questionable priority system upon which we base our selection of stimuli, a lack of motivation to concentrate, and/or a limited attention span, our listening efficiency will be diminished.

Just as *hearing* (for example, "You don't hear a word I say!") and *listening* are often erroneously used as synonyms, *attending* (for example, "Can't you pay attention to what I say?") and *listening* are often incorrectly equated. The listening process encompasses more than the two processes of receiving and attending. We can, for example, hear and attend to a foreign language, but if we cannot assign meaning to the aural stimuli, we have not engaged in the total listening process.

Assigning Meaning The third component, assigning meaning, refers to the interpretation or understanding of the stimuli heard and/or seen and attended to. In this process, the listener's goal is to attach meaning as similar as possible to that intended by the message sender; however, we must realize that assigning meaning is a very personal process. Therefore, because of the senders' and receivers' differences in past experiences, present feelings, and even future expectancies, we often do not reach the desired goal.

Theories on How Meaning Is Assigned. Various theories have been posited as to how meaning is assigned. Among these are the image theory, classical conditioning, linguistic reference, meaning as an implicit response, meaning as a mediating response, and meaning as a behavioral disposition.[81]

Lundsteen favors the image theory. Utilizing evidence established by memory research and theories proposed by Anderson,[82] she suggests that listeners go through two separate processes: "acoustical encoding" (the translation of the aural data into internal speech) and "semantic encoding" (the translation of the aural data into tentative, perceptual images or internal pictures).[83] After having formed these initial images, we search through images held in our memory store in order to find possible "matches" for the data. We may then compare the cues we have selected with previous knowledge and experience so that we can form further tentative images. If we have not found a "match" yet, we may test our cues by questioning and summarizing, or we may return to our memory store for further search. Once we have matched the cues with the aural input by way of forming tentative images, searching, comparing, testing, and decoding, we achieve meaning. We then decide what the aural stimuli means to us.[84]

Although Barker does not elaborate upon how meaning is assigned, he notes that there are two levels of meaning. The first level, the primary meaning assignment, is associated with the classical conditioning responses to the aural stimuli. After integrating past experience with this primary meaning, however, listeners arrive at a secondary meaning. This is the meaning listeners believe was intended by the message sender.[85]

As comprehensive listeners, we must make a concerted effort to concentrate on the sender's message.

Photo by Robert Tocha.

Weaver supports—with slight modification—the theory of meaning as a behavioral disposition.[86] This theory is based upon a system of categories into which the mind sorts and assigns aural stimuli. Although the system was devised by Bruner, Goodnow, and Austin in 1956,[87] Roger Brown made the categorical system widely known.[88] Categories are stored in the memory. After we have selected an aural stimulus for attention (for instance, *bicuspid*), we search our memory to find the category in which this stimulus "fits" (where memories of other stimuli with a similar pattern are stored). We cannot assign meaning until we have found a "match." Having found the "match" (*tooth,* in our example), we then ascribe meaning (know approximately what the stimulus means) because of the category evoked; the stimulus then assumes the meaning of the category (in this case, a *double-pointed jaw tooth*).

The memory system has thousands of categories. Each word and each recurrence in the nonlinguistic world has a referent; each referent is a category. Also, in itself, the name of each referent is a category. Brown exemplifies this last statement by citing the following: At the beginning of a course, an instructor generally uses many new words. When the instructor first uses a new word, he or she establishes a novel or original category to be filled in with later experience. At first, the category is empty because nothing is signaled by the new word except the existence of a category.[89]

Each category, "a human construction imposed on an array of objects or events,"[90] has characteristic features called attributes. An attribute is "any dimension on which objects and events can differ."[91] Attributes are criterial (essential) and noncriterial (nonessential). When we use some value of an attribute to determine the category membership of an event or object, that attribute is criterial for the categorization. In other words, that value is what a referent must have to belong to that category; it is the attribute that experience has shown to be invariably present. Experimental studies demonstrate that individuals abstract the recurrent features or attributes (while they ignore or overlook the nonessential variations) and then, when developing categories or meanings, generalize them to all other objects of events which contain these features. Also, these studies reveal that a considerable part of our category system operates below the level of accessibility; thus, we often do not know why we derive the meaning we do.[92]

An attribute is not criterial if it can be changed in value without having an effect on categorizing judgments; its presence should not detract from the criterial attributes when we are categorizing. Although noncriterial attributes (if recognzied as such) do not determine assignments to a category, they are part of the meaning evoked when we hear the name of the category. Failure to distinguish between criterial and noncriterial attributes can result in the incorrect assignment of meaning. For example, if we think that the noncriterial attribute *dishonest* is criterial when assigning meaning to *politician,* our assignment of the stimulus to a category will be greatly affected when *politician* and *dishonest* become associated. This problem is a common "block" to listening.

In our system of categories, there are four kinds: *single attribute, disjunctive, relational, and conjunctive.* The memory system has thousands of categories of each of these four kinds.

An example of a *single attribute category* is the category named *birds* because birds have only one criterial or essential attribute that distinguishes them from other mammals: this essential attribute is feathers. Indeed, birds have other attributes, but these other attributes are nonessential. Many of us may think that having wings that support flight is an essential attribute of birds; however, this attribute is neither universal among birds nor confined to birds. Some birds—such as ostriches and kiwis—cannot fly, and some animals that can fly—such as bats and bees—are not birds.

The second kind of category, the disjunctive category, consists of any referent that has any one of two or more essential attributes. The category named *out* as it applies to baseball illustrates the *disjunctive category.* Among the many ways that a baseball player can make an *out* are the following: he may strike out, fly out, run out of the baseline when his purpose is *not* to avoid interfering with a defensive player, bunt the ball foul on a third strike, interfere with the catcher when there are less than two outs and a teammate is on third base, ground out if a defensive player reaches first base before he does, be tagged out when he is caught stealing, or be hit by a batted ball as he is running the bases. If you are knowledgeable about baseball, you no doubt can think of additional attributes that are essential to this category named *out*. However, we believe that we have listed a sufficient number of essential attributes to illustrate that a baseball player would be called out if he were the source or the receiver of any of the many essential attributes that constitute an out.

An illustration of *the relational category* is the category named *quadrilateral*. A quadrilateral is a relational category because its essential attributes are relational or interrelated: there are four sides, and there are four angles. Without these features, a figure would not be a quadrilateral. We know that the square, rectangle, and rhombus are members of the general category named *quadrilateral* because these figures have this category's essential relational attributes. On the other hand, we know that an octagon does not belong to the quadrilateral category because an octagon's essential attributes are different from the essential attributes of a quadrilateral. Thus, the category named *octagon* is a distinct relational category whose essential attributes are these: there are eight sides, and there are eight angles. These examples, indeed, illustrate that a referent belongs to the relational category when there is a definite relationship between or among the referent's parts.

Into the final kind of category, *the conjunctive category*, we assign a referent that often requires our making a value judgment. A referent belonging to this category has no set number of essential attributes; however, the referent must have a sufficient number of essential attributes. What is a sufficient number? There is no fixed number. The number of essential attributes depends upon the judgment of the person who is assigning meaning to the referent. For example, if we were to ask a group of people to define a leader, each would assign the category named *leader* to the conjunctive category and then make a value judgment regarding what the essential attributes of a leader are. One person may believe that there are four essential attributes: trustworthiness, expertness, self-control, and sensitivity. Another may believe that, in addition to the four attributes just listed, a leader should possess impartiality and forcefulness. Still another may believe there are only two essential attributes: charisma and determination. If former President Harry S. Truman were alive today, he might list only one essential attribute: feistiness. After you have finished reading this book, we trust that each of you will include the desire and ability to listen effectively as an essential attribute of a leader. Hopefully, this one example of a referent belonging to the conjunctive category has illustrated that a referent in this category is often the source of misunderstanding when we are assigning meaning. Misunderstanding may result because each of us makes a personal judgment regarding what the referent's essential attributes are and whether the referent has a sufficient number of these attributes.

The complexity of the system of categorization can be illustrated further by noting that attributes are of two sorts and that categories are arranged in hierarchies. There are two sorts of attributes: formal (referring to the form and structure of the referent, such as the size, shape, and weight of various knives—butcher, kitchen, pocket, and hunting) and functional (referring to the use of the referent, such as the tasks various knives perform—slice, peel, file, and kill). For example, a power mower is a part of a larger hierarchy called *mowers* as well as a part of a larger hierarchy called *tools*. Thus, every referent in the universe is susceptible to multiple categorization since it can usually be assigned to several different formal and functional hierarchies. As a result of the complexity of categories, a single referent is often meaningless until a subcategory is specified by qualifiers (modifiers). Therefore, if a communicator wishes to communicate successfully, he or she must be specific in the words or sounds he or she transmits, and the listener must make every attempt to receive and attend to each stimulus, since meaning is assigned according to the category of subcategory evoked.[93]

We establish most of our categories by actual or vicarious experiences. Therefore, each person's categories are different. When we first experience a new object or event, we begin to establish such a category. We learn the criterial and noncriterial attributes of the aural stimulus, assign it to one of four kinds of categories, and then assign meaning to it. After a category has been established, any other stimulus that we believe has the same criterial attributes—common features that we first abstract and then generalize from—is assigned to that category. The meaning that is evoked by the category or subcategory in which the stimulus is placed is then assigned to the stimulus.[94]

How categories are used when we listen can be illustrated. In oral communication, we generally listen to several names such as are in this sentence: The steel-headed, forked hammer cracked. The word, *hammer* (a form-class word), is a general category that has its own criterial and noncriterial attributes. *The, steel-headed,* and *forked* are modifying names that summon forth subcategories of a general category, *hammer*. When we are assigning meaning, we cannot do so until we search our memory and find the category into which the stimulus "fits," and the brain makes only one search for category assignment at a time. In this specific example, one subcategory (the sum of the attributes of the four words) is evoked by the entire phrase: *The steel-headed, forked hammer;* the meaning—claw hammer—is then assigned. A second general category, *cracked,* is evoked by the action word. We then assign a complete meaning to the sentence. From this example, we can see that if we as listeners miss one word, for example, *forked,* we would assign the wrong meaning—riveting hammer, boilermaker's hammer, bricklayer's hammer, ball peen hammer, prospecting hammer, blacksmith's hammer, or cross peen hammer—as a result of our incorrect categorization. In this example, it is assumed that we have a category for claw hammer. However, if we do not have a category for a given stimulus (as in the case when we hear a new word or a strange sound), we can only guess at its meaning. Thus, we can very easily make an incorrect match; we cannot really understand if we do not know the category in which the stimulus "fits."

Incorrect Categorization. There are many reasons why incorrect categorization frequently occurs. The major reason is that each person has a different category system; that is, because each person is unique, each develops meanings based on his or her own personal experiences. For example, while the speaker's meanings for the words *mother* or *boss* may be those meanings that the speaker has for his or her own mother or boss, the listener's meanings may be for those that the listener has for his or her own mother or boss. In *Through the Looking-Glass,* Humpty Dumpty illustrates the personal quality of meaning assignment when he says to Alice, "When *I* use a word . . . , it means just what I choose it to mean—nothing more nor less."[95] To Humpty Dumpty, a word may, indeed, mean what he chooses it to mean; however, to his dialogue partner, it may have a very different meaning, for although messages may be transmitted between speakers and listeners, meanings cannot be. Meanings do not reside in words; rather, meanings reside in each individual user, and they are determined by each user's point of view.

This personal point of view, better known as one's frame of reference, consists of all that makes each person a unique individual. It consists of one's attitudes, knowledge, communication skills, life experiences, socio-cultural patterns, background, present feelings and thoughts, expectations of self and others, values, beliefs, personality factors, interests, concerns, fears, pressures, tensions, needs, biases, prejudices, stereotypes, fantasies, morals, convictions—everything that makes up the sum total of the individual. All of these elements which govern the way one views the world create the perceptual filter through which the listener screens each message before assigning a personal meaning to the message. Jiddu Krishnamuriti, in *The First and Last Personal Freedom,* stresses the impact that each individual's perceptual filter has on one's listening:

> To be able to really listen, one should abandon or put aside all prejudices, preformulations, and daily activities. When you are in a receptive state of mind, things can be easily understood; you are listening when your real attention is given to something. But unfortunately most of us listen through a screen of resistance. We are screened with prejudices, whether religious or spiritual, psychological or scientific; or with our daily worries, desires, and fears. And with these for a screen, we listen. Therefore, we really listen to our own noise, to our own sound, not to what is being said.[96]

Not only do the listener's frame of reference and perceptual filter alter the meanings of the speaker's words, but also they affect the listener's selection of information to process. In order to preserve internal balance, the listener tends to be selective in what he or she exposes him or herself to, attends to, perceives, and remembers.[97] Thus, the listener seeks information which is consistent with his or her personal beliefs and information which confirms one's personal expectations, and the listener perceives what he or she wants to or is set to perceive (see, hear, and believe) so as to be able to assign meanings which conform to expected meanings. Thus, rather than seeking out information that may prove him or her wrong, paying attention to information with which he or she may disagree, checking out one's perceptions against those of others who have different views, and retaining information that is inconsistent with his or her beliefs, the listener often chooses to continue categorizing from his or her own frame of reference rather than from the speaker's frame of reference.

Furthermore, the listener's frame of reference affects assignment of meaning when his or her emotional biases are aroused or triggered. Now serving primarily as an emotional filter, the listener's perceptual filter is a powerful source of meaning distortions. Each listener has certain words, phrases, ideas, topics, and people (including some speakers themselves) to which old emotions associated with previous emotional events still cling. Thus, these emotional triggers arouse immediate, unthinking, positive or negative reactions within the listener. What may create a positive reaction in one listener may create a negative reaction in another. For example, if Mr. Jefferson and Mr. Bentley of the television show, "The Jeffersons," heard someone mention "air pollution," each would have a different emotional reaction. Mr. Jefferson, the owner of a drycleaning business, would react positively because to him air pollution probably means more cleaning business, whereas Mr. Bentley would react negatively because to him air pollution likely means a health hazard. Whether the emotional triggers produce within a particular listener a positive reaction as *justice, equal opportunity, free enterprise, land conservation, Jesse Jackson,* or *Billy Graham* may (or may not) or a negative reaction as *bureaucracy, women's work, merit pay, nuclear arms control* (or *proliferation*), *Jerry Falwell,* or *James Watt* may (or may not), they have a powerful impact on the listener's assignment of meaning. As Leo Buscaglia observes, they can cause "a permanent inprint [sic], a freezing of reality, through which all future learning and perception would then be filtered."[98] Indeed, emotional triggers result in incorrect categorization, because the listener receives little or none of the message if he or she is overreacting emotionally. For example, if the listener resents or dislikes a particular speaker, his or her negative reactions may prevent him or her from listening to the speaker's message and, thus, prevent him or her from assigning any meaning. Or if the listener does listen to the speaker's message, he or she may listen in a selective manner (primarily to his or her own mind rather than to the speaker's message) and, thus, assign meanings which have been colored by his or her own feelings rather than by the so-called "enemy's." Another example is that if the listener feels that his or her self-image is being threatened or attacked by an emotional trigger, that individual may become so involved in defending the self as to focus on his or her feelings rather than on the remainder of the speaker's message.

Moroever, if the listener encounters opposition to deeply-rooted views, he or she is apt to become emotionally "deaf" and, thus, either spend the listening time reflecting on some aspect of the speaker's message or planning a strategy to refute or destroy the opponent's point of view rather than listening to the speaker's complete message. Recently, Joe, a friend of ours, described a communication situation in which he had found himself a victim of emotional "deafness." Joe's best friend since early childhood had asked him if he would serve as best man in his wedding. Knowing that his friend and fiancee had for some time been planning to marry in two years, Joe responded, "Yes, but isn't this a bit soon to be asking me?" Joe's friend replied, "No, we're getting married next month. Sue's pregnant. . . ." When Joe heard "pregnant," he became emotionally "deaf" as a listener. No longer listening to his friend, Joe was listening only to himself: "He's the last person in the world I'd ever expect to hear this from. Why, he's always been so 'straight'—a good Catholic—active in the church. How could he have forgotten what we learned and agreed upon in our Bible Study classes—that premarital sex is unequivocally wrong, that sex is to be shared only between man and wife. . . ." To many listeners, "pregnant" would not be an emotional trigger; however, to Joe, who had thought that he and his best friend shared the same view regarding premarital sex, "pregnant"—in this communication interaction—deafened him as a listener. Although these examples illustrate the effects of negative emotional triggers, the listener must also be aware of the effects of positive emotional triggers: the listener may admire the speaker so much or may be so positively influenced by certain words, phrases, etc., that he or she will accept whatever is said without question. Indeed, both negative and positive triggers contribute to incorrect categorization.

It is helpful, therefore, to be aware of how the listener's frame of reference and perceptual filter affect his or her assignment of meaning. However, as William S. Howell stresses, awareness is not a solution in itself: "Recognizing differences in perception among interacting people helps us understand the gap of misunderstanding but does little to reduce it."[99] To reduce misunderstanding, the listener must develop the desire and ability to enter another's frame of reference—to attempt to see the message from the speaker's point of view—especially when the speaker's point of view differs greatly from that of the listener. For one to enter into another's world, another's frame of reference, Hugh Fellows recommends that the communicator (here serving as both listener and speaker) participate in the following mental activity:

> You are walking alongside a stream of water and you hear a tiny voice say, "I am a fish. I have never seen a man, but I have heard men talk. Tell me, please: What are shoes?" Try to put into words what you would say to the fish to make him understand what shoes are. (You cannot say simply, "They are covering for one's feet," for if he has never seen a man he would not know what feet are.)[100]

To explain to the fish what shoes are, one must literally enter the fish's world—his frame of reference—and use terms, which the fish already knows, to help the fish relate that with which he is not familiar to that with which he is familiar. Unfortunately, few listeners are willing to enter so completely into another's frame of reference in order to avoid incorrect categorization.

Reducing misunderstanding also necessitates that the listener recognize his or her emotional triggers and endeavor to minimize their effect on meaning assignment. The first step is to recognize one's own emotional biases. Although one cannot be *completely* free of emotional biases, one can become aware of them and, thus, recognize when they are working against his or her accuracy of meaning assignment. The second step is to control one's emotional reactions. Although the listener often may not be able to regulate the outer environment, he or she can control the inner environment. Rather than exposing one's emotional biases to others so that those who desire to control him or her can achieve that control, the listener should curb his or her emotional reactions so as to maintain self-control. Perhaps each listener would do well to go through the same kind of emotional desensitizing training that many in law enforcement positions must undergo. The importance of maintaining emotional control is explained by Robert Lucas, former gunnery sergeant and instructor of military police at Camp Legeune, North Carolina:

> Military and civilian law enforcement personnel are trained to recognize the words that tend to trigger a personal emotional response so that they maintain control of themselves should an occasion arise when they are subjected to verbal abuse wherein these trigger words are directed at them. . . . [T]o effectively do their jobs and assist in crisis intervention situations, they must remain detached and objective. If they are triggered into losing their objectivity and become emotionally involved, they are no longer an objective third party mediator who can help solve the problem, but instead become part of the problem.[101]

Although each listener may never be in a position in which he or she must assist in a crisis intervention situation, he or she will likely be involved in several personal crises in which emotional triggers will be directed at him or her. Thus, in order to avoid becoming a *part of the problem* in these crisis situations, the listener, like law enforcement personnel, must maintain emotional control. However irritating a speaker may be or however offensive his or her ideas may be to the listener, the listener who has emotional control is in a better position to detect the speaker's illogical thinking on issues with which the listener strongly disagrees as well as to detect the speaker's errors on issues with which the listener agrees. In addition, the listener who seeks out ideas which might prove him or her wrong as well as those that might prove him or her right may prevent self-enslavement by emotional biases, which may, in fact, be held on irrational grounds.

Although controlling one's emotional triggers is quite difficult, it is not impossible. It requires that one develop his or her own self-training program as

Buchminster Fuller did in order to gain control of his linguistic environment. In *Love,* Leo Buscaglia describes Fuller's program:

> Buchminster Fuller is said to have been so concerned with his being controlled by words that he spent two years, mostly alone, studying what words meant specifically to him. Only after a two-year period did he feel sufficiently free from language traps to use language as an agent for bringing things closer rather than pushing them away, for making language his tool.[102]

Each listener may not wish to spend as much time alone as Fuller did in gaining control of his linguistic environment, but each should have the same goal as Fuller had. By knowing one's emotional triggers, by employing self-discipline to curb one's emotional reactions, by listening to those speakers whom one dislikes as well as those whom one likes, by delaying judgment until one has listened to the speaker's complete message, by remaining open to views that differ from one's own views, by searching for evidence that might prove the speaker or oneself wrong or right, by conserving emotional energy that should be directed toward attending to what the *speaker means* when *he or she uses a word, phrase,* etc., and by accepting the uniqueness of each individual, the listener can, in fact, minimize the impact that his or her emotional triggers have on him or her and, thus, incorrectly categorize far less frequently.

Other common causes of listeners not assigning the meaning intended by the message source are the listeners' limited knowledge, narrow experiences, inadequate vocabularies, and rigidity in category assignment. Fortunately, as listeners increase their knowledge, broaden their experiences, enlarge their vocabularies, and temper their stubbornness, errors in categorization can be minimized. Each listener must demonstrate flexibility in recategorizing stimuli if that person sincerely desires to assign more reliable meanings to the stimuli to which he or she attends.

Up to this point, we have reduced the number of listening components included in the previously-cited definitions to three: *receiving* (which includes hearing, apprehending, and sensing); *attending to* (which includes concentrating, receiving, and selecting); and *assigning meaning* (which includes analyzing, understanding, registering, interpreting, relating to past experiences and future expectancies, engaging in further mental activity, assimilating, converting meaning to the mind, receiving, identifying, recognizing, comprehending, and evaluating). We have not, however, resolved whether or not two other components initially presented should be included in the listening process.

Remembering and Responding. It is our belief that remembering—the process of storing stimuli in the mind for the purpose of recalling them later—is probably involved in all aspects of listening and is, thus, inherent in the listening process when a listener actively engages in the total listening process. The importance of remembering can be seen as it relates to the holding of accumulated sound while we are initially receiving and attending to a message.[103] Also, it is relevant to the act of attending to, since, in general, only those stimuli to which we attend reach the LTM. Moreover, as we categorize input data, we must search our memory bank for a "fit" in order to assign meaning. Since remembering as it relates to listening has been discussed under the listening components of receiving, attending to, and assigning meaning, we do not feel that remembering should be included as a separate component of the listening process; its inclusion would only be repetitious. Although we do not limit the symbols involved in listening to verbal sounds only, we agree with Lundsteen's view regarding where the process of listening ends: "The term listening is appropriate when the person reaches the part in the series of steps where his experience brings meaning to verbal symbols."[104]

In analyzing responding (also referred to as reacting), we think that it is critical to determine whether covert (internal response perceivable only to the listener) or overt (external response perceivable to others) response is meant. If covert response is meant, the response could be a part of (1) the receiving process as our auditory and sensory mechanisms respond to the original stimulus, (2) the attention process since the very act of attending to the stimulus is a response by the system, or (3) the assignment of meaning process when we respond by categorizing the stimulus so that it matches the intended meaning of the source. However, if overt response is indicated, we do not consider responding to be a part of the listening process. When listeners respond overtly, they are no longer listeners; instead, they become the senders in the communication process. Weaver demonstrates that responding is beyond the listening process:

> Let us assume that the singe word "come" is a command. Whether you obey it or not does not concern the process of listening. You have "heard" it, which means you have received and attended to the data. The listening process concerns only the selecting of such stimulus data in order to "receive" it and the cognitive structuring of it.[105]

In his statement, Weaver also has called attention to a frequently held view that we, too, believe needs clarification. Briefly mentioned in chapter 1, this view is that many people think listening means agreement. We often hear a person say "Steve just refuses to listen to anything I say." A sender often makes this type of statement because the listener does not agree with the content of the sender's message. This disagreement does not mean that the listener did not listen; the listener just did not agree. We wish to emphasize that listening does not necessarily mean agreement.

Additional Characteristics of Listening

Three additional listening characteristics enumerated in the definitions cited at the beginning of this section have not yet been treated. These qualities are that listening is *creative,* is *purposeful,* and is *a process.*

Creative Listening. Although Hook used the term *creative listening* to stress that "mental response is essential,"[106] listening scholars now view the creative aspect of listening in a different light. They recognize that as listeners each of us bring to the listening situation his/her own knowledge, experiences, attitudes, beliefs, mental set, category attributes, biases, personality, language, perceptions, and everything else that makes each of us a unique individual. Because each of us is unique and each of us develops his or her concepts personally, concepts can never mean the same for two individuals. We can give only that which we possess, and when assigning meaning, we must—in a creative way—apply that which we bring with us to that which we receive and attend to. The creative aspect of listening can be observed when several people listen to one message and derive several different meanings.

Purposeful Listening. Is listening purposeful? It is generally believed that there are purposes for listening.[107] The most commonly stated purposes are to appreciate, to evaluate, and to comprehend. Other purposes—similar to those for reading, the other receptive language skill—are to associate or classify, to organize or synthesize, and to engage in problem solving.[108] Still other objectives, as cited by the Commission on the English Curriculum of the National Council of Teachers of English, are to stimulate thinking, to respond to the challenge of new ideas and interests, to bolster a point of view already held, and to increase one's power to use language effectively.[109] Recognizing that there are many purposes for listening and that a listener cannot have all listening purposes stimultaneously, we recommend that the listener consciously determine the purpose most suitable to the listening occasion during the early stages of a communicative act.

Dynamic Listening. The last characteristic which has been cited in several of the former definitions is that listening is *a process.* We, too, believe that listening is an ongoing, dynamic process—a process involving three separate but interrelated processes (receiving, attending, and assigning meaning), all of which occur almost simultaneously and yield a particular end result: listening.

Wolvin-Coakley Structural Definition and Model of Listening

This chapter has illustrated that the complex term *listening* cannot be adequately defined in one sentence. A thorough understanding of the processes involved in listening necessitates a detailed explanation. And only after this understanding has been acquired can a definition of listening, stated in one sentence, be meaningful. Having carefully analyzed existing definitions in view of past and current listening research and having searchingly explored our own understanding of the listening act, we have chosen to define listening as *the process of receiving, attending to and assigning meaning to aural stimuli.* For the purpose of this text, this structural definition of listening will be used. Our definition of the listening process might be depicted as a sequential process model (fig. 3.3).

Figure 3.3.
Wolvin-Coakley Model of the Listening Process.
Drawing by Ted Metzger, Visual Technics.

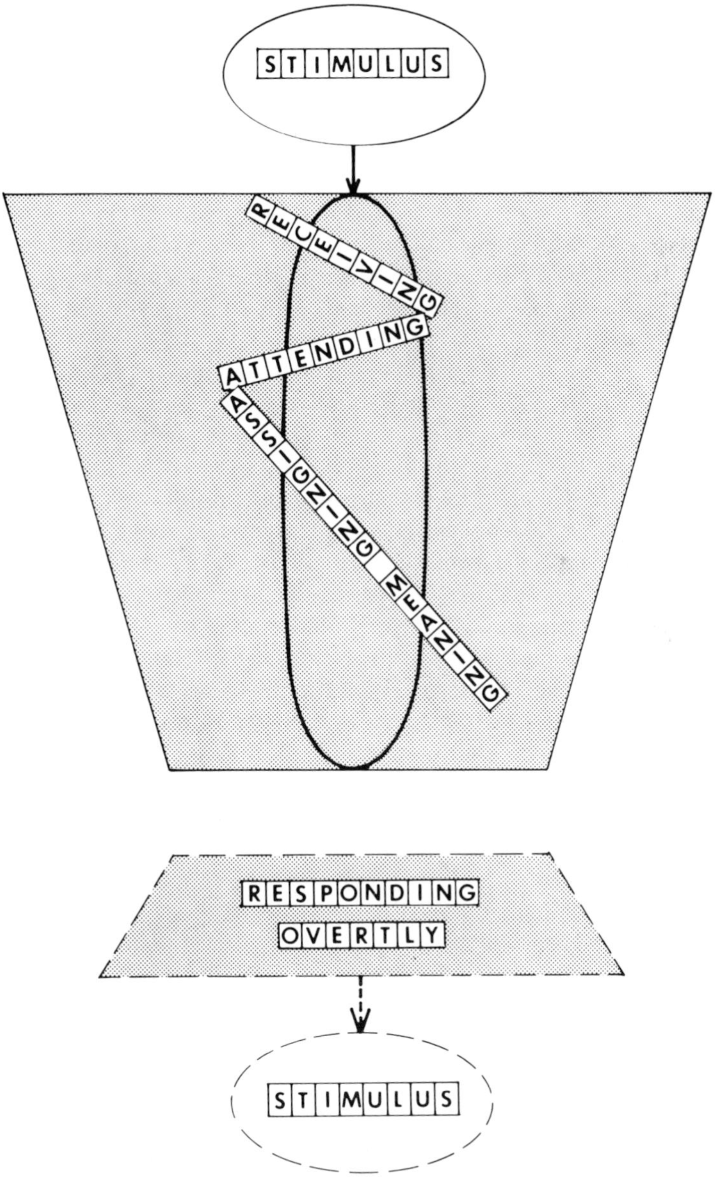

This model is designed to illustrate the process of listening, the decoding of the stimulus through the auditory and visual senses. As you study the model, keep in mind that, throughout the listening process, our listening is enhanced or diminished by the efficiency of the sensory system and by the listening objectives which we set for ourselves.

The first aspect you should note in the model is that it contains two separate, conical-shaped parts: the listening cone (the upper cone) and the feedback cone (the lower cone). The listening cone is wider at the top and more narrow at the bottom to indicate that a given stimulus (aural or visual) can be interpreted in as many ways as there are listeners; and since the assignment of meaning is a very personal matter, an individual will limit the meaning to "fit" his or her own system of categories. The feedback cone, on the other hand, is more narrow at the top and wider at the bottom to exemplify that if a listener chooses to respond overtly, the listener—who then becomes the source—draws on his or her personal system of categories to encode the message and sends a stimulus which is open to varied interpretations by various listeners.

Next, you should observe that the listening cone contains the three components that we consider integral to listening: receiving, attending, and assigning meaning. To portray the intricate interaction of these three separate but interrelated processes, we have overlapped the components.

Another aspect you should notice is that a cylinder runs through the core of the listening cone. This cylinder represents the processes of remembering and covertly responding. Listeners remember the stimulus as they "run" it through the three listening processes, and they probably respond covertly to the stimulus as they "use" it while they are decoding the stimulus.

When studying the feedback (or overt response) cone, you should note that broken lines outline the cone and surround the stimulus. The broken lines illustrate that the process of overtly responding may or may not occur when listeners engage in the listening process. The stimulus indicates that an overt response is a second message. If listeners send feedback, they become the sources of the feedback messages and create a different stimulus in the process.

The last aspect you should observe is the dotted lines which run diagonally throughout both cones. These dotted lines represent the perceptual filters through which listeners operate while they are decoding and through which sources operate while they are encoding. Furthermore, the dotted lines serve to emphasize that the total communication process is a very personal and complex process.

SUMMARY

In this chapter, we have presented a detailed description of contemporary views and conclusions about listening. First, we have cited studies which provide experimental evidence that listening is a distinct activity. Second, we have traced the evolution of a listening definition from 1925 to the present. Third, we have critically questioned and examined—in light of past and current research findings and theories—seventeen definitions of listening and four definitions of *auding* in order to determine what stimuli, what components, and what characteristics are involved in the listening act. Lastly, we have presented our structural definition—and a sequential process model—of listening: *Listening is the process of receiving, attending to, and assigning meaning to aural stimuli.*

SUGGESTED ACTIVITIES

1. Before reading the chapter section entitled "A Definition of Listening," answer all questions (except number one) that are posed after the presentation of definitions. With the class, discuss your views concerning what the process of listening entails.
2. List the characteristics of a good definition. Then, evaluate the strengths and weaknesses of the cited listening and auding definitions (including the definition presented by us). Also, determine which of the cited definitions is the strongest.
3. List ten sounds which you hear in a normal day. Then, rank order the sounds according to the amount of auditory fatigue each sound causes you.
4. Identify five words you have acquired through unique personal experiences and which, as a result of these experiences, you have specialized meanings. Some of these words can be shared with the class.[110]
5. Identify five words that evoke highly emotional feelings in you; then analyze what personal experiences have influenced these reactions. Some of these words can be shared with the class.
6. List three words whose once empty categories have become meaningfully filled since this course began. Some of these words can be shared with the class.
7. Discuss at least five purposes for which you have listened during the past five days.
8. Create your own definition and model of the listening act. All definitions and models should be mimeographed, shared with the class, and then carefully analyzed and evaluated by the student and instructor.
9. Go to a public place, such as a shopping mall, department store, health club, sporting event, playground, amusement park, golf course, beach, library, or cafeteria. For several minutes, close your eyes and listen to all of the sounds that are present; then, list the sounds you heard. Repeat the listening experience, but this time focus your attention on listening only to nonhuman sounds; list the nonhuman sounds you heard. Next, focus your attention on listening only to human sounds, such as paralanguage, words, phrases, sentences, etc.; list the human sounds you heard. This exercise will demonstrate how you use selective attention.
10. List at least five specific beliefs, views, attitudes, and/or biases which you presently have regarding general subjects such as government, family, marriage, religion, economics, health, death, success, freedom, and/or entertainment. Trace each belief, etc., back to its origin. Share a few of your beliefs,

etc., and their origins with the class to determine in what ways you and other students have similar/dissimilar frames of reference. How did these likenesses/differences affect your listening to other students as they shared their beliefs, views, attitudes, and/or biases?

11. Listen to and view a televised episode of *People's Court,* and point out examples of ineffective listening. Also, identify possible causes (emotional "deafness," selective listening, concentration on defending self rather than on listening to the speaker's complete message, etc.) of ineffective listening.
12. Throughout the semester, you should keep a journal of your listening experiences. Each day, you should record one or more listening experiences in "diary" fashion. The following format may be most helpful:

    Date:
    Type of Listening (Appreciative, Discriminative, etc.):
    (We recognize that you will not fully appreciate these categories until you have covered chapters 5 through 9. For the time being, leave this section blank and plan to go back, at a later date, to designate the types of listening you have done.)
    Description of the Listening Event:
    Your Response As a Listener:
    What You Learned about Your Listening:
    Try to provide a variety of experiences in the various types of listening. Avoid recording just experiences you have at work, etc., but rather go to some events you might otherwise never attend so that you can broaden your listening skills as you prepare this journal. At the end of the semester, submit your journal to your instructor.
    The following are examples of possible journal entries:

    September 18
    Therapeutic Listening
    Today I listened as a friend described the options available to her family about her mother's illness. Her mother has terminal brain cancer and recently underwent an unsuccessful operation and radiation therapy. The decision must be made as to whether to have her undergo another operation or to leave things as they are and let the woman die in peace.

    I served as a sounding board, offering no advice, but trying to give comfort and support. She finally decided to leave things as they are. I'm sure that her opportunity to talk through the situation with me was helpful.

    I know people can solve their own problems, but I certainly realize how important it is to have that other person as a "sounding board" to articulate your thoughts and come up with a solution. If only more people would listen to others. . . .

October 10
Appreciative Listening

Tonight I went to the Kennedy Center Concert Hall to see Al Jarreau. The warmup act was Dave Valentine. His violinist did incredible things with the violin! Then Al Jarreau came on. The man's voice is an instrument in itself. I realized that parts of his album that I thought were instrumental were actually his voice. The drummer would beat, and he would copy the sound to the exact pitch.

It was a very sensual experience. I wonder why certain music has such power. I love music and have learned how to avoid picking it apart but, instead, just letting it "happen" to me at a concert such as this one. It's a wonderful way to appreciate an artist's work.

October 29
Critical Listening

Today I listened to the 90–minute presidential debate. Ronald Reagan proved to be true to form. After listening to him talk, I trusted him even less than I had before the debate. I thought that he used his acting techniques (expressing surprise, disbelief, etc.) to win points. I found this approach to be very distasteful. The man who will be in that office for the next four years should be a sincere person, and that sincerity should be apparent with no necessary tricks.

Jimmy Carter impressed me more because he said what I knew in 1976—that there is no simple answer to complex questions. Reagan turned me off completely with his ready cure for all the "ills of the country." Also, when Carter challenged statements that Reagan was known to have made, Reagan said that he had been misinterpreted, which was definitely not true.

Also, I noticed that quite often in Reagan's answers and sometimes in Carter's responses, the point got lost. What made me very angry was Ronald Reagan using the example of talking to black youths and being sympathetic to our plights or situation, when I know full well that he's not going to be very helpful.

I guess I get too emotional when it comes to black issues, and I certainly need to work on controlling my emotions if I want to be truly objective in my evaluations.

November 28
Discriminative Listening

I talked to my brother yesterday, and he said that he thought my mother (who is a manic depressive personality) was going into a manic phase. He wanted me to call her in Ft. Lauderdale and see if I could tell. She has had this illness for at least five years, so by just listening to her talk, we can usually pick up on the warning signs. I called her this morning to check it out. I was listening for an increased pace in her speech, higher pitch in her voice, disjointed thoughts, and irrational thinking. After listening to her, I decided that she hadn't gone into this phase yet, but I could tell it was coming on. It's very important to detect it immediately so that adjustments can be made in her medication.

I am pleased that I've been able to sharpen my discriminative listening skills and deal with what could be an important medical situation. I wish more physicians and nurses could have this training!

NOTES

1. John Caffrey, "Auding Ability at the Secondary Level," *Education* 75 (January 1955):303–310; John Caffrey and T. W. Smith, "Preliminary Identification of Some Factors in the Davis-Eells Games," cited by Donald Spearritt, *Listening Comprehension—A Factorial Analysis* (Melbourne, Australia: G. W. Green and Sons, 1962), pp. 14–15; J. E. Karlin, "A Factorial Study of Auditory Function," *Psychometrika* 7 (December 1942): 251–279; Clair N. Hanley, "Factorial Analysis of Speech Perception," *Journal of Speech and Hearing Disorders* 21 (March 1956): 76–87.
2. Spearritt, *Listening Comprehension—A Factorial Analysis.*
3. *Ibid.*, pp. 21–22.
4. Carl H. Weaver, *Human Listening: Processes and Behavior* (Indianapolis: Bobbs-Merrill Company, 1972), p. 132.
5. W. Tucker, "Science of Listening," *19th Century* 97 (April 1925): 548.
6. Paul Tory Rankin, "The Measurement of the Ability to Understand Spoken Language" (Ph.D. dissertation, University of Michigan, (1926), *Dissertation Abstracts* 12 (1952): 847.
7. Julius N. Hook, *The Teaching of High School English* (New York: Ronald Press, 1950), p. 238).
8. Kenneth O. Johnson, "The Effect of Classroom Training upon Listening Comprehension," *Journal of Communication* 1 (May 1951): 58.
9. Walter Barbe and Robert Meyers, "Developing Listening Ability in Children," *Elementary English* 31 (February 1954): 82.
10. James I. Brown and G. Robert Carlsen, *Brown-Carlsen Listening Comprehension Test* (New York: Harcourt, Brace and World, 1955), p. 1.
11. Dana S. Still, "The Relationship between Listening Ability and High School Grades" (Ph.D. dissertation, University of Pittsburgh, 1955), p. 45.
12. M. S. Jones, "A Critical Review of Literature on Listening with Special Emphasis on Theoretical Bases for Further Research in Listening" (M. A. thesis, North Carolina State College, 1956), p. 12.
13. Dominick A. Barbara, "On Listening—the Role of the Ear in Psychic Life," *Today's Speech* 5 (January 1957): 12.
14. Richard Hampleman, "Comparison of Listening and Reading Comprehension Ability of Fourth and Sixth Grade Pupils," *Elementary English* 35 (January 1958): 49.
15. Thomas R. Lewis, "Listening," *Review of Educational Research* 28 (April 1958): 89.
16. Charles Robert Petrie, Jr., "What Is Listening?" in *Listening: Readings,* ed. Sam Duker (New York: Scarecrow Press, 1966), p. 329.
17. Larry L. Barker, *Listening Behavior* (Englewood Cliffs, New Jersey: Prentice-Hall, 1971), p. 17.

18. Sara W. Lundsteen, *Listening: Its Impact on Reading and the Other Language Arts* (Illinois: NCTE/ERIC, 1971),p. 9.
19. Weaver, *Human Listening: Process and Behavior,* p. 12.
20. Robert O. Hirsch, *Listening: A Way to Process Information Aurally* (Dubuque, Iowa: Gorsuch Scarisbrick, Publishers, 1979), p. 1.
21. Lyman K. Steil, "On Listening . . . and Not Listening," *Executive Health* 18 (December 1981): 3.
22. Donald P. Brown, "Teaching Aural English," *English Journal* 39 (March 1950): 128.
23. *Ibid.,* p. 130.
24. Donald P. Brown, "What Is the Basic Language Skill?" *ETC* 14 (Winter 1956–1957): 104.
25. John Caffrey, "Auding," *Review of Educational Research* 25 (April 1955): 121.
26. Edna Lue Furness, "Listening: A Case of Terminological Confusion," *Journal of Educational Psychology* 48 (December 1957): 481.
27. G. L. Horrworth, "Listening: A Facet of Oral Language," *Elementary English* 43 (December 1966): 857–858.
28. Lundsteen, *Listening: Its Impact on Reading and the Other Language Arts,* p. 9.
29. The reader should note that our statement of the listening process is very much a description which is derived from a human information-processing model of the cognitive psychologists. This information-processing model is not without its critics among psychologists, critics who argue that the information process is not so simple as the model would suggest and that the information stimulus is not merely transferred from one stage to another to ultimate storage in the long-term memory. Rather, some psychologists argue, the process is much more interrelated so that memory, for instance, plays a key role *throughout* the sequence of dealing with a stimulus. We certainly agree that any view of listening should not be perceived as a simple serial progression of stages, because the process is highly dynamic and interrelated at any given time. For reviews of the research on information-processing, see Roy Lachman, Janet L. Lachman, and Earl C. Butterfield, *Cognitive Psychology and Information Processing: An Introduction* (Hillsdale, New Jersey: Lawrence Erlbaum Associates, 1979), chapter 14 and Arthur Wingfield and Dennis L. Byrnes, *The Psychology of Human Memory* (New York: Academic Press, 1981), pp. 16, 147–148.
30. Weaver, *Human Listening: Processes and Behavior,* pp. 6–7.
31. Ray L. Birdwhistell, as cited in Mark L. Knapp, *Nonverbal Communication in Human Interaction,* 2nd ed. (New York: Holt, Rinehart and Winston, 1978), p. 30; Albert Mehrabian, *Silent Messages* (Belmont, California: Wadsworth Publishing Company, 1971), pp. 43–44; an interesting discussion of the functions of nonverbal cues is offered by Dale G. Leathers, *Nonverbal Communication Systems* (Boston: Allyn and Bacon, 1976).
32. For readings on the intricacies of visual discrimination, see Charles H. Graham, ed., *Vision and Visual Perception* (New York: John Wiley and Sons, 1965).
33. For a complete discussion of the physiology of hearing, see Hayes A. Newby, *Audiology* (New York: Appleton-Century-Crofts, 1972).
34. Arthur S. Freese, "An Implant Pierces Walls of Deafness," *Parade,* 10 June 1979, pp. 20, 22.
35. Denise Grady, "A Sound Approach to Better Hearing," *Discover* 3 (November 1982): 92.

36. "We Hear You, Mr. President," *The New York Times,* 11 September 1983, p. 22E.
37. Newby, *Audiology.*
38. Table from Alexander Cohen, Joseph Anticaglia, and Herbert H. Jones, "Sociocusis—Hearing Loss from Non-Occupational Noise Exposure," *Sound and Vibration* (November 1970): 13. Reprinted by permission of the publisher.
39. "Hearing Loss: Ways to Avoid, New Ways to Treat," *U.S. News and World Report,* 18 October 1982, pp. 85–86.
40. "Rock Fallout," *Parade,* 10 December 1978, p. 23.
41. The Environmental Protection Agency Office of Noise Abatement and Control (Washington, D.C. 20460) has published a number of excellent pamphlets on various aspects of noise pollution. See especially their "Noise: A Health Problem."
42. Daniel Rapoport, "Seattle: Laws, Residents' Attitudes Preserve Air of Tranquility," *The Washington Post,* 5 November 1980, p. A-29.
43. Sheldon Cohen, "Sound Effects on Behavior," *Psychology Today* 15 (October 1981) 49.
44. Charles M. Solley and Gardner Murphy, *Development of the Perceptual World* (New York: Basic Books, 1960), p. 178.
45. Neville Moray, "Attention in Dichotic Listening: Affective Cues and the Influence of Instructions," *Quarterly Journal of Experimental Psychology* 11 (February 1959): 56–60; A. T. Welford, "Evidence of a Single-Channel Decision Mechanism Limiting Performance in a Serial Reaction Task," *Quarterly Journal of Experimental Psychology* 11 (November 1959): 193–210; Anne M. Treisman and G. Geffen, "Selective Attention and Cerebral Dominance in Perceiving and Responding to Speech Messages," *Quarterly Journal of Experimental Psychology* 20 (May 1968): 139–150; Neville Moray, *Listening and Attention* (Baltimore, Maryland: Penguin Books, 1969).
46. D.E. Broadbent, *Perception and Communication* (London: Pergamon Press, 1958); Neville Moray, *Attention: Selective Processes in Vision and Hearing* (London: Hutchinson Educational LTD, 1969), pp. 28–30.
47. J. A. Deutsch and D. Deutsch, "Attention: Some Theoretical Considerations," *Psychological Review* 70 (1968): 80, 84.
48. *Ibid.,* p. 84.
49. Moray, "Attention in Dichotic Listening: Affective Cues and the Influence of Instructions," pp. 56–60; I. Oswald, A. Taylor, and M. Treisman, "Discrimination Responses to Stimulation during Human Sleep," *Brain* 83 (1960):440–453; C. E. Howarth and K. Ellis, "The Relative Intelligibility Threshold for One's Own Name Compared with Other Names," *Quarterly Journal of Experimental Psychology* 13 (November 1969): 236–239.
50. Anne M. Treisman, "Contextual Cues in Selective Listening," *Quarterly Journal of Experimental Psychology* 12 (November 1960): 246.
51. *Ibid.,* pp. 242–248; Moray, *Attention: Selective Processes in Vision and Hearing,* pp. 30–32; Moray, *Listening and Attention.*
52. Ulric Neisser, *Cognitive Psychology* (New York: Appleton-Century-Crofts, 1967), pp. 79–107.
53. Daniel Kahneman, *Attention and Effort* (Englewood Cliffs, New Jersey: Prentice-Hall, 1973).
54. James C. McCroskey, "Human Information Processing and Diffusion," in *Speech Communication Behavior,* eds. Larry L. Barker and Robert J. Kibler (Englewood Cliffs, New Jesey: Prentice-Hall, 1971),p. 172.

55. *Ibid.*
56. Sir Frederic C. Bartlett, *Remembering* (Cambridge: Cambridge University Press, 1932), p. 190.
57. Weaver, *Human Listening: Processes and Behavior,* pp. 33, 37.
58. Lynn Hasher and Rose T. Zacks, "Automatic and Effortful Processes in Memory," *Journal of Experimental Psychology: General* 108 (1979): 356–388.
59. Magdalen D. Vernon "Perception, Attention, and Consciousness," in *Attention* ed. Paul Bakan (Princeton, New Jersey: D. Van Nostrand Company, 1966), pp. 37–57.
60. R. C. Atkinson and R. M. Shiffrin, "Human Memory: A Proposed System and Its Control Processes," in *The Psychology of Learning and Motivation: Research and Theory,* Vol. 2, eds. Kenneth W. Spence and Janet T. Spence (New York: Academic Press, 1968), pp. 89–195; D. A. Norman and D. E. Rumelhart, "A System for Perception and Memory," in *Models of Human Memory,* ed. D. A. Norman (New York: Academic Press, 1970), pp. 19–64.
61. George Sperling, "The Information Available in Brief Visual Presentations," *Psychological Monographs* 74 (1960): 1–29: Ralph N. Haber and L. G. Standing, "Direct Measures of Short-Term Visual Storge," *Quarterly Journal of Experimental Psychology* 21 (February 1969): 43–54; Emmanuel Averbach and A. S. Coriell, "Short-Term Memory in Vision," *Bell System Technical Journal* 40 (January 1961): 309–328.
62. Christopher J. Darwin, Michael T. Turvey, and Robert G. Crowder, "An Auditory Analogue of the Sperling Partial Report Procedure: Evidence for Brief Auditory Storage," *Cognitive Psychology* 3 (April 1972): 255–267; A. D. Baddeley, *The Psychology of Memory* (New York: Basic Books, 1976); Robert Efron, "The Minimum Duration of a Perception," *Neuropsychologia* 8 (January 1970): 57–63; D. W. Massaro, *Experimental Psychology and Information Processing* (Chicago: Rand McNally, 1975).
63. Lachman, Lachman, and Butterfield, *Cognitive Psychology and Information Processing: An Introduction,* p. 211.
64. D. A. Norman, "Memory While Shadowing," *Quarterly Journal of Experimental Psychology* 21 (February 1969): 85–93; M. I. Posner, "Short Term Memory Systems in Human Information Processing," in *Attention and Performance,* ed. A. F. Sanders (Amsterdam: North-Holland Publishing Company, 1967), pp. 267–284; R. M. Shiffrin and R. C. Atkinson, "Storage and Retrieval Processes in Long-Term Memory," *Psychological Review* 76 (March 1969): 179–193.
65. Posner, "Short Term Memory Systems in Human Information Processing," p. 276.
66. Dewey Rundus, "Analysis of Rehearsal Processes in Free Recall," *Journal of Experimental Psychology* 89 (July 1971): 63–77.
67. G. A. Miller, "The Magical Number Seven, Plus or Minus Two: Some Limits on Our Capacity for Processing Information," *Psychological Review* 63 (1956): 81–97.
68. Robert N. Bostrom and Enid S. Waldhart, "Components in Listening Behavior: The Role of Short-Term Memory," *Human Communication Research* 6 (Spring 1980): 123.
69. Arthur W. Melton, "Implications of Short-term Memory for a General Theory of Memory," *Journal of Verbal Learning and Verbal Behavior* 2 (July 1963): 5.
70. Lachman, Lachman, and Butterfield, *Cognitive Psychology and Information Processing: An Introduction,* p. 286.

71. John A. Ellis, "Transfer Failure and Proactive Interference in Short-Term Memory," *Journal of Experimental Psychology: Human Learning and Memory* 3 (March 1977): 211–221 Robert E. Warren and Natalie T. Warren, "Dual Semantic Encoding of Homographs and Homophones Embedded in Context," *Memory and Cognition* 4 (September 1976): 586–592.
72. D. A. Norman and D. G. Bobrow, "On the Role of Active Memory Processes in Perception and Cognition," in *The Structure of Human Memory,* ed. Charles N. Cofer (San Francisco: W. H. Freeman and Company, 1976), pp. 114–132; Fergus I. M. Craik and Robert S. Lockhart, "Levels of Processing: A Framework for Memory Research," *Journal of Verbal Learning and Verbal Behavior* 11 (December 1972): 671–684.
73. Richard C. Atkinson and James F. Juola, "Search and Decision Processes in Recognition Memory," in *Contemporary Developments in Mathematical Psychology,* Vol. 1, eds. David H. Krantz, et al. (San Francisco: W. H. Freeman and Company, 1974), pp. 243–293; Richard M. Shiffrin and Walter Schneider, "Controlled and Automatic Human Information Processing: II. Perceptual Learning, Automatic Attending, and a General Theory," *Psychological Review* 84 (March 1977): 127–190.
74. Lachman, Lachman, and Butterfield, *Cognitive Psychology and Information Processing: An Introduction,* p. 273.
75. *Ibid.,* p. 297.
76. M. Haider, "Neuropsychology of Attention, Expectation, and Vigilance," cited by Weaver, *Human Listening: Processes and Behavior,* p. 42.
77. Kahneman, *Attention and Effort,* p. 9.
78. Barker, *Listening Behavior,* p. 32.
79. Wilson Bryan Key, *Media Sexploitation* (New York: New American Library, 1977); Wilson Bryan Key, *Subliminal Seduction* (New York: New American Library, 1974); Wilson Bryan Key, *Clam Plate Orgy* (New York: New American Library, 1981).
80. See a summary of this research in Wallace C. Fotheringham, *Perspectives on Persuasion* (Boston: Allyn and Bacon, 1966), pp. 97 and 150. Current work with the technique is described by Barbara Armstrong, "Computers: Subliminal Self-Help?" *The Washington Post,* 16 November 1983, p. B5.
81. Roger Brown, *Words and Things* (New York: Free Press of Glencoe, 1958), pp. 82–109.
82. R. C. Anderson, "Control of Student Mediating Processes during Verbal Learning and Instruction," *Review of Educational Research* 40 (June 1970): 349–369.
83. Lundsteen, *Listening: Its Impact on Reading and the Other Language Arts,* p. 37.
84. *Ibid.,* pp. 37–41.
85. Barker, *Listening Behavior,* p. 33.
86. Weaver, *Human Listening: Processes and Behavior,* pp. 42–59.
87. Jerome S. Bruner, Jacqueline J. Goodnow, and George A. Austin, *A Study of Thinking* (New York: John Wiley and Sons, 1956).
88. Roger Brown, *Words and Things.*
89. *Ibid.,* p. 206.
90. *Ibid.,* p. 14.
91. *Ibid.,* p. 10.
92. S. C. Fisher, "The Process of Generalizing Abstraction; and Its Product, the General Concept," *Psychological Monographs* 21 (1916): 1–213; C. L. Hull, "Quantitative

Aspects of the Evolution of Concepts: An Experimental Study," *Psychological Monographs* 28 (1920): 1–86; Edna Heidbreder, "The Attainment of Concepts: III. The Process," *Journal of Psychology* 24 (1947): 93–138.
93. Weaver, *Human Listening: Processes and Behavior,* pp. 55–56.
94. *Ibid.,* p. 47.
95. Lewis Carroll, *Through the Looking-Glass* (New York: International Collectors Library, n.d.), p. 230.
96. Jiddu Krishnamuriti, *The First and Last Personal Freedom* (New York: Harper and Row, 1975), quoted in Ronald B. Adler, Lawrence B. Rosenfeld, and Neil Towne, *Interplay,* 2nd ed. (New York: Holt, Rinehart and Winston, 1980), p. 153.
97. James C. McCroskey, "Human Information Procesing and Diffusion," pp. 170–173.
98. Leo Buscaglia, *Love* (New York: Fawcett Crest Books, 1972), p. 147.
99. William S. Howell, *The Empathic Communicator* (Belmont, California: Wadsworth Publishing Company, 1982), p. 48.
100. Hugh P. Fellows, *The Art and Skill of Talking with People* (Englewood Cliffs, New Jersey: Prentice-Hall, 1964), pp. 38–39.
101. Robert W. Lucas, "Trigger Words." Unpublished paper, College Park, Maryland: University of Maryland, 1983. Used by permission.
102. Buscaglia, *Love,* pp. 150–151.
103. Lundsteen, *Listening: Its Impact on Reading and the Other Language Arts,* p. 26.
104. *Ibid.,* p. 41.
105. Weaver, *Human Listening: Processes and Behavior,* p. 6.
106. Hook, *The Teaching of High School English,* p. 238.
107. Harlen M. Adams, "Learning to Be Discriminating Listeners," *English Journal* 36 (January 1947): 13–14; George Murphy, "We Also Learn by Listening," *Elementary English* 26 (March 1949): 127–128, 157; Barbe and Meyers, "Developing Listening Ability in Children," pp. 82–83; Donald E. Bird, "Listening," *NEA Journal* 49 (November 1960): 32; Ralph G. Nichols, "Listening Instruction in the Secondary School," in *Listening: Readings,* ed. Duker, p. 240; Barker, *Listening Behavior,* pp. 10–13.
108. Lundsteen, *Listening: Its Impact on Reading and the Other Language Arts,* pp. 32–33.
109. Commission on the English Curriculum of the National Council of Teachers of English, *The English Language Arts* (New York: Appleton-Century-Crofts, 1952), p. 334.
110. Robert O. Hirsch, *Listening: A Way To Process Information Aurally,* p. 17.

Concepts You Will Encounter

Homophily
Responsible Decision-Making
Listening Strategies
Self-Understanding
Johari Window
Self-Disclosure
Stereotypes
Discriminative Preferences
Self-Motivation
Active Listening
Feedback
Listening Factors
Time
Age
Sex
Self-Concept
Hemispheric Specialization
Physical/Psychological States
Receiver Apprehension

Listening as a Communication Function

4

Listening, as the process of receiving, attending to, and assigning meaning to aural stimuli, is very much a communication function. As we have seen, communication is a transactional process in which the source and the receiver *share* the communication experience as they simultaneously send and receive messages. Thus, the ongoing nature of the communication transaction requires that we—as receivers/sources—participate as decoders of the source's messages and as encoders of our own feedback messages.

Listening as Sharing

Much of the communication effectiveness of both listeners and speakers results from a principle termed "homophily." Homophily represents the degree to which interacting individuals have significant similarities in such attributes as education, background, social status, beliefs, values (in contrast to "heterophily" in which interacting individuals have significant differences). When the source and the receiver have common characteristics which enable them to share the message, communication undoubtedly becomes more effective. Furthermore, Rogers and Bhowmik emphasize that "effective communication between source and receiver leads to greater homophily in knowledge, beliefs, and overt behavior."[1]

The principle of homophily is particularly important to communicators who must interact with persons from other cultures. Business executives and diplomats, for example, must understand that the individuals with whom they are communicating in international settings may not necessarily share their frames of reference or even their language code. Consequently, they must be trained in the communication patterns of different cultures so that they will be able to adapt to differing communication conventions and to understand the impact of these differences on the communication transaction.

Listening as Decision-Making

Just as communication results from the homophilous sharing of messages by source and receiver, so, too, is communication the result of careful, responsible decision-making throughout the system. The source must select the original stimulus and translate that stimulus into a message. The development of the message requires decision-making: deciding in which code (verbal and/or nonverbal) to best express the message, through which channel(s) to present the message, in what context, and to whom. Although all of these decisions may occur instantaneously as they often do, for example, in conversation, the skillful communicator is at all times aware of what he or she is doing while making these communication decisions.

Communication as responsible decision-making should not be viewed, however, as the sole function of the source. For centuries, communication scholars have focused on the source of the communication by formulating the strategies for developing and structuring speeches, for understanding audiences, and for presenting ideas through effective delivery. Until recent times, little if any attention has been focused on the listener. As communication scholars have come to understand the psychology of processing human communication, they have also recognized the central role that the listener must assume in the communication process. This central role assumes at least equal participation by the listener. But equal participation can result only from careful, responsible decision-making throughout the process.

Viewing listening as a communication act implies that the listening communicator must have understandings and skills about the listening process in order to function effectively. First of all, the listener must make decisions about the reception of and attention to the stimulus. It is possible to decide to hear or not to hear the sound, for example, just by the simple control of the on-off knob on the radio. We make these receiving decisions on the basis of whether or not we have the time and/or energy to listen, whether or not we perceive we have anything to gain from the listening, whether or not we desire to listen to the particular source of the communication, whether or not we feel satisfied with the communication channel, and a host of other influences which can affect this initial decision.

Once the listener has decided to receive and to attend to the message, it is necessary to make choices about assigning meaning to the stimulus. Assignment of meaning requires decisions about the categorization of the stimulus within the category system, decisions about the interpretations of the terms used by the speaker, decisions about the degree of emotional involvement which the listener can allow in these interpretations, as well as numerous other decisions which allow for the linguistic and semantic processing of the stimulus within the individual's language system. Recognizing the semantic principle that meanings reside in people—not directly in the symbols that we use to communicate—leads to recognizing that decisions about the verbal message also extend to the nonverbal message. It is essential for the listener to recognize the nonverbal messages and to interpret these messages as they can complement, contradict, or replace the verbal messages.

Although the actual listening process stops with the assignment of meaning, the listening communicator also has a responsibility to provide some form of feedback in the system. Consequently, the listener must make choices about the form and the function of the feedback he or she intends to send to the source. At this stage in the communication process, however, the listener becomes the sender of the feedback message.

Thus, to participate in a communication transaction in which the listener has the responsibility of decoding the messages of others and also of encoding feedback messages, the listener must make choices. A listener must decide

not to listen,
to listen actively,
to listen for a purpose,
to set aside biases and attitudes in order to understand the message,
to concentrate on the message, not the speaker,
to overcome emotional barriers to listening,
to know why he/she is listening at a given time,
to know how he/she is listening at a given time,
to understand the process of listening—and the process of communication—in order to know what he/she is (or should be) doing as a listening communicator throughout this process.

It may interest the reader to note that we have included as one choice to decide not to listen. A listener has a responsibility to him- or herself and to the other person to make this choice if it is appropriate. You may choose not to listen, for example, if you do not have the time to listen. If you have a pressing deadline for a project at work, it would be appropriate to attend to the project and not break your concentration to try to listen to another person. It would be likely that the listening in such a situation would not be particularly satisfying for either party. You would feel frustrated because you need to get on with the project, and the other person would feel frustrated because you are not truly "tuned in" as a listener.

You may need to decide not to listen, also, if you are suffering from what might be termed "information overload." There are times when we all receive too much information at one time, so that it becomes difficult to process it meaningfully. Information overload must be much like the experience of a young child at a theme park—the child cannot possibly take in all the stimuli at one time. Indeed, this example might be descriptive of us as adults as well.

The decision-making process is not easy. The lifetime of experiences, attitudes, knowledge, and skills that make up our frame of reference—our very self—influences the way we deal with these choices. How we react to situations and process them through our own perceptions is a dominant force in our decision making. A listener might decide to listen with careful comprehension, for example, if he or she perceived the outcome to be rewarding. Listening so as to thoroughly comprehend a lecture in order to do well on a test over the material may be a familiar choice to most of us.

Many decisions we make as listeners relate to others as well as to ourselves. We may listen with empathy to someone we would like to have as a friend, but we may listen more comprehensively if the other person is a stranger who wants to discuss a faulty product. Each listener must make choices based on the relationship he or she has, or wants to have, or does not want to have with the other person.

Whether the decisions affect the listener, the other person, or both, every listening choice creates its own problems, generates its own difficulties, and pays its own rewards. As human beings, listeners make their choices and then must live with the positive or negative consequences of those decisions. It would seem, then, that the responsible listener must be aware of the choices he or she faces, make those choices within some sort of valid framework for him- or herself and the other person, and then be prepared to live with or to change the results of the choices he or she makes. As listening communicators, we have responsibilities both to ourselves and to others. These responsibilities impose upon us certain key listening strategies which are necessary in any communication transaction.

Listening Strategies

Understanding the Self

The first strategy for effective listeners is to understand ourselves as communicators. Just as the sources of the communication messages should be trained in self (intrapersonal) communication, so too should listeners know themselves. Brooks states the case eloquently:

> To see one's self accurately; to understand and know one's self clearly and honestly; to have acquired those abilities and characteristics associated with a strong, wholesome, self-concept—these objectives are directly related to liking one's self, being confident in one's self, and in relating and living effectively and satisfyingly with others.[2]

Learning about yourself has become a major focus of the popular self-help books and workshops (Werner's est, Dyer's *Your Erroneous Zones,* etc.). A useful technique for beginning this self-analysis is through the Johari Window.[3]

The Johari Window (fig. 4.1) accounts for the dimensions of the self. As the diagram indicates, there are four basic areas of the self: free, blind, hidden, and unknown. Area 1 is the open, public self. Area III, the hidden area, could be systematically diminished through communicating information about yourself to others—a process of self-disclosure.

Figure 4.1.
The Johari Window.
From *Of Human Interaction* by Joseph Luft by permission of Mayfield Publishing Company. Copyright © 1969 by the National Press.

	Known to Self	Not Known to Self
Known to Others	I Free Area	II Blind Area
Not Known to Others	III Hidden Area	IV Unknown Area

The blind area consists of all information which other persons know about you but which you do not know about yourself. This may be information which individuals are reluctant to reveal to you. Some enterprising individuals have formed companies in metropolitan areas to handle the communication of such messages. One firm in Washington, D.C., for instance, will send a message to your boss that he has bad breath—for a fee of $5.00!

The unknown area represents all aspects of a person which really are not known to the individual or to others. While some persons may argue that the more you communicate about yourself and create an "open" window, the more you diminish your unknown area, others may contend that we can never specify the unknown and, thus, never narrow our unknown area.

Through self-disclosure, a communicator can design his or her own window so that the configurations may change. Each individual's window, of course, will have different proportions. An open individual may have a window which resembles that in figure 4.2.

The value of self-disclosure for improved mental health has been documented by the pioneer of this technique, Sidney Jourard, who stated

> . . . no man can come to know himself except as an outcome of disclosing himself to another person. . . . When a person has been able to disclose himself utterly to another person, he learns how to increase his contact with his real self, and he may then be better able to direct his destiny on the basis of knowledge of his real self.[4]

Figure 4.2.
The Johari Window as modified through self-disclosure.
From *Of Human Interaction* by Joseph Luft by permission of Mayfield Publishing Company. Copyright © 1969 by the National Press.

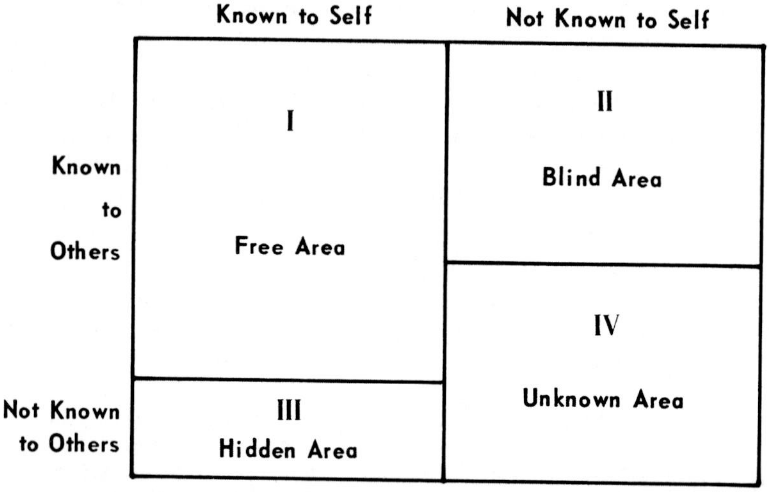

Although there are great advantages to the process of self-disclosure, it should be recognized that the process also carries with it considerable risk. As one sets about disclosing the dimensions of one's self to another person, the other individual must be able to accept the information which is disclosed. Consequently, a great deal of trust in the relationship is necessary for self-disclosure to be meaningful, and this trust results from continuous negotiation of the relationship. Most readers probably can recall a situation when they disclosed some confidential aspect about themselves to a friend or school mate who, in turn, managed to communicate that information to the entire circle of friends or fellow students. As in all relationships, it then became necessary to reconsider the relationship with this informant and decide to continue the friendship and further self-disclosure or to terminate the relationship. The risks involved in this disclosing process, however, are well worth the sacrifices we all make in developing and maintaining human relationships and in defining our own self-concept through the process.

This process of understanding yourself can be of value to you as a listener in knowing something about your self-concept and how it affects your listening behavior. Understanding your self-concept also can lead to a better self-understanding of your attitudes not only toward messages you receive but also toward the receiving process itself. Just as a negative attitude about our listening behavior may be fostered, we may come to have a distorted attitude about the process as a passive act. As our model of the listening process would indicate, listening is a very active, dynamic act. Through social conditioning at home and at school, however, it is possible that listeners have come to view this process as a very passive phenomenon: sit back and let the teacher talk.

Not only are we conditioned to view listening as a rather passive process, but also most listeners may be conditioned to prefer to rely on visual stimuli for information. Some research has been conducted on visual discrimination as it relates to receiver preferences for stimuli. Researchers have concluded that three factors may account for our preference for visual stimuli: the potential for discriminability, the informative value, and the saliency of the stimulus itself.[5]

Our channel preferences may be tied up in our educational process. Research in reading indicates that most young learners prefer to learn through listening in the early years. At about the age of twelve, the learner begins to prefer to learn information through reading rather than listening.[6]

Understanding our visual discrimination as it relates to auditory discrimination can help us to become more discerning in our reception of stimuli. McLuhan and Fiore noted our tendency not to trust the auditory input:

> Most people find it difficult to understand purely verbal concepts. They *suspect* the ear; they don't trust it. In general we feel more secure when things are *visible,* when we can "see for ourselves." We admonish children, for instance, to "believe only half of what they *see,* and nothing of what they *hear.*" All kinds of "shorthand" systems of notation have been developed to help us *see* what we *hear.*
>
> We employ visual and spatial metaphors for a great many everyday expressions. . . . We are so visually biased that we call our wisest men *vision*aries, or *see*rs![7]

This distrust of auditory input may have an effect on our discrimination of auditory stimuli. If, indeed, we prefer to receive information visually, that preference could lead us to more careful attention to and discrimination of visual communication codes. However, in spite of our preference, we must not disregard auditory communication codes.

Just as understanding our attitudes toward our channel preferences aids us in knowing our listening self, so does knowing our value system. How you process the information you receive through the category system depends to a great extent upon how consistent your categories are with what you value. Thus, as a receiver, you run the risk of stereotyping nonverbal and verbal messages and drawing false conclusions from these.[8] Certainly, nonverbal, physical characteristics make up the first impressions that individuals have of others, and "despite people's best intentions, their initial impressions of others are shaped by their assumptions about such characteristics."[9] These assumptions are stereotypes that individuals hold. Snyder points out that "these assumptions are not merely beliefs or attitudes that exist in a vacuum; they are reinforced by the behavior of both prejudiced people and the targets of their prejudice."[10] Walter Lippmann once explained the concept of stereotype:

> . . . an ordered, more or less consistent picture of the world, to which our habits, our tastes, our capacities, our comforts, and our hopes have adjusted themselves. They may not be a complete picture of the world, but they are a picture of a possible world to which we are adapted. In that world people and things have their well-known places, and do certain expected things. We feel at home there. . . .[11]

Psychologist Daniel Katz views stereotyping as necessary to the linguistic process in that stereotyping is the only way that one can quickly assimilate and thus interpret a new stimulus. Yet Katz warns that stereotyping emotionally limits the intellectual process. Because an individual has very narrow experiences, this person must assimilate information to his or her own frame of reference. This limitation of experience, thus, is essentially made up by a person's tendency to assign all of a group or classification to one simple cognitive category. One who has had little or no interaction with persons of a particular ethnic group will tend to stereotype (or to assimilate to his or her own frame of reference) messages about persons of that ethnic group. "The mere fact we lack the experience or the imagination to understand another point of view," cautions Katz, "does not mean that we realize our inadequacy and remain open-minded about it."[12] Rather than recognize the limitations of stereotyping, most individuals will proceed with processing the stereotype in order to handle the information that is being communicated and, consequently, make it meaningful to their own frame of reference.

Although it is apparent that stereotyping is certainly part of the verbal, linguistic process of assigning meaning to a stimulus, it should be recognized that listeners can run risks with stereotyping nonverbal stimuli as well. Your authors caution that many of the principles offered by popular writers on the subject of "body language" can perpetuate stereotypes. Though certainly increasing awareness of nonverbal communication, some of the popular treatments of the subject tend to overgeneralize and almost encourage listeners to stereotype the nonverbal message which is being sent, whether it be how to recognize the sexually available woman or man or how to recognize the status-seeking individual.

Despite the oversimplification inherent in attempting to interpret nonverbal codes, research indicates that there are some nonverbal acts or events which can serve as perceivable stimuli for a listener. These stimuli can carry meaning to the listener only if, as in verbal communication, the intent of the stimuli and the code are shared by the two communicators.

It is desirable, therefore, for the listener to know when he or she is stereotyping verbal and nonverbal messages and to recognize the limitations that these "short cuts" bring to the communication. Coming to terms with our own stereotyping behavior can be a significant part of knowing the listening self.

Understanding our own listening behavior, then, involves discovering our self-concept, attitudes, and values as they relate to our listening responses. We owe it to ourselves to know how we are responding and sincerely attempt to avoid any of the pitfalls in the process.

Motivating the Listening Self

As a second listening strategy, we should strive for individual motivation in the process. As we have defined listening as an active process, involving complex interaction of our sensory channels, responsible listeners should recognize that they cannot remain passive partners in the communication.

Carl Weaver notes that developing a desire to listen is basic to effective listening. Unfortunately, developing this desire is not a simple behavioral act, for, as Weaver notes, "most people do not really want to listen, but to talk."[13] He concludes that the desire to listen requires that the listener suppress the desire to talk and develop a desire to learn. We have a capacity to listen, composed of all the dimensions treated in this book; but this capacity to listen is not meaningful unless we combine it with a willingness to listen.[14]

The impact of motivation on listening comprehension was demonstrated in a recent study in which subjects were asked to comprehend and recall information presented by means of compressed speech tapes. Subjects in one of the groups were promised extra credit points commensurate with their comprehension scores as an added incentive to performing well as listeners. The results of this experiment indicate that the motivated group actually scored higher, leading researchers to conclude that the capacity to listen combined with willingness to listen affects listening performance.[15]

Since listening requires active behaviors, good listeners will assume the responsibility for their own motivation to listen and not passively wait for the speaker to provide such motivation. Indeed, this overreliance on the speaker to carry the burden in the communication process results in serious barriers to effective communication transactions. Further, such passive behavior on the part of most of us as listeners almost represents a cultural conditioning: we have come to rely on the speaker for motivation. The speaker who fails to provide such motivation frequently is tuned out. Such an attitude toward the motivation to listen is irresponsible, because it represents a renunciation of the equal responsibility to make a communication work.

Building intrinsic motivation to listen is not easy. There is no specific drive to listen. Rather, a combination of factors enters into our motivation: drives, habits, predispositions, cognitive states. If the listening experience can fulfill basic needs, then motivation can be maintained at a high level. This maintenance can be strengthened by efforts on the part of the listener to establish goals and identify specific purposes for listening before entering the listening situation.

Likewise, the listener can enhance intrinsic motivation to listen by establishing his or her own rewards system.[16] Rather than relying on external rewards (gold stars from teachers, etc.), we can motivate ourselves by providing our own satisfactions for effective listening. Often this reward system can result from establishing and then achieving the goal in a listening situation. For instance, you may set as your goal the acquisition of new information from a technical briefing in a field with which you are not familiar. Your internal reward can come from the satisfaction of knowing that you did listen well and that you did gain new information.

We ought to consider the effect of social conditioning on our listening motivation as well. We tend to emphasize the passive nature of listening in American society. School children are expected to "Be quiet and listen." Adults are advised to "Just sit back and listen" by emcees, personnel trainers, and even ministers. We should reorient our communication to the advice, "Sit *up* and listen."

To establish internal motivators, obviously, requires the listener to place greater premium on effective listening behavior. It would seem, therefore, that we have a serious responsibility to ourselves to place a higher priority on listening motivation.

Listening Actively

A third strategy for effective listening is listening actively, consistently participating in the communication process. Since communication is a transactional process, it is necessary that listeners assume at least fifty percent of the burden in that communication. The motivated listener will be an active listener, participating actively with the source throughout the transaction. Although it may seem simplistic to advise someone to listen, it is unfortunate that many people do not assume the responsibility for active listening. We know listeners who become too anxious to let the speaker carry the burden of the communication, listeners who too frequently dismiss their own poor listening with "Oh, he's a boring speaker" or "What a worthless subject." Such responses serve as convenient excuses for not assuming responsibility to participate actively in the communication.

Active listening throughout the communication transaction should be regarded as a parallel to our right to free speech. Just as speakers have the right to speak out in our democratic society, listeners also have the right to free listening. As we have seen, we can make choices to listen or not to listen. But once we have made the decision to listen, that decision should be accompanied by a commitment to listen with responsibility. The active listener is willing to meet this obligation and to listen to an entire message before passing judgment.

The importance of this willingness to listen was demonstrated recently on college campuses. Several notable but controversial speakers, including United Nations Ambassador Jeane Kilpatrick, social activist Eldridge Cleaver, and Saudi Arabian Sheik Ahmed Zaki Yamani, were heckled by members of campus audiences. The incidents led a coalition of organizations in higher education to issue a statement deploring the heckling. In their call, the coalition stressed: "Unless there is freedom to speak and to teach, even for those with whom we differ on fundamentals . . . and unless there is freedom for all to listen and to learn, there can be no true college or university. . . ."[17] It is clear that, as communicators, we should be willing to participate equally in the process. Such participation extends to our responsibility to hear the speaker out before we decide to accept or reject that person's message. People who share the communication transaction and allow speakers the opportunity to present their messages serve as active listeners throughout the process.

Sending Feedback

A fourth strategy which characterizes the listener as an effective communicator is the strategy of sending feedback. Feedback—the response or reaction of the listener as perceived by the source in the communication transaction—plays a very valuable role in the entire process. The feedback we send to individuals can have a significant effect on them. First, it can greatly affect the development of their self-concept. As we have seen, self-concept results very much from our perceptions of how others perceive us. A person who receives positive feedback gains in self-confidence. On the other hand, negative feedback can be disruptive and discouraging to a speaker and thus diminish the self-confidence which the speaker may have as a communicator.[18]

Feedback from listeners also can regulate speakers' actions, such as how they organize their remarks as they are communicating to listeners. The denial of feedback has been found to be disruptive to speakers and to result in speeches which are less coherent, less accurate, and more wordy.[19] The listener who intends to actively participate in the communication transaction, then, must decide to send feedback which will be supportive to the speaker's efforts to further the communication process.

Supportive feedback can be valuable not only to individuals but also to organizations. In an informative study which demonstrates the impact of feedback on an organization, Tubbs and Widgery trained managers and supervisors in a large automotive factory to send to workers feedback about their job performance. As a result of the training in feedback skills, managers and supervisors improved their communications with their workers. The factory workers, in turn, were found to improve their job performance and to be more satisfied with their work.[20]

Many organizations have come to recognize the benefits of feedback in conducting the business of the organization. Raymond Dreyfack urges executives to use feedback techniques by questioning the speaker and/or repeating what the individual has said as "a virtual guarantee of efficiency."[21] "In communicating," he stresses, "it is as important to make good feedback—or checkback—habitual as it is important from a health standpoint to make deep breathing habitual."[22] The payoff for effective feedback ultimately is increased productivity for the organization and more supportive interpersonal relationships for individuals.

A classic study on the use of feedback illustrates the impressive potential for strengthening the communication transaction for both the speaker and the listener. In this study, Leavitt and Mueller asked a speaker to describe a diagram to another person. In different treatments, the level of feedback was shifted so that, in some situations, the speaker received no direct verbal or nonverbal response whatsoever, while in other situations the speaker could at least look at the listener, ask questions, or enter into a complete conversation about the diagram with the listener. The research demonstrated that the more feedback there was between the speaker and the listener, the more accurate was the listener's interpretation of the message. Likewise, with increased feedback, both listener and speaker became confident that the message was communicated with accuracy, and, as feedback increased, both received greater satisfaction from the communication. Introducing feedback into the communication system, however, increased the amount of time required for the communication transaction.[23]

Despite the time required, feedback can strengthen the communication and create a true transaction for the communicators. To be effective, however, the listener's feedback should be open, honest, constructive, and meaningful to the speaker. Barker offers ten basic guidelines for sending feedback effectively:

1. Send feedback that is appropriate to the speaker's message.
2. Be certain the speaker perceived the feedback.
3. Make certain the feedback is clear in meaning.
4. Send the feedback quickly.
5. Beware of overloading the system.
6. Delay in performing any activity that might create an unintentional effect.
7. Keep feedback to the message separate from personal evaluation.
8. Use nondirective feedback until the speaker invites evaluation of his message.
9. Be certain that you understand the message before you send directive feedback.
10. Realize that early attempts at giving more effective feedback may seem unnatural but will improve with practice.[24]

As general guidelines for sending feedback, Barker's suggestions can prove to be useful. Listeners need to sharpen their feedback skills and recognize that they are sending verbal and nonverbal messages through the feedback channel. Since sending feedback is a continuous process while we are communicating with someone, it is essential that the feedback express what it is we want to communicate to the other person.

A good listener will avoid sending distracting, unintentional feedback through responses which may not be appropriate to the situation. And a good listener will recognize that open, honest feedback certainly is the best form of communication. We realize, however, that honest feedback may sometimes have a negative effect on a speaker and lead to ending the communication. Consequently, the listener should assess carefully the possible effects of his or her response and judge accordingly.

To develop skill in the use of feedback, we, as listeners, "should not only be providing some kind of feedback, but we should be aware of the other person's response to that feedback."[25] Perceptions of the other person's response to feedback require total involvement in the communication transaction. The listener must be aware not only of the feedback he or she is sending but also of how that feedback is being received. Should you find, for instance, that the speaker is being antagonized by the responses you are giving, then you ought to consider adjusting the feedback messages so as not to create a defensive communication climate.

One of the most dramatic examples of the need for developing sensitive feedback skills is in the classroom. Students should learn how to send teachers useful and supportive feedback which can facilitate the learning process. Students who read their notes or student newspapers in class often fail to realize what their "silent messages" communicate to a teacher who is presenting a lecture. Or the student who responds to a teacher's questioning look with "I'm sorry that I've missed the last two weeks. Have we done anything important?" clearly needs to analyze the impact of the message which he or she is sending. Attention to the feedback which a student sends to a teacher—as well as the feedback that a teacher sends to a student—can serve to create a positive, supportive communication bond that ought to enhance the learning process.

Developing useful, supportive feedback skills can be a major task for all sensitive listeners. Feedback skill results from conscious effort; you must know what you are doing as a communicator. Practice and experience can enable one to develop and perfect these skills. As Barker points out in his tenth recommendation, however, concentration on feedback skills may seem unnatural at first. However, listeners may find that using feedback skills over a period of time leads to a comfortable level for communicating feedback messages to speakers.

Indeed, sending feedback is an important listening strategy, just as knowing one's self, developing self-motivation to listen, and listening actively serve as devices to enhance the communication transaction between listeners and speakers in conversations, in the classroom, on the job, and in all aspects of life. It is evident, then, that the listener is a communicator, maintaining at least equal responsibility for the communication process as it is being transacted by those involved. As a communicator, the listener must make use of these key communication strategies in order to fulfill his or her responsibilities.

Factors Influencing the Listening Process

Just as there are strategies which affect the listener's participation in the communication process, so, too, are there key influences which will affect our listening performance. Clearly, as listeners we are affected by the many aspects of the entire communication process: the source of the message; the message itself; the channel(s) through which the message is transmitted; the communication environment; the noise surrounding the communication. And, as listeners, we are affected by some key factors which influence the way we function at any given time in the listening process. Research in listening behavior stresses the significance of these influencing factors.

Time

The influence of time on all communicators is significant. Indeed, time has become such a precious commodity to Americans today that we even try to practice principles for success as *The One Minute Manager.* Tubbs and Moss point out that "time is one of the most relevant variables in the study of human communication."[26] Time can affect the intensity of the communication relationship (A group meeting for only one hour each week for an extended period of time would have less intensity than a group that meets for a marathon weekend.); time can change the channel of communication (A parent and a child move from nonverbal to verbal communication as the child develops verbal language skills.); and time can alter the style of the communication (A couple who have been together for a long period of time probably uses fewer words; each is able to anticipate the other's thoughts and feelings.).[27]

Listening communicators are continuously influenced by various dimensions of time. The time which is manifested in the aging process itself can affect one's listening efficiency. The physical deterioration of the hearing mechanism over a lifetime, for example, can reduce the listener's auditory acuity. And the time it takes to actually listen is a significant factor. Research illustrates that listeners can listen (and think) about four times faster than the normal conversation rate, so we have a great deal of "lag time" in the system for attention to wander and to lose focus.[28]

Time also becomes a factor in the listening process in that the time in which the communication occurs, such as the time of day, can affect one's attentiveness and overall motivation to listen. Speakers often cite differences that they notice in audiences for luncheon speeches as contrasted with after-dinner speeches or breakfast presentations. The amount of time that one has available to listen has a profound effect on the process as well. If the listener is rushed or unable to devote much time to the process, then the listening may well be short-circuited. Most of us probably have experienced conferences with a busy adviser, salesperson, or executive who really did not have time to listen and nonverbally communicated a desire to end the conversation. It can be a very frustrating experience for both speaker and listener if, indeed, there is not enough time to listen. Time certainly plays a significant role in the communication process.

Age

A listener may very well "grow" with age and gain greater experience and sensitivity so as to achieve effective listening. Likewise, an individual's sensory mechanisms, particularly hearing affected by presbycusis, may deteriorate with age and thus increase one's difficulty in receiving the message.[29] Research also has inferred that young people may have shorter attention spans but have greater memory capacity. Such conclusions may not be warranted, however, as more contemporary studies demonstrate few if any distinctions between younger and older subjects.[30]

Sex

Research does point out that men and women have different attention styles and perhaps even different cognitive processing styles. These factors can affect the way men and women, even at a very early age, respond in different ways to the same stimuli. Although some early researchers concluded that men were superior to women as listeners, careful study of the literature does not substantiate such generalizations. It is clear, however, that the sex roles of men and women are so dominant in American culture that there is a great likelihood that individuals are conditioned while young to respond according to those ascribed sex roles. While the feminist movement is working to break down these sex role stereotypes, some brain researchers are discovering that male and female brain structures are different.[31]

Self-Concept

Another significant influence on the communication process is the listener's self-concept. The effect of the self-concept on listening behavior has not been researched to any great extent. Research in reading, however, supports the idea that better self-concepts can improve reception: "Sufficient evidence has been found . . . and enough support from authorities in education and psychology has been accumulated to suggest that many disabled readers can be helped by improving their self-concepts."[32]

For most of us, our listening self-concept is too negative. Throughout our lives, we have probably experienced few rewards for good listening. Instead, we have been subjected to negative reinforcement: "You're not listening to me." "Sit down and listen to me." "You don't listen." "Why don't you ever listen to me?"

Such messages must have a significant impact on the ability to function as a listener. If you are told often enough that you are not a good listener, you will start to believe that you are a poor listener and will behave accordingly. Research in psychology supports the idea that an individual will behave in accordance with his or her self-concept and "live up to the label" through a self-fulfilling prophecy.[33]

The influence of the significant others who shape the self-concept can be profound. In a study of the listener's self-concept, one of your authors discovered that students reported that parents, friends, and other family members were most instrumental in shaping their perceptions about themselves as listeners. As hypothesized, all too frequently these significant others were reported to be instrumental in shaping negative perceptions of these students' listening behavior.[34]

Hemispheric Specialization

In recent decades, clinical and experimental research on the brain has led to the formation of the dual-brain theory; that is, the brain consists of two halves or cerebral hemispheres (the left and right hemispheres), which are connected by the corpus callosum (a thick bundle of never fibers) which mediates "a constant flow of information from one hemisphere to the other."[35] This dual-brain theory posits (1) that each hemisphere governs the actions of the opposite side of the body, with the left hemisphere controlling the right side and the right hemisphere controlling the left side; (2) that each hemisphere specializes in a different mode of processing information, with the left hemisphere processing highly-structured information logically and analytically by thinking in words, numbers, and symbols and the right hemisphere processing patterns of information spatially, holistically, nonverbally, and perceptually by mainly thinking in pictures and images[36] (as illustrated in fig. 4.3); and (3) that each hemisphere has its own functions. Exploring the differences in hemispheric functions by studying subjects with intact brains as well as subjects with brain damage, researchers have found that some of the major hemispheric functions appear to be as follows:

Left Hemisphere	**Right Hemisphere**
verbal—reading, writing, speaking, and listening to verbal messages; thinking in word symbols	*nonverbal*—projecting and perceiving nonverbal cues
linguistic—being competent in the grammar, syntax, and semantics of language	*nonlinguistic*—seeing objects, events, etc., as they are without names/words connected to them; lacking the linguistic elements of grammar, syntax, and semantics
analytical—reducing the whole to its parts	*holistic*—seeing in wholes
logical/rational—reasoning	*emotional*—responding to/with feeling
mathematical/digital—computing, measuring, and timing	*intuitive*—having insight; responding with "ah ha" premonitions
linear—perceiving objects, events, etc., in their true relation to one another	*creative*—exhibiting inventiveness/imagination
syntactical—arranging information in an orderly/systematic manner	*spatial/relational*—recognizing patterns, configurations, shapes, forms, etc., even though part of the data may be missing
objective—being independent of mind	*perceptual*—seeing in three-dimensions; having depth perception
articulate—expressing oneself clearly/distinctly	*visual*—thinking in images/pictures
ordered—organizing; categorizing information	*artistic*—having skill in such activities as art, music, dance
	aesthetic—enjoying stimuli
	novel—responding to new/unknown stimuli; being innovative[37]

Moreover, Hogen has noted these possible differences: the left hemisphere may be superior in detecting sameness and may cause one to use "I think. . . ." more often, to be efficient at name identification and concept identification tasks, and to possess "right-ear advantage for auditory perception of spoken sounds, words, digits, consonants, words in music, and recognition of speakers' voices"; the right hemisphere may be superior in detecting differences and may cause one to use "I feel. . . ." more often and to be efficient at physical identification and fact recognition.[38]

During given tasks, both hemispheres may work together (hemispheric enhancement), or they may interfere with each other (hemispheric conflict). Ideally, there should be internal cooperation between the hemispheres; however, the left hemisphere seems to dominate within most individuals (especially right-handed persons). What are the reasons for the left cerebral dominance? George Prince, author of *Mindspring,* believes that "because we operate in such a sequential-seeming world and because the logical thought of the left hemisphere is so honored in our culture, we gradually damp out, devalue and disregard the input of our right hemispheres. It is not that we stop using it altogether; it just becomes less and less available to us because of established habit patterns."[39] Roger Sperry's and his followers' view, as summarized by Fincher in *Human Intelligence,* is as follows:

> Our society . . . , especially in the fields of science and education, is inherently prejudiced against the intellect of the right, or nonlanguage, hemisphere. It is the linguistic, the abstract side of ourselves we test and educate and reward—and by such powerful social strategem catapult to an overarching prominence in the human scheme of things.[40]

Many researchers who have studied creativity claim that "the educational process concentrates on the functions of the logical brain while neglecting the creative brain."[41] One of these researchers is Edwards, author of *Drawing on the Right Side of the Brain;* she conjectures that "long and exclusive emphasis on the verbal mode in education may have the effect of diminishing an individual's ability to make cognitive shifts in information-processing mode as required for specific tasks."[42] Whatever the reason(s) may be for left hemispheric dominance, the left hemisphere appears to be quite proficient in restricting the actions of the right hemisphere and even assuming control of the tasks at which the right hemisphere excels. Thus, interference between the hemispheres prevents maximum performance as well as maximum understanding.[43]

Research also indicates that gender may be related to hemispheric specialization.[44] The female brain tends to be less specialized than the male brain is; for example, adult females appear to have verbal and spatial abilities on both sides of the brain.[45] Another gender difference is that the left hemisphere generally develops first in the female while the right hemisphere generally develops first in the male; thus, many little girls read and write better than many little boys.[46] Also, each gender seems to excel in certain abilities. For instance, males appear to excel in certain types of spatial perceptions, mathematics, mechanical tasks, responsiveness to verbal cues, and detection of simple pitch patterns, melodies, and environmental sounds, while females appear to be superior in verbal skills, to process information faster, to respond more readily to facial cues, to be more empathic, to be less distracted by visual images while listening, and to be better able to remember names and faces of former classmates.[47] Moreover, females appear to be more perceptive about people; that is, they are more skilled

Figure 4.3. Advertisement by SAAB-SCANIA of America, Inc.
Reprinted by permission of SAAB-SCANIA of America Company.

A CAR FOR THE LEFT SIDE OF YOUR BRAIN.

The left side of your brain, recent investigations tell us, is the logical side.

It figures out that $1+1=2$. And, in a few cases, that $E=mc^2$.

On a more mundane level, it chooses the socks you wear, the cereal you eat, and the car you drive. All by means of rigorous Aristotelian logic.

However, and a big however it is, for real satisfaction, you must achieve harmony with the other side of your brain.

The right side, the poetic side, that says, "Yeah, Car X has a reputation for lasting a long time but it's so dull, who'd want to drive it that long anyway?"

The Saab Turbo looked at from all sides.

To the left side of your brain, Saab turbocharging is a technological feat that retains good gas mileage while also increasing performance.

To the right side of your brain, Saab turbocharging is what makes a Saab go like a bat out of hell.

The left side sees the safety in high performance. (Passing on a two-lane highway. Entering a freeway in the midst of high-speed traffic.)

The right side lives only for the thrills.

The left side considers that *Road & Track* magazine just named Saab "The Sports Sedan for the Eighties." By unanimous choice of its editors.

The right side eschews informed endorsements by editors who have spent a lifetime comparing cars. The right side doesn't know much about cars, but knows what it likes.

The left side scans this chart.

Wheelbase	*99.1 inches*
Length	*187.6 inches*
Width	*66.5 inches*
Height	*55.9 inches*
Fuel-tank capacity	*16.6 gallons*
EPA City	*19 mpg**
EPA Highway	*31 mpg**

The right side looks at the picture on the opposite page.

The left side compares a Saab's comfort with that of a Mercedes. Its performance with that of a BMW. Its braking with that of an Audi.

The right side looks at the picture.

The left side looks ahead to the winter when a Saab's front-wheel drive will keep a Saab in front of traffic.

The right side looks at the picture.

The left side also considers the other seasons of the year when a Saab's front-wheel drive gives it the cornering ability of a sports car.

The right side looks again at the picture.

Getting what you need vs. getting what you want.

Needs are boring; desires are what make life worth living.

The left side of your brain is your mother telling you that a Saab is good for you. "Eat your vegetables." (In today's world, you need a car engineered like a Saab.) "Put on your raincoat." (The Saab is economical. Look at the price-value relationship.) "Do your homework." (The passive safety of the construction. The active safety of the handling.)

*1982 SAAB PRICE** LIST*

900 3-Door	*5-Speed*	*$10,400*
	Automatic	*10,750*
900 4-Door	*5-Speed*	*$10,700*
	Automatic	*11,050*
900S 3-Door	*5-Speed*	*$12,100*
	Automatic	*12,450*
900S 4-Door	*5-Speed*	*$12,700*
	Automatic	*13,050*
900 Turbo 3-Door	*5-Speed*	*$15,600*
	Automatic	*15,950*
900 Turbo 4-Door	*5-Speed*	*$16,260*
	Automatic	*16,610*

All turbo models include a Sony XR70, 4-Speaker Stereo Sound System as standard equipment. The stereo can be, of course, perfectly balanced: left and right.

The right side of your brain guides your foot to the clutch, your hand to the gears, and listens for the "zzzooommm."

Together, they see the 1982 Saab Turbo as the responsible car the times demand you get. And the performance car you've always, deep down, wanted with half your mind.

**Saab 900 Turbo. Remember, use estimated mpg for comparison only. Mileage varies with speed, trip length, and weather. Actual highway mileage will probably be less. **Manufacturer's suggested retail price. Not including taxes, license, freight, dealer charges or options desired by either side of your brain.*

A CAR FOR THE RIGHT SIDE OF YOUR BRAIN.
SAAB
The most intelligent car ever built.

at "listening between the lines" (sensing the difference between what people say and what they mean and detecting nuances that reveal the true feelings of others).[48]

The dual-brain theory has many implications relevant to the listening process and listening behavior. The major implication of the theory is that we may listen differently due to our being left- or right-hemisphere oriented. As we have noted, there are hemispheric differences in the types of information attended to, modes of information-processing employed, communication codes used, and functions performed. In addition, there is experimental evidence that memory may be related to hemispheric differences. Paivio has found that the right hemisphere has an advantage for visual memory since it is easier to remember pictures than words; yet, he has also found that "naming enhances memory for pictorial items and image coding increases memory for words."[49] These findings seem to indicate that hemispheric cooperation should contribute to memory improvement. Unfortunately, however, there frequently is hemispheric interference rather than cooperation when one is processing messages consisting of verbal and visual (nonverbal) components.[50] This observation is only one example of the many findings that illustrate how hemispheric conflict prevents maximum performance in processing (including remembering) information as well as in listening; however, by establishing internal cooperation between the two hemispheres, individuals may significantly improve their efficiency in both information-processing and listening.

Physical and Psychological States

A person's physical and/or psychological state at any given time will influence listening behavior. If an individual does not feel well or is worried about something at work, for example, then it will be difficult to concentrate and attend to the message with effective listening.[51]

Receiver Apprehension

The psychological state and/or the negative self-concept can further affect us as listeners by inducing what might be termed receiver apprehension. Although to date most of the research on this construct has focused on the communication apprehension of the source, Wheeless has pioneered some study of the listener's apprehension, which he conceptualizes as "the fear of misinterpreting, inadequately processing, and/or not being able to adjust psychologically to messages sent by others."[52] The little research focused on receiver apprehension suggests that "the anxiety or fear stemming from the listening situation may in turn result in inefficient listening."[53] For example, the listener who is anxious may have to learn how to relax before he or she can listen effectively to a lecturer, an interviewer, the boss, or to a family member.

The listener as communicator, then, is influenced by a number of factors which can affect his or her behavior as a listener at any given time throughout the communication transaction. These key factors—including time, age, sex, self-concept, hemispheric specialization, physical/psychological state, and receiver apprehension—can deter or can facilitate listening efficiency, depending upon the nature of the influence at the time. It should be clear, however, that a listener can overcome any negative, deterring influence by systematically employing the listening strategies in the communication. The listener who strives to know and to motivate himself or herself, to listen actively, and to send appropriate feedback can become a more effective listening communicator.

The improvement of listening behavior requires effort. Understanding your own listening behavior is a first step, but building the additional strategies necessary to improve your listening behavior must follow. Lundsteen has noted that "superior performance in listening skill probably not only requires possession of a wide range of basic competencies, but also the ability to *mobilize* them for a particular communicative situation and then to apply them beyond the listening moment."[54] Building competency with these strategies takes practice. Once you understand how you function as a listener and how effective listeners *should* function, you must practice using the listening strategies for your own improvement. This involves practicing improved skills, for, as Duffin cautions, "since 'practice makes perfect' only if it is correct practice, practicing existing listening habits probably serves to reinforce ineffective listening behaviors and attitudes."[55]

Through understanding and through practice, then, the listener can acquire knowledge and skills in order to grow as an effective listening communicator. Dominick Barbara has eloquently described the objective for which the listening communicator should strive:

> To discover order and honesty in his perceiving, Man must have the courage to face the truth within himself. His listening must remain free of prejudiced distortions, false condemnations, and personal resentments. Furthermore, he must be honest enough to develop a realistic understanding of his own motives and the actions to which he is driven by them. The more able he is to listen on a rational, responsible and humanistic basis, the more readily will Man ultimately realize himself and discover his most constructive possibilities.[56]

SUMMARY

In this chapter, we have stressed that listening is a communication function. Throughout the process, the listener and the speaker communicate with each other, and the more homophilous the communicators are (the more they share common attibutes), the more effective that communication can be. The listener, as a communicator, must make decisions throughout the listening process to receive and to attend to that message, to assign meaning to that message, and to utilize appropriate listening strategies in order to participate effectively in the communication transaction. These strategies include developing an understanding of the self as a listener, motivating that listening self, listening actively throughout the process, and sending appropriate feedback to the speaker.

Just as these strategies, if carefully chosen and applied throughout the communication process, can influence the outcome of the communication transaction, so, too, can certain key factors affect the listener during the process. The listener's age, sex, self-concept, hemispheric specialization, physical and psychological states, and receiver apprehension all can combine with the time factor to affect the way a listener will function at any point in the transaction.

As listening communicators, then, individuals must know themselves and be sensitive to others as they assume equal participation in the communication transaction. It is clear that the speaker alone should not be forced to carry the burden for successful communication. The listener shares that responsibility and makes his or her decisions accordingly.

SUGGESTED ACTIVITIES

1. Interview two people who are especially effective as listeners (perhaps professional counselors or friends/family members who are "noted" for listening). Ask them to reflect on their techniques and on their sense of responsibility to themselves and to other communicators.
2. Interivew a politician who has recently conducted an election/re-election campaign. Ask the person about the general responsiveness of his or her audiences and his or her impression of how seriously his or her listeners had taken their responsibilities as listeners. What do you perceive to be the general state of listening responsibility in the United States?
3. Participate in a self-disclosure conversation with another person on some topics that you have not discussed before. After the discussion, draw your Johari Window and discuss it with your partner. Does it reflect the extent to which you did self-disclose? What did you learn, then, about your self-concept through the Window?
4. Create a list or a chart of those ideas and beliefs which are important (of value) to you. Then, prepare another list or chart of those things which you value. What do these lists or charts tell you about yourself? What do they tell you about your listening behavior? Do these values influence the perceptions through which you listen? How?
5. Practice the skill of sending feedback to speakers in interviews, group discussions, and public speeches. Make a conscious effort to apply the principles described in this chapter. Ask the speakers to whom you send feedback what their impressions are. Does your feedback communicate the messages you intend? Are you effective in sending feedback?
6. Design your plan for listening improvement. Make a list of those aspects which you wish to improve and detail what strategies you plan to implement in order to improve. Arrange a conference with your instructor to discuss the strategies so as to insure that your plans will lead to improvement of your listening behavior.
7. Go to your library and locate current literature on the key factors which influence listening behavior: time, age, sex, self-concept, hemispheric specialization, physical/psychological state, receiver apprehension. Summarize the literature in a paper which can then provide the subject matter for a class discussion on these salient listening factors.

8. Make an effort to identify your stereotypes. List those which you can recognize, and consider how you came to develop these particular stereotypes. What are some of the more "universal" stereotypes which characterize American values?

NOTES

1. Everett M. Rogers and Dilip K. Bhowmik, "Homophily-Heterophily: Relational Concepts for Communication Research," in *Speech Communication Behavior,* eds. Larry L. Barker and Robert J. Kibler (Englewood Cliffs, New Jersey: Prentice-Hall, 1971), p. 214.
2. William D. Brooks, *Speech Communication,* 3rd ed. (Dubuque, Iowa: Wm. C. Brown Company Publishers, 1978), p. 56.
3. Joseph Luft, *Group Process: An Introduction to Group Dynamics* (Palo Alto, California: National Press, 1963).
4. Sidney M. Jourard, *The Transparent Self* (New York: Van Nostrand Reinhold Company, 1964), p. 5.
5. Cynthia R. Gilner et al., "A Developmental Investigation of Visual and Haptic Preferences for Shape and Texture," *Monographs of the Society for Research in Child Development* 24 (September 1969): 36.
6. See, for example, Donald D. Durrell, "Listening Comprehension Versus Reading Comprehension," *Journal of Reading* 12 (March 1969): 455–460.
7. From *The Medium Is the Massage* by Marshall McLuhan and Quentin Fiore. Coordinated by Jermone Agel. Copyright © 1967 by Bantam Books, Inc. Reprinted by permission of the publisher. All rights reserved.
8. For a dated but interesting review of research on stereotyping, see William L. Brembeck and William S. Howell, *Persuasion* (Englewood Cliffs, New Jersey: Prentice-Hall, Inc., 1952), pp. 108–119.
9. Mark Snyder, "Self-Fulfilling Stereotypes," *Psychology Today* 16 (July 1982): 60.
10. *Ibid.*
11. Walter Lippmann, *Public Opinion* (New York: Macmillan Company, 1922), p. 95.
12. Daniel Katz, "Psychological Barriers to Communication," in *Messages,* ed. Jean M. Civikly (New York: Random House, 1974), p. 326.
13. Carl Weaver, *Human Listening: Process and Behavior* (Indianapolis: Bobbs-Merrill, 1972), p. 82.
14. Weaver notes this distinction and emphasizes the importance of the willingness to listen, *Ibid.,* pp. 7–8.
15. Michael J. Beatty, Ralph R. Behnke, and Deidre L. Froelich, "Effects of Achievement Incentive and Presentation Rate on Listening Comprehension," *The Quarterly Journal of Speech* 66 (April 1980):193–200.
16. Motivation researchers have come to regard motivation as equivalent to reinforcement. See, for example, Robert C. Bolles, *Theory of Motivation* (New York: Harper and Row Publishers, 1967), ch. 15.
17. Press Release, American Council on Education, Washington, D.C., March 29, 1983.
18. Gardiner surveyed over fifty studies of feedback and drew similar conclusions as to the effect of feedback. See James C. Gardiner, "A Synthesis of Experimental Studies of Speech Communication Feedback," *Journal of Communication* 21 (March 1971): 17–35.

19. This research is summarized in Robert E. Kraut, Steven H. Lewis, and Lawrence W. Swezey, "Listener Responsiveness and the Coordination of Conversation," *Journal of Personality and Social Psychology* 43 (October 1982): 718–731.
20. Stewart L. Tubbs and Robin N. Widgery, "When Productivity Lags, Check at the Top: Are Key Managers Really Communicating?" *Management Review* 67 (January 1978): 20–25.
21. Raymond Dreyfack, *What An Executive Should Know about Listening More Effectively* (Chicago: The Dartnell Corporation, 1983), p. 12.
22. *Ibid.*, p. 13.
23. Harold J. Leavitt and Ronald A. H. Mueller, "Some Effects of Feedback on Communication," in *Interpersonal Communication: Survey and Studies,* ed. Dean Barnlund (Boston: Houghton Mifflin, 1968), pp. 251–259.
24. Larry L. Barker, *Listening Behavior* (Englewood Cliffs, New Jersey: Prentice-Hall, 1971), pp. 123–124.
25. Stewart L. Tubbs and Sylvia Moss, *Human Communication* (New York: Random House, 1983), p. 43.
26. *Ibid.*, p. 44.
27. *Ibid.*, pp. 44–47.
28. See Ralph G. Nichols and Leonard A. Stevens, *Are You Listening?* (New York: McGraw-Hill Book Company, 1957), chapter 7.
29. For summaries of some of this research, see Barker, *Listening Behavior,* pp. 45–46 and Weaver, *Human Listening: Processes and Behavior,* pp. 13–14.
30. For a review of this research, see Arthur Wingfield and Dennis L. Byrnes, *The Psychology of Human Memory* (New York: Academic Press, 1981), pp. 365–368. See also Alex Cherry Wilkinson and Ronald Koestler, "Repeated Recall: A New Model and Tests of Its Generality from Childhood to Old Age," *Journal of Experimental Psychology* 112 (1983): 423–451.
31. See Weaver, *Human Listening: Processes and Behavior,* pp. 70–78, for a review of the research on sex differences.
32. Ivan Quandt, *Self-Concept and Reading* (Newark, Delaware: International Reading Association, no date), p. 31.
33. For an interesting review of some of the research on the self-fulfilling prophecy, see Robert Rosenthal, "Self-Fulfilling Prophecy," *Readings in Psychology Today* (Del Mar, California: CRM Books, 1967), pp. 466–471.
34. Andrew D. Wolvin, unpublished manuscript, "The Listener's Self-Concept."
35. Jack Fincher, *Human Intelligence* (New York: G. P. Putnam's Sons, 1976), p. 55.
36. Marilyn Ferguson, *The Aquarian Conspiracy* (Los Angeles: J. P. Tarcher, 1980), pp. 298–300; Betty A. Edwards, "The Effect of Verbal/Visual Interactions on Drawing Ability," in *Nonverbal Communication Today,* ed. Mary Ritchie Key (Berlin: Mouton Publishers, 1982), pp. 35–37.
37. Roger W. Sperry, "Hemisphere Disconnection and Unity in Conscious Awareness," *American Psychologist* 23 (October 1968): 723–733; Ferguson, *The Aquarian Conspiracy,* pp. 78–79, 297–300; Edwards, "The Effect of Verbal/Visual Interactions on Drawing Ability," pp. 33–53; George Prince, "Putting the Other Half of the Brain to Work," *Training HRD* 15 (November 1978): 57–60; Mary C. Kirkland, "What Are the Choices?" *Future* 20 (May/June 1982): 24–27; Leonard J. Shedletsky, "Can We Use Our Brains to Define Communication?" *The Encoder,* Fall 1980, pp. 30–40; Daniel Goleman, "Special Abilities of the Sexes: Do They Begin in the Brain?" *Psychology Today* 12 (November 1978): 48–59, 120; Joyce Brothers, "Men and Women—

The Differences," *Woman's Day,* February 9, 1982, pp. 58, 60, 138, 140, 142; Harold A. Sackheim, Reuben C. Gur, and Marcel C. Saucy, "Emotions Are Expressed More Intensely on Left Side of Face," *Science* 202 (October 1978): 434–436; James Mann, "What Is TV Doing to America?" *U.S. News and World Report* 93 (2 August 1982): 27–30; Howard Gardner, "The Music of the Hemispheres," *Psychology Today,* June 1982, pp. 91–92; J. Sonnenfeld, "The Communication of Environmental Meaning: Hemispheres in Conflict," in *Nonverbal Communication Today,* ed. Key, pp. 17–29; O. M. Hogen, "An Introduction to Bilateral Communication," cited by Robert O. Hirsch, *Listening: A Way to Process Information Aurally* (Dubuque, Iowa: Gorsuch Scarisbrick Publishers, 1979), pp. 28–30; P. Andersen, J. Garrison, and J. Andersen, "Implications of a Neurophysiological Approach for the Study of a Nonverbal Communication," *Human Communication Research* 6 (1979): 74–89.

38. Hogen, "An Introduction to Bilateral Communication," pp. 29–30.
39. Prince, "Putting the Other Half of the Brain to Work," p. 58.
40. Fincher, *Human Intelligence,* p. 73.
41. Kirkland, "What Are the Choices?" p. 24.
42. Edwards, "The Effect of Verbal/Visual Interactions on Drawing Ability," p. 34.
43. *Ibid.,* p. 36; Prince, "Putting the Other Half of the Brain to Work," p. 58.
44. Carol Johmann, "Mind: Sex and the Split Brain," *Omni* 5 (August 1983): 26, 113.
45. Shedletsky, "Can We Use Our Brains to Define Communication?" p. 33; Goleman, "Special Abilities of the Sexes: Do They Begin in the Brain?" pp. 48–59, 120; Brothers, "Men and Women—The Differences," p. 142.
46. Brothers, "Men and Women—The Differences," p. 140; Goleman, "Special Abilities of the Sexes: Do They Begin in the Brain?" pp. 48–59, 120.
47. Brothers, "Men and Women—The Differences," p. 142; Goleman, "Special Abilities of the Sexes: Do They Begin in the Brain?", pp. 48–59; Ferguson, *The Aquarian Conspiracy,* p. 299; Hogen, "An Introduction to Bilateral Communication," p. 29.
48. Brothers, "Men and Women—The Differences," p. 142.
49. Allan Paivio, "On Exploring Visual Knowledge," in *Visual Learning, Thinking and Communication,* eds. Bikkar S. Randhawa and William E. Coffman (New York: Academic Press, 1978), p. 116.
50. Sonnenfeld, "The Communication of Environmental Meaning: Hemispheres in Conflict," p. 28.
51. Several of these factors are summarized in Barker, *Listening Behavior,* chapter 3.
52. Lawrence R. Wheeless, "An Investigation of Receiver Apprehension and Social Context Dimensions of Communication Apprehension," *Speech Teacher* 24 (September 1975): 263.
53. Katie Paschall and Anthony J. Clark, "An Investigation of the Effects of Receiver Apprehension and Source Apprehension on Listening Comprehension," (Paper presented at the Fifth Annual Convention of the International Listening Association, Scottsdale, Arizona, March 8, 1984), p. 12.
54. Sara W. Lundsteen, *Listening: Its Impact at All Levels on Reading and the Other Language Arts* (Urbana, Illinois: ERIC Clearinghouse on Reading and Communication Skills, 1979), p. 75.
55. John Duffin, "DLA's: Teaching Listening Skills with Videotape," *Teacher Talk* 2 (Fall 1982), pp. 5–6
56. Dominick A. Barbara, *The Art of Listening* (Springfield, Illinois: Charles C. Thomas Publisher, 1958), p. 191.

Concepts You Will Encounter

Auditory Discrimination
Language Development
Phonology
Paralanguage
Sensitivity
Speech Patterns/Dialects
Visual Discrimination
Kinesics
Artifacts
Appearance
Proxemics
Chronemics
Touch
"Civil Inattention"
"Eyebrow Flash"
Affect Displays
Adaptors
Displacement Signals
Territorial Markers
Emblems
Neurolinguistic Programming
Self-Monitoring Behaviors
Illustrators
Mirroring
Quasi-Courtship Behaviors
Regulators
Ingratiating Behaviors
Respectful Behaviors
Deception Cues
Nonverbal Leakage Cues

Skills You Should Develop

Refining Skills Included in Weaver and Rutherford's Hierarchy
Recognizing the Sound Structure of Our Language
Detecting and Isolating Vocal Cues
Understanding Dialectal Differences
Recognizing Environmental Sounds
Detecting and Isolating Nonverbal Cues

Discriminative Listening

5

One purpose for listening is discriminative listening: listening to distinguish the aural stimuli. Depending upon the communication context, however, the stimuli also may be visual, such as a smile, a clenched fist, or a shrug of the shoulder.

Discriminative listening is placed first among the five purposes of listening because it is basic to the other four purposes. As the following examples illustrate, the listener who has developed effective discriminative listening skills is a more efficient listener when engaging in each of the other four purposes of listening. For example, the comprehensive listener who can detect changes in the sender's pitch, volume, and/or rate is better equipped to determine when the sender is moving from one main idea to another. Also, if the comprehensive listener is sensitive to dialectal differences, he or she can more quickly recognize the sender's intended meaning. Likewise, the therapeutic listener who recognizes the structure of the language and vocal cues is better able to determine the degree of the sender's distress by reason of his or her use of vocal characterizers (such as speaking at a barely audible volume), vocal segregates (such as frequently pausing and/or vocalizing pauses with sounds such as *uh* and *umm*), and speech nonfluencies (such as starting the same sentence twice and/or beginning with one thought and then jumping to another thought without completing the first). Furthermore, the critical listener who is skilled in detecting and accurately interpreting nonverbal cues can more readily determine from the sender's leg, foot, and hand movements as well as facial expressions whether or not the sender is "speaking" the truth. Finally, the appreciative listener who can detect the sounds of the individual instruments in an orchestra can increase his or her enjoyment of the total artistic expression while the appreciative listener who recognizes the distinct as well as subtle differences in sounds' intensity, pitch, and duration can heighten his or her appreciation of the voices of singers like Beverly Sills and Luciano Pavarotti.

Uses of Auditory Discrimination

Throughout our lives, we rely heavily on our auditory discrimination ability. We begin the development of discriminative listening as we learn to perceive and identify the sounds in our environment and then to use these sounds in order to adapt to that environment. During our first few months of life, we recognize the human voice and respond to it. Later, we turn our heads in search of the direction from which sounds are coming, and shortly thereafter we move toward the sources of the sounds. During our lolling stage, we listen to our own sounds and repeat them. Then we begin to imitate the sounds that make up our world—the sounds of family members, pets, and our environment. We are learning a language, which at this stage consists of coos, cries, happy tones, angry tones, loud noises, soft noises, close sounds, distant sounds, vowel sounds, consonant sounds, chirping sounds, perking sounds, continuous sounds, sporadic sounds, nonsensical sounds, sensible sounds, nasal tones, throaty tones, high-pitched sounds, low-pitched sounds, twangy sounds, and drawling sounds. As we grow older, we continue to enlarge our inventory of sounds and to test our ability to discriminate among varied sounds. Indeed, listening discriminatively, whether it be to detect the arrival of a rainstorm or the sincerity in a sender's voice, is essential to our acquiring information which enables us to adapt more effectively to our environment.

The Importance of Auditory Discrimination

The importance of auditory discrimination is documented in research on the language acquisition of children. It is generally agreed that the effective development of both oral and reading vocabularies depends upon our auditory discrimination. One specialist in language development, Perkins, notes the role of auditory discrimination in the process of our oral language development:

> Long before his first true word is spoken, the infant has been working on his system for deciphering the mysterious stream of jabber he hears when people talk. The fact that he can recognize meaning of what is spoken before he himself can speak reveals the ability to recognize at least gross differences in sounds on which meaning hinges before he can produce these differences. This ability is often called *auditory discrimination*. Less is known about how this capacity to recognize differences develops than about development of capacity to produce speech sounds.[1]

Ebel, summarizing the research on the development of reading skills, concludes that "the strength of many developmental reading programs appears to lie in their success in improving auditory discrimination of language sounds."[2] Neuman also surveyed the literature and noted that the research consistently supports one major conclusion: "[T]he child who is unable to hear and distinguish sounds will most likely have difficulty in learning to read."[3] Thus, auditory discrimination ability has played, and continues to play, an important role in the development of our listening, speaking, and reading effectiveness.

As adults, it is essential that we possess highly developed auditory discrimination skills so that we can help others develop their discriminative ability. Many of us who are teachers, speech therapists, or parents especially need to develop our discriminative ability, for we are responsible for guiding a child's language acquisition. Only through careful auditory perception can we discriminate the child's language development (through, for example, *wabbit* and *yights* to *rabbit* and *lights*) and provide the necessary guidance.

As adults, we also need to develop our discriminative ability so that we can help ourselves become more efficient listeners. According to Fessenden, the first level of listening involves the isolation of the individual aspects of a message. This level does not include evaluation or analysis; it involves only "the recognition of the presence of specific, independent items."[4] Our proficiency in recognizing specific items depends especially on our auditory discrimination ability, and without highly developed auditory discrimination skills, we cannot achieve our goal of becoming complete listeners.

Skills Involved in Auditory Discrimination

Developing our auditory discrimination skills is an ongoing process. When we are quite young, we begin to develop many of the essential auditory skills. As we grow older, we often need to refine those discriminative skills that are underdeveloped; also, we need to acquire and cultivate additional discriminative skills in order for us to master discriminative listening.

Refining Skills Included in Weaver and Rutherford's Hierarchy

A list of many of the auditory discriminative skills which we begin to develop early in our lives has been compiled by Weaver and Rutherford. After surveying the literature dealing with the development of discriminative as well as other listening skills, Weaver and Rutherford developed a hierarchy of auditory skills grouped according to the estimated time periods at which the various skills are generally developed. Although the authors of the hierarchy have distinguished between environmental skills (skills pertaining to sounds other than verbal) and discrimination skills (skills pertaining to verbal sounds), both sections are relevant to the development of auditory discrimination:

Environmental Skills

Prenatal

Fetal movement in response to sound.

Infancy

Responds reflexively to sudden loud noises.
Responds to loud noises by crying.
Listens to the human voice.
Is quieted by sound.
Changes activity in response to the human voice.
Turns head in search of sound (VH*).[5]
Learns that people and objects make sound.
Learns that objects make sound with manipulation.
Localizes sound sources and moves toward them (VH*).

Preschool

Associates a sound with an object.
Repeats a sequence of sounds.
Learns that unseen objects make sounds.
Learns that sound sources can be labeled or named.
Given three noisemakers, can find the one that sounds different.
Can identify people and animals by sound.

Kindergarten-Grade 3

Learns that sounds differ in intensity (VH*).
Learns that sounds differ in pitch (VH*).
Learns that sounds differ in pattern.
Learns that sounds differ in duration (the length of time they can be heard).
Learns the concept distance in relation to sound localization and movement (VH).

Grade 4-Grade 6

Identifies sounds in the environment at certain times of day and evaluates them in terms of orientation and mobility (VH).
Promotes growth of echo perception and spatial orientation (VH).

Discrimination Skills

Infancy

Responds differentially to sounds.
Responds to his name.
Begins imitating speech sounds.

Preschool

Separates certain sounds from background sounds.
Identifies like sounds and different sounds.
Can match verbal sounds.

Kindergarten-Grade 3

Learns that sounds differ in intensity (VH*).
Learns that sounds differ in pitch (VH*).
Learns that sounds differ in pattern.
Learns that sounds differ in duration.
Recognizes differences in word sounds.
Recognizes differences in initial consonants (cat-mat) auditorily.
Recognizes differences in final consonants (mat-map) auditorily.
Recognizes differences in medial sounds (map-mop) auditorily.
Recognizes discrete words within a sentence.
Recognizes sequence of words within a sentence.
Identifies accented words within a sentence.
Identifies number of syllables within a word.
Identifies accented syllable within a word.
Changes accent from one syllable to another.
Recognizes initial and final consonant sounds.
Recognizes short vowel sounds.
Recognizes long vowel sounds.
Recognizes rhyming words.
Recognizes and discriminates word endings (s, ing, er).
Discriminates temporal order of sounds within words.[6]

Recognizing that responding to sound during the prenatal and early infancy stages is the first auditory skill developed, several specialists advocate behavioral communication between parent and child. They encourage the pregnant mother to use soothing words, sing lullabies, and listen to calming music to help the unborn child begin to experience life with emotional and intellectual stimulation.[7] Mozart's music, for example, has been found to calm six-month-old fetuses, while rock music stimulates intense kicking in the mothers' wombs.[8] Likewise, newborn babies prefer such auditory stimulation as classical music, their parents' voices, and the sound of the mother's heartbeat. Advocates of infant stimulation point to studies which illustrate that infants who have been stimulated (primarily by auditory means) develop faster, have longer attention spans, and are generally more curious.[9]

To assist children in developing other skills listed in the hierarchy of auditory skills, we can devise numerous exercises. For example, exercises—such as having children, with their eyes closed, (1) focus on sounds outside the room, inside the room, and within their bodies, (2) distinguish changes in cadence when they listen to the tapping of a pencil, and (3) determine differences in intensity of the clapping of hands—can help children develop three previously cited auditory skills. These skills are (1) spatial location—locating from where the sound is coming; (2) frequency spectra—determining how often sounds occur; and (3) loudness—determining the intensity of the sound that reaches the ear.[10] Exercises devised to assist children in developing other auditory skills listed in Weaver and Rutherford's hierarchy can likewise be beneficial.

Although the skills listed by Weaver and Rutherford are concentrated at the lower educational levels, many of these skills can be further developed throughout a person's life. Developing our auditory discrimination skills, we repeat, is an ongoing process.

Recognizing the Sound Structure of Our Language

A skill that we cultivate after our primary grade years is that of recognizing the sound structure of our language. If, for example, we are proficient in the previously cited skill of recognizing the various vowel and consonant sounds in the initial, medial, and final positions (a skill that we generally develop early in our schooling) and we know that English words do not begin with *sr,* we will not mishear *this rip* as *this srip*. Or if we are trying to identify words at the beginning of a sentence, where they are quite unpredictable, and we know that *mg* cannot start a word in English, we will not perceive a sentence beginning with *I'm g . . .* as anything but *I'm* plus the start of a new word (whereas we could perceive a sentence beginning with *I'm a* as *I may* or the start of *I'm making*).[11] Research indicates that when we are categorizing stimuli, our initial decisions are made on a phonetic basis.[12] Goss, in his listening model which is based on an information-processing perspective, directs attention to the listener's need to make phonetic decisions in the initial phase of listening. During this phase, which Goss refers to as the signal processing (SP) stage, the listener must segment and structure the speech signal into potentially meaningful units.[13] For example, the listener who recognizes the sound structure of the language would know that a rapidly spoken "Idrankitfirst" could be segmented and structured in two ways: "I drank it first" or "I'd rank it first." The examples in this section illustrate that if we wish to improve our discriminative listening and, thus, our assigning of meaning, we must increase our understanding of phonology (the structure of sound).

Detecting and Isolating Vocal Cues

Effective discriminative listeners must develop the skill of isolating vocal cues—noting how a message is vocalized. Becoming efficient in this skill involves developing our sensory awareness to and increasing our understanding of paralanguage (vocal characteristics—pitch, inflection, tension, volume, intensity, rate, quality, tone, and dynamics of the speaking voice—and nonverbal vocalizations such as *ah*).

We must be able to distinguish whether the paralanguage reinforces or contradicts the verbal message. When the paralanguage is contradictory, research shows that listeners rely more heavily on the vocal expression to infer the sender's feelings.[14] Mehrabian believes that a reasonably safe generalization regarding the impact of nonverbal communication, including vocal expression, can be made:

> When any nonverbal behavior contradicts speech, it is more likely to determine the total impact of the message . . . touching, positions (distance, forward lean, or eye contact), postures, gestures, as well as facial and vocal expressions, can all outweigh words and determine the feelings conveyed by a message.[15]

Mehrabian illustrates how this generalization may apply to a recorded message or a telephone conversation; if the vocal expression contradicts the verbal message, the vocal expression will determine the total impact. The impact will be negative if the words are positive and the vocal expression is negative, or the impact will be positive if the words are negative and the vocal expression is positive.[16] Thus, if we become more aware of vocal cues and learn to distinguish both obvious and subtle differences in paralanguage, we may be better able to understand the messages of others, whether they be political candidates, job supervisors, or family members.

Understanding Dialectal Differences

On a less involved level, auditory discrimination can enhance listeners' sensitivity, particularly in their understanding of and their reactions to the speech of others. As listeners, we tend to stereotype speech patterns as a Southern drawl, a Midwestern twang, New York Brooklynese, "Havahd." In 1970, Dubin conducted a study that illustrates listeners' stereotyped reactions. He asked personnel interviewers in the Washington, D.C., area to react to tapes of speakers demonstrating the following dialects: general American white, general American black, light black, southern American white, and strong black. Predictably, the interviewers (who were not told what dialects they were listening to) more frequently selected the speaker with the standard white dialect for upper-level managerial positions and the speakers with the nonstandard dialects for lower-level positions.[17]

In a more recent study conducted by Terrell and Terrell, six black college women—using equivalent bogus letters of recommendation and job experience—were randomly sent to be interviewed by 100 southwestern personnel managers. During the interviews, half of the women spoke black English dialect while half spoke standard English. The secretly-made tapes of the interviews revealed that interviewees speaking black English " 'were given shorter interviews and fewer job offers' " than those speaking standard English.[18] Furthermore, of those offered jobs, the black-English speakers " 'were offered positions paying significantly less money than standard English speakers.' "[19] Being aware of various regional and local dialects and understanding the differing dialectal characteristics through auditory discrimination can diminish the frequency with which we misunderstand words pronounced differently than we pronounce them as well as diminish our stereotyped reactions.

Recognizing Environmental Sounds

Likewise, sensitivity to environmental sounds through more careful discriminative listening can enhance our listening efficiency. Stories about the discriminative listening sensitivity which mothers develop to listen to their infants exemplify this level. Comedians such as Rich Little develop extraordinary discriminative listening sensitivity in order to incorporate into their routines the mimicking of others' voices. Owners of automobiles also must develop discriminative listening skills. Most of us, as commuters, depend upon our cars to transport us to where we want to go. And our cars tell us their general state of health. Describing the many ways racing experts such as A. J. Foyt and local auto mechanics tune in to their cars, Robert Ross says that "you will learn by listening whether to take your car home to fix it yourself, or to a service station for minor repairs, or to a more expensive garage for major surgery."[20] Similarly, those in business must listen with discrimination. For example, one of your authors' students manages an ice cream shop. He must carefully listen to the sounds of the freezers, for any malfunction of the machines could ruin the ice cream products and prove to be quite costly. Another business owner who listens discriminatively is the prominent poultry producer on Maryland's Eastern Shore, Frank Perdue. He points out in one of his television commercials that he has learned to listen to his chickens! Indeed, in a listening program designed by one of your authors' former students, the firm has installed sound monitors in the various poultry buildings to enable the staff to listen to the chickens. They communicate a great deal about their general state of health through the sounds they emit. Clearly, listening to sounds in the environment can be an important part of coping with the demands of control in that environment.

Unfortunately, the findings of a study conducted by two of your authors' students reveal that many listeners do not adequately listen with discrimination to environmental sounds. The instrument used in this study was a tape recording of fifty sounds ranging from the clicking of a pen and the perking of coffee to a bellowing elephant in a zoo. Students at different grade levels in various urban, suburban, and rural schools were asked to identify the sounds. The results were interesting; they illustrated how nondiscriminative we can be. The researchers concluded that the problem is not so much that we are not exposed to a variety of sounds but that we do not attend consciously to the sounds.[21] Thus, by expending more attention energy in perceiving the sounds of our environment, we can improve our recognition of these sounds.

Measurements of Auditory Discrimination

A standardized measure of listening discrimination may be obtained through the utilization of the *Seashore Measure of Musical Talents.* This test provides separate measures for pitch, loudness, rhythm, time, timbre, and tonal memory. The tests have been used since 1919 as measures of musical aptitude, but they do provide reliable indicators of our general auditory discrimination.[22]

Another test, the *Test of Non-Verbal Auditory Discrimination* (TENVAD), is patterned after the *Seashore Measure of Musical Talents.* This taped test consists of 50 pairs of tones in the same five subtests as the *Seashore* test. Each subtest has 10 pairs of tones that are the same or different in some way. Designed to be administered to groups of primary grade children who record their responses in test booklets, this test can be a useful tool for planning instructional programs in the primary grades.[23]

A third test that assesses the auditory discrimination of young children (ages 5 through 8) is *The Auditory Discrimination Test.* Two equated forms of the test measure a child's ability to distinguish between phonemes used in English speech.[24]

Visual Discrimination

Detecting and Isolating Nonverbal Cues

As effective listeners, we also must frequently apply visual discrimination; that is, we must distinguish visual stimuli whenever we have the opportunity to view the sender(s). Although research in listening has primarily focused on auditory discrimination and reception, it is clear that listening is not synonymous with hearing. Indeed, analysis of messages in human interactions indicates that the greatest impact of the meaning of a message may well stem from what is communicated through the visual channel. Ray Birdwhistell, for instance, has determined that in a normal, two-person conversation, 35 percent of the meaning of the message is carried verbally, while as much as 65 percent is conveyed through nonverbal channels.[25] Albert Mehrabian's formula for determining the impact of the various channels in communicating feeling messages attributes even more importance to the nonverbal channels with 38 percent of the message's meaning coming from the vocal, 55 percent coming from the facial, and only 7 percent coming from the verbal.[26]

The prominence of the visual channel is probably not even within the consciousness of many listeners. In a poignant story, Connie Broughton, a young mother, describes how she learned the importance of the listener using the visual channel. In an argument with her five-year-old daughter, Broughton insisted that she was listening to her; however, the daughter—not believing her mother's verbal message—replied, "But you're not looking at me."[27] The incident led Broughton to begin consciously making eye contact with all of her children when she was conversing with them. This mother realized that listeners who maintain eye contact with senders nonverbally communicate that they are listening.

Not only can using the visual communication system convey to others that we are listening, but also it can enable us, as listeners, to understand better the messages of others. Research suggests that the visual system especially conveys more affective (emotional) information than do the verbal or vocal systems and that this affective information is highly reliable.[28] The face, for example, reveals much of how the sender feels at any given time, while the body reveals the intensity of a particular feeling.

One of three principal ways that senders use nonverbal messages is to complement verbal messages. They shake their heads affirmatively, for example, to accompany a "yes" response. Or they firmly grasp others' hands as they say, "It's so good to see you." As listeners, we generally believe these senders, for "[t]he people we trust are usually those people whose nonverbal behavior consistently confirms and reinforces the content of their verbal communication."[29]

Nonverbal messages also can contradict verbal messages. For instance, communicators respond with "Yes, I'm listening" while they continue to attend to a newspaper or a television program. Or a father does not succeed at suppressing a smile while he is reprimanding his son. When these nonverbal messages do contradict the verbal messages, we tend to trust what we derive from the nonverbal messages. The old adage, "Actions speak louder than words," certainly holds true in our visual interpretations.

At other times, nonverbal messages can replace verbal messages. Americans who travel in foreign countries, for example, often must communicate by way of gestures and other nonverbal means when they do not know the native verbal code. Because each culture has its own nonverbal language, replacing the verbal language can be difficult. To illustrate, suppose you are an American in Greece, and you want the elevator operator to take you to the fifth floor. Making this request requires that you hold up your hand to show all five fingers while the palm of your hand is directed toward you. If you are unaware of the significance of the direction of your palm, you may turn your palm toward the elevator operator and find yourself the receiver of an unexpected insult. Why? In Greece, the palm turned toward the operator would be interpreted as an obscene gesture!

Our understanding of a sender's message often depends on our ability to "listen" with our eyes.
Photos by Robert Tocha.

Indeed, awareness of cultural differences can prevent misunderstandings between senders and receivers who do not share the same nonverbal language code.

While being held a prisoner of war by the North Vietnamese, Jeremiah Denton, Jr., realized the value of replacing a verbal code with a nonverbal code. When featured in a North Vietnamese propaganda film, Denton and other American POW's stated that they were being treated in compliance with the requirements of the Geneva Convention. An alert intelligence man who viewed the film, however, noted that Denton was blinking. The intelligence staff carefully scrutinized the film and discovered that Denton was blinking "torture" in Morse code. Denton's knowledge of the Morse code enabled him to communicate an important nonverbal message to America. However, "his knowledge would have been in vain had there not been someone who was able to listen with his eyes."[30] Indeed, the listener who "listens" with visual discrimination can receive significant messages.

In addition to using nonverbal messages in these three principal ways, communicators use nonverbal language in many forms. Perhaps the most revealing visual form is *kinesics,* or the language of the face and body. Through posture, bodily movements, gestures, facial expressions, and eye contact, communicators convey numerous messages ranging from "I have some exciting news to share with you" to "I don't have time to listen now." Though some scholars are attempting to equate body language to verbal language and develop nonlinguistic categories, Knapp maintains that kinesics probably does not have the same structure as spoken language. Rather, he notes, various bodily movements can communicate "liking or dislike for another, status, affective states or moods, intended and perceived persuasiveness, approval seeking, quasi-courtship behavior, need or desire for inclusion, leakage and deception clues, interpersonal warmth, and various interaction 'markers' to accompany certain spoken behaviors."[31]

Two other nonverbal visual forms are *artifacts* and *appearance.* From other people's use of artifacts (such as clothing, makeup, jewelry, insignia, plaques, art objects, vehicles, equipment, furniture, offices, and homes) observant listeners can detect messages of status, style, and self-esteem. The importance of some of these artifacts (especially clothing, makeup, and jewelry) as message-senders is attested by the growing enterprise of "wardrobe engineering," in which consultants assist individuals (usually those who desire to advance socially, economically, and/or professionally) in selecting the proper colors and styles to communicate the desired image. John Molloy initiated much of this interest in his popular *Dress for Success,*[32] and now wardrobe engineering has become so specialized that "color consultants" are available to determine the proper shades of colors for individual skin tones, eyes, and hair.

Furthermore, listeners can use the visual channel to interpret messages conveyed through the nonverbal form of *proxemics,* or the language of space and distance. The spatial distance that communicators keep between themselves is significant, especially as North Americans tend to keep considerable distance away from those who, they feel, are invading their "bubble of personal space." Indeed, one of the first observations visitors to the United States make is this distance. In contrast, Latin Americans, for example, communicate at a much closer distance; Hall describes how this cultural difference can create misunderstandings: "[W]hen they [Latin Americans] move close, we [North Americans] withdraw and back away. As a consequence, they think we are distant or cold, withdrawn and unfriendly. We, on the other hand, are constantly accusing them of breathing down our necks, crowding us, and spraying our faces."[33]

The visual channel also assists listeners in discriminating *chronemics,* or the language of time, as well as the language of *touch.* One's punctuality in keeping an appointment, fulfilling an assignment, or arriving at the office can convey many messages such as one's attitude, priorities, and sense of responsibility. Moreover, the amount of time one is willing to give to another person can convey messages such as one's liking, concern for, and involvement with another person. Touch, too, conveys many messages through the visual channel when the listener is the

As listeners, we often convey—through our facial expressions—our responses to the sender's message.

Photo by Robert Tocha.

observer of the touching and by means of skin conduction when the listener is the receiver of the touching. The listener as a discriminating observer and receiver of touching—or the lack of touching—can derive such messages as liking or disliking, encouragement or apathy, warmth or coldness, playfulness or anger.

Clearly, nonverbal cues we receive as listeners can reveal a great deal to us. Through kinesics, artifacts, appearance, proxemics, chronemics, and touch (as well as paralanguage, which is sent through the auditory channel), individuals can complement, contradict, or replace their verbal messages with nonverbal ones. The discriminating listener, therefore, must be able to distinguish among these messages in order to assign more accurate meanings to them. It is helpful to note how this skill can be used in a hypothetical (yet realistic) situation which we have designed in order to describe the dimensions of nonverbal communication. As you read through the letter-coded scenario about our student, you can follow it along with our commentary, which describes what is occurring nonverbally at any given point in the situation.

Scenario

It is 6:30 P.M. *on July 18. Having parked his car in Lot BB at the University of Maryland, Bob starts walking up the hill toward Hornbake Library where the first session of his listening class will meet in Room 4205 at 7:00.*[a] *The campus appears desolate except for one other person walking down the hill toward Bob. At a distance of approximately fifteen feet, the two strangers glance at each other and then look down and away until they have passed one another.*[b] *Reaching the top of the hill, Bob unexpectantly meets Maria, a girl who had been in his business course the previous semester. Upon seeing Bob, Maria raises her eyebrows,*[c] *smiles,*[d] *and stops at a distance of one-and-a-half feet from Bob.*[e] *Bob steps back a foot or two,*[f] *crosses his arms,*[g] *and asks Maria how she has been. After a short while of conversing, Maria asks Bob why he has not called as he had said he would. Bob rubs the back*

Commentary on Scenario

a. Time communicates. Formal time, labeled by Hall and measured by a calendar or clock, suggests that one be prompt. One's punctuality may indicate one's perception of the importance of or respect for the event (and the other participants) as well as one's sense of responsibility.[34]

b. Goffman refers to the behavior illustrated here as "civil inattention." When two urban, white North American strangers approach each other on neutral ground in an uncrowded space, they glance at one another to acknowledge each other's presence when they are just within recognition distance (at a distance somewhere between 12 and 32 feet), and then they look down and away to avoid eye contact until they have passed one another. Any violation of this behavior may indicate an invitation to a more intimate encounter—which could be a pickup, a handout, or some kind of information. People in the West and in small towns, however, may be more likely to look at and greet strangers, as are blacks, who often greet other blacks whom they do not know.[35]

c. The "eyebrow flash," consisting of the rapid raising of the brows, is a sign of recognition.[36]

d. This smile is used for greeting friends. In a study in which Bayes examined ratings of interpersonal warmth, she found that "smiling is the best single predictor of warmth."[37] Morris refers to the smile (one of the many affect displays, which are behaviors that reflect emotional states) as "the most important social bonding signal in the human gestural repertoire."[38]

e. Hall has identified four main distances at which most white, middle-class North Americans interact with one another. In the incident between Bob and Maria, the first two of these distances are evident. The first distance, the intimate distance, ranges from six to eighteen inches and is reserved for very special people (and pets). To prevent intruders from entering this intimate zone, Americans typically carry with them an invisible, two-foot (arm's length) "spatial bubble of privacy," which may expand or contract, depending upon the given situation. Each communicator's two-foot bubble (which is not necessary spherical) allows communication partners to maintain the second distance—the personal distance—which ranges from one and a half to four feet and is used, for example, when two people are chatting on the street. Due largely to Maria's Latin American heritage, Maria normally interacts at close range and, thus, unintentionally (or perhaps intentionally in this situation) invades Bob's spatial bubble and violates his intimate zone.[39]

f. To protect himself from Maria's intrusion into his intimate zone, Bob steps back in order to establish a personal distance.[40] See *e*.

g. One classification of gestures is adaptors, which are "behaviors which once served a useful purpose, but which now are part of the individual's habit repertoire."[41] One type of adaptor is the self-adaptor, which involves self-touch and which may emerge unconsciously as an indication of the user's inner state (especially the inner state of anxiety). Bob, in a tense situation here, engages in the self-adaptor gesture of folding his arms across his body.

of his neck, tugs at his ear,[h] *and then responds, "Well, I've . . . uh . . . been working . . . uh . . . overtime; I've wanted . . . uh . . . to call, you know, but I just . . . uh . . . I have just been too busy."*[i] *Leaning toward Bob*[j] *and placing her hand on his arm,*[k] *Maria asserts, "Well, I've been eagerly awaiting your call." A tight smile crosses Bob's mouth,*[l] *and, as he glances toward the library and makes small circles away from and back toward Maria,*[m] *he says that he will call her soon but that he must be getting to class now. Moistening her lips, expanding her chest, and slightly narrowing her eyelids, Maria, in a soft, low-pitched voice, says, "I'll be waiting."*[n]

After entering the library, Bob takes the elevator to the fourth floor. While on the elevator with two other people, Bob claims his third of the elevator—the back wall—while the other two passengers claim the two side walls; each person faces forward, keeps his/her eyes glued to

h. Rubbing the back of one's neck and tugging at one's ear are two examples of self-adaptors—here indicating tenseness. See *g.*

i. When one is in a state of anxiety (at times stemming from deception), one frequently uses vocal segregates ("momentary interjections into the stream of speech"[42]) such as pauses and sounds (*uh, um, er,* and *ah*), as well as speech nonfluencies, like starting the same sentence twice ("I was . . . uh . . . I was sleeping when he left.") or beginning a new sentence without completing the previous sentence ("Mary said she'd . . . The work has to be completed by tonight!"). In the situation illustrated, Bob uses both vocal segregates and speech nonfluencies.

j. Forward leans often convey liking.[43] Maria's forward lean may indicate her liking of Bob as well as her desire to enter his intimate zone.

k. Touching conveys greater liking and facilitates interpersonal attraction.[44] As in *e,* a cultural difference is being illustrated here: Latinos are highly tactile people[45] whereas North Americans are generally low-contact people who tend to consider touching as being an intimate/personal act that carries sexual overtones. In an interesting study, Jourard observed the amount of touching individual pairs engaged in during one-hour sittings in coffee houses in different countries; he found that 180 touches were engaed in by Puerto Ricans, 110 by French, none by English, and 2 by Americans.[46]

l. Although the face is considered to be the best indicator of emotion, it is also the most controllable part of the body when a situation dictates that one must mask an emotion.[47] In Bob's situation, he controls the mouth and lower facial muscles (which are the most easily controlled facial muscles)[48] in order to simulate a smile and disguise his true feelings.

Since women tend to be more adept than men at reading the face, Maria may have noted Bob's forced smile; however, Maria may have chosen to ignore the "leak" since, as Rosenthal and DePaulo suggest, women may be penalized more than men for being so perceptive at reading "leaks" and thus learn to ignore social lies since social life calls for overlooking them.[49]

m. Turning away and making small circles away from and back to the person with whom one is conversing are signals that one desires to terminate the conversation.[50]

n. By using three of the many courtship signals, Maria indicates her attraction to Bob.[51] Additionally, Maria uses her voice to reveal affection; Davitz has found that affection is usually shown by soft volume, low pitch, steady inflection, regular rhythm, and slurred enunciation.[52]

the lighted row of floor numbers, and remains silent. Bob exits as the elevator reaches the fourth floor.[o]

At 6:45, Bob enters Room 4205. Surveying the room already occupied by several students and the instructor, who greets him with a smile and a warm hello,[p] *Bob notes the three rectangular tables aligned vertically with eight chairs at each table and chooses to sit at the middle table where no student is yet seated. Wanting to view directly the front of the room where the instructor will likely be positioned, Bob selects the seat at the head of the middle table.*[q] *As he waits for class to begin, he makes several observations. He sees the instructor organizing the course materials and setting up the audio tape recorder; he notes her bronze tan, casual yet stylish clothes and hair style, and well-conditioned body and thinks that she may make each three-hour class session more bearable.*[r] *He observes the other students who are quietly rummaging through papers, leafing through the textbook, and ob-*

o. There are unwritten "rules" of elevator etiquette. Bob and his elevator companions demonstrate some of these rules; among other rules are not looking at other passengers (who are strangers), not touching, keeping hands folded in front of the body unless the elevator is crowded and then keeping hands at one's sides, and not talking to strangers.[53]

p. See *d*.

q. Where one chooses to sit in a room containing fixed furniture can foster or inhibit communicative interaction. In a regular classroom, students sitting up the middle as well as in the central front rows tend to participate more.[54]

r. One's appearance (clothes, hair, face, skin, physique, etc.) conveys many messages such as one's sex, age, race, status, personality, group membership, attitudes, values, occupation, sexual availability, etc. In the situation described, Bob regards the instructor's tanned skin as being healthy-looking and attractive; he views her choice of clothing and hair style as signals that she is fashionably feminine, she is informal and concerned with comfort, and she is sociable and extroverted (since she is wearing bright and saturated colors). Also, he associates her physique (classified as a mesomorphic—muscular—type) with her being athletic, self-reliant, powerful, energetic, confident, competitive, adventurous, optimistic, determined, cheerful, enthusiastic, enterprising, and outgoing.[55] He sees her as being physically attractive and possessing favorable personality characteristics.

serving the surroundings as he is.[s] *And, he observes the room where he will spend the next six weeks on Monday and Wednesday evenings; he immediately finds relief in the fact that the room is comfortably air-conditioned and not sticky-hot as the Maryland summer weather is outside.*[t]

Before long, the room—with a seating capacity of thirty-five—contains nearly twenty students. Mark, who seats himself two chairs to Bob's right,[u] *introduces himself to Bob, and the two begin conversing about their course expectations. Janice enters the room, notes Bob's attractive appearance,*[v] *places her notebook and umbrella on the table space to Bob's left,*[w] *and exits to the ladies' room. A few moments later, Janice returns and seats herself to Bob's immediate left.*

At 7:00,[x] *the instructor begins her introduction to the course. Standing rigidly behind a chair whose back she tightly clutches and speaking rather rapidly in a somewhat shrill voice,*[y] *she shares with the*

s. Displacement signals, such as repeatedly opening and closing the clasp of a bracelet, repeatedly checking a ticket prior to an airplane flight, tapping a cigarette that has no ash, dusting dust-free furniture, etc., are small behaviors in which one may engage when he/she is in a tense situation.[56] Rummaging through papers and leafing through the textbook may be displacement signals in which students who are together for the first time may engage.

t. Griffitt and Veitch have found that room temperature affects one's psychological disposition as well as one's social behavior with others; high room temperatures produce more negative feelings than do lower, more moderate and comfortable room temperatures.[57]

u. Liebman suggests that prevailing social norms promote closer interpersonal distances between females than between males.[58]

v. Individuals who rate others as attractive choose closer seating distances.[59]

w. "Territorial markers"—personal possessions such as books, umbrellas, coats, open notebooks, etc.—are used to reserve space when the owner of the item(s) temporarily vacates the spatial area (such as a library, cafeteria, or classroom).[60]

x. See *a*.

y. Rather than using tables or desks as many communicators do, the instructor—who is experiencing anxiety at the class's first meeting—uses a chair to create a physical barrier between her and her students. She likewise signals anxiety in her bodily posture, her clutching of the chair, and her voice.[61]

class her interest in listening and the course goals. Bob looks intently at the instructor, leans forward, and frequently smiles and nods affirmatively as she speaks;[z] *he shares her interest in listening and the course goals. The instructor then introduces the students to a taped listening test which they are to take. During the introduction, Kay enters the classroom*[a2] *and takes an empty chair to Janice's left. Eyeing Kay askance, Janice reluctantly removes her umbrella and purse from the area in front of Kay and places them under her chair.*[b2] *As the instructor is giving directions regarding the personal data that is to be filled out on the test form, Kay asks Janice if she has an extra pencil; Janice, clicking her tongue,*[c2] *searches through her purse until she finds a pencil for Kay. The instructor now turns on the tape, and Janice realizes that she will have to complete the personal data information after she has completed the test.*

z. Maintaining eye contact, leaning forward, smiling, and nodding affirmatively are reinforcing signals that indicate attentiveness, liking, warmth, agreement, support, interest, affirmation, approval, cooperation, and responsiveness.[62]

a2. See *a*.

b2. Fisher and Byrne, investigating the reaction of males and females whose personal space was invaded while they were sitting in a library, found that males reacted more negatively to invasions directly across from them, while females reacted more negatively to invasions from the side.[63] In the illustrated example, Janice indicates her negative feelings towards Kay's invasion (in a room where fourteen other chairs remain unoccupied) by looking askance—a sign of disapproval.[64]

c2. The "tsk, tsk" clicking sound of the tongue is a vocal emblem indicating disapproval.[65]

During the first four parts of the listening test, the students mildly laugh at various points[d2] *and appear to be actively involved. However, during the last part of the test, consisting of a ten-minute lecture, many different student behaviors are evidenced. Kay "checks out" the room and the other students; Pat's eyelids slowly droop; Gordon repeatedly checks his watch; Deanna has a blank, out-of-focus look; Mike drums his fingers on the table; Irene props her head up with the palm of her hand; Sherry makes excessive postural shifts and jiggles a foot;*[e2] *and Bob, who is right-handed, frequently blinks and regularly moves his eyes horizontally to the left and downward to the left.*[f2] *At the end of the test, many students emit deep sighs.*[g2]

Following the test, the instructor distributes the course syllabus and answers students' questions about the course requirements. As she responds to the students' questions and comments, her hands are now free, she maintains a more open body stance as she stands closer to the d2. Laughing is a vocal adaptor—here indicating a positive response.[66]

e2. The actions displayed by the students in the illustrated situation are signs of inattention, disinterest, boredom, and preoccupation with something other than the test lecture.[67]

f2. One sign of attentive listening may be blinking; the blink rate is typically every three to ten seconds.[68]

According to Neurolinguistic Programming (NLP), a model developed by John Grinder and Richard Bandler, every individual tends to have a "primary representational system" (PRS)—the sensory system/mode that is favored/most frequently used when one is processing information. The three major sensory modes are visual, auditory, and kinesthetic, and they are linked to distinctive patterns of eye movement. Proponents of NLP, observing Bob's horizontal eye movements to either side and downward movement to the left, would claim that Bob favors the auditory sensory mode of processing information.[69]

g2. Sighing is another vocal adaptor—here indicating relief.[70]

students, her rate is slower, and her pitch is more natural.[h2] *Placing an index finger along her cheek and grouping the remaining fingers below her mouth,*[i2] *Kay—speaking in a harsh and loud voice*[j2]*—strongly objects to the class attendance requirement. Sharon, who has reservations during the summer at Virginia Beach, purses her lips*[k2] *as the instructor explains the importance of attending each class session due to the laboratory format of the course. Running his fingers through his hair and frowning,*[l2] *Arthur also protests this requirement. As Arthur begins stating his protest, Bob adjusts his bodily positioning so that he can see Arthur more clearly.*[m2] *As the protests are being made, the instructor—viewing the group interaction as a potent example of the communication process in action—remains silent*[n2] *as she busily notes communicative attitudes and behaviors to which she will refer during the next class session. (Meanwhile, Steven, having been "caught" looking at Marjorie's legs, rubs his eyes as if to imply that his eyes were not* h2. The instructor is now signaling that she is relaxed. See *y*.

i2. Placing one's chin in one's palm, extending an index finger along one's cheek, and grouping the remaining fingers below one's mouth may be an indication that the listener is making a critical evaluation of the speaker.[71]

j2. A harsh, loud voice may indicate anger/hostility.[72]

k2. Pursing one's lips may be a signal that one has taken a defensive position.[73]

l2. Running one's fingers through one's hair may indicate frustration, while frowning generally indicates disapproval.[74]

m2. Those who wish to listen to the sender's aural and visual message will shift their body orientations (if they need to) in order to see the sender.[75]

n2. Silence communicates. In this situation, silence communicates that the instructor is interested in and desirous of understanding the communication interaction among the students.

working properly.[o2]*) Amid the mumblings of Kay, Sharon, and Arthur (who, incidentally, have adopted similar bodily postures*[p2]*), Toni—arising from her seat at the front of the middle table*[q2]*—loudly clears her throat,*[r2] *momentarily places her hands on her hips,*[s2] *and then, using a short chopping motion of her hands,*[t2] *emphatically states in clipped enunciation,*[u2] *"I've taken thirty courses at this university, and each course has requirements. This course is no different." Then, with a wave of her hand,*[v2] *she concludes, "If any student cannot meet the requirements of this course, he or she should accept the penalties or drop the course!" Toni's remarks are acknowledged by Rodney's A-Okay sign*[w2] *and with a loud applause*[x2] *by all other students except Kay, who locks her arms across her chest, crosses her legs, and says, "Harumph";*[y2] *Sharon, who narrows her eyes and shakes her head from side to side;*[z2] *and Arthur, who leans back, looks toward the ceiling, and deeply sighs* o2. According to Scheflen, individuals often perform self-monitoring behaviors to serve as "an excuse or rationalization for what they have done."[76] In the illustrated situation, Steven, who is caught by Marjorie as he is looking at her legs, imposes a self-monitor by rubbing his eyes as if to indicate that his eyes were working improperly.

p2. In situations where tension and conflicting views exist (as in our classroom situation), those who hold the same view may adopt similar postures.[77]

q2. A person may communicate dominance by occupying an "important" seat.[78] See *q* regarding Toni's choice of seats.

Standing, when all other interactants are sitting, is a power move that signals dominance.[79]

r2. See *j2* regarding loudness of volume.

Clearing one's throat is a vocal adaptor that commonly indicates that one is preparing to speak and desires to call others' attention to him/herself.[80]

s2. Placing one's hands on one's hips while one is standing with legs apart may signal determination.[81]

t2. A baton is a type of illustrator (a nonverbal behavior that is used to accentuate, punctuate, index, signal, specify, clarify, amplify, and underscore accompanying speech).[82] In the illustrated situation, an aggressive Toni uses a baton (the rhythmic chopping motion of her hands) with the intent of having her "ideas cut through the confusion of the situation, to an imposed solution."[83]

u2. Clipped enunciation (i.e., chopping off or shortening syllables) is a vocal signal of anger.[84]

v2. One frequently dismisses an argument with a wave of his/her hand.[85]

w2. Am emblem, which is a nonverbal behavior that can be translated into a word or phrase, is performed with awareness and intent. Rodney's A-Okay sign is an emblem that means "all right"/"good."[86]

x2. Applauding by clapping one's hands indicates that a performance (here, Toni's presentation) is pleasing to the applauder.[87]

y2. Locking one's arms across one's chest and crossing one's legs—both self-adaptors—may indicate attitudes of defensiveness as well as withdrawal.[88]

"Harumph" is a vocal emblem of disapproval.[89]

z2. Narrowing one's eyes and horizontally shaking one's head signal disapproval, disagreement, and perhaps a closed mind.[90]

as he clenches his fists.[a3] *The instructor announces a fifteen-minute break. . . .*

Although it is now 10:05 P.M., *and Bob, a special agent with the FBI, is tired, he knows that his attendance at the retirement party will be helpful in his career advancement, so he decides to drive the few blocks to the Chesapeake Grande Hotel. Upon entering the crowded*[b3] *hotel party room, Bob spots his best friend, Jim, who is a special agent in his field office, and he walks across the red carpet*[c3] *to join Jim. They exchange small talk and then observe several of the party guests. They see their office secretary standing among a large group*[d3] *under the dimly-lit chandelier;*[e3] *they see two of the career board members sitting with their backs leaning against the arms of a small sofa and their legs crossed toward one another as they are conversing;*[f3] *and they cannot help but notice the beautiful, middle-aged wife of one of the assistant directors flirtatiously toying with her wine glass*[g3] *as she talks with the* a3. A cluster (or group) of nonverbal behaviors carries more meaning than a single nonverbal signal. In the illustrated situation, the cluster of behaviors—leaning backward, casting one's eyes "toward the heavens" while heaving a great sigh, and closing one's eyes—indicates negativity, annoyance, and close-mindedness.[91]

b3. Although Griffitt and Veitch found that a crowded room situation led subjects to report negative reactions and less liking toward strangers,[92] Cozby's argument that crowding "may be seen as good or bad, depending upon the individual's current goals and whether the presence of others facilitates or inhibits these goals"[93] was supported when he found that subjects liked a crowded room for a party situation while they disliked a crowded room for a study situation.[94]

c3. Color may influence one's feelings. Wexner had found that various colors are often associated with various moods: blue typically connotes security, comfort, tenderness, and calm; red, excitement, stimulation, defiance, hostility, and protection; yellow, cheerfulness, jovialness, and joyfulness; black, power and strength; black and brown, despondence, dejection, unhappiness, and melancholia; orange, distress; and purple, dignity.[95]

d3. Standing conversational groups consisting of more than three persons tend to form squares or circles with their bodies.[96]

e3. A dimly-lit room provides a feeling of warmth and tends to be more conducive to intimate conversation.[97]

f3. The adoption (or imitation) of bodily movements as well as verbal styles (such as joke-telling and question-asking) by conversationalists in pairs or groups is referred to as mirroring. Also identified as interactional synchrony, mirroring—which is a common feature of human social interaction—tends to enhance rapport between/among the interactants, for it signals that the interactants are open to and with one another.[98]

g3. A person's use of object-adaptors (artifacts which are played with, stroked, punched, wielded, etc.) may give clues to the user's emotional state.[99]

newest (and youngest) special agent in their field office. The two men share a silent message that says, "She surely doesn't miss any new talent!"[h3]

As they move toward the bar, Bob turns his attention away from Jim's message as he detects the scent of Opium perfume emanating from a lady whom they pass; Bob immediately thinks of his former lady friend, Susan, and how her Opium perfume had affected him. . . .[i3] *While Bob is getting a drink, Jim sees Dave Dawe, who is Bob and Jim's supervisory special agent—the man whose appraisal of Bob's performance will contribute significantly to Bob's career advancement goals. With his index finger,*[j3] *Jim beckons Bob to him, and, as Jim tells Bob that Dave is here, Jim directs his chin*[k3] *toward where Dave Dawe is standing.*

After straightening his tie,[l3] *Bob approaches Dave; the two men acknowledge one another, smile, extend their hands,*[m3] *and firmly shake* h3. Over a period of time, many close dialogue partners develop a coded silent language that consists of messages covering numerous situations from "They're interested" to "I think you've said enough" to "It's time to leave."

i3. Smell can communicate. Generally, a pleasant odor tends to foster communication (for example, the using of an aerosol spray to improve the odor in the communication environment), while an unpleasant odor tends to inhibit communication (for example, avoiding someone whose body odor is undesirable).[100] However, in the illustrated situation, a pleasant odor (which has a direct impact on Bob's emotions) actually inhibits the communication between Bob and Jim.

j3. One beckons to someone by holding up the palm of the hand and waggling just the index finger or all the fingers; this nonverbal behavior is an emblem that signals, "Come here."[101]

k3. A pointer is an illustrator that points to some object. The pointer that Jim uses is the chin nod.[102] See *t2*.

l3. Scheflen has described preening as one type of "quasi-courtship behaviors"; preening behaviors consist of straightening the tie, rearranging clothing, smoothing or stroking the hair, flattening a crease, reapplying makeup, etc.[103]

m3. Among the nonverbal greeting behaviors in which two people who know one another engage are the following: the two sight one another, frequently nod, wave or smile, approach one another, engage in mutual gaze, present the palm of a hand, and usually make bodily contact through a handshake, embrace, or kiss.[104]

hands.[n3] *Just as they begin conversing while they are directly facing one another*[o3] *at a distance of approximately three to four feet,*[p3] *Steve Brent, who is also desirous of a promotion to supervisory special agent, joins the two men. During the next fifteen minutes, Steve is extremely attentive to Dave; he maintains a positive tone of voice, smiles almost continuously, engages in unrelenting eye contact, nods vigorously, asks numerous questions of Dave (even when Dave keeps his hand in mid-gesture at the end of a sentence or when Dave combines a change in inflection with a pause but also includes upward eye contact*[q3]*), and frequently responds to Dave's comments with expressions of "uh huh," "yes," "how interesting," "you're absolutely right," "I totally agree," etc.*[r3] *Bob also is attentive; however, his attentiveness—consisting of appropriate smiles, head noddings, forward leans, responsive eye contact, and relevant comments at appropriate times (made after Dave comes to the end of some of the hand-movements that accompany his speech* n3. The way in which one shakes another's hand communicates feelings and attitudes. These three styles of handshakes tend to be interpreted as follows: firm handshake—greater liking and warmth; loose handshake—aloofness and unwillingness to become involved; and limp handshake—lack of affection/friendliness.[105]

o3. How communicators orient their bodies when they are standing can foster or inhibit interaction. The face-to-face body orientation fosters the most effective interaction followed—in descending order of effectiveness—by standing at a ninety-degree angle, standing shoulder-to-shoulder, and standing back-to-back.[106]

p3. Hall has identified the third distance as social-consultative distance, which ranges from four to twelve feet and is used during business transactions or social exchanges.[107] See *e*.

q3. Regulators are nonverbal behaviors that control and direct (or serve as traffic signals for) the flow of interaction between/among speakers and listeners. Although hands, body, and voice all serve as regulators, the eyes appear to be the primary regulator.[108] Among the numerous regulators that signal that the speaker desires to continue talking are the following: the speaker raises his/her volume when another interrupts and speaks louder than the other if the other continues to speak; the speaker keeps a hand in mid-gesture at the ends of sentences; the speaker combines a change in inflection with a pause but also includes upward eye movement; and the speaker avoids eye contact at pauses (possibly filled with segregates—*uh, um, ah,* etc.) when he/she is considering how to complete a thought.[109] In the illustrated situation, Steve apparently is ignorant of turn-taking signals.

r3. Mehrabian has identified a cluster of social behaviors which he has labeled ingratiating behaviors. This cluster includes "frequent questioning, smiling and other pleasant vocal and facial expressions, frequent verbal agreement such [as] 'Uh-huh,' 'Yes,' or 'Same here,' and the complete exclusion of negative and unpleasant remarks."[110] (These are the behaviors in which Steve engages in the illustrated situation.) Ingratiating behavior, because of its positive quality, is related to affiliative (or liking/preference) behavior; however, it differs from affiliative behavior because it often creates an interaction that is strained/uncomfortable. The ingratiator, using excessive positiveness to insure a positive reaction, makes his/her communication partner(s) feel compelled to reciprocate with pleasantness. The ingratiator is frequently judged to be false/insincere as well as dependent/submissive.[111]

or after Dave has ended a sentence with a drop of inflection followed by a pause and a gaze at his listeners[s3]*)—is by no means as excessive or extreme as Steve's is.*[t3]

Finally, the subject of promotions is brought up by Dave. To determine whether Bob and Steve have met the promotion requirement of having been a relief supervisor for two years, Dave—accompanying his question with rising pitch, elevated eyebrows, and upward head movement[u3]*—asks them, "How long was each of you a relief supervisor in your former field office?" Steve, all the while maintaining his smiling expression, slowly responds, as he makes frequent postural shifts and repeatedly rubs his cheek with his left hand, "Well, Sir, I was a relief for a year on the Bank Robbery Squad, and I was a relief for a year on the Applicant Squad."*[v3] *Bob then directly replies, "And I was a relief a year on the Organized Crime Squad and a relief for another year on the Security Squad." The three men continue to converse for several* s3. Among the numerous regulators which signal that the speaker desires to yield the floor are the following: the speaker terminates hand gestures accompanying speech; the speaker ends on a prolonged rising or falling pitch; the speaker ends by trailing off in volume or by saying "you know," "or something like that," etc.; and the speaker returns his/her gaze to the listener(s) and gives the listener(s) a prolonged look at the end of his/her utterance.[112] Apparently, Bob—in the situation illustrated—is knowledgable of turn-taking signals. See *q3*.

t3. Mehrabian also has identified a cluster of social behaviors that he has labeled respectful behaviors. He notes that although this "includes a submissive quality, it lacks the undesirable aspects of ingratiation. Respectful behavior, which is more reserved, is characteristic of interactions with a higher-status person who is liked, such as a liked employer."[113] Bob's behavior in the illustrated situation is respectful behavior. See *r3*.

u3. An eyebrow raise and an upward head movement often accompany a rising pitch (a vocal illustrator) when one asks a question.[114]

v3. In a well-known study on deception, Ekman and Friesen found that the best sources of deception cues (nonverbal leakage)—from the most revealing to the least revealing—are (1) legs/feet, (2) hands, and (3) face. Although, as Ekman and Friesen suggest, the face is the best nonverbal sender of feeling messages (followed by the hands and legs/feet), the face is also the part of the human anatomy of which the possessor is most consciously aware and over which he or she can exercise the most control (followed again by the hands and legs/feet); thus, the face is the best "liar" while the hands and legs/feet are better at "telling the truth." Being overattentive to the face, as many people are when they are attempting to detect deception, can, therefore, hinder individuals from detecting the cues of the more revealing sources—the legs/feet and the hands; unfortunately, one's hands, legs, and feet are often obscured from view, and the listener cannot observe them.[115]

Studies indicate that some of the nonverbal leakage cues signaling deception are the following: tense (unnaturally still) leg positions, less body orientation toward the listener(s), frequent postural shifts, abortive flight movements, and restless and repetitive foot and leg activity; suppressed hand movements (achieved by sitting on hands, putting them in one's pocket(s), clasping one hand with the other in order to allow them to hold each other down, etc.) normally used as illustrators, frequent hand-to-face actions (such as the chin stroke, lip press, cheek rub or dig, eyebrow scratch, and—especially—the mouth cover and nose rub), and frequent use of the hand shrug; increased smiling, decreased nodding, and tiny, fleeting, and truth-leaking facial expressions which most people never perceive.[116]

One additional and interesting speculation is that left-handed gestures may be more truthful in revealing feelings, since the right-hemisphere is believed to house emotions.[117]

In the illustrated situation, Steve is lying about the length of time he has served as a relief supervisor; there is no indication, however, that his deception has been detected.

additional minutes, and then Dave—turning slightly away from Bob and Steve and looking toward the door[w3]*—announces that he must start for home. Bob and Steve, following Dave's glance toward the door,*[x3] *add that they, too, must be going. The men bid one another good evening and walk away in different directions.*

Bob searches the room for Jim, whom he finally finds, and then walks over to him. Jim comments that he had noticed that Steve had immediately joined Bob and Dave when the two had just begun conversing and asks about Steve's contributions to the conversation. Bob, maintaining an expressionless face, snorts and responds sarcastically, "Steve certainly made our conversation stimulating."[y3] *Laughing, Jim remarks, "I'm sure* he did,"[z3] *and he and Bob start to the door. . . .*

w3. Turning away and looking away are abbreviated leave-taking signals when conversationalists are standing.[118]

x3. See *f3*.

y3. Mehrabian and his colleagues conclude from their experiments that in the communication of feelings and attitudes, the impact of the words is only about 7 percent; the vocal expression, 38 percent; and the facial expression, 55 percent. Thus, when the voice and face contradict (are inconsistent with) the words (as in the illustrated situation), the nonverbal behaviors are more likely to determine the total impact of the message.[119]

z3. See *y3*.

As our commentary illustrates, there are many nonverbal messages being sent to the discriminating listener who listens with more than his or her ears. Indeed, the effective listener, as Gerald Egan notes, must "listen" to all of the preceivable cues which the sender emits:

> One does not listen with just his ears: he listens with his eyes and with his sense of touch, . . . he listens with his mind, his heart, and his imagination. He listens to the words of others, but he also listens to the messages that are buried in the words or encoded in the cues that surround the words. . . . He listens to the voice, the demeanor, . . . the gestures . . . and the bodily movements of the other. He listens to the sounds and to the silences. He listens not only to the message itself but also to the context, or in Gestalt terms, he listens to both the figure and the ground and to the way these two interact.[120]

Effective discriminatory listening, then, requires careful concentration, keen observation, and conscious recognition of the auditory and/or visual stimuli. Visual and auditory acuity—developed through an understanding of the dimensions involved, motivation, sensory awareness, concentration, experience, practice, and care of the hearing and seeing mechanisms—can help us to listen with discrimination. There is so much in the world around us that we may be missing because we only see and hear it; we are not listening to it with any level of discrimination.

SUMMARY

In this chapter, we have discussed discriminative listening—listening to distinguish the aural stimuli. First, we have noted the role that auditory discrimination plays in our listening effectiveness, language acquisition, and reading development. Also, we have presented a hierarchy of auditory discrimination skills that are developed during a child's early years—from infancy through grade six—and are strengthened throughout a person's life. Knowing this developmental sequence of discrimination skills and becoming adept in these skills can provide the adult with the tools necessary to assist a child in developing proficient auditory discrimination skills. Too, we have discussed additional discriminative skills that adults should possess: among these are recognizing the sound structure of our language, detecting and isolating vocal cues, becoming more sensitive to and understanding dialectal differences, and being more sensitive to environmental sounds. Finally, we have stressed the importance of applying visual discrimination in communication settings where an awareness and understanding of nonverbal communication can enhance the listener's understanding of the message conveyed by a sender whom the listener has the opportunity to observe. By developing and strengthening our discriminative listening skills, we can broaden our world of sound and sight as well as improve our understanding of the messages of others.

SUGGESTED ACTIVITIES

1. Prepare a list of twenty words; each list will consist of some words that are similar in sounds (such as yes, yet, gold, cold, low, blow, jaw, flaw, etc.). Participants will be paired and will sit back to back. One participant (the sender), stating each word only once, will clearly read his or her list while the partner (the listener) writes down what he or she hears. Then, the participants will exchange roles. There will be no feedback between partners. Participants may change partners as often as time permits. Before changing partners, each participant should score him- or herself by checking the sender's list. This practice helps listeners discriminate sounds and words.
2. Study the differences among the three major regional dialects (eastern, southern, and general American); these differences are discussed in the following texts: Wilhelmina G. Hedde, William N. Brigance, and Victor M. Powell, *Patterns in Communication* (Philadelphia: J. B. Lippincott Company, 1973), pp. 30–36, and Harlen Martin Adams and Thomas Clark Pollock, *Speak Up!* (New York: Macmillan Company, 1964), pp. 434–436. Then, attempt to pronounce the following words as a native from Boston, Georgia, and Cleveland would pronounce them: there, laugh, court, car, better, board, Alaska, after, years, past, ask, path, answer, hot, four, house, high, class, and Florida. This practice helps you become more aware of and more sensitive to differing dialectal characteristics.
3. Participants will sit in a circle and close their eyes. Each individual will vocalize "oh" in a way as to express a different emotion. Participants will interpret the meaning of each "oh." This practice helps listeners become more sensitive to emotions expressed in vocal cues.
4. Each student is to bring to class five sound-producing objects (such as a whistle or a pair of dice that can be rolled or shaken). Students are to conceal their items until the exercise has been completed. One at a time, each student—while being out of view of the other students—should produce a sound with each of his/her objects while the other students listen to identify each sound and list each sound-producing object. Students will check their answers and discuss reasons for the ease or difficulty they had in identifying individual sounds.
5. To test your ability to discriminate among the sounds of various musical instruments, listen to an orchestra performance, and then focus your attention on the sounds of individual instruments such as the harp, saxophone, oboe, cello, clarinet, and violin.
6. Turn the sound off, and watch a dramatic or comic television program. Take notes on what you believe is occurring in the program. Have a friend watch the same program (with the sound on) on another set. At the conclusion of the program, discuss your interpretations with your friend. How well did you "listen" to the nonverbal messages which the actors/actresses communicated?

7. Interview someone from another culture to determine the differences that exist between his or her culture and yours with respect to nonverbal communication aspects such as spatial distance, eye contact, voice patterns, touching behavior, regard for time, clothing, gestures, bodily movements, and regulatory cues. Which of these aspects are potential sources of communication barriers between communicators from the interviewee's culture and your culture? Discuss your findings with the class.
8. Each student is to describe—in one sentence—a situation that might produce a distinct emotional reaction. Students are then to exchange cards. Each card holder will portray an emotion which the situation suggests, and students will interpret the emotions being portrayed.
9. Recall your first memory of touching and being touched. What were your feelings? What are your present feelings about touching and being touched? Are you satisfied with these feelings? During what communication situations would you like to be touched more/less? During what communication situations would you like to touch more/less? Experiment with your touch behavior. Discover what happens when you touch more/touch less.
10. Experiment with eye contact by violating "civil inattention" behavior. Rather than glancing at an approaching stranger (in an uncrowded space on neutral ground) and then looking away until the two of you have passed one another, keep looking at the stranger until he or she has passed. Observe the stranger's reactions and report them to the class.
11. Experiment with head nods by reinforcing the speaker with appropriate head nods and then not moving your head. How did the speaker react? Report your findings to the class.
12. Experiment with spatial distance. Violate the personal space of one person and/or maintain an inappropriately faraway distance from someone else with whom you are conversing. Note your dialogue partner's reactions and report them to the class.
13. Occupy a seat where someone has left a "territorial marker" (a personal possession such as a book, umbrella, coat, etc.). Note the reactions of the person who had "reserved" his or her space when he or she returns. Report the person's reactions to the class.
14. List various ways that a speaker *nonverbally* indicates (or attempts to indicate) his or her status to listeners. How do you react to these status signals? Share your reactions with the class.
15. The next time you converse with someone, attempt to mirror his or her posture. Determine if mirroring assists you in identifying the other's feelings.
16. Collect comic strips or cartoons that show characters smiling, block out the captions/messages, and bring the comic strips/cartoons to class. Share them with the class, and have students give their interpretations of the meanings of the differently depicted smiles.

17. Make a deliberate effort to change your nonverbal behavior when you communicate with someone whom you dislike. Notice whether your behavioral changes result in the other person altering his/her behavior or whether there are changes in your feelings toward the other person.
18. Discuss how the following quote by Andre Kostelanetz applies to you: "We listen too much to the telephone and we listen too little to nature. The wind is one of my sounds. A lonely sound, perhaps, but soothing. Everybody should have his personal sounds to listen for—sounds that will make him feel exhilarated and alive, or quiet and calm. . . . As a matter of fact, one of the greatest sounds of them all—and to me it is a sound—is utter, complete silence."[121]

NOTES

1. William H. Perkins, *Speech Pathology* (St. Louis: The C. V. Mosby Company, 1971), p. 115.
2. R. L. Ebel, ed., *Encyclopedia of Educational Research* (New York: MacMillan Company, 1969), p. 1083.
3. Susan B. Neuman, "Effect of Teaching Auditory Perceptual Skills in Reading Achievement in First Grade," *Reading Teacher* 34 (January 1981):422.
4. Seth Fessenden, "Levels of Listening—a Theory," *Education* 75 (January 1955): 34–35.
5. Discrepancies in the time when some skills are said to develop in sighted and visually handicapped persons are indicated by (VH*), and skills that apply only to the visually handicapped are indicated by (VH).
6. Susan W. Weaver and William L. Rutherford, "A Hierarchy of Listening Skills," *Elementary English* 51 (November/December 1974): 1148–1149. Reprinted with permission of the publisher.
7. Sarah Ban Breathnach, "The World According to the Unborn . . . and After," *Washington Post,* 10 January 1983, p. B5.
8. Carol Atwater, "It Can Get Pretty Lively in the Womb," *USA Today,* 2 August 1983, pp. 1–2.
9. Breathnach, "The World According to the Unborn . . . and After," p. B5.
10. Daniel Tutolo, "Attention: Necessary Aspect of Listening," *Language Arts* 56 (January 1979): 34–35.
11. Ronald A. Cole, "Navigating the Slippery Stream of Speech," *Psychology Today* 12 (April 1979): 78–79.
12. *Ibid.,* p. 80; George Mandler, "Words, Tests and Categories: An Experimental View of Organized Memory," in *Studies in Thought and Language,* ed. J. L. Cowan (Tucson, Arizona: University of Arizona Press, 1970), pp. 128–129.
13. Blaine Goss, "Listening As Information Processing," *Communication Quarterly* 30 (Fall 1982): 304–307.
14. Albert Mehrabian, *Silent Messages* (Belmont, California: Wadsworth Publishing Company, 1971), p. 56.
15. *Ibid.,* p. 45.
16. *Ibid.,* p. 43.
17. Harvey L. Dubin, "Standard and Non-Standard Phonological Patterns as Related to Employability" (M. A. thesis, University of Maryland—College Park, 1970), p. 51.

18. Janet Raloff, "Language," *Science News* 122 (December 4, 1982): 360.
19. *Ibid.*
20. Robert O. Ross, *Listen to Your Car* (New York: Walker Publishing Company, 1981), p. 16.
21. Larry Dobres and Cathy Gaffney, Discriminative Listening Project (University of Maryland—College Park, 1972).
22. Carl F. Seashore, Don Lewis, and Joseph G. Saeveit, *Seashore Measure of Musical Talents,* rev. ed. (New York: The Psychological Corporation, 1960).
23. Norman A. Buktenica, "Auditory Discrimination: A New Assessment Procedure," *Exceptional Children* 38 (November 1971): 237–240.
24. Joseph M. Wepman, *The Auditory Discrimination Test,* rev. ed. (Chicago, Illinois: Language Research Association, 1973).
25. Mark L. Knapp, *Nonverbal Communication in Human Interaction* (New York: Holt, Rinehart and Winston, 1972), p. 12.
26. Mehrabian, *Silent Messages,* p. 44.
27. Connie Broughton, "When Mother's Intuition Isn't Enough," *Redbook* 159 (May 1982):56.
28. Dale Leathers, *Nonverbal Communication Systems* (Boston: Allyn and Bacon, 1976), p. 236; Gail E. Myers and Michele Tolela Myers, *The Dynamics of Human Communication* (New York: McGraw-Hill Book Company, 1973), p. 180.
29. Myers and Myers, *The Dynamics of Human Communication,* p. 180.
30. John W. Drakeford, "From Tuning Out: The Most Debilitating Social Disease," *New Woman,* July 1983, p. 67.
31. Knapp, *Nonverbal Communication in Human Interaction,* p. 113.
32. John T. Molloy, *Dress for Success* (New York: Warner Books, 1976).
33. Edward T. Hall, *The Silent Language* (Greenwich, Connecticut: Fawcett Publications, 1959), p. 185.
34. Hall, *The Silent Language.*
35. Erving Goffman, *Behavior in Public Places* (New York: The Free Press, 1963), pp. 83–88; Edward Hall and Mildred Hall, "Body Talk," in *Communicating Interpersonally,* eds. R. Wayne Pace, Brent D. Peterson, and Terrence R. Radcliffe (Columbus, Ohio: Charles E. Merrill Publishing Company, 1973), pp. 128–129.
36. Albert E. Scheflen, *Body Language and the Social Order* (Englewood Cliffs, New Jersey: Prentice-Hall, 1972), p. 37.
37. Marjorie S. Bayes, "Behavioral Cues of Interpersonal Warmth," *Journal of Consulting and Clinical Psychology* 39 (October 1972): 337.
38. Desmond Morris, *Manwatching* (New York: Harry N. Abrams, Inc., Publishers, 1977), p. 259.
39. Hall and Hall, "Body Talk," pp. 129–130.
40. *Ibid.,* p. 129.
41. Randall P. Harrison, *Beyond Words* (Englewood Cliffs, New Jersey: Prentice-Hall, 1974), p. 137.
42. *Ibid.,* p. 108.
43. Mehrabian, *Silent Messages,* p. 22.
44. *Ibid.;* Alvin Boderman, Douglas W. Freed, and Mark T. Kinnucan, " 'Touch Me, Like Me': Testing an Encounter Group Assumption," *Journal of Applied Behavioral Science* 8 (September/October 1972): 527–533.

45. Robert Shuter, "Proxemics and Tactility in Latin America," *Journal of Communication* 26 (Summer 1976):46–52.
46. Sidney M. Jourard, "An Exploratory Study of Body-Accessibility," *British Journal of Social and Clinical Psychology* 5 (August 1966): 221–222.
47. Daniel Goleman, "Can You Tell When Someone Is Lying to You?" *Psychology Today* 16 (August 1982): 20.
48. P. Ekman, W. V. Friesen, and P. Ellsworth, *Emotion in the Human Face: Guidelines for Research and an Integration of the Findings* (New York: Pergamon Press, 1972).
49. Goleman, "Can You Tell When Someone Is Lying to You?", pp. 22–23.
50. Mehrabian, *Silent Messages,* p. 3.
51. Morris, *Manwatching,* pp. 245–251; Scheflen, *Body Language and the Social Order,* pp. 15–20.
52. Joel R. Davitz, ed., *The Communication of Emotional Meaning* (New York: McGraw-Hill, 1964).
53. Barbara Burtoff, "You: Going Up? Down?" *Washington Post,* 24 November 1980, p. B-5.
54. Harrison, *Beyond Words,* p. 153.
55. Keith Gibbins, "Communication Aspects of Women's Clothes and Their Relation to Fashionability," *British Journal of Social and Clinical Psychology* 8 (December 1969): 301–312; Michael Argyle, *Bodily Communication* (New York: International Universities Press, 1975), pp. 323–344; Harrison, *Beyond Words,* pp. 131–133; Juan B. Cortes and Florence M. Gatti, "Physique and Motivation," *Journal of Consulting Psychology* 30 (October 1966):408–414; Morris, *Manwatching,* pp. 213–221.
56. Morris, *Manwatching,* pp. 179–181.
57. William Griffitt and Russell Veitch, "Hot and Crowded: Influences of Population Density and Temperature on Interpersonal Affective Behavior," *Journal of Personality and Social Psychology* 17 (January 1971): 92–98.
58. Mariam Leibman, "The Effects of Sex and Race Norms on Personal Space," *Environment and Behavior* 2 (September 1970): 208–246.
59. A. R. Allgeier and Donn Byrne, "Attraction toward the Opposite Sex As a Determinant of Physical Proximity," *Journal of Social Psychology* 90 (1973): 213–219.
60. Franklin D. Becker, "Study of Spatial Markers," *Journal of Personality and Social Psychology* 26 (June 1973): 439–445.
61. Harrison, *Beyond Words,* pp. 148–149; Argyle, *Bodily Communication,* pp. 263, 281, 347; Morris, *Manwatching,* p. 133.
62. Harrison, *Beyond Words*, pp. 126–127; Argyle, *Bodily Communication,* p. 260; Bayes, "Behavioral Cues of Interpersonal Warmth," pp. 333–339; G. R. Breed, "The Effect of Intimacy: Reciprocity or Retreat?" *British Journal of Social and Clinical Psychology* 11 (1972): 135–142.
63. Jeffrey D. Fisher and Donn Byrne, "Too Close for Comfort: Sex Differences in Response to Invasions of Personal Space," *Journal of Personality and Social Psychology* 32 (July 1975):15–21.
64. Scheflen, *Body Language and the Social Order,* p. 108.
65. Harrison, *Beyond Words,* p. 110.
66. *Ibid.,* p. 111.
67. Morris, *Manwatching,* pp. 186–187; Gerald I. Nierenberg and Henry H. Calero, *How to Read a Person like a Book* (New York: Pocket Books, 1973), pp. 121–124.
68. Argyle, *Bodily Communication,* p. 230.

69. Daniel Goleman, "People Who Read People," *Psychology Today* 13 (July 1979): 66–78.
70. Harrison, *Beyond Words,* p. 111.
71. Nierenberg and Calero, *How to Read a Person like a Book,* p. 59.
72. Davitz, *The Communication of Emotional Meaning.*
73. Nierenberg and Calero, *How to Read a Person like a Book,* p. 35.
74. Scheflen, *Body Language and the Social Order,* p. 108.
75. Argyle, *Bodily Communication,* p. 310.
76. Scheflen, *Body Language and the Social Order,* pp. 112–113.
77. Harrison, *Beyond Words,* p. 133.
78. Argyle, *Bodily Communication,* pp. 308–309.
79. Scheflen, *Body Language and the Social Order,* p. 19.
80. Harrison, *Beyond Words,* p. 111.
81. Argyle, *Bodily Communication,* pp. 273–275.
82. Harrison, *Beyond Words,* p. 134.
83. Morris, *Manwatching,* p. 58.
84. Davitz, *The Communication of Emotional Meaning.*
85. Hall and Hall, "Body Talk," p. 127.
86. Harrison, *Beyond Words,* p. 138.
87. *Ibid,* p. 103.
88. Argyle, *Bodily Communication,* pp. 266, 281.
89. Harrison, *Beyond Words,* p. 110.
90. *Ibid.,* pp. 126–127; Scheflen, *Body Language and the Social Order,* p. 108.
91. Nierenberg and Calero, *How to Read a Person like a Book,* pp. 68, 84, 91–92; Mehrabian, *Silent Messages,* p. 22.
92. Griffitt and Veitch, "Hot and Crowded: Influences of Population Density and Temperature on Interpersonal Affective Behavior," pp. 92–98.
93. Paul C. Cozby, "Effects of Density, Activity, and Personality on Environmental Preferences," *Journal of Research in Personality* 7 (June 1973): 46.
94. *Ibid.,* pp. 45–60.
95. Lois B. Wexner, "The Degree to Which Colors (Hues) Are Associated with Mood-Tones," *Journal of Applied Psychology* 38 (December 1954): 432–435.
96. Scheflen, *Body Language and the Social Order,* p. 34.
97. Mark L. Knapp, *Nonverbal Communication in Human Interaction,* 2nd ed. (New York: Holt, Rinehart and Winston, 1978).
98. Adam Kendon, "Movement Coordination in Social Interaction: Some Examples Described," *Acta Psychologica* 32 (April 1970): 101–125; Susan Dellinger and Barbara Deane, "People-Watching for Hidden Emotions," *Self* 3 (April 1981): 76–79.
99. Harrison, *Beyond Words,* p. 137.
100. R. W. Moncrieff, *Odour Preferences* (New York: John Wiley, 1966).
101. Harrison, *Beyond Words,* pp. 22, 138–141.
102. *Ibid.,* p. 134.
103. Albert E. Scheflen, "Quasi-Courtship Behavior in Psychotherapy," in *Nonverbal Communication: Readings with Commentary,* ed. Shirley Weitz (New York: Oxford University Press, 1974), pp. 182–198.
104. Adam Kendon and Andrew Ferber, "A Description of Some Human Greetings," in *Comparative Ecology and Behavior of Primates,* eds. Richard P. Michael and John H. Crook (London: Academic Press, 1973), pp. 591–668.

105. Mehrabian, *Silent Messages,* p. 7.
106. Harrison, *Beyond Words,* pp. 151–152.
107. Hall and Hall, "Body Talk," pp. 129–130.
108. Dellinger and Deane, "People-Watching for Hidden Emotions," pp. 76–79.
109. Argyle, *Bodily Communication,* p. 166; Harrison, *Beyond Words,* pp. 111,126.
110. Mehrabian, *Silent Messages,* p. 63.
111. *Ibid.,* pp. 59–65.
112. Argyle, *Bodily Communication,* p. 166; Harrison, *Beyond Words,* p. 126.
113. Mehrabian, *Silent Messages,* p. 65.
114. Harrison, *Beyond Words,* p. 110; Argyle, *Bodily Communication,* p. 160.
115. Paul Ekman and Wallace V. Friesen, "Nonverbal Leakage and Clues to Deception," *Psychiatry* 32 (February 1969): 88–106.
116. *Ibid.;* Albert Mehrabian, "Nonverbal Betrayal of Feeling," *Journal of Experimental Research in Personality* 5 (March 1971): 64–73; Morris, *Manwatching,* pp. 106–111.
117. Harrison, *Beyond Words,* p. 138.
118. Mehrabian, *Silent Messages,* p. 3.
119. *Ibid.,* pp. 42–47.
120. Gerald Egan, "Listening As Empathic Support" in *Bridges Not Walls,* 2nd ed., ed. John Stewart (Reading, Massachusetts: Addison-Wesley Publishing Company, 1977), p. 228.
121. *The International Dictionary of Thoughts,* s.v. "Silence."

Concepts You Will Encounter

- Comprehension
- Understanding
- Memory
- Loci System
- Link System
- Phonetic System
- Peg-Word System
- Mnemonic Devices
- Chunking
- Concentration
- Vocabulary
- Structural Analysis
- Contextual Clues
- Correlation Coefficient
- Speech Speed / Thought Speed
- Compressed Speech
- Main Ideas
- Transitions
- Organizational Patterns
- Details
- Inferences
- Notetaking
- Outlining
- Precis
- Fact Versus Principle
- Mapping
- Items in a Sequence
- Oral Directions
- Questions

Skills You Should Develop

- Capitalizing on the Differential between Speech Speed and Thought Speed
- Listening for Main Ideas
- Listening for Significant Details
- Drawing Justifiable Inferences
- Being an Effective Notetaker
- Recalling Items in a Sequence
- Following Oral Directions
- Formulating Meaningful Questions

Comprehensive Listening

6

The third purpose for listening goes beyond the discrimination of aural, and sometimes visual, stimuli to the understanding of the message. This listening for understanding is called comprehensive listening. The comprehensive listener is successful if the message that he or she receives, attends to, and assigns meaning to is as close as possible to that which the sender intended. Remembering plays a major role in comprehensive listening when the listener's purpose is not only to understand the message being presented but also to retain it for future use.

Uses of Comprehensive Listening

In all phases of our lives, we listen to understand. Much of the educational process is based on comprehensive listening. We must carefully listen to lectures and class discussions in order to understand and retain an extensive amount of information. At work, we are often expected to learn new skills and new procedures through training programs which frequently utilize lecture and discussion methods for imparting knowledge. In our professional lives we also listen to briefings, reports, seminars, conferences, oral papers, and other oral messages. In our personal lives, too, we listen to understand. We listen to our insurance agents explain our various policies, auto mechanics explain why our car is not operating properly, our accountant inform us of items that are now tax deductible, our children describe how their baseball game was won, our physician explain a diagnosis, media personalities share their views on current issues, and countless other people with informative messages. To be effective comprehensive listeners in each of these phases of our lives, we must concentrate on the message strictly to understand, not to make a critical judgment of it.

Variables Related to Comprehensive Listening

A careful reading of the research conducted in the field of listening shows us that of the five purposes for listening, comprehensive listening has received the most attention. A major reason why it has been studied so frequently is that it is the most "testable." A study which provides a pre-test of information, a presentation of the information, and then a post-test covering the presented information can yield results from which we can make some generalizations about the listening comprehension of the persons in the study. Although test results provide some clues regarding the listening efficiency of the comprehensive listener, such data also illustrate some of the many variables which tend to influence the listener's comprehensive ability.

Memory

One of the variables directly related to comprehensive listening is memory. In fact, according to proponents of the schema theory, we cannot process information (which we must do as we listen at any level) without bringing the memory into play throughout the system. They further suggest that we draw up schemata or "scripts" which "represent relationships among concepts rather than among words"[1] and which perform three important functions: (1) they establish expectations of what we are going to encounter in our activities; (2) they serve to structure our comprehension of activities when described by others; and (3) they guide recall of our experiences and/or information.[2] Thus, since comprehensive listening involves information-processing and since we often measure comprehensive listening by a person's ability to remember information which has been presented, memory is a significant variable.

Extensive research on human memory has provided us with valuable information that can greatly aid us in improving our memory. Before we examine some of this information, however, it is useful to consider some theories on why we forget or, stated in another way, why we cannot retrieve information that we have stored in our memory system. Among the theories of forgetting are (1) fading theory: information that is not used frequently enough tends to fade from memory; (2) distortion theory: information is often distorted due to its becoming similar to and eventually indistinguishable from other stored information; (3) suppression theory: information that may have unpleasant associations or may be emotionally painful to recall tends to be consciously (through perhaps not subconsciously) forgotten; (4) interference theory: previously learned information interferes with presently learned information while subsequently learned information interferes with previously learned information; and (5) processing break-down theory: no part, or only a portion, of the information sought (as in the tip-of-the-tongue phenomenon) can be recalled due to an individual's poor retrieval cues or weak or ambiguous coding system in the LTM.[3] This last theory is, indeed, critical since "successful memory performances depend on a compatibility between the strategies of retrieval and the strategies of the original encoding."[4]

Memory specialists, such as Lorayne, Cermak, and Montgomery, postulate a number of reasons why we do not remember. One major reason that we may "forget" (as many of us would say) information is that we do not pay attention to it and thus do not remember it in the first place. We frequently observe this type of "forgetting" when we are introduced to several people in succession. Later, when conversing with one of these individuals, we may say, "I'm sorry; I've forgotten your name," when, in actuality, we never learned (remembered) the name initially. As we have noted in Chapter 3, usually only information which has been attended to reaches the LTM. Memory specialists cite additional reasons for our forgetting; among these are poor organizational methods of storing information, distractibility, a lack of caring for people, and a lack of motivation to improve our ability to remember.[5]

Besides knowing some of the theories and reasons for forgetting, knowing *what* is more easily remembered and *how* information is more easily remembered can assist us in impeding the forgetting process. What information is more easily remembered? Research shows that we remember more easily information which is (1) meaningful, useful, and of interest to us, (2) particularly striking/out of the ordinary, (3) organized, and (4) visual.[6] In addition, we remember best that information which we learned well during our first exposure to it, with which we associate pleasant feelings, and with which we associate (by relating in some way such as comparing and/or contrasting) previously-learned, familiar information.[7]

Knowing how information is more easily remembered is critical to memory improvement. According to Montgomery, a memory training specialist, there are prerequisites we must meet in order to improve our memory: have a strong desire to improve our memory, concentrate on improving our memory, and care about people. Once we have met these initial requirements, Montgomery recommends that we then practice improving our memory.[8] In a 1980 experimental study of the LTM, Ericsson, Chase, and Faloon found that "there is seemingly no limit to improvement in memory skill with practice."[9] The effects of motivation and practice on retention and recall are vividly illustrated by a waiter whom your authors know. Michael Barber, a waiter at the Iron Gate Restaurant in Virginia Beach, Virginia, has the capacity to elaborate in great detail the entire menu of this gourmet restaurant. No menus are issued to diners, so the entire gourmet offering, which changes nightly, must be explained by the waiter. Moreover, Michael takes the orders of all persons in the party without writing down any of the details (and diners are offered a vast array of appetizers, entreés, desserts, wines, etc.) and delivers, without error, these orders to the correct individuals. When we asked Michael how he had developed his tremendous memory capacity, he stressed that it was necessary for him to (a) want to work from memory, i.e., *motivation*—and (2) *practice* with the information until he felt satisfied with the explanation of the evening's menu.

Through studying the processes of information storage and retrieval, researchers and practitioners have discovered many techniques we can practice in order to improve our memory. All of these procedures depend extensively upon our intention to remember and our ability to attend to incoming information, organize/structure the information, form associations, and rehearse. Many other techniques also rely upon our ability to create vivid mental images—images that are visual and striking in color, action, exaggeration, and absurdity. Researchers and memory training specialists have determined that by using these skills, we will remember more effectively, whether we are remembering issues in a speech, items in a list, numbers in a series, rules, names, etc.

One of the oldest memory techniques is the *loci system,* which involves learning a sequence of familiar, yet uncrowded, locations (loci) and matching the to-be-remembered items with the locations. Greeks in antiquity worked to perfect this system which they used to remember their orations. The rooms of your home or various areas in a specific room are good loci. To remember the five purposes of listening that are described in a lecture, for example, you might mentally travel around your family room and associate, by creating unbelievable, ridiculous, and comical images, a different area with each purpose. You might clearly visualize the stereo as appreciative listening, the crackling fire as discriminative listening, the sofa as therapeutic listening, the desk where you usually read the newspaper as comprehensive listening, and the draperies that you intensely dislike as critical listening. To recall the purposes, you would visualize in turn each of the previously-assigned sequence of areas where the room items are located and, thereby, discover each purpose. The same set of loci can be used over and over for remembering new items. This system has been found to facilitate the learning of ordinarily difficult material.[10]

A second technique is the *link system,* which involves vividly and imaginatively linking (or associating) the first to-be-remembered item to the second item, the second to the third, and so on through the use of ridiculous images that you must clearly visualize in your mind. For instance, if you wanted to remember a shopping list consisting of carrots, cigars, milk, and an all-purpose cleaner, you might mentally picture a blue carrot smoking a footlong cigar and wiping up an ocean of spilled milk with a tiny container of all-purpose cleaner. To prevent your forgetting the first item (to which all other items are linked), you should also associate the first item with a location which will remind you of the item. Thus, for your grocery list, you might visualize a carrot bending over a grocery cart. Both imagery and linking have been found to increase recall ability.[11]

Another complex yet highly effective technique with endless possibilities of aiding in learning and recall is the *phonetic system.* This consists of associating or connecting numbers, phonetic sounds, and words representing these numbers and sounds with the items to be remembered. This system involves four steps: (1) learning the association between numbers and a ten-sound phonetic alphabet, consisting only of consonants; (2) forming and learning words that correspond to the numbers; (3) forming a strong visual image of each word that corresponds to each number; and (4) forming a strong visual association between each item to be remembered in sequence with each word formed and visualized (in steps two and three). In this system, the first three steps, which must be known very well, are permanent; only the to-be-remembered items in step four change.

To use this system, one must first learn the associations between numbers and a phonetic alphabet. Since memory training specialists slightly vary their versions of the phonetic alphabet, we will not present a standard alphabet. For the purpose of describing this system, we have chosen to present Montgomery's version:

1=t, d, th	6=j, ch, sh, tch, dg, soft g
2=n	7=k, ng, q, hard c, hard g
3=m	8=f, v, ph
4=r	9=p, b
5=l	0=z, s, soft c[12]

To assist one in remembering this alphabet, there are cues, such as 1 is represented by t (which has a single downstroke), 2 is represented by n (which has two downstrokes), . . . 9 is represented by p (which resembles 9), o is represented by z (which is the last alphabet letter as well as the first letter of the word *zero,* the name of 0). Moreover, one who is familiar with voiced and voiceless sounds will recognize that these sounds (such as t and d, j and ch, k and hard g, f and v, p and b, and z and s) are paired. Having learned and associated the numbers and sounds, you then form a concrete word to represent each number; for example, 1, which is represented by t, d, th, might be *tie;* 2, represented by n, might be *Noah;* . . . 14, represented by t, d, th and r, might be *tree* (or it could be *tar, tear, tier, trio,* etc.). Remember, vowel sounds and y, h, and w do not count in this system; thus, in the example of each word that could possibly be the learned word for 14, only t and r, which represent 1 and 4=14, remain when the vowel sounds are omitted. After having learned the number and phonetic sounds, as well as each word you will associate with each number/phonetic sound, you next associate a strong visual image of each word that corresponds to each number. For example, a mental picture of *tea* will always represent the number *1*. Having learned (really learned) the three permanent steps of this system, you are equipped to utilize the system as an aid in remembering items in and out of sequence as well as backwards, by twos, by threes, etc. To remember lists of words, such as supplies which you must obtain from the supply room, you mentally link—in a strong visual image—each learned word with the supply item occupying that numbered position; if the fourteenth supply item were scissors, you might picture a gigantic tree (Remember, 14=t+r=tree.) with thousands of silver scissors as branches. This system is also useful for remembering numbers. For instance, to remember the telephone number, 996–8043, you would utilize what you learned in step one and convert the numbers to their corresponding letters: p p j f z r m. Then you would create a word, phrase, or sentence that includes these letters (as well as vowels and y, h, and w, that do not count when you are decoding); your phrase might be one similar to this one: *P*a*p*a *J*oy o*f* *z*oo *r*oo*m*. To recall the telephone number, you would recall the phrase and then decode it.

Rhyming, too, can facilitate learning and recall. How many of us recall a rhyme in order to determine, for example, the number of days in March ("Thirty days hath September. . . .") or the spelling of *receive* and *freight* ("Use *i* before *e,* except after *c,* or when sounded like *a* as in *neighbor* and *weigh*; the exceptions are the *weird foreigner seizes neither leisure* nor sport at its *height.*")? A more complex rhyming device is the *peg-word system.* This system involves three steps: (1) learning a number-word rhyme; (2) associating vivid mental images with each number-word combination; and (3) using vivid association to interact (link) each to-be-remembered item in its sequence with the corresponding item in the peg-word sequence. The first two steps, which must be learned well (forward and backward), are permanent; only the to-be-remembered items change. The rhyme, though it differs slightly among memory training specialists, may be as follows: "One is bun, two is glue, three is key, four is store, five is drive, six is mix, seven is heaven, eight is ape, nine is dine, and ten is pen."[13] Having learned the complete rhyme, you then associate a mental picture with each number-word combination in the rhyme; for example, for "one is bun," you might visualize a gigantic red hamburger bun sun-tanning atop McDonald's golden arches. After creating your own images for the complete rhyme and knowing both rhyme and images well, you associate each item to be learned with its corresponding number-word/image in the peg-word sequence. To illustrate, suppose you use the peg-word system to remember the tasks you have been told to accomplish during the day. For the first task, to type a letter of complaint to the Consumer Protection Agency, you might visualize yourself angrily typing as you are sitting in a leaking swimming pool that is being held up by the sun-tanned, red hamburger bun that is atop McDonald's golden arches; the remaining tasks would also be visually associated—in order of priority—with the peg-word rhyme. This system has been proven to result in high levels of recall.[14]

Mnemonic devices, or memory tricks, also are commonly used to improve the memory. Two closely-related mnemonic devices are acronyms and acrostics. Acronyms are letter cues such as NATO (North Atlantic Treaty Organization), EPA (Environmental Protection Agency), AIDS (Acquired Immune Deficiency Syndrome), PUSH (People United to Serve Humanity), and USFL (United States Football League). Similar to acronyms are acrostics, made up of words or sentences whose letters or the first letter of each word represents an item of information to be remembered. An acrostic which one of your authors remembers from her elementary school days is one that her teacher taught to help the students learn to spell the word *geography:* George's eldest oldest girl rode a pig home yesterday. Other examples of acrostic sentences are (1) *Every good boy does fine* (representing the lines on the treble clef: EGBDF); (2) *Bless my dear aunt Sally* (presenting the correct order for algebraic operations: brackets, multiply, divide, add, and subtract); (3) *Do men ever visit Boston?* (relating the ranking of English titles: duke, marquis, earl, viscount, and baron); and (4) *Mother visits every Monday, just stays until noon period* (presenting the sequential order of the planets: Mercury, Venus, Earth, Mars, Jupiter, Saturn, Uranus, Neptune, Pluto). These four examples assist one in remembering items in sequential order. To remember items which are not sequential, you might list the first word of each item to be remembered, then rearrange the letters until you create a word, phrase, or sentence. To illustrate this technique, you might remember the cabinet posts by creating the sentence, *Hail the D.C. jets* (representing secretaries of health, agriculture, interior, labor, transportation, housing and urban development, energy, defense, commerce, justice, education, treasury, and state). Examples of acrostic words are HOMES (representing the Great Lakes: Huron, Ontario, Michigan, Erie, and Superior); PAIL (representing the four types of skin cuts: puncture, abrasion, incision, and laceration); STAB (representing four members of a quartet: soprano, tenor, alto, and bass); and ROY G. BIV (representing the ordered colors of the visible spectrum: red, orange, yellow, green, blue, indigo, and violet).

Still another memory technique is *categorical clustering*, an organizational technique which one uses systematically to modify incoming information by imposing structure on unstructured information. This technique, although not helpful in recalling items in a sequence, will assist one in free recall. For example, if you were given a list of words, such as rose, dog, apple, mouse, daisy, lemon, etc., to recall, you would cluster the items categorically (rose/daisy, apple/lemon, dog/mouse, etc.) and thus remember them more easily. There is substantial evidence that this technique facilitates recall.[15]

Finally, a memory technique described as *chunking* involves combining single elements into larger units. Although this technique can be useful in transferring information to the LTM (as it is, for example, for those who learn the English alphabet by dividing the 26 letters into 3 chunks with each chunk containing 2 elements, each element containing 2 units, and each unit containing 1 to 4 letters: "[(ab-cd) (ef-g)] [(hi-jk) (lmno-p)] [(qrs-tuv) (w-xyz)]"[16]), it is frequently used to retain items in the STM (for example, while one is taking the first two parts of the *Brown-Carlsen Listening Comprehension Test*[17] or the first two parts of the *Kentucky Comprehensive Listening Skills Test*[18]). As you may recall from Chapter 3, Miller determined that the STM can hold only approximately seven units.[19] The letters, *r, o, s, e, p, a,* and *n,* would make up seven units; however, if you were to utilize chunking, combining the seven single units into larger units (forming the words, *rose* and *pan*), you would then have two units, and your STM would still have the capacity to hold five additional units. To illustrate further the chunking technique, suppose you are asked to recall these seven words: *sacrifice, fly, run, and, hit, drag,* and *bunt.* A person unfamiliar with baseball terminology would probably use seven units (the seven words) to retain this information, while a baseball fan would likely utilize only three units by chunking, or combining, these seven units into three: *sacrifice fly, run and hit,* and *drag bunt.* Thus, we see that chunking allows us to retain more information in the STM. Another way to use chunking is to create one word to represent several letters in sequence; for instance, to retain the letters *t, n, i,* and *o,* you might use one unit, the word *attention*—a word that contains in sequence the four letters/four units. One must be aware, however, that the use of chunking in this way will be effective in retaining information only if one can correctly decode the chunk and recall its components; in other words, remembering *attention* will not be useful if you do not recall the correct sequential letters which the word represents (*t, n, i,* and *o,* not *a, e, t,* and *n*). Still another way that chunking can be used is to recall numbers. For instance, to remember a long number, such as 8153219, you might break up the number into a series of two- or three-digit numbers (81–532–19, 815–32–19, etc.).

A concern of many listeners is not how to improve their memory of dictionary terms or multiple-digit numbers; rather, it is how to remember people's names. Although there is no specific technique for remembering names, there are several steps one can take and a number of strategies one can use in order to remember names more effectively. You will observe that many of these steps/strategies, such as attending to, rehearsing, associating, and visualizing images, are based upon what we have already learned about memory improvement. Lorayne and Lucas describe remembering names in a series of three steps: learning the name, learning the face, and linking the name and the face.[20] To remember the name, you must first hear the name correctly and attend to it; that is, you must really listen to it. If you did not clearly hear it, ask the person to repeat it until you do clearly hear it. Second, discuss the person's name with him/her; ask for its spelling, its pronunciation, and/or its origin, ask whether the name has a special meaning, and/or ask whether the person knows of a special way to assist you in remembering the name. Third, consider whether or not you know anyone with a similar name; if you do, tell the person. Also, rehearse the name silently in order to help transfer the name to the LTM. Additionally, state the person's name several times during the conversation—when you are introduced, while you are conversing, and when you are leaving. Later, repeat the name to yourself and write it down. Lastly, associate the name with some ridiculous image. If the person's name is Cal Ripkin, for example, visualize a monstrous cow and its kin—miniature purple cows—ripping down a fence, piece by piece, so that they can graze in a more fertile field. The second step is to remember the face. Look, really look, at the person; concentrate on his/her face. Then select an outstanding feature (or any feature if none is outstanding) that will help you remember the face. Let us say, for example, that Cal Ripkin's outstanding facial feature is his receding hairline. The last step is to link the name and the face. To link the name and face, add an additional image to the mental picture that you have already created. For our example, we might visualize the monstrous cow stacking each ripped-down fence piece on its horns (across its forehead). With this mental addition, you have linked the name to the face. It is essential that you remember the purpose of creating the absurd mental pictures: you are forcing yourself to be aware—to concentrate; you are attending to the name and face and, thus, increasing the chances that you will transfer the information to the LTM. Two additional memory strategies that do not involve creating ridiculous images but can facilitate learning and recalling names are composing a rhyme about a person's name (such as, Steady Eddie Murray is never in a hurry.) and associating the person's name with his/her work (such as, Jim Palmer throws a palm ball in the gym.).

The effectiveness of the memory techniques presented in this section is supported by experimental findings in the laboratory as well as by experiential findings outside of the laboratory. Unfortunately, unless a person is trained or given specific instructions regarding how to use these techniques, he/she does not spontaneously utilize many of these techniques. Since memory is so closely related to comprehensive listening, one way that a listener can improve such comprehensive listening is to improve the ability to remember. An effective way to begin this improvement is to use these as well as other memory techniques which are limited only to one's own creativity.

Concentration

Another significant variable to effectiveness in comprehensive listening (as well as in any type of listening) is the listener's ability to concentrate or pay attention. Concentration on the sender's message, in fact, may be the listener's most difficult task. Quite frequently, we hear senders complaining about their intended listeners' lack of concentration/poor attention, and almost just as frequently, we hear listeners bemoaning their own lack of concentration/poor attention. Indeed, concentration is a pervasive problem that has long existed—long before television, the medium commonly mentioned as a major cause of listeners' poor attention spans. Approximately twenty years before television became a household item in most American homes, former President Franklin Delano Roosevelt suspected that those who passed through receiving lines did not really pay attention to what he said to them. His suspicions were confirmed when he reportedly said to one dignitary, as they shook hands, "I shot my grandmother this morning," and the dignitary replied, "How lovely! What a splendid celebration."

Unfortunately, recent studies and testimonials indicate that the attention of listeners apparently has not improved since Roosevelt's finding. For example, psychophysiologist Thomas Mulholland tested the attention spans of forty young television viewers by attaching to each an instrument that shut off the television set whenever each youngster's brain produced many alpha waves (which are normally associated with daydreaming or falling asleep). Mulholland found that even though the children were told to concentrate, only a few could keep the television set on for more than thirty seconds.[21] To your authors' knowledge, no similar experiment has been conducted in the classroom; however, those in education are well aware of the frequent complaints of teachers regarding students' poor attention spans. Although children may have difficulty concentrating, they are often quick to recognize that adults do not always pay attention either. Two third-grade students, for instance, made these comments about their parents: "They don't look at me, or they just walk away" and "Sometimes you think they're listening to you, and maybe they're walking around or talking to someone else."[22] Adults' lack of concentration extends to television viewing, according to William F. Buckley; commenting on a 1983 Public Broadcasting Service series highlighting great orators in American history, Buckley notes one of the problems that the series' directors had to confront: "The television audience . . . is not trained to listen—unstroked, no peanuts or candy bars, no fireworks or bullets or one-liners—to 15 uninterrupted minutes."[23] Concentration also is a problem adults have at work; Watson and Smeltzer found that while business students ranked internal distractions and business practitioners ranked environmental distractions as the most serious barrier to effective listening at work, both groups ranked inattentiveness as the third most serious barrier.[24]

Although few research studies have investigated *why* listeners do not concentrate and have poor attention spans, many reasons have been adduced. One of these is that listeners may feel that time constraints require them to divide their attention energy between/among various stimuli rather than to give their undivided attention to any one stimulus. At home, they do family and household tasks, read, watch television, eat, do homework, etc., *while* they engage in conversations. At school, they prepare yesterday's unfinished assignments, plan today's events, prearrange tomorrow's activities, etc., *while* they participate in classroom lecture-discussions. At work, they study schedules, perform job tasks, and design future projects, etc., *while* they take part in telephone and face-to-face communication interactions. Even after dividing their attention energy by day, however, they still frequently do not get sufficient rest at night, and, thus, their lack of alertness the following day further adds to their inability to concentrate on senders' messages. Being so time-oriented in a fast-paced society, they often become selfish and impatient; they think they cannot afford to give their time to only one stimulus, and they are too impatient to attend to senders who, for example, provide detailed accounts of events, are repetitious, have poor communication skills, discuss subjects with which the listeners think they are familiar enough, etc. Hence, many listeners attend to only portions of senders' messages, assign incomplete meanings, and then direct their attention energy to other pressing concerns.

Misdirection of attention energy, due to causes other than time constraints, is a second possible reason for poor concentration. According to Erving Goffman, standard forms of misinvolvement include (1) external preoccupation—rather than focusing on senders' messages, listeners are easily distracted by external stimuli and, thus, concentrate on unrelated stimuli such as the hot room, the sound of an airplane, a person walking down the hall, the senders' appearance; (2) self-consciousness—focusing on how well or how poorly they are doing as interactants in communication situations; (3) interaction-consciousness—focusing on how the interactions are going as, for instance, hosts and hostesses would during dinner parties; and (4) other-consciousness—focusing on other participants (their positive or negative communication skills, personal qualities, viewpoints,etc.).[25] These four forms of misdirected attention energy, coupled with listeners expending energy on rehearsing what they are going to say during their "turns" to speak rather than on listening to others' verbal and nonverbal messages, all contribute to listeners' poor concentration. A reason closely related to

Goffman's second form of misinvolvement is that listeners may be too ego-involved. They may focus on internal distractions such as physical pains, hunger, inappropriate clothing, injured feelings resulting from senders' use of emotional triggers, personal concerns, etc., rather than concentrating on senders' messages. Or listeners may be so "sure" that they "know" what the senders are going to say that they focus on planning their responses rather than on listening to the senders' complete messages. A fourth possible reason is that they lack curiosity or drive; thus, rather than attending to what they do not know or what they do not understand, they—preferring comfort and laziness to challenge and exertion—avoid that which demands concentration. Still another reason may be that they have become conditioned not to pay attention to various stimuli. For instance, many messages are repeated so often that listeners have become used to attending to different portions of the same message each time it is repeated; our world is so noisy that listeners have learned to tune out many stimuli; and there is so much information presented daily that listeners have mastered ways to avoid information overload.

Underlying the five reasons for lack of concentration are three additional reasons: lack of self-discipline, lack of self-motivation, and lack of responsibility. There is no doubt that listeners must be disciplined, motivated, and responsible if they are to concentrate on and be attentive to senders' messages. Just as mountain climbers and car racers must discipline themselves to direct their undivided attention to their tasks, so must listeners develop mental discipline to control distractions. Self-discipline is much more easily practiced when listeners are personally motivated to listen. If each listener had the same motivation to listen in all other listening situations as he or she has when being told he or she has been awarded a scholarship, been promoted, or won the grand prize in a contest, concentration would seldom be a listening problem. Unfortunately, listeners do not have this same motivation in all other listening situations. But they can develop a high degree of motivation if they approach each listening experience as opportunists looking for what will bring them personal rewards—enjoyment/pleasure, friendship/love from those important to them, respect from those whom they admire, praise from those who "count," fulfillment of basic needs, monetary gains, job advancements, and/or information they can use in some way that will be beneficial to them. Since listeners are not prophets and, thus, do not know when these rewards will come or when the results will prove to be beneficial, they must concentrate on each sender's complete message so that they will not prevent themselves from gaining rewards that may be useful to them (now or in the future)—in their personal lives, schooling, and/or jobs—or to individuals important to them. Listening for "what is in the message for me or for someone important to me" will provide each listener with intrinsic motivation to concentrate. Having an opportunistic attitude not only helps listeners to provide their own motivation to listen (rather than depending on senders to provide this incentive) but also helps them to accept responsibility for the success of each communication interaction. Accepting responsibility entails single-minded involvement in each sender's message, not ruling out a message as "uninteresting" or useless until the entire message has been searched for some personal value, being responsive, and caring how their listening behavior affects the senders. In addition, each listener assumes more responsibility and improves his or her concentration by practicing the following behaviors: (1) being honest with the sender when he or she is having difficulty letting the sender's message in due to being too tired, too busy, or too pressured by other concerns and then establishing another time to continue the interaction; (2) engaging in self-questioning in order to be more attentive: Am I giving my single-minded attention to the sender? Why or why not? Am I inwardly listening to myself and outwardly listening to the sender? What am I considering more important than the sender's message? Can these concerns be set aside until a later, more appropriate time? Am I paying attention to paying attention, or am I paying attention to the sender's message?; (3) making it a habit to write down any personal concern which appears while he or she is listening and then dealing with the concern after, rather than during, the listening experience; (4) listening with the intent to ask the sender the most penetrating question he or she can think of; (5) listening with the intent to share each sender's message with another person and then actually sharing the message with someone within the next few hours; (6) listening—at the group, public, and mass levels of communication—as if the sender were speaking to him or her individually; and (7) practicing the appropriate listening skills—as they are presented in this book—in each communication situation in which he or she is an active participant.

Vocabulary

Still another variable that appears to influence the listener's comprehensive ability is size of vocabulary. Although the precise relationship between listening and vocabulary has not been determined, "it can be concluded tentatively that size of listening vocabulary is probably an important variable in listening comprehension."[26] Since the assignment of meaning is an integral part of the listening process, we must have a sufficiently developed vocabulary so that we can expand our system of categorization and minimize our categorical errors. Only then can we assign more reliable meanings to the stimuli to which we attend.

As communicators, we have four functional vocabularies that vary in size. Until we reach approximately age twelve, our largest functional vocabulary is our listening vocabulary (followed, in order, by our speaking, reading, and writing vocabularies). After age twelve, our listening vocabulary is generally surpassed by our reading vocabulary (and followed, in order, by our writing and speaking vocabularies).[27] Although our listening vocabulary generally ranks, throughout our lives, as either our largest or second largest functional vocabulary, it is still quite limited when we consider that the average adult's personal vocabulary consists of only about 20,000 words (which is a small fraction of the estimated 600,000 to 1 million words in the English language).[28] After noting how the average adult communicator's functional vocabularies vary in size, the reader may initially conclude that if the speaking vocabulary of the average adult speaker is smaller than the listening vocabulary of the average adult listener, a listener should encounter few problems in assigning meaning. However, the reader will quickly dismiss this conclusion when he or she considers that individuals' general vocabularies are as unique as are individuals themselves. While two communicators may share many words, the same two communicators may not share many others. Thus, to improve our listening effectiveness, we must continually work toward improving our listening vocabularies so that we can narrow the vocabulary gap (as well as the understanding gap) which exists between us as listeners and others as speakers.

There are many steps we can take to improve our general as well as our listening vocabularies. According to Pauk, the first step is "to develop a genuine interest in words."[29] Fortunately, some of us have already developed this interest. It may have been instilled by another individual, perhaps an instructor, a writer, or a parent, who was enthralled with words and shared his or her fascination with us. Or it may have arisen within us, perhaps by chance, as we completed our first crossword puzzle, consulted our first dictionary or thesaurus, or composed our first composition. If, on the other hand, we have yet to develop a genuine interest in words, we should strive to remedy this deficiency by taking courses (such as courses in vocabulary building, word study, dialects, or language history) or by establishing our own self-study programs (such as studying vocabulary books, thesauri, and general, specialized, and unabridged dictionaries, developing a program built around the material in this section, or completing the vocabulary exercises listed at the end of this chapter). Regardless of how our interest in words—their origins, meanings, functions, structures, subtle differences, and beauty—begins, this interest will provide the impetus we need to continue building our vocabularies.

In addition to developing a genuine interest in words, we should develop vocabulary acquisition skills. Two basic skills which will assist us in learning new words and their meanings are the abilities to analyze the structure and the contexts of words. The first skill, structural analysis, requires that we initially learn key root words as well as common prefixes and suffixes. Then, when we encounter unfamiliar words, we can break them down, if possible, into their component parts (that is, their prefixes, root words, and suffixes) and apply our previously learned knowledge of structure to the unfamiliar words so that we can determine their meanings. To illustrate the word power that structural analysis can give us, we shall consider the following fourteen words which, according to James I. Brown, "contain prefix and root elements found in over 14,000 relatively common words or close to an estimated 100,000 of unabridged dictionary size":[30]

Word	Prefix	Common Meaning	Root	Common Meaning
precept	pre-	before	capere	take, seize
detain	de-	away, down	tenere	hold, have
intermittent	inter-	between, among	mittere	send
offer	ob-	against	ferre	bear, carry
insist	in-	into	stare	stand
monograph	mono-	alone, one	graphein	write
epilogue	epi-	upon	legein	say, study of
aspect	ad	to, towards	specere	see
uncomplicated	un-	not	plicare	fold
	com-	together, with		
nonextended	non-	not	tendere	stretch
	ex-	out, beyond		
reproduction	re-	back, again	ducere	lead
	pro-	forward, for		
indisposed	in-	not	ponere	put, place
	dis-	apart, not		
oversufficient	over-	above	facere	make, do
	sub-	under		
mistranscribe	mis-	wrong	scribere	write
	trans-	across, beyond[31]		

Having learned these twenty prefixes and fourteen root words, along with eight common suffixes (*able*—capable of; *ate*—to make; *ed*—indicating the past participle verb form or an adjective; *ence*—act or quality of; *er* or *or*—one who; *ous*—characterized by; and *tion*—act or state of), we can determine—through structural analysis—the meanings, for example, of the following words:

adscript	epigraph	monologue	remise
complice	explicate	nondeferrable	scrivener
defect	inductile	obstinate	subtend
deference	inexplicit	oversubscribe	tenacious
desist	intercessor	prescript	transposition
distend	misinferred	prospectus	untenable

The second skill, learning the meanings of unfamiliar words from their contexts, requires that we initially learn contextual clues which speakers frequently use. Then, when we, as listeners, encounter unfamiliar words, we apply our knowledge of contextual clues by noting the meanings of familiar words which surround the unfamiliar words and determining whether or not they provide us with clues to the meanings of the unfamiliar words. There are two main types of contextual clues with which we should be familiar: semantic (word meaning) and syntactic (sentence structure) clues. Among the semantic clues are the following:

synonym clues (often signaled by *and*): Jim's dull, *lethargic*, and sluggish manner made us question the success of his recovery.

contrasting clues (often signaled by *but, not, although, however, nevertheless, instead,* and *rather*): Janet's spaghetti sauce has always been quite flavorful, but the sauce she made today is *insipid.*

description clues: Some animals are *herbivorous.* They feed chiefly on grasses, plants, and seeds.

example clues (often signaled by *for example, like, such as, in the way that,* and the pronouns *this, that, these,* and *those*): At their daughter's graduation party, the Chobots *regaled* the guests with a rock band, a fortune teller, and a delicious meal.

summary clues: At home, Susan willingly helps her younger siblings. At school, she actively participates in class discussions and activities. At work, she eagerly completes her tasks. Indeed, Susan's display of *alacrity* makes others envious of her.

explanation clues (often signaled by *that is, by, I mean, or, is, in other words,* and *in short*): The romance was *ephemeral*—that is, short-lived.

experience clues (relating one's own experiences to the context): His mouth was *agape* as he, standing within the Roman Colosseum, was filled with awe and wonder. (The listener has experienced this facial expression when he or she has been filled with awe and wonder.)

mood, intent, tone, or situation clues: Lisa's arguing, pleading, and threatening had no impact on changing her father's original decision; he remained *adamant* regarding his refusal to allow Lisa to work at the beach during the summer.

The second type of contextual clues is syntactic or sentence structure clues. Among these clues are those found in *sentence patterns* (such as in "Psoriasis is one example. . . .", *psoriasis* is a noun, *is* is a verb, *one* is an adjective, *example* is a noun); *inflectional endings* (such as in "He deferred. . . .", deferr*ed* signals a verb); *markers* (such as in "A heliotrope is. . . .", *a* signals a noun; in "After the neolithic period. . . .", *after* signals an adverb clause; in "She has retained. . . .", *has* signals a verb; and in "Between the cold photosphere and. . . .", *between* signals a prepositional phrase); and, possibly in oral sentences, pauses (such as in "An example of a predator—an animal that hunts and kills other animals for food—is a lion", the dashes of the written sentence represent pauses in an oral statement).

Although using contextual clues is generally recognized as being "the best single way of developing word power,"[32] we cannot doubt the effectiveness of a final way of improving our vocabularies: learning new words by having first-hand experiences which are associated with the words. For example, when we take a computer course, attend a computer exhibit, or operate a computer, we learn terms such as *interface, modem, cursor,* and *expansion slot.* Thus, by broadening our personal experiences and subjecting ourselves to a wide variety of listening experiences—especially experiences involving complex material which is more challenging than that to which we are generally accustomed, we can broaden our word power and therefore improve our comprehensive listening.

Additional Variables

Relationships between listening and many other variables have been investigated by listening scholars; however, many factors have contributed to the delay of precise conclusions regarding the variables that influence listening comprehension. Among these contributing factors are (1) there has been a lack of scientifically controlled experiments, (2) not enough is known about the validity and reliability of the listening tests utilized in the studies, and thus many of the "listening" tests may be measuring abilities other than listening, while many of the variables may involve measurement of the same general abilities, and (3) much of the research has not been coordinated and collated. Although these factors have prevented "conclusive" results, the following additional variables—as measured by statistical correlations[33]—currently appear to be slightly to moderately related to listening comprehension: *age* (with students gradually improving as they advance through school),[34] *intelligence* (with the estimated correlation being .46);[35] *motivation* (with subjects—who had been forewarned that recall tests would follow the presentation of material, promised monetary rewards for listening and recalling, and mentally prepared by the anticipatory sets created by the experimenter—scoring significantly higher on listening tests than those subjects who had not been forewarned, promised rewards, or mentally prepared);[36] *scholastic achievement* (with correlations ranging from .24 to .82);[37] *speaking ability* (with correlations ranging from .36 to .79);[38] *reading comprehension* (with the average correlation estimated at being about .53 by Erickson and .59 by Duker);[39] *verbal ability* (with correlations ranging from .37 to .76);[40] *language and study skills* (with correlations ranging from .25 to .67);[41] *organizational ability* (with correlations ranging from .36 to .53);[42] *rate of presentation* (to be discussed later in this chapter); and *cultural status* (with correlations ranging from .33 to .48).[43] The relationships between listening and the following variables are presently less conclusive than the variables previously discussed: *sex, personality characteristics, interest in the subject matter discussed, auditory acuity, experience in listening, speech training, notetaking ability, visibility of the speaker, the speaker's use of gestures, speaker effectiveness, souce credibility, difficulty of material, time of day, room temperature and ventilation, seating, position in family,* and *size of family.* As we can see, additional and more controlled research investigating the relationships between listening and these variables, as well as other variables, is greatly needed in order for us to better understand the variables involved in listening comprehension.

Skills Involved in Comprehensive Listening

Although at present we do not know all of the variables or all of the subskills involved in listening comprehension, scholars in the field of communication and related areas of study have provided us with several findings which, when put into practice, can enhance our listening comprehension.

Capitalizing on the Differential between Speech Speed and Thought Speed

Ralph G. Nichols, whose research in comprehensive listening pioneered the field, cautions that the efficient comprehensive listener should be careful not to waste the differential between speech speed and thought speed. As listeners, we can think about 500 words per minute while the normal speaking rate is about 125 to 150 words per minute. Thus, we may have close to 400 words of thinking time available to us each minute we are listening.

Because we can think so much faster than speakers can speak, we tend to "tune in" and "tune out" during the message; while we are "tuning out," we are attending to other stimuli. We can imagine the danger here when some other stimulus attracts more attention than the message; we then cease concentrating on the message. The efficient comprehensive listener will be certain to "tune in" with regularity; instead of attending to external and/or internal stimuli, he or she will actively use the spare thinking time by mentally paraphrasing (in his or her own words) what has been presented, relating the message content to what he or she already knows and/or has experienced, mentally reviewing and summarizing what has been presented, identifying and determining the relationship between/among main ideas, weighing the evidence used, applying points of support to his or her own life, predicting the speaker's next point and then confirming or negating the prediction, formulating questions, noting and assigning meaning to nonverbal messages being presented, and listening for what is not said. Nichols emphasizes the importance of our using our spare thinking time efficiently:

> Not capitalizing on thought speed is our greatest single handicap. The differential between thought speed and speech speed breeds false feelings of security and mental tangents. Yet, through listening training, this same differential can be readily converted into our greatest asset.[44]

A relatively new research technique may help the comprehensive listener reduce the time differential between speech speed and thought speed. Communication scholars have been studying the effects of compressed speech—speech that consists of increasing the word rate of a previously recorded message without essential alteration. The process was first applied by having the speaker speak more rapidly. It was then accomplished by speeding up the recorder. Next, a cut-and-splice method was employed. Now, material can be compressed electronically. Until 1950, most scholars believed that "increasing rate led to a decrease in listening efficiency."[45]

Recently, however, researchers have demonstrated that (1) speed of speech can be effectively doubled without impairing intelligibility[46] and that (2) speaking rates can be increased with 50 percent compression without loss of comprehension.[47] The optimal speaking rate for comprehension appears to be between 275 and 300 words per minute.[48]

Since we think much more rapidly than the normal conversational speech rate, it is evident that we can handle auditory input at a much faster rate; many recent studies have supported this view. Foulke, et al., studying the effect of compressed speech on the comprehension ability of 291 blind children, found that there was no significant loss of comprehension of messages recorded up to 275 words per minute.[49] It has also been found that sighted students benefit from using time-compressed speech. In 1974, Short, using a Syracuse University population of 90 students, found that subjects who used variable speed compressors saved significant amounts of time (an average time savings of 32 percent) and scored significantly higher on post-tests than those subjects who learned the same material at normal speed. In addition, 70 percent of those who used variable speech adapted to it quickly and liked listening at faster than normal rates.[50]

Currently, compressed speech is being used in many segments of society, including business, education, and public services. In industry, it has been found to be a cost effective tool. In addition to providing its users with a time-saving means to review recorded dictation, check recorded meetings, reports, and telephone answering tapes, and compile taped inventory records, it has been found to improve the concentration and comprehension of new employees when it has been utilized in training programs. In the field of education, it has led to substantial savings in time. Instructors can preview auditory material faster, media specialists can review media seminar tapes in less time, and students—as they listen to taped lecture material—can decrease their review time while they increase their comprehension ability. Still another educational application of compressed speech is its use in tutorial programs. Rome, who originated the use of speech compressors in the autotutorial program at Western Connecticut State College, believes speech compressors have a promising future:

> We can finally provide something effective for those students who do not learn best through the visual modality. With the introduction of lower cost rate-controlled recorders, we have a viable alternative for learning which may rival the printing press as a way of disseminating information.[51]

Law enforcement officers and hospital personnel, too, have found compressed speech useful. It can assist them in providing professional training, reviewing and previewing auditory data, checking logged calls and interviews, rapidly transferring information between shifts, and providing professional updating. The current use of compressed speech indicates that compressed speech offers widespread potential for application in improving the listening and learning of those involved in these as well as many other segments of society.[52]

The use of compressed speech has extended beyond business, education, and public services to television, radio, and video-tapes. Both television commercials and television programs are presently being time-compressed. An estimated one out of ten commercials is compressed,[53] generally by a subtle, barely perceptible 15 percent. Although 15 percent compression may not seem very significant to us, to advertisers it means cutting costs. For instance, if a 34 to 35-second commercial were aired during the 1983 Superbowl, it would have cost $414,000. The same commercial, run in 30 seconds, would have saved the advertiser $54,000. Not only do advertisers save money by compressing the rate of their commercials, but also they increase the attention and retention of their listeners if researchers in the advertising field can further substantiate the research findings of LaBarbera, Shoaf, and MacLachlan, who found that subjects who listened to (and viewed) commercials increased in speed by 25 percent had higher levels of attentional effort and greater recall two days later than did subjects who listened to (and viewed) commercials played at their regular speed.[54] Perhaps this comparison by Michael Klasco, director of research and development at Integrated Sound Systems, Incorporated, a New York time-compressor manufacturer, best explains the higher levels of attention energy: "If you're driving 30 m.p.h., you tend to daydream, but at 90 m.p.h. you pay attention."[55] Television programs, too, are being compressed throughout the country.[56] For example, *Chinatown* was compressed by a 10 percent speedup (cutting 11 minutes and 8 seconds) by CBS when it was aired in 1981, and Washington, D.C.'s WRC-TV daily shortens the *Muppet Show* by 1 minute while Houston's KHTV regularly shortens *Star Trek* and *Charlie's Angels* to allow three minutes of news each hour that these programs are aired. Furthermore, radio stations that play Top 40 songs often time-compress them, and video-tape production houses are compressing movies to fit onto 90-minute cassettes (rather than the more expensive 120-minute cassettes) for home use.[57]

Speech compressors or rate-controlled recorders are now readily available and fairly inexpensive, and they could offer you interesting demonstrations as to the possibilities of reducing time and improving listening comprehension. One speech controller is the VSC Speech Controller, also known as the Variable Speech Control tape recorder; weighing 4.3 pounds, this recorder is manufactured by the Variable Speech Control Corporation (VSC). In addition to including all of the features of a standard recorder, it has a slide lever (labeled VSC rate) graduated from 0.6 to 2.5. These numbers, indicating the amount of slowdown or speedup of the tape, allow the user to control the playback rate of any standard audio cassette without distortion of pitch or creation of a "chipmunk" or "Donald Duck" effect; that is, a tape originally recorded at 150 words per minute (wpm) could be played from 90 wpm (if the slide lever were placed at 0.6) up to and including 375 wpm (if the lever were placed at 2.5). VSC manufactures the VSC Model C-4 Soundpacer, which is a compact, portable, battery-operated model that includes all of the features of a standard recorder as well as speed control graduated from 0.8 to 2, pitch control, and a microcassette adaptor.[58] Another speech compressor, particularly designed for use by the blind and other print-handicapped persons, is the Library of Congress's Cassette-Book Machine—C-80 Series. The C-80 is portable and provides both time compression and expansion. By means of the AmBiChron® Pitch Restorer, the C-80 maintains natural pitch over a playback speed range from less than 0.8 normal speed to above 2.5 normal speed. The AmBiChron integrated circuit is available commercially and can be used for automatic pitch restoration over a much wider range of time compression and expansion than is provided in the C-80.[59] A third speech compressor is the Lexicon Model 1200 Audio Time Compressor, manufactured by Lexicon, Incorporated; this "broadcast quality" compressor allows the user to play back recorded audio or video tapes and film at variable speeds ranging from 200 percent to 50 percent of the initial recording time without altering original pitch.[60] Each of these compressors holds much promise for the individual who wishes to become a more efficient comprehensive listener.[61]

Despite the technological advances in compressed speech, however, its usefulness to the general listener remains limited. Just as speed readers have difficulty applying the speed-reading techniques to difficult technical material, "speed listeners" report little carry-over to complex listening situations.

Listening for Main Ideas

One important skill which can help to enhance our efficiency in using the speech speed-thought speed differential is knowing for what we should listen. Several scholars suggest that the efficient listener listens to acquire the main ideas from the message; he or she should concentrate primarily on the main points rather than on the supporting data. If you consider that we tend to be able to recall—at a later time—no more than 25 percent of what we listen to today, it is evident that we should strive to concentrate on understanding the key concepts of a message rather than the details which exemplify the concepts.

There are several ways we can become more adept at identifying the main idea(s) of an oral message, provided that the speaker clearly knows his or her purpose and direction. We must strive to identify the main idea of the entire message as well as the main concepts presented within the message. To help us identify the principal idea of the entire message (known also as the central idea or thesis statement), we must become aware of the positions where most senders place the main idea. It may be stated in the title, stated shortly after the introduction has been presented, repeated throughout the speech (since senders often repeat important concepts), stated in the summary of the speech, or subtly implied (suggested) in the speech as a whole and recognized only after we have listened to the complete message. If the main idea is stated, we must learn to identify transitions which speakers use when they are introducing or discussing the main idea; some of these transitions are the following: "I want to make one impression on you, and that is. . . ."; "Today, we are going to discuss. . . ."; "Simply stated, the issue is. . . ."; "Let us today examine why. . . ."; "Today, we will be covering. . . ."; "There are three methods that we. . . ."; "Our subject this evening is. . . ."; "And so we can conclude that. . . ."; "In conclusion, then, I want you to understand that. . . ."; "To summarize, . . ."; "In summing up, we must remember that. . . ."; and "As can be seen, . . ."

In addition to knowing where the main idea is often expressed and what transitions are frequently used to introduce a main idea, efficient listeners must also know what nonverbal behavioral changes speakers often use when they are stating a main idea. If we become skilled in listening to and watching for these changes in rate, volume, pitch, bodily movements, gestures, eye contact, and other nonverbal cues, we will be able to identify more readily the main idea of a message. Moreover, when we are identifying the main idea, we must exercise caution that we not make it too broad (by including more than is in the message) or too narrow (by including only some concepts); we must be specific, yet comprehensive enough to include all of the relevant concepts that have been presented.

When identifying the principal concepts within a message (those concepts which are used to establish the main idea of a speech), we must have knowledge of many general organizational patterns. Among these patterns are the following:

Unfolding

Introduction
Statement of thesis sentence
Statement of first point
Discussion of first point
Statement of second point
Discussion of second point
Statement of third point
Discussion of third point, etc.
Conclusion

One-point

Introduction
Statement of thesis sentence
Example
Example
Example, etc.
Conclusion

Partitioning

Introduction
Statement of thesis sentence
Restatement of thesis and division
Statement of first point
Discussion of first point
Restatement of first point
Statement of second point
Discussion of second point
Restatement of second point
Statement of third point
Discussion of third point
Restatement of third point, etc.
Conclusion—Summary[62]

Furthermore, we must be aware of the previously mentioned nonverbal cues and numerous other transitions, such as "first," "along with," "not only . . . but also," "finally," "next in importance," "in addition to this," "on the other hand," "also," "following this step is," "a somewhat similar method is," "above all," "of even more importance," "in connection with this," "equally important," and "together with this." If we train ourselves to listen primarily for main ideas/concepts, we will not become so preoccupied with facts and details that we overlook the main ideas; we must be first idea listeners and then fact/detail listeners.

Listening for Significant Details

After we have become proficient in listening for main ideas, we should then develop the skill of listening for significant details which the speaker uses to support his or her main ideas. These details may be in the form of facts, examples, statistics, restatements, anecdotes, personal incidents, analogies, references to reliable sources, descriptions, contrasts, definitions. As we listen for essential details, we must again be aware of transitions which indicate that details are following. Some of these transitions are "for example," "to illustrate this point," "this can be seen by," "for instance," "by way of illustration," "that is," "to explain," "in other words," "comparable to," "the fact is," "on the contrary," "according to," "namely," "to be more specific," "a case in point is," and "to describe." By recognizing these transitional words, we can more readily identify supporting details. We must, however, distinguish between those details which are relevant and those which are irrelevant to the main ideas that the speaker is presenting, and we must separate what we have learned in the past from what we are listening to now if we hope to be accurate in our listening. Identifying the main ideas and supporting details and understanding the interrelationships between the ideas and details will aid us in assigning more reliable meanings to the sender's message.

Drawing Justifiable Inferences

Another skill which the comprehensive listener should develop is the ability to draw justifiable inferences. Inferences (implications) are data that are not stated but are implied. Efficient listeners will not only listen to what is explicitly stated but also listen for what is implicitly suggested. Because each listener draws his or her own inferences, they are very personal and subject to error. Weaver stresses the importance of making inferences and the difficulty of separating personal meanings or interpretations from the speaker's meanings: "It is likely that the most important part of our communication is the part we infer. And yet we do this through our screen of personal biases, our needs, and our affective states."[63] The more we know about ourselves and our personal biases, needs, and emotions, the less likely we are to make errors in drawing inferences. The following steps will help us in drawing justifiable inferences:

1. Fully understand the stated ideas.
2. Reason by logical thinking to the inferred idea.

3. Determine the fairness or justice of the inferred idea.
4. Base reasoning on the idea stated by the sender; do not be misled by your personal opinions, feelings, biases, or "what seems reasonable" but is not stated by the communicator.

Let us illustrate how we can apply these four steps when we are listening. Suppose we hear a woman who is running for county executive make this statement about her opponent: "How can you think of voting for him? He didn't even attend his own mother's funeral!" Our first step is to understand fully the stated idea, which—in our example—is in the form of a question and a statement. The question is why or for what reason(s) are we thinking of voting for her opponent; the statement is that her opponent was not present at his mother's funeral. Once we fully understand the stated idea, we should then apply the second step: reason by logical thinking to the inferred idea. In our example, the woman running for office wants us to vote for her; she does not want us to vote for her opponent. She wants to give us a reason for not voting for him. She *hopes* that we will infer, from her stated idea, that if her opponent did not care enough about his mother to attend her funeral, he certainly would not be responsive to the needs and concerns of us, most of whom are strangers. She *hopes* that if we draw the inference she wants us to draw, we will not want him to be our representative, and therefore we will not vote for him.

Our next step is to determine whether the inference we have drawn is justifiable or fair. We have drawn the inference that she had hoped we would, but we do not have to accept what she silently said. Is the critical issue regarding her opponent's qualifications for county executive whether or not he attended his mother's funeral? Regardless of our personal feelings concerning the manner in which a person should cope with the death of a family member, a person's presence or absence at the funeral of a family member should not be the critical issue upon which we base our voting preference. We do not know, in fact, that he did not attend his mother's funeral. Nor do we know why he was not present at the funeral, if he were not present. He could have been someplace where he could not have been reached, he could have been a prisoner of war or a hostage, or he could be a person who prefers remembering a loved one as she or he was in life rather than in death. If we carefully analyze the justification of each inference we draw, as we have carefully analyzed this one, we will become more efficient listeners. Hopefully, this example has helped you to understand how to apply the first three steps that assist listeners in drawing justifiable inferences.

Let us now illustrate how listeners can apply the fourth step: base our reasoning on the stated idea rather than on personal views. Suppose that we later hear the woman's opponent speak. In his speech he makes the following statement: "I spent the first fifteen years of my life in the slums and on welfare, and now I'm running for county executive." He *hopes* that we will infer from this statement that because he is a man who has overcome his poor beginnings and has become a strong, determined leader despite his early hardships, he can help us overcome our problems. However, this time we are misled by our personal views, and our personal meanings lead us to draw these inferences: Here is a man who, having been on welfare himself, will raise our taxes in order to provide more revenue for welfare assistance programs; then, he will provide more handouts to all the lazy, no-good people in our country. Because we often allow our personal views to be the basis of our reasoning, as we did in this illustration, we frequently make errors when drawing inferences.

Being aware of these four steps and practicing them should assist us in drawing justifiable inferences when the speaker does not explicitly state his or her position, specific details, or relationships. Such steps, then, can enhance our comprehension of the overall message.

Being an Effective Notetaker

Though few studies have correlated notetaking and efficient listening behavior, notetaking, when done properly, can be valuable to listener comprehension in many ways. One value is that notetaking can improve our ability to concentrate in lecture settings as well as in public listening situations. Experiments indicate that the behavioral involvement required for notetaking increases our attention to the message and thus increases the probability that we will be able to retrieve the message content later.[64] A second value is that notetaking can motivate us to take the initiative in putting the message content into our long-term memory system. To facilitate this storing process, we must make the message content meaningful by rehearsing it and linking it to our existing store of information. A third value is that notetaking tends to make us more aware of various communication aspects, such as organizational patterns (or lack of them), transitions, main ideas, supporting details, relevant (as well as irrelevant) content, etc. Still another value is that notetaking can "lock in print" information which we may need to refer to at a later time. Shortly after we have taken our notes, we should review them, clarify them, add to them, note any points about which we need additional information and obtain that information (from the sender or other sources) as soon as possible, summarize the notes in a brief sentence or two, list any ideas which may have come to us after we had listened to the presentation, and, if necessary, restructure them so that they will be more meaningful to us now as well as at a later time. Reviewing (rehearsing) our notes will also aid us in retaining the information more permanently. One recommended method of reviewing notes is the Cornell System. This system requires that listeners take notes on main ideas in a right-hand "Record" column, and then after the speaker's completion of the message, they summarize the recorded data by jotting down only key words and phrases in the left-hand "Recall" column. Shortly thereafter users of this notetaking method cover the right-hand column, and then, using only the key words and phrases, they attempt to reconstruct the right-hand column as they recite the message content in their own words; later reviews are conducted in the same manner.[65] This system of reviewing can assist us in retaining message content.

There are several points we should consider when we take notes. The first is that we should determine whether or not we need to take notes. Are we going to use the material presented immediately? Can we retain the information without taking notes? Do we have high concentration abilities? If the answer is *yes* to these questions, we probably do not need to take notes. If, however, we must retain the information for future reference, it is recommended that we take notes in a manner that will enhance rather than detract from our listening. Secondly, we should be physically, mentally, and psychologically prepared to take notes. Physically, we should have pen and paper ready, we should have a firm surface on which to write, we should be sitting upright, and we should be giving our attention to the speaker. Mentally, we should, prior to the listening situation, obtain background information about the topic and the speaker. Psychologically, we should have a positive, open-minded attitude toward the communicative situation. Also, we should not begin taking notes too soon after the speaker has begun his or her presentation. However, if the speaker names (or lists on the board) the main ideas to be discussed under the principal topic and mentions the order in which they will be presented, taking brief introductory notes may be useful as a check to see whether our main ideas correspond with those initially designated by the speaker. Further, we can use the introductory notes to determine the relationships between/among the main ideas as well as the relationship between the main topic and the main ideas. On the other hand, if the speaker does not introduce the main ideas at the beginning of the presentation, we should wait several minutes until we have determined the speaker's organizational pattern, or his or her lack of an organizational pattern, and then we must adjust our notetaking style to the speaker's style of presentation.

If we are to be good listeners, we must be flexible notetakers. When we do take notes, we must not take them in a mechanical fashion for the sole purpose of external storage; our task is not accomplished unless internal rehearsal of the message accompanies the act of notetaking. In addition, while we are taking notes, we should make them as brief as possible so that they will not interfere with our listening, phonetically record unfamiliar words, note any points we missed and—rather than distracting another listener to ask him or her about the point we missed—wait until the speaker has finished before we inquire about the point we missed, set aside a section to list any word, phrase, idea, etc., which evokes an emotional reaction so that we can dismiss it until we have completed the listening experience, and jot down any question(s) that we may have as we are listening. Finally, we must determine what method of notetaking we should use, for there are several methods.

Probably the most commonly-used method of notetaking is the outlining method. The strengths of this system are that notes are neat, organized, easily filed, useful for review, and helpful in developing our ability to coordinate items of equal rank and subordinate items of less importance. There are, however, two major weaknesses to this system: the system is impractical if the speech does not follow some definite plan of organization (and less than one half of the speeches we hear are carefully organized), and listeners often become so preoccupied with the symmetry and the mechanics (indentations, capitalizations, I, A, i, a, etc.) that they become confused and lose important concepts and supporting details of the message. Before we begin to outline our notes, we must listen for several minutes so that we can detect the structure; if the speaker's material is organized, then we may choose this method for our notetaking. However, if the speaker's material is unorganized, we must choose another method. Remember Nichols's advice: "There are few things more frustrating than to try to outline an unoutlinable speech."[66] When we do choose to outline our notes, we must be skilled in identifying the central ideas, noting the significant details, understanding interrelationships between ideas and details, recognizing which ideas are important and which ones are of little concern, noting transitional devices, and knowing well the mechanics of outlining. (See fig. 6.1 for a sample of the outlining method of notetaking.)

Another method of notetaking is the précis method. When we use this system, we listen for several minutes, we mentally summarize what is being said, and then—at widely-spaced time intervals—we record a summary of what we have heard by writing a short paragraph or a one- or two-sentence abstract. We repeat these three steps until the message has been completed. The strengths of this system are that our notes are brief, easily filed, and useful for review; also, this method can be used for both organized and disorganized messages. One major weakness is that this system requires too much writing at one time. During the periods of writing, the speaker goes on, and the listeners are losing portions of the message. A second weakness is that significant details are often slighted or omitted. Still another weakness is that often we may not have time to write a complete précis; if we only have enough time to write down a key word or phrase, we should—as soon as possible after the speech—expand our notes so that they will be more meaningful to us when we review them later. If we use this method of notetaking, we must be skilled in recognizing the common structure of most concepts (with the speaker going from the main idea to supporting details—the deductive approach—or going from supporting details to the main idea—the inductive approach); recognizing transitional devices which are signals that a main point follows ("More important than . . . is . . . ," "Now that we have considered . . . , let's look at a second consideration," "Another main point is . . . ," etc.); knowing when to listen, when to mentally summarize, and when to write the abstract (at the end of spoken units of thought); and knowing what to include in our précis (the thesis sentence, generalizations or main concepts, and the final appeal which the speaker makes). (See fig. 6.2 for a sample of the précis method of notetaking.)

A third method of notetaking is the fact versus principle method. When using this system, we divide our paper vertically in half. In the right-hand column, we list the important principles (main ideas) and number them in Roman numerals; in the left-hand column, we list the important facts (verifiable supporting data) which we may need to recall later and number them in Arabic numbers. If a

Figure 6.1. The outlining method of notetaking.

Notetaking Methods

I. Outlining—perhaps most common
   A. Strengths
      1. Neat
      2. Organized
      3. Fileable
      4. Reviewable
      5. Helpful in skill development
         a. Of coordinating items
         b. Of subordinating items
   B. Weaknesses
      1. Impractical for disorganized speaker
      2. Distractible for notetaker preoccupied with format
   C. Preparation
      1. Listening to detect speaker's structure
      2. Choosing appropriate notetaking style
   D. Skills needed
      1. Identifying central ideas
      2. Noting significant details
      3. Understanding interrelationships between/among ideas and details
      4. Distinguishing between/among important and unimportant items
      5. Recognizing transitional devices
      6. Knowing mechanics of outlining

II. Précis method

III. Fact versus principle method

IV. Mapping method

Figure 6.2. The precise method of notetaking.

Steps include listening, mentally processing input, and periodically recording brief summaries/abstracts (précis) of input.

Strengths include brief, fileable, and reviewable notes and useability for all message structures.

Weaknesses include losing incoming data while writing, slighting significant details, and lacking time to complete précis.

Skills needed include recognizing inductive and deductive structures and transitional devices; knowing when to complete the three steps; and knowing what to include in précis.

question arises as we listen, we state it at the bottom of the appropriate column. The strengths of this system are that the notes are brief and easily filed; also, this system is especially workable for disorganized messages, it flows naturally as the speaker develops the message, and it provides a clear means for recalling key concepts as they were developed. The system also has weaknesses; often our understanding of the basic structure of the message is lost, and it is often difficult to distinguish between facts and principles. If we use this method of notetaking, we must be skilled in distinguishing between supporting data and main ideas, differentiating between relevant and irrelevant data, understanding interrelationships between main ideas and details, recognizing transitional devices, and noting a possible interrelationship among the principles. Finally, it is crucial that shortly after the message has been completed, we structure our notes so that we can give order to the speaker's message (if it were disorganized). (See fig. 6.3 for a sample of the fact versus principle method of notetaking.)

A fourth method of notetaking is mapping, which is organizing our notes in a visual manner resembling a map. Using this method requires that we list each main idea, as it is presented, in the center of our paper (in the center, or, depending on the number of main ideas presented, to the far left or right of the center and to the immediate left or right of center) and then circle each listed main idea. As significant details are presented, we write them on lines which we connect to the main idea which they support. Finally, we place minor details on lines that we connect to the significant details which the minor details further amplify. The strengths of this system are many: the notes are brief, easily filed, useful for review, and helpful in our ability to coordinate items of equal rank with subordinate items of less importance; the system is useful for both organized and disorganized messages but is especially workable for disorganized messages or messages whose organizational structures do not emerge early in the speakers' presentations; it is a particularly effective system for the visually-oriented notetaker; it allows the notetaker to utilize actively both his/her left and right hemispheres since it involves analytical, verbal, visual, and creative processes; and its visual images aid in the notetaker's retention of the information recorded. Although notetakers who are proficient in mapping find few disadvantages to the system, two possible weaknesses should be noted. Listeners may become too preoccupied with the creative process of drawing the "map" and omit important concepts and supporting details, or listeners may spend too much time adjusting their papers in order to list the supporting and minor details. If we use this method of notetaking, we must be skilled in distinguishing between supporting data and main ideas, understanding the interrelationships between main ideas and details, and recognizing transitional devices.[67] (See fig. 6.4 for a sample of the mapping method of notetaking.)

Figure 6.3. The fact versus principle method of notetaking.

Facts

1. Divide paper into two vertical columns.
2. Label left-hand column *facts.*
3. Label right-hand column *principles.*
4. List important to-be-remembered facts (verifiable supporting data) in left-hand column.
5. Number facts in Arabic numbers.
6. List important to-be-remembered principles (key ideas) in right-hand column.
7. Number principles in Roman numerals.
8. List any question that arises at the bottom of the appropriate column.
9. Notes are brief.
10. Notes are fileable.
11. Method is quite suitable for disorganized messages.
12. Method flows naturally as speaker develops message.
13. Method aids user in recalling key concepts as speaker developed them.
14. Basic structure of message may be lost.
15. Distinguishing between facts and principles may be difficult.
16. User must distinguish between supporting details and main ideas.
17. User must differentiate between relevant and irrelevant data.
18. User must understand interrelationships between main ideas and details.
19. User must recognize transitional devices.
20. User must note possible interrelationships between/among principles.
21. If necessary, user should give structure/order to notes after message has been completed.

Are my notes brief enough?
Should I restructure my notes in outlining form?
Should I indicate the interrelationship between facts and principles by placing the number of each fact under the principle that the fact supports? (Yes, I have done so.)

Principles

I. This notetaking method follows a specific format.
(1, 2, 3)

II. Users of this notetaking method follow specific procedures.
(4, 5, 6, 7, 8)

III. This notetaking method has recognized strengths.
(9, 10, 11, 12, 13)

IV. This notetaking method has recognized weaknesses.
(14, 15)

V. The user of this notetaking method must possess specific listening skills.
(16, 17, 18, 19, 20)

VI. There is a follow-up step to this notetaking method.
(21)

Figure 6.4. The mapping method of notetaking.

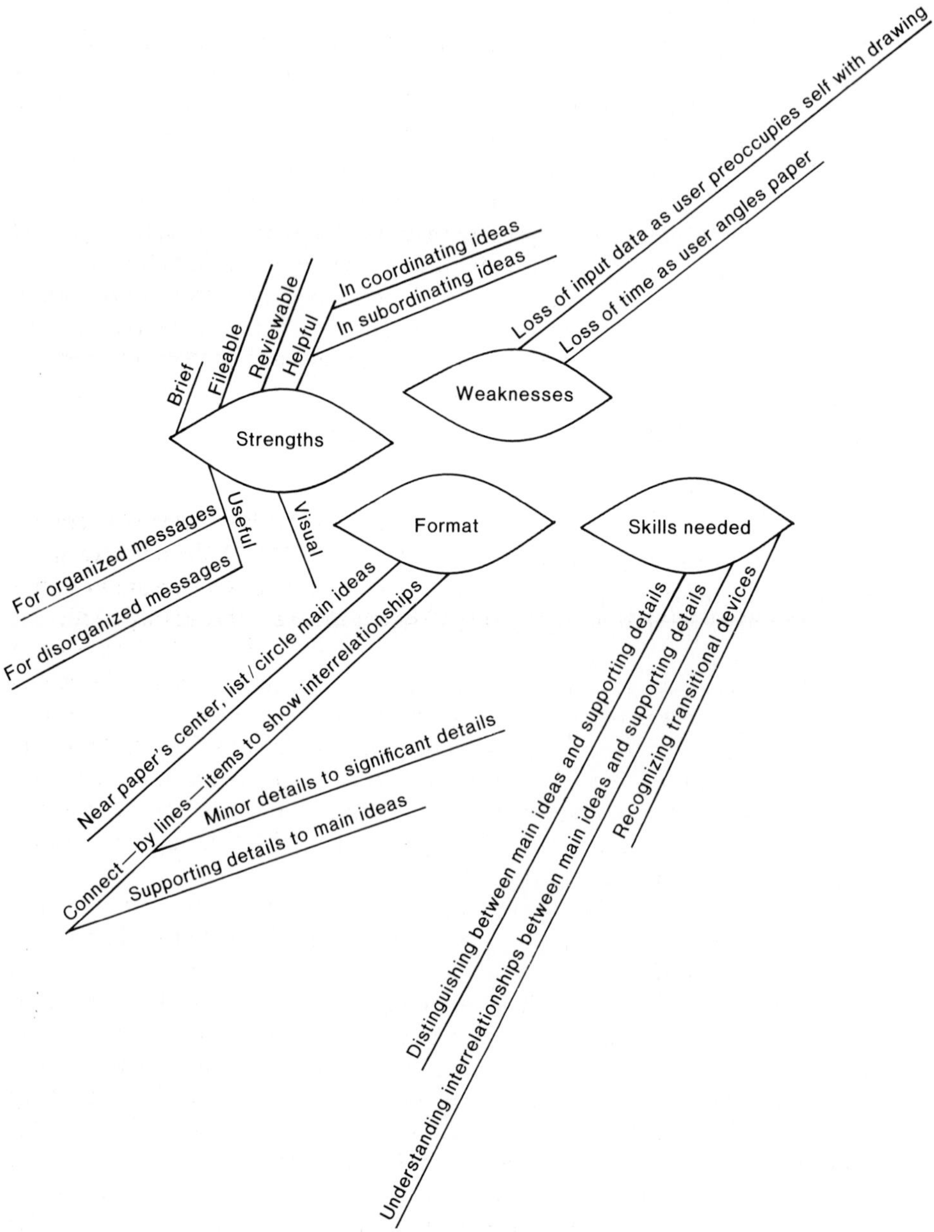

Recalling Items in a Sequence

Another skill that listening scholars frequently recommend for proficiency in comprehensive listening is the ability to recall items in a sequence. As listeners, we often need to recall simple sequences when we are orally given phone numbers, route directions, shopping lists, names of new acquaintances, lists of tasks, dates of upcoming events, addresses, and numerous other data. A typical example of a situation in which listeners need to utilize this ability can be found in the most widely-used listening test, the *Brown-Carlsen Listening Comprehension Test*. Brown and Carlsen include *immediate recall* as one of the five listening skills that their test measures. One of their test items in Form AM is the following: "In the statement, 'Send three boxtops with your name and address and 20 cents to Box 24, Denver 18, Colorado, to receive the special gift offer,' the *number of cents* to be enclosed is ____ ?"[68] As we look at this example and recall similar examples from our daily lives, we become aware of the importance of being able to recall items in a sequence. In addition to attending carefully to the sequential stimuli, we can utilize appropriate memory techniques (discussed earlier in this chapter) to aid us in developing this skill.

Following Oral Directions

A skill that is closely related to sequential ordering and is considered necessary for comprehensive listeners to develop is the ability to follow oral directions. Lundsteen includes this skill in a list of comprehensive skills which are most frequently mentioned in listening literature.[69] Also, Brown and Carlsen include this skill as one of the five listening skills which their test measures.[70] Moreover, the Speech Communication Association has included this skill in its list of minimal competencies in speaking and listening for high school graduates.[71] Our need to develop this skill can readily be seen when we consider how frequently we are required to follow oral directions. We often need to apply this skill when we perform job tasks, order items introduced on the radio or television, perform household maintenance tasks, exercise, play a game unfamiliar to us, apply a medical treatment, and in numerous other activities.

Not following oral directions in these as well as other areas can be costly to us and to others. For example, a friend of ours asked his wife to videotape *An Officer and a Gentleman* one evening. Having given her directions on how to record the televised movie without recording the commercials, he went to his business meeting. Two days later when he sat down to view the movie, he found that she had only recorded the commercials. Neither did another friend, John, follow directions well. John was told to buy ten fifty-cent combination lottery tickets for his boss. Rather than purchasing combination tickets, John bought straight tickets, one of which was 572, and the winning number that day was 752. These two examples are minor compared to what another friend who is the owner of an industrial insulation company encountered. *Not wanting* a particular job that was estimated to cost $1,500,000, the owner decided that the best way to be on record for bidding the job but not being awarded the contract was to overprice the company's bid. Thus, he told one of his estimators to bid $1,800,000. Rather than bidding $1,800,000, the estimator bid $1,080,000. Consequently, the job was given to our friend's company, and the company lost an estimated $420,000. Whether the listener be an airline pilot, a medical surgeon, or—in our examples—a wife or employee, the problem is still the same: we often make costly errors because we do not listen carefully to oral directions.

To develop this skill, we must apply much of what we have learned to do when we develop the previously discussed skill—recalling items in a sequence. However, this new skill—one that, too, can be developed through our use of memory aids—often requires us to recall sentences and longer phrases rather than short phrases and words. We must carefully attend to the oral stimuli; by concentrating intensely, we can insure that the oral directions will be stored in our LTM. Also, practice in improving our concentration ability as we listen to oral directions can aid us in becoming more efficient in this skill.

Formulating Meaningful Questions

A final skill useful to the comprehensive listener is that of asking questions. On the surface, asking questions does not appear to be a listening skill; however, Lundsteen has found that *to formulate simple questions* is frequently included in listening scholars' lists of important comprehensive listening skills.[72] When we consider that the goal of comprehensive listening is to understand the sender's message, we realize that if we ask a sender to clarify a point which we find confusing, which we find inconsistent with what we already know, or which we believe can be interpreted differently, we demonstrate that we are sharing the responsibility for accurate communication; thus, we are increasing the chance of reaching our goal of understanding.

But how often do we ask questions when we wish to have a point clarified or when we need additional information? Patterson and Cosgrove, investigating the frequency with which children ranging from preschoolers to fourth graders asked questions when they needed more information, found that only fourth graders spontaneously asked questions. The researchers have suggested that "although active, effective listening may often require students to ask questions, teachers may inadvertently foster the belief that good listening requires listeners to remain silent."[73] Patterson further stresses that failure to ask questions is not limited to elementary students; she has also found that few students ask questions in the courses she teaches at the University of Virginia. When she surveyed the students in her Introductory Child Psychology course, she found that although 94 percent of the students admitted not having understood something presented in class at least once or twice, 70 percent said they had never asked a question in class. Among their reasons for not asking questions were "fear of looking stupid and a desire not to make themselves conspicuous."[74] The fear of looking stupid or appearing ignorant is frequently a listener's rationale for not asking a question. This fear is particularly strong when the listener is greatly influenced by peer pressure and/or when the listener perceives the speaker's respect and liking for him or her as being important. However, if the listener would realize that question-asking is indicative of interest and a desire to learn and that the only "dumb" question is the one that was never asked, he or she would probably dispel the fear of appearing ignorant as a reason for not questioning. Two other reasons which listeners frequently give for not questioning are that they are too proud or too confused to know what question to ask. Pride should be discarded for the same reasons that fear should be dispelled. Confusion, however, should be confronted honestly; the listener should admit confusion by stating, "I'm confused about the last point you made (or how the example relates to the main idea or what the second main idea has to do with the topic of discussion, etc.)." Still another reason why listeners may not ask questions is that the sender does not provide a climate which is conducive to questioning. Many teachers, parents, bosses, etc., create a feeling of unapproachability when they respond to listeners' questions in the following ways: Teacher to student—"Can't you understand plain English?"; parent to child: "No, I don't know why the dish ran away with the spoon! Now go out and play and quit asking such stupid questions!"; boss to employees at the end of a staff meeting: "None of you have any questions, do you?" Such responses definitely affect our willingness to ask these persons questions. Nevertheless, if we have a sincere desire to become more effective comprehensive listeners, we must put aside our pride or discomfort and ask questions when we do not understand.

Once we have developed the willingness to ask questions, we also must learn when, how often, and how to ask them. We should wait until the sender (whether it be a speaker, a boss, or a close friend) has completed his or her message before we ask questions; often, we interrupt (or wish to interrupt) someone so that we can ask a question prematurely, whereas, if we had waited for the sender to finish, the sender would have answered our question in the course of his or her message. The frequency with which we should ask questions lies somewhere between a car going 75 miles per hour and a car that is out of gas. Most of us know someone who interrupts to question much too often (and probably perceives questioning as a substitute for listening rather than questioning as a follow-up to listening), and most of us know someone who questions so rarely that we wonder whether he or she is even interested in what we are saying. Also, we should not ask questions that are irrelevant or distracting. Does it really matter whether we saw a furniture truck in front of our friend's house on Tuesday or Wednesday when our friend is describing his or her newly acquired chairs and couch? The manner in which we ask questions, too, is important. Hayakawa believes that good listeners ask questions that "avoid all implications (whether in tone of voice or wording) of skepticism or challenge or hostility. They must clearly be motivated by curiosity about the speaker's view."[75] Using a condescending or angry tone or asking a question that is "loaded" or is embarrassing to the speaker should not be a part of effective listeners' communication behavior. Hayakawa further states that the most useful kind of question for clarification may be one phrased in this manner:

When we ask a question, we must be willing to listen to the answer.
Photo by Robert Tocha.

" 'I am going to restate in my words what I think you mean. Then would you mind telling me if I've understood you correctly?' "[76] Finally, when we ask a question, we must be willing to listen to the answer, even if we disagree with it or if the answer takes much longer than we had hoped it would, because, after all, we ask questions so that we can increase our understanding of the sender's message.

A Recommended Approach for Improving Understanding

We would like to conclude this chapter on comprehensive listening by describing an approach that will help us check our understanding of a sender's message. The need to test the quality of our understanding has been stressed by many people who deal with helping others to communicate more effectively. Carl Rogers, a well-known psychotherapist, believes that the major barrier to interpersonal communication is our tendency to react to a highly emotional statement by evaluating it from our own frame of reference. To avoid this barrier, he proposes that we listen with understanding; that is, we try to peceive the expressed message from the sender's frame of reference.[77] Hayakawa stresses that understanding should also be our goal when we attend a conference; he points out that "too often, the fact that misunderstanding exists is not apparent until deeper misunderstandings have already occurred because of the original one."[78] Most of us have attended business conferences, civic meetings, or social events where we have listened to a heated discussion involving two people who were not discussing the same issue. The discussion starts with Mrs. Fleming making a statement that Mr. Burr hears differently than Mrs. Fleming intended. Mr. Burr tries to refute what he thought Mrs. Fleming said. Not understanding Mr. Burr's protest, Mrs. Fleming defends her original message with further statements. Mr. Burr then interprets these statements in the light of the original message that he misunderstood, and he responds by moving further away from Mrs. Fleming's original statement. The discussion becomes more and more heated, and the comprehensive listener's goal of understanding becomes more and more unreachable. Supporting Rogers's view, Hayakawa suggests that we can avoid such entanglements if we engage in "entering actively and imaginatively into the other fellow's situation and trying to understand a frame of reference different from your own."[79] Two others who recognize the importance of checking our understanding are Edelson and Venema, who help married couples ease their communication problems. Edelson, a University of Wisconsin social scientist, believes that accuracy is the one communication ingredient that is really important. When recommending basic steps toward improved communication, he cautions, "Make sure everything you said was accurate and it was understood . . . it's okay to ask questions if they [*sic*] understood what you were saying."[80] He further stresses that being accurate is the responsibility of both the speaker and the listener, who has to ask, "Am I hearing that right?"[81] Venema, a clinical psychologist, recommends the following approach for developing better understanding:

> An active, involved listener does a lot of talking. He uses words to "mirror back" what he thinks the other is communicating. This approach permits correction of errors. It also sends a message back to the speaker: "This person is really trying to hear what I'm saying."[82]

Each of these specialists we have just cited recognizes the need for improved understanding, and each has recommended certain guidelines we can use to test the quality of our understanding; however, Rogers's approach is probably the one that is most frequently recommended by communication scholars.

Rogers's approach is one that we highly recommend. Although we also discuss aspects of this approach in the chapter on therapeutic listening, we do not believe that its use is limited to therapeutic situations. Certainly, it is an approach that has much value in comprehensive listening as well since understanding is the listener's goal. There is one rule that must be observed when we are using this approach: " 'Each person can speak up for himself only *after* he has first restated the ideas and feelings of the previous speaker accurately and to that speaker's satisfaction.' "[83] Simply stated, the approach involves two people engaging in a dialogue; as the two discuss some item of interest, the listener must restate what he or she thinks the speaker has said to the speaker's satisfaction before the listener (who then becomes the speaker) can contribute a further idea to the discussion. This will be a slow process, but it is an excellent approach for improving understanding, which is the goal of the comprehensive listener.

SUMMARY

In this chapter, we have examined comprehensive listening—listening for understanding. We have illustrated that comprehensive listening plays a significant role in all phases of our lives and that many variables—including memory, concentration, size of vocabulary, age, intelligence, motivation, scholastic achievement, speaking ability, reading comprehension, verbal ability, language and study skills, rate of presentation, and cultural status—appear to be slightly to moderately related to listening comprehension; however, we have stressed that additional research investigating these variables, as well as others,must be conducted in order for us to determine the specific variables which are most directly related to listening comprehension. Additionally, we have listed, discussed, and suggested ways to improve eight skills which appear to be involved in comprehensive listening: capitalizing on the differential between speech speed and thought speed, listening for main ideas and significant details, drawing justifiable inferences, being an effective notetaker, recalling items in a sequence, following oral directions, and formulating meaningful questions. Finally, we have described an approach that will help us to improve our understanding and, thus, help us to reach our goal as comprehensive listeners.

SUGGESTED ACTIVITIES

1. Try deliberately to improve your concentration ability in the classes that are giving you the most difficulty. Keep a log of your concentration habits. List the times you started listening and the times you found yourself "tuning out." Also, record why you stopped listening and what you found yourself thinking about when you realized you were not concentrating on the class discussion or lecture. Keep this log for a certain period of time; then turn it in to the instructor.[84]
2. Prepare a statement which includes at least one word with which many college students would be unfamiliar. Read your statement to the class (only once); the listeners are to identify the unfamiliar word(s) and guess at its/their meaning(s). When a student guesses correctly, that student is to explain what contextual clues led him or her to make the proper guess. When a student guesses incorrectly, another student should be given the opportunity to define the word. Students are then to discuss how the size of one's vocabulary affects listening comprehension.[85]
3. Five or six class members, assuming fictitious names and backgrounds, will form a receiving line. Other class members, designated as guests, will go through the receiving line. Each member of the receiving line will introduce each guest to the person standing next to him or her by stating the name of the guest, together with the name of and some background information on the person next in line. Each guest will state that person's name and comment on the given background information.
4. Class members will roleplay a situation involving three participants. One will be assigned the role of foreman or boss while two will be assigned the role of new employees. The foreman will teach a set of new procedures to the first

new employee. That employee will then teach the procedures to the second new employee. The rest of the students will note the problems involved in following (and perhaps giving) oral directions.

5. Several class members will be designated as senders. They will prepare specific, step-by-step directions for completing some simple task such as putting staples into a stapler, opening a window, opening a bottle. Each sender will be paired with a receiver. One at a time, each listener will follow, in front of the class, the sender's directions. The sender may not add directions which he or she does not have written down, and the receiver may not do anything that she or he has not been told to do; the receiver may not communicate with the sender, either. Participants will then discuss how this exercise has helped them to discover the difficulty of giving and following oral directions accurately.[86]
6. Conduct a survey to determine the memory techniques which others use to remember information. Share your findings with the class.
7. Discuss how the following quotation from Walter Kolesnik can be applied to improved listening and remembering: "The intensity of our interest in an activity as well as the amount of effort that we expend on it depends on our feeling of personal involvement in that activity."[87]
8. A member of the class will speak for two or three minutes about an activity, trip, sporting event, course, etc., which he/she has experienced. While the speaker is making his/her presentation, you are to list any of the speaker's words/phrases that lead you to focus on your own experience(s); besides these words, list one or two words that you associate with the speaker's expressions. This exercise will show you how listeners freely associate the speaker's thoughts with their own experiences, and, at times, tune out the speaker and become preoccupied with their own thoughts.[88]
9. Learn the meanings of the following suffixes, then collect, from your listening experiences, examples of words containing these suffixes, attempt to define the words, and share the words with the class: *-ancy, -ard, -ate, -ent, -esque, -ism, -ory, -ster.*
10. Learn the meanings of the following prefixes, then collect, from your listening experiences, examples of words containing these prefixes, attempt to define the words, and share the words with the class: *astro-, contra-, dyna-, epi-, neo-, pseudo-, retro-, ortho-.*
11. View a half-hour educational program on television and listen for three or four words with which you are not familiar. Attempt to write down the sentence in which each word is used. Share your words with the class to determine whether they, as listeners, can determine the meaning of each word from its context.
12. Keep a list of all new words that you, as a listener, encounter; also, write down the sentences in which the words are used. Using the dictionary, define these words, and then share them with the class.
13. To improve your vocabulary, consider using Hugh Fellows's plan: Each day, read an article from a magazine that contains short articles on a wide variety

of subjects. Note with a check each word whose meaning is unfamiliar to you. After having read the article, look up the meaning(s) of each word checked. If you believe the word will be useful to you, write it—*just the word*—down. Then, go back to the article and observe how the word is used. The next day, review the words you have listed. Look a word up again if you have forgotten its meaning. Continue reviewing your list of words, reading a new article, and adding words to your list daily.[89]

14. Each student will prepare a set of written directions (consisting of four to six steps) on how to perform some simple task, such as how to remove ink stain from a piece of clothing. One student will then present his/her set of instructions to the class. After he/she has finished presenting, he/she will randomly select a class member to repeat orally the instructions. Discuss possible reasons why the class member could or could not repeat the instructions; consider the speaker's clarity, accuracy, organization, and word choice, the environmental influences, the listener's attention, etc. Repeat the assignment two or three more times. Do the communicators improve in their ability to send and receive messages? Why or why not?

NOTES

1. Arthur Wingfield and Dennis L. Byrnes, *The Psychology of Human Memory* (New York: Academic Press, 1981), p. 130.
2. R. Schank and R. Abelson, *Scripts, Plans, Goals and Understanding* (Hillsdale, New Jersey: Lawrence Erlbaum Associates, 1976).
3. Guy R. Lafrancois, *Psychology for Teaching,* 3rd ed. (Belmont, California: Wadsworth Publishing Company, 1979), pp. 169–170; Thomas G. Devine, *Teaching Study Skills* (Boston: Allyn and Bacon, 1981), pp. 282–285.
4. Wingfield and Byrnes, *The Psychology of Human Memory,* p. 8.
5. Harry Lorayne and Jerry Lucas, *The Memory Book* (New York: Ballantine Books, 1974); V. J. Rex, "Memory Massage," *Future,* September/October 1980, pp. 32–35; Robert L. Montgomery, "How to Improve Your Memory," *U.S. News and World Report* 87 (August 27, 1979): 55; Robert L. Montgomery, "Executive Memory" (Paper presented at the Second International Listening Association Convention, Denver, Colorado, March 4, 1981), p. 2.
6. Lafrancois, *Psychology for Teaching,* pp. 168–169.
7. Madeline Hunter, *Retention* (El Segundo, California: TIP Publications, 1967.
8. Montgomery, "How to Improve Your Memory," p. 55.
9. K. Anders Ericsson, William G. Chase, and Steve Faloon, "Acquisition of a Memory Skill," *Science* 208 (June 6, 1980): 1182.
10. Gordon H. Bower and Judith S. Reitman, "Mnemonic Elaboration in Multilist Learning," *Journal of Verbal Learning and Verbal Behavior* 11 (August 1972): 478–485.
11. A. Paivio, *Imagery and Verbal Processes* (New York: Holt, Rinehart and Winston, 1971), p. 332; Frances L. Prestianni and Rose T. Zacks, "The Effects of Learning Instructions and Cueing on Free-Recall," *Memory and Cognition* 2 (January 1974): 194–200; W. D. Rohwer, Jr., "Elaboration and Learning in Childhood and Adolescence," *Advances in Child Development and Behavior* 8 (1973): 1–57.
12. Montgomery, "Executive Memory," p. 10.

13. *Ibid.*, p. 7.
14. B. R. Bugelski, Edward Kidd, and John Segman, "Image As a Mediator in One-Trial Paired-Associate Learning," *Journal of Experimental Psychology* 76 (January 1968): 69–73.
15. Endel Tulving and Zena Pearlstone, "Availability Versus Accessibility of Information in Memory of Words," *Journal of Verbal Learning and Verbal Behavior* 5 (August 1966): 381–391.
16. Donald A. Norman, *Memory and Attention* (New York: John Wiley and Sons, 1969), p. 119.
17. James I. Brown and G. Robert Carlsen, *Brown-Carlsen Listening Comprehension Test* (New York: Harcourt, Brace and World, 1955).
18. Robert N. Bostrom and Enid S. Waldhart, *Kentucky Comprehensive Listening Skills Test* (Lexington, Kentucky: The Kentucky Listening Research Center, 1983 rev. ed.).
19. G. A. Miller, "The Magical Number Seven, Plus or Minus Two: Some Limits on our Capacity for Processing Information," *Psychological Review* 63 (1956): 81–97.
20. Lorayne and Lucas, *The Memory Book,* pp. 50–72.
21. James Mann, "What Is TV Doing to America?" *U.S. News and World Report* 93 (August 2, 1982), pp. 27–30.
22. Lori Ubell, "How To Listen to a Child," *Parade,* July 31, 1983, p. 16.
23. William F. Buckley, Jr., "Has TV Killed Off Great Oratory?" *TV Guide,* February 12, 1983, p. 38.
24. Kittie W. Watson and Larry R. Smeltzer, "Barriers to Listening: Comparison between Business Students and Business Practitioners" (Paper presented at the Fourth Annual International Listening Association Convention, St. Paul, Minnesota, March 4, 1983).
25. Erving Goffman, "Alienation from Interaction," in *Communicating Interpersonally,* eds. R. Wayne Pace, Brent D. Peterson, and Terrence R. Radcliffe (Columbus, Ohio: Charles E. Merrill Publishing Company, 1973), pp. 144–153.
26. Charles Robert Petrie, Jr., "The Listener," in *Listening: Readings,* ed. Sam Duker (New York: Scarecrow Press, 1966), p. 337.
27. Devine, *Teaching Study Skills,* pp. 124–125; George F. Tuttle and Johnny I. Murdock, "A Competency-Based Model for Teaching Listening within Organizational Environments" (Presentation made at the Sixty-Ninth Annual Speech Communication Association Meeting, Washington, D.C., November 10, 1983).
28. Roy M. Berko, Andrew D. Wolvin, and Darlyn R. Wolvin, *Communication: A Social and Career Focus,* 2nd ed. (Boston: Houghton Mifflin Company, 1981), p. 76; Devine, *Teaching Study Skills,* p. 128.
29. Walter Pauk, *How to Study in College,* 2nd ed. (Boston: Houghton Mifflin Company, 1974), p. 86.
30. James I. Brown, *Programmed Vocabulary* (New York: Appleton-Century-Crofts, 1964), p. v.
31. *Ibid.*, p. vi.
32. Devine, *Teaching Study Skills,* p. 135.
33. A correlation coefficient is a commonly used numerical measure of the degree of relationship between two or more variables. The correlation coefficient ranges in value from −1.00 for perfect negative correlation through .00 for no correlation to +1.00 for complete positive correlation; thus, a low correlation coefficient indicates a weak relationship between variables, and a high correlation coefficient indicates a strong relationship between variables.

34. Evan L. Wright, "The Construction of a Test of Listening Comprehension for the Second, Third, and Fourth Grades" (Ph.D. diss., Washington University, 1957, *Dissertation Abstracts* 17 (1957): 2226–2227; Richard Hampleman, "Comparison of Listening and Reading Comprehension Ability of Fourth and Sixth Grade Pupils," *Elementary English* 35 (January 1958): 49–53; Vern L. Farrow, "An Experimental Study of Listening Attention at the Fourth, Fifth, and Sixth Grade" (Ph.D. diss., University of Oregon, 1963), *Dissertation Abstracts* 24 (1964): 3146; James I. Brown and G. Robert Carlsen, *Brown-Carlsen Listening Comprehension Test* p. 15; John Caffrey, "Auding Ability at the Secondary Level," *Education* 75 (January 1955): 308; Edwyna F. Condon, "An Analysis of the Difference between Good and Poor Listeners in Grades Nine, Eleven, and Thirteen" (Ph.D. diss., University of Kansas, 1965), *Dissertation Abstracts* 26 (1965): 3106; Allen G. Erickson, "Can Listening Efficiency Be Improved?" *Journal of Communication* 4 (Winter 1954): 128–132; Althea Beery et al., *Sequential Tests of Educational Progress: Listening Comprehension* (Princeton, New Jersey: Educational Testing Service, 1957).
35. Erickson, "Can Listening Efficiency Be Improved?" p. 131.
36. Charles M. Kelly, "Listening: Complexity of Activities—and a Unitary Skill?" *Speech Monographs* 34 (November 1967): 456; Henry T. Moore, "The Attention Value of Lecturing without Notes," *Journal of Educational Psychology* 10 (1919): 467–469; Franklin H. Knower, David Phillips, and Fern Keoppel, "Studies in Listening to Informative Speaking," *Journal of Abnormal and Social Psychology* 40 (January 1945): 82–88; Daniel W. Mullin, "An Experimental Study of Retention in Educational Television," *Speech Monographs* 24 (March 1957): 31–38; Ralph G. Nichols, "Factors in Listening Comprehension," *Speech Monographs* 15 (1948): 161; David G. Ryans, "Motivation in Learning," in *Growth, Teaching, and Learning,* ed. H. H. Remers et al. (New York: Harper and Brothers, 1957), p. 125; Charles T. Brown, "Studies in Listening Comprehension," *Speech Monographs* 26 (November 1959): 288–294.
37. John A. Haberland, "A Comparison of Listening Tests with Standardized Tests," *Journal of Educational Research* 52 (April 1959): 301; Robert J. Baldauf, "A Study of a Measure of Listening Comprehension and Its Relation to the School Achievement of Fifth Grade Pupils" (Ph.D. Diss., University of Colorado, 1960), *Dissertation Abstracts* 21 (1960): 2979.
38. Joel Stark, "An Investigation of the Relationship of the Vocal and Communicative Aspects of Speech Competency with Listening Comprehension" (Ph.D. diss., New York University, 1956), *Dissertation Abstracts* 17 (1957): 696; Annette Vister Evans, "Listening Related to Speaking in the First Grade" (M.A. thesis, Atlanta University, 1960).
39. Erickson, "Can Listening Efficiency Be Improved?", p. 131; Sam Duker, "Listening and Reading," *Elementary School Journal* 65 (March 1965): 322.
40. Edward J. J. Kramer, "The Relationships of the Wechsler-Bellevue and A.C.E. Intelligence Tests with Performance Scores in Speaking and the Brown-Carlsen Listening Comprehension Test" (Ph.D. diss., Florida State University, 1955), *Dissertation Abstracts* 15 (1955): 2599; Ramon Ross, "A Look at Listeners," *Elementary School Journal* 64 (April 1964): 370; Nancy Mead, "Assessing Listening Ability: Relationships with Verbal Ability and Racial/Ethnic Bias" (Paper delivered at the Sixty-fourth Annual Meeting of the Speech Communication Association, Minneapolis, Minnesota, November, 1978), p. 9.
41. Brown and Carlsen, *Brown-Carlsen Listening Comprehension Test,* p. 18.

42. Charles Robert Petrie, Jr., "Listening and Organization," *Central States Speech Journal* 15 (February 1964): 8–9.
43. Thomas Wood Smith, "Cultural Bias and Listening," in *Listening: Readings,* ed. Sam Duker, p. 128; Ramon Ross, "A Look at Listeners," p. 370.
44. Ralph G. Nichols, "Listening Is a 10–Part Skill," *Nation's Business* 45 (July 1957): 4.
45. Paul W. Keller, "Major Findings in Listening in the Past Ten Years," *Journal of Communication* 10 (March 1960): 34.
46. Sanford E. Gerber, "Dichotic and Diotic Presentations of Speeded Speech," *Journal of Communication* 18 (September 1968): 272–282.
47. Grant Fairbanks, Newman Guttman, and Murray S. Miron, "Auditory Comprehension of Repeated High-Speed Messages," *Journal of Speech and Hearing Disorders* 22 (March 1957): 20–22.
48. David B. Orr, "Time Compressed Speech—A Perspective," *Journal of Communication* 18 (September 1968): 288–292.
49. Emerson Foulke et al., "The Compression of Rapid Speech by the Blind," *Exceptional Children* 29 (November 1962): 134–141.
50. Emerson Foulke, ed., *Proceedings: Third Louisville Conference on Rate Controlled Speech* (New York: American Foundation for the Blind, 1975).
51. Linda Olsen, "Technology Humanized: The Rate-Controlled Tape Recorder," *Media and Methods* 15 (January 1979): 67.
52. For more specific information regarding the use of compressed speech in business, education, and public services, contact Variable Speech Control (VSC) Corporation, 185 Berry Street, San Francisco, California 94107; the telephone number is 415/495–6100—TELEX 340–328.
53. John Hill Kirk, "Time Compression Speeds the Gift of Gab," *USA Today,* 12 October 1982, p. 3–B.
54. James MacLachlan, "What People Really Think of Fast Talkers," *Psychology Today* 13 (November 1979): 113–117.
55. John Leo and Nancy Pierce Williamson, "As Time Goes Bye-Bye," *Time,* July 19, 1982, p. 78.
56. Tom Shales, "The Incredible Shrinking Shows," *The Washington Post,* 18 January 1983, p. D-1.
57. Leo and Williamson, "As Times Goes Bye-Bye," p. 78; Lexicon's Model 1200 brochure, entitled "Case Histories in Manipulating Time," 1983.
58. The address and phone number of Variable Speech Control Corporation (VSC) can be found in footnote number 52 of this chapter.
59. The address of AmBiChron is 67 Smith Street, Lynbrook, New York 11563; the telephone number is 516/599–3489.
60. The address of Lexicon is 60 Turner Street, Waltham, Massachusetts 02154; the telephone number is 617/891–6790/Telex 923468.
61. To receive information regarding the ordering of rate-controlled recorded speech and/or descriptions of commercially available speech compressors, contact Emerson Foulke, Perceptual Alternative Laboratory, University of Louisville—Graduate School, Louisville, Kentucky 40292, or call 502/588–6722.
62. Roy M. Berko, Andrew D. Wolvin, and Darlyn R. Wolvin, *Communicating: A Social and Career Focus* (Boston: Houghton Mifflin Company, 1977), pp. 234–241.

63. Carl H. Weaver, *Human Listening: Processes and Behavior* (Indianapolis: Bobbs-Merrill Company, 1972), p. 70.
64. D. E. McHenry, "The Effects of Certain Learner, Task, and Response Variables on Immediate and Delayed Aural Comprehension of Meaningful Verbal Material" (Ph.D. diss., University of Denver, 1974), cited in Paul G. Friedman, *Listening Processes: Attention, Understanding, Evaluation* (Washington, D.C.: National Education Association, 1983), p. 11; Francis J. DiVesta and G. Susan Gray, "Listening and Note Taking," *Journal of Educational Psychology* 63 (February 1972): 8–14.
65. Pauk, *How to Study in College,* pp. 126–133.
66. Ralph G. Nichols, "Do We Know How to Listen? Practical Helps in a Modern Age," *Speech Teacher* 10 (March 1961): 122.
67. For a further explanation of the mapping notetaking method, see Tony Buzan, *Use Both Sides of Your Brain* (New York: E.P. Dutton and Company, 1976), pp. 83–106.
68. Brown and Carlsen, *Brown-Carlsen Listening Comprehension Test,* p. 4.
69. Sara W. Lundsteen, *Listening: Its Impact on Reading and the Other Language Arts* (Illinois: NCTE/ERIC, 1971), pp. 52–53.
70. Brown and Carlsen, *Brown-Carlsen Listening Comprehension Test,* p. 4.
71. Ronald E. Bassett, Nilwon Whittington, and Ann Stanton-Spicer, "The Basics in Speaking and Listening for High School Graduates: What Should Be Assessed?" *Communication Education* 27 (November 1978): 298.
72. Lundsteen, *Listening: Its Impact on Reading and the Other Language Arts,* pp. 52–53.
73. Charlotte J. Patterson, "Teaching Children to Listen," *Today's Education* 67 (April/May 1978): 53.
74. *Ibid.*
75. S. I. Hayakawa, "How to Attend a Conference," *ETC* 3 (Autumn 1955): 5–9.
76. *Ibid.*
77. Carl R. Rogers and F. J. Roethlisberger, "Barriers and Gateways to Communication," *Harvard Business Review* 30 (July 1952): 46–52.
78. S. I. Hayakawa, "How to Attend a Conference."
79. *Ibid.*
80. "To Ease Marital Strife, Try Really Listening," *The Evening Sun* 15 November 1976, p. A-3.
81. *Ibid.*
82. Marion Wells, "Listening Says You Really Care," *Grit* 15 January 1978, p. 16.
83. Rogers and Roethlisberger, "Barriers and Gateways to Communication," p. 48.
84. Andrew D. Wolvin and Carolyn Gwynn Coakley, *Listening Instruction* (Urbana, Illinois: ERIC Clearinghouse on Reading and Communication Skills, 1979), p. 16.
85. *Ibid.,* pp. 16–17.
86. *Ibid.,* pp. 25–26.
87. Walter B. Kolesnik, *Motivation: Understanding and Influencing Human Behavior* (Boston: Allyn and Bacon, 1978), p. 105.
88. Debra Duxbury Cary, "Listening As a Discipline," *ILA Listening Post,* September 1982.
89. Hugh P. Fellows, *The Art and Skill of Talking with People* (Englewood Cliffs, New Jersey: Prentice-Hall, 1964), pp. 72–73.

Concepts You Will Encounter

Therapeutic Listening
Focusing Attention
Attending Behaviors
Defensive Climate
Supportive Climate
Action-Reaction Principle
Empathy
Risk
Self-Disclosure
Trust
Interrupting Response
Unrelated Response
Tangential Response
Discounting Response
Philosophizing Response
Blaming Response
Evaluative Response
Advising Response
Sounding Board
Discretion
Honesty
Patience
Faith
Probing Response
Feeling Response
Feelings
Perception-Checking
Thought Response
Paraphrasing
Feeling/Thought Response

Skills You Should Develop

Focusing Attention
Demonstrating Attending Behaviors
Developing a Supportive Communication Climate
Listening with Empathy
Responding Appropriately

Therapeutic Listening

7

The third purpose of listening, therapeutic listening, is listening to provide a troubled sender with the opportunity to talk through a problem. The effective therapeutic listener utilizes not only many of the discriminative and comprehensive listening skills presented in chapters 5 and 6 but also five additional skills which are essential to this unique type of listening.

Before we present the fundamental skills of therapeutic listening, each reader should consider and record on paper what he or she would actually say in response to the following hypothetical messages if these messages were conveyed to the reader by three of his or her friends. If you record your own responses, you can then analyze and assess your present therapeutic listening responses as you read this chapter and discover how an effective therapeutic listener should respond to a troubled sender.

Message sent by a forty-five-year-old female friend:

> *I don't know what to do. I'm just. . . . Tony and I just don't seem to have anything. . . . I mean, we just don't share anything special anymore. He's always too busy for me with work and consulting and . . . playing poker with the guys. . . . He never seems to have time for us . . . for us to talk about us—about our marriage and how empty it is. I don't feel that. . . . He seems to think of me only as the kids' mother, the house's keeper, and the family's social planner . . . I'm no longer his special lady, and I want to be . . . I desperately want to. . . . We used to be content just holding each other and sharing a special smile and. . . . Now, we hardly ever touch . . . except when we pass each other in the bathroom or. . . . And we don't even look at each other . . . I mean, really look at each other. There just doesn't seem to be anything left to hold us together . . . except the kids . . . and they'll be going out on their own soon.*

Message sent by a seventeen-year-old nephew:

> *My parents are impossible! They really are! I don't even know why they had me. . . . Yea, I know: they wanted someone to mold in their own image. I'm serious. They certainly don't think I can think for myself. According to them, there's only one way to think, and that's* their *way. They* know *what friends I should have, what activities I should participate in, what schools I should attend, what courses I should take, what career I should pursue, what. . . . They know* everything *that's "best for me." I only wish they knew* me, *but they won't give me a chance to let them know who I am.*

Your response:

Message sent by a co-worker who has just been told that his promotion application has been denied:

> *I can't believe it! I just can't believe it! After all the work I've done to make that ________ Jones look good, that hypocrite passed me over again! I didn't get my promotion.*

For this example, you are to check each of the following responses that you might tend to give.

_____ 1. *I would interrupt him before he had finished his message.*
_____ 2. *"Hey, what time are we scheduled to play racquetball this afternoon?"*
_____ 3. *"Promotions are a pain! I was in grade for what seemed like years! I didn't think I'd ever get my thirteen."*
_____ 4. *"Forget it. It's water over the dam now."*
_____ 5. *"Hey, cheer up. You'll get your promotion soon."*
_____ 6. *"Your problem is that you still think diligence pays off. Maybe it did in high school where you received a college scholarship. But, buddy, the reward system is different here. Those in power here are people-users, people-abusers, people-bruisers, and people-choosers. And, you've just been used, abused, and bruised. But, you haven't been 'choosed' because you don't know how to play the game. The game of organizational politics consists of doing what you have to do to become the boss's chosen one."*

_____ 7. *"Well, I told you you'd better learn how to take constructive criticism without getting so defensive and hostile."*

_____ 8. *"You probably haven't demonstrated enough initiative on the job."*

_____ 9. *"Why don't you discuss the issue with the inspector general?"*

_____ 10. *"Well, I'll tell you what you should do. Transfer over to D-4, the new section that's being formed. Rumor has it that Collins, the woman who'll be the branch chief, really takes care of her own and is not afraid to speak up for her people in front of the promotion board. I realize that your experience is in system maintenance rather than in system design, but, heck, you could take a short course or two and pick up the needed knowledge quickly. Then, you'd fit right in and get your promotion faster. Plus, you'd be rid of Jones."*

_____ 11. *"What explanation did Jones give you for the turning down of your application for promotion?"*

_____ 12. *"You sound as if you really feel betrayed."*

_____ 13. *"You think Jones let you down, huh?"*

_____ 14. *"Am I correct in understanding that you feel betrayed because you think Jones has let you down?"*

The Need for Therapeutic Listening

The need for an empathic listener exists in nearly everyone. Indeed, this need has become pervasive in American society. In San Francisco, for example, a firm entitled "Conversation" has been established to fill this need for therapeutic listeners. For five dollars a half hour, the firm provides listeners who let people talk to them. The growth of the telephone "Hot Line" operations in most major American cities also demonstrates the need for therapeutic listeners. These "hot lines," designed to provide support to troubled persons, are serviced by individuals who are trained in therapeutic listening techniques—techniques which enable them to help troubled callers disclose their problems. Many of these "hot lines," usually staffed by volunteers, have become specialized so that they offer services to particular groups of people, such as students on college campuses, rape victims, abused persons, employees of specific organizations, etc. Coupled with these "hot lines" is the development of crisis centers which also provide therapeutic listening support (as well as professional help) to persons in need: battered wives, abused children, drug abusers, rape victims, homeless individuals, distressed parents, suicidal individuals, and many others.

The need for effective therapeutic listening has been recognized by many experts. Dr. Robert Wicks, a psychologist-author, states that he "would like to see people not quickly sending everyone to a professional."[1] Instead, Wicks urges people to resist the impulse to give advice and instead spend time listening to the person's problem. After all, observes Ray Jones, "When you need someone to turn to in time of trouble or crisis, you turn to someone who . . . will listen. . . ."[2]

Beier and Valens, in their interesting work on *People Reading,* stress the importance of listening to your children:

> Listening to a young person can easily be an act of love. Listening with concern but without judging is an art, and it helps the child explore his motivations, his style, and the compromises he has so far achieved. . . . It means giving him a safe place where he can speak at his own speed and explore new options, however unrealistic they may appear to us.[3]

Psychologists recognize that the importance of listening to children also extends to the teenage, adolescent years as well as beyond these years. Psychologist-author, Manford Sonstegard, has developed a series of workshops on "Listening to Teens." In his work, Sonstegard advises parents to be willing to listen to their teens "without always making value judgments. And be willing to concede that parents don't always know the right answer.[4]" Indeed, as the following example illustrates, parents who are effective therapeutic listeners are not expected to have the "right answers" for their children's problems. After a troubled married daughter had called her, Colleen Onnen of Cherokee, Iowa, was worried that she had not helped her daughter with her problem. But the mother was wrong, for shortly after the first call had been completed, the daughter called her back and thanked her for having been such a good listener: "Mom, it was so good to be able to dump it all on you and know that you'd understand. I didn't expect you to fix anything; I just needed to talk."[5] Clearly, one of the most valuable skills of parenthood is developing the ability to listen empathically to their children. A lifetime of family communication can be sustained through listening with empathy to family members in need of those who will listen.

Just as workshops on family communication have become popular, so, too, have workshops on couple communication. These workshops are designed to facilitate the development of communication skills such as empathic listening in couple relationships. In one such workshop, Dr. Jeffrey Moss, a social worker, conducts a seminar on "Communication Skill Building and Problem Solving in the Couple Relationship." Moss contends that listening with empathy is important because being a couple "is never easy. Feelings become hurt, angers mount, disagreements grow, and as a result there is a need to give vent to these feelings."[6] Moss stresses that effective listening does not require that you take on your partner's problems. "Rather, to be a good listener is to be a sounding board for your mate's thoughts and feelings. You help the other person clarify feelings which have plagued him/her."[7]

The need for listening with empathy extends to the workplace. B. D. Sorrell notes that the effective manager must "convey the idea that he understands and appreciates what the speaker said. This requires listening with empathy."[8] The effective manager or supervisor must also recognize the need to listen with empathy to employees troubled by personal problems. Meyer and Meyer observe that "[i]t has long been recognized that personal problems affect workers' productivity," but only recently "have corporations begun to examine closely the link between personal problems and productivity."[9] Indeed, the supervisor skilled in therapeutic listening may greatly contribute to workers' increased productivity. Therapeutic listening in organizations also applies to the advances in labor relations. Unionized workers today increasingly have turned to negotiations for renewing contracts and for setting forth salary and employment conditions in their agreements with their employers. When negotiations of salary and working conditions take place, both management and labor are encouraged to listen with understanding to the positions advanced by each side. Such efforts to achieve careful, empathic listening can facilitate the advancement of both management and worker needs and understandings and, thus, lead to successful, continuing labor relationships.

Therapeutic listening plays an essential role in educational organizations as well. Teachers are encouraged to listen with empathy in order to help their students grow as persons. To develop an atmosphere in which student self-exploration is possible, teachers should demonstrate "understanding of and skill at communicating these concepts of empathy, respect, and genuineness."[10] Such skill is useful to teachers in communicating with their students as well as with other school personnel and with parents. Some school systems place such a premium on effective teacher communication (including therapeutic listening) that they offer workshops to assist teachers in developing their skills.

The development of therapeutic listening skills is important to yet another professional group—those individuals who must deal directly with terrorists. Throughout the world, political figures, corporate officials, diplomats, and military officers have become targets of terrorists. Attacks of terrorism range from bombing military installations, hijacking airplanes, and kidnapping ambassadors to threatening destruction of the White House and Washington Monument in Washington, D.C. One of the major strategies on which terrorism experts have come to rely is that of therapeutic listening: attempting to understand the terrorist's point of view and providing a willing listener in the process of negotiating the release of the victim(s) and/or negotiating an end to the threatened attack. United States Department of State officials and Department of Defense security officers have come to understand the value of therapeutic listening as a means of dealing with terrorism, both for the attackers and for the victims of these vicious attacks.

While it is evident that there is a great need for therapeutic listeners in our society, it may not be so evident that we *are* able to function as therapeutic listeners when others come to us with problems (provided that these problems are not of a serious psychological nature). A recent study by two psychologists compared the results of two groups of patients who suffered neurotic depression or anxiety reactions. One group was treated by psychotherapists, and the other group was treated by college professors who demonstrated ability to form understanding relationships. The results of the study indicated that the patients treated by professors showed, on the average, as much improvement as patients treated by professional therapists.[11] It is possible for people to serve a therapeutic function as listeners.

Skills Involved in Therapeutic Listening

Focusing Attention

The effective therapeutic listener gives his or her *full* attention to the sender; that is, he or she focuses completely on the sender rather than dividing his or her attention energy between/among the sender and some other concern(s). The attentive listener does not become preoccupied with personal concerns such as lint or a loose thread on his or her clothing, an annoying hangnail, the time, or his or her own unrelated thoughts. Nor does he or she engage in such energy-consuming activities as reading the newspaper, watching television, concerning self with items on his or her desk, or looking at each person who passes in the hall. Rather than creating or tolerating distractions which compete for his or her attention, the effective therapeutic listener attempts to establish a receptive listening environment that is quiet and has an atmosphere of privacy by closing the door of the room or the office in which the interaction is occurring; holding phone calls; discouraging interruptions; turning off the radio, stereo, or television; and engaging in any other act that will keep the communication interaction as free as possible of external distractions. Additionally, he or she makes a conscious effort to free him or herself of personal concerns, or internal distractions, by directing all of his or her attention energy to the sender and the sender's concern.

Demonstrating Attending Behaviors

To indicate that he or she is focusing attention on the sender, the listener—utilizing every part of his or her body—engages in appropriate attending behaviors. By demonstrating attending behaviors, the listener conveys a message that represents an open invitation to the sender to talk:

> I'm interested in you as a person, and I think that what you feel is important. I respect your thoughts, and even if I don't agree with them, I know they are valid for you. . . . I . . . want to understand you. I think you're worth listening to, and I want you to know that I'm the kind of person you can talk to.[12]

One attending behavior that has been proven to indicate a positive therapeutic attitude and has been judged as an important nonverbal behavior for showing empathy is eye contact.[13] The effective therapeutic listener does not frequently shift his or her gaze, look around the room, stare, or maintain an out-of-focus look. Rather, he or she maintains an appropriate and comfortable gaze (an individual gaze when the listener directly looks at the sender even though the sender may be looking elsewhere as he or she is speaking and a mutual gaze when the listener and sender directly look at one another).[14]

The following example illustrates how important eye contact is as an attending behavior:

> While a mother is washing dishes, her five-year-old daughter, Kenzie, enters the kitchen and says, "Mama."
>
> "Yes, Kenzie?" the mother responds sweetly.
>
> Ten seconds of silence elapse.
>
> "Ma-ma," Kenzie repeats.
>
> "What dear?" the mother asks (still in a sweet tone).
>
> Ten seconds of silence elapse.
>
> "M-a-a-ma!" Kenzie again repeats.
>
> "What?" the mother asks less sweetly.
>
> Ten seconds elapse.
>
> "Ma-a-a-ama!" Kenzie yells.
>
> "*What* do you want?" the mother yells back.
>
> Then, Kenzie says something such as, "I have two blue dresses," "I saw a bird in the back yard," or "What are you doing?"
>
> This type of dialogue and behavior continues until one day the mother finally shouts at Kenzie, "I'm listening!"
>
> "But you're not looking at me," replies Kenzie.
>
> The mother suddenly realizes that she, in fact, hadn't been looking at her daughter—at least not until she had become angry with her. With this realization, she now understood why Kenzie had tried to make her angry: to get her to look at Kenzie.
>
> From that day on, the mother consciously tried to make eye contact with Kenzie whenever they communicated. Her five-year-old had taught her what giving eye contact can mean to a child: "Looking at a child eye to eye gives her assurance. She knows you are really paying attention, knows that you really care."[15]

This example depicts a troubled child who, despite her young age, understood long before her mother did how essential eye contact is as an attending behavior. Unfortunately, there are many individuals who never learn what Kenzie's mother learned from her daughter.

Attending behaviors also include the listener's bodily positioning. Three bodily behaviors that have been shown to be indicative of a positive therapeutic attitude and judged to be demonstrative of empathy are (1) direct (face-to-face) body orientation, (2) forward trunk leans, and (3) close (yet not uncomfortably close) interactional distances.[16] Another attending behavior of the body is an open, receptive posture—a posture free of body crosses (since body crosses may convey that the listener has little desire to interact with the sender). These open, natural, and relaxed bodily behaviors—unlike noninclusive body orientation, excessive postural shifts, fidgeting, greater interactional distance, and closed bodily posture that suggest restlessness, uneasiness, and unresponsiveness—reflect listener interest and involvement.

Four additional attending behaviors are nodding the head, maintaining responsive facial expressions, verbalizing brief and encouraging expressives, and speaking in a warm and pleasant voice tone. Research shows that there is a significant positive relationship between perceived helping effectiveness and frequency of positive head nodding and smiling.[17] Besides smiling at the appropriate times, the listener should convey other facial expressions that indicate involvement; for example, to signify a lack of understanding, the listener may knit his or her brow or drop his or her jaw. Above all, the concerned listener should avoid presenting an "expressionless" face; a lack of facial responsiveness can quickly destroy a communication interaction. Research also shows that the listener's verbalization of expressives indicates to the sender that the listener is attending to the sender's message.[18] Examples of these signal cues are vocal segregates such as "mm-hmm," "uh huh," "ah," "umm," etc., and brief comments such as "oh," "I see," "yes," "right," etc. By verbalizing these expressives, the listener demonstrates an important attending behavior and encourages the sender to continue speaking. Likewise, research indicates that another positive attending behavior is the listener's use of a generally warm, quiet, and pleasant tone—a tone that communicates caring and involvement.[19]

Showing thoughtful consideration for the sender's comfort is still another type of attending behavior in which the therapeutic listener should engage. This type of behavior may entail offering the sender a chair, a tissue, a drink of water, time to gain self-composure, and—depending upon the listening situation—a host of other nonverbal comforting acts.

Closely related to comforting behavior is touching, a potent therapeutic attending behavior. Although non-Anglo-Saxon and non-Germanic Americans tend to be physically expressive, Americans in general are viewed as low-contact or, quite often, non-contact individuals. Thus, by not touching, many American listeners are missing numerous opportunities to assist troubled senders. According to research findings, touching results in greater self-exploration by senders, touching facilitates openness, honesty and trust, touching reduces stress and tension, and touching, "used lovingly as a therapeutic tool, can get through to troubled people who are otherwise unreachable, and can go a long way toward healing their emotional wounds."[20] The effective therapeutic listener, therefore, should consciously attempt to make touching (hugging, holding a hand, etc.) a part of his or her attending behavior.

A final attending behavior is silence. Attentive and active silence, like touching, can carry a powerful message: "I have interest in and concern for you; your thoughts and feelings are of worth because you are of worth." In the field of psychotherapy, the value of silence has long been recognized. Psychoanalyst and author, Theodor Reik, in *Listening with the Third Ear,* discusses the powerful effects that the therapeutic listener's silence can have on the sender:

> Silence has a calming, beneficial effect. The patient interprets it preconsciously as a sign of quiet attention. . . . This silence seems to ask him to speak freely. . . . The active power of silence . . . has a force that pulls the patient forward, driving him into deeper layers than he intended. . . . [T]he silence of

the analyst works upon the patient encouragingly, and works even more strongly than words could.[21]

Though many listeners become anxious when there is silence and thus cut off the silence prematurely due to their own anxiety, the therapeutic listener must recognize, as Reik notes, that silence can be an effective attending behavior. However, the listener also must recognize that a prolonged silence may be an open invitation for the listener to ask the sender to share his or her present thoughts and feelings with the listener.

The nine attending behaviors presented in this section help to communicate the listener's concern and involvement. Moreover, they make the sender feel valued and worthwhile.

Developing a Supportive Communication Climate

Suppose a woman sends the following message to Karl, her co-worker: "I've taken just about all that I'm going to take from Betty. If she makes one more 'put down' remark about me in front of the boss, I'm going to have it out with her."

Karl's responding message will likely set the communication climate for the continuation (or, possibly, termination) of this interpersonal dialogue. If he chooses to respond by rolling his eyes, emitting a deep breath, and saying, "Oh, Susan, you're just too sensitive," he is apt to be creating a defensive communication climate. On the other hand, if he chooses to respond by looking directly at Susan, showing concern in his eyes, and saying, "Sounds as if you're quite disgusted with Betty's belittling you in Mrs. Walker's presence," he is apt to be creating a supportive communication climate.

The effective therapeutic listener provides a supportive communication climate—a climate in which the sender feels free, safe, and comfortable to express him or herself. By providing a supportive atmosphere, the listener communicates a message that says, "I'm here; I care. Although I may not agree with you, I accept you, and I'm interested in you, your thoughts, and your feelings." Knowing that the listener has interest in and unconditional regard for the sender, the sender feels secure and free to let down his or her guard, to self-disclose without the fear or threat of being personally attacked, and to explore—at his or her own pace—various options without feeling anxious that the listener may regard some (or even all) of them as being totally unrealistic and/or foolish. Truly, the creation of a supportive communication climate promotes self-exploration and thus facilitates problem-solving for the sender.

Just as the sender benefits from a supportive communication climate, so do both the listener and the sender-listener relationship benefit. Perhaps the greatest benefit to the listener is a fuller understanding of the sender's thoughts and feelings—from the sender's frame of reference rather than from the listener's own frame of reference. Perhaps the greatest benefit to the dialogue partners' relationship is the open communication resulting from mutual trust and acceptance, which are essential to developing and maintaining positive interpersonal relationships.

As the introductory example in this section illustrates, the listener plays a major role in creating a communication climate by the way he or she nonverbally and verbally responds to the troubled sender. Rather than responding with acceptance, many listeners unfortunately offer responses which communicate nonacceptance and, thus, create a defensive communication climate which usually results in the sender becoming defensive (and, therefore, bringing the action-reaction principle into play with both communicators becoming defensive) or silent (and, therefore, terminating the communication interaction).

To avoid communicating nonacceptance, the listener should be aware of responses that senders perceive as indicating disapproval. According to Dr. Thomas Gordon, author of the popular *Parent Effectiveness Training* and *Leader Effectiveness Training,* the twelve most commonly-expressed, nonaccepting responses are the following:

1. Ordering, directing, commanding ("You have to. . . .")
2. Warning, admonishing, threatening ("You'd better not. . . .")
3. Moralizing, preaching, exhorting, imploring ("It's your duty to. . . .")
4. Advising, giving suggestions or solutions ("What you should do is. . . .")
5. Persuading with logic, lecturing, aruging, teaching ("Experience says that. . . .")
6. Judging, criticizing, disagreeing, blaming ("You'd be foolish to. . . .")
7. Praising, agreeing, evaluating positively, buttering up ("You're such a good. . . .")
8. Name-calling, ridiculing, shaming ("How naive can you be?")
9. Interpreting, analyzing, diagnosing ("Your problem is that. . . .")
10. Reassuring, sympathizing, consoling, supporting ("Tomorrow will be better.")
11. Probing, questioning, interrogating ("Why did you. .")
12. Distracting, diverting, kidding, avoiding, withdrawing, humoring ("Hey, have I told you. . . ?")

Gordon notes that these "typical twelve" responses are highly inappropriate as therapeutic responses, the very kinds of responses that professional therapists and counselors strive to avoid when they are establishing a supportive communication climate.[22]

To understand further how to avoid developing a defensive communication climate as well as how to develop a supportive communication climate, the listener should note the classic study of communication climate conducted by Jack R. Gibb. Gibb identified six types of characteristics which can arouse defensiveness and six contrasting characteristics that can create supportive communication climates.[23] These contrasting characteristics—exemplified by responses that the parents of a recent high school graduate might give after their son has remarked, *"I don't know if I want to go to school, join the military, or get a job; I'm having a tough time deciding"*—are as follows:

Defensive Climates	**Supportive Climates**
1. Evaluation—judging others from one's own frame of reference; accusing; blaming *"You never have been any good at making decisions."*	1. Description—imposing no judgments on others; describing thought and feeling perceptions; questioning to gain information *"We sense that you are confused about what direction to take in your immediate future."*
2. Control—directly attempting to change others (whom the sender views as inadequate) so that they will do what the sender wants them to do/see as the sender does; attempting to restrict others' options *"If you want our support, you'll go on to school and prepare yourself for a good-paying job."*	2. Problem-Orientation—expressing a desire to share in the defining of a mutual concern and the seeking of a solution or allowing others to work through their own problems *"Is there any way we can help you with this difficult decision?"*
3. Strategy—manipulating others through dishonesty/trickery *"We have several friends in high places; they're just waiting for an educated young man with a degree in electrical engineering."*	3. Spontaneity—being honest and direct; being free of deception/hidden motives *"These three options do give you a great deal to consider, don't they?"*
4. Neutrality—expressing an attitude of cold detachment/uncaring indifference *"We don't care what you choose to do. Do what you want."*	4. Empathy—identifying with another's problems, accepting and sharing feelings, and expressing understanding *"We understand the anxiety and confusion that you're feeling as you're making this decision."*
5. Superiority—expressing an attitude of being better than others; raising feelings of inadequacy in others *"You're not old enough or experienced enough to make this decision that will affect the rest of your life. We'll decide; we know the 'real world'."*	5. Equality—recognizing and respecting the individual worth of others; recognizing others' ability to explore their own problems and reach their own tentative solutions; being willing to share in participative planning/problem-solving *"We respect your judgment, son, and we will willingly listen as you work through your options."*

Defensive Climates	Supportive Climates
6. Certainty—having preconceived notions about how something should be, what ideas are "true"/"right"—without considering anyone else's ideas; being unwilling to change; appearing dogmatic	6. Provisionalism—being open to and willing to investigate information/ideas; being willing to reconsider one's own behavior, ideas, attitudes; being willing to share in problem-solving
"You will go on to college, and we don't want to hear another word about it."	*"Shall we explore what you see as the pluses and minuses of each option?"*

In this example, what the son needs is understanding, caring, and accepting listeners—not critics, controllers, manipulators, nonparticipants, superiors, or authorities.

A supportive communication climate provided by a listener can, indeed, assist a troubled sender in exploring a problem that does not directly involve the listener him/herself. However, there are many occasions when the sender believes that the listener/the listener's behavior is, in fact, the problem. On such occasions, defensiveness may again appear—with the listener displaying the defensive behavior. As a result, his or her listening effectiveness may greatly suffer. To illustrate, let us begin with the listener's spouse making this statement: *"I am fed up with doing all the work around this house while all you do is sit around and watch television. I've never in my life seen anyone as lazy as you!"* (This sender undoubtedly does not know how to express his/her feelings without creating a defensive communication climate; however, neither do many, many other people so this illustration is not atypical.) Listening to this message—like listening to most hostile messages that come from a spouse, friend, boss, child, sibling, or anyone significant to the listener—often is quite difficult. Having received this message, the listener—whose self-esteem has been threatened and diminished by the sender's name-calling, accusing, and evaluating—will most likely become defensive (if he or she does not totally withdraw from the communication interaction). Feeling defensive here seems quite natural; however, one should realize that it interferes with listening effectiveness. When a person becomes defensive, he or she frequently becomes controlled by emotions and stops listening. Rather than expending energy on solving the problem at hand, he or she focuses his or her attention energy on the aroused and festering feelings or on rehearsing what to say and how to say it in order to protect/defend his or her self-image, "win the battle" by destroying the "opponent's" viewpoint, make a verbal counterattack, etc.

The effective therapeutic listener faces a strong challenge in situations like this one. It would be so easy to reply, "And who does all of the lawn work, maintains the car and pool, does the garden work, buys the groceries, . . . while you play bridge, ride your bike, lounge around the pool,. . . . If you want to see someone who's lazy, go look in the mirror!" Indeed, it would be easy to respond in this manner, but it would hardly be productive. With the action-reaction principle in effect, much that could be gained may never come to be: the feelings of one's partner may never be explored; the problem-solving process may never be undertaken; knowledge about one's self may never be known; further dialogue may never be encouraged; and potential hostility and a damaged relationship may never be prevented.

When the listener considers the potentially negative effects of defensive behavior, he or she may realize that although it may be much more difficult to (1) control one's emotions (or to acknowledge and express one's emotional tensions to the sender in order to release them and be free to listen), (2) focus on understanding the sender's message rather than defending one's self, and (3) make a response such as, *"Sounds as if you're feeling overwhelmed with the amount of housework you have to do and you'd like my help,"* any of these three behaviors would, indeed, be more productive. Moreover, these supportive listening behaviors are likely to create the more positive effect of the action-reaction principle, as Carl Rogers, in *On Becoming a Person,* maintains: with one party's dropping of defensiveness comes the other party's dropping of defensiveness.[24] Furthermore, creating a supportive communication climate should be the goal of the effective therapeutic listener.

The two listener responses made to the sender's message in the example introducing this section call attention to still another component which strongly affects the communication climate: the nonverbal message that the listener conveys. Just as effective therapeutic listeners should provide supportive verbal feedback, they should also provide supportive nonverbal feedback in order to develop a supportive communication climate. Frequently, one's verbal message indicates acceptance while, on the contrary, one's nonverbal message may indicate nonacceptance. For example, if one responds by saying, "I really enjoy working with you," but does not look at his or her dialogue partner and turns his or her body away, the response is likely to create defensiveness.

To create a supportive, rather than a defensive, communication climate, the listener should first become aware of what nonverbal behaviors tend to produce each climate, and then he or she should consciously engage in the behaviors that are more likely to produce an atmosphere of acceptance. Some of the many nonverbal behaviors that tend to create each communication climate are the following:

Defensive Climates	**Supportive Climates**
leaning back (possibly with both hands supporting the head) or away	leaning forward
positioning body to exclude partner, pointing feet or entire body toward the exit	positioning body to include partner
turning face away from partner	turning face toward partner
shaking head horizontally (negatively)	nodding head vertically (affirmatively)
assuming incongruent (dissimilar) body posture	assuming congruent (similar) body posture

Defensive Climates	Supportive Climates
making excessive postural shifts, fidgeting, tapping or jiggling a foot, maintaining a fixed or rigid body posture	maintaining a relaxed/involved body posture
elevating one's self, "standing tall"	maintaining same elevation as partner
holding head and/or body erect, tilting head back	tilting head slightly to the side
increasing distance between self and partner or invading partner's personal space	maintaining a close and comfortable distance from the partner
maintaining a closed body posture (crossing or locking arms/legs or camouflaging body crosses)	maintaining an open body posture
crossing legs away from partner	crossing legs toward partner
avoiding tactile contact with partner	touching partner
engaging in highly expansive gestures	engaging in natural gestures
shifting gaze, staring, looking around, casting eyes down, not blinking, peering over glasses, looking down one's nose, directing one's eyes "toward the heavens"	maintaining an appropriate eye gaze with partner
flickering flat hand(s), clenching fists, steepling fingers, rubbing nose or eyes, tapping or strumming fingers, propping head up with hand, pointing or shaking index finger at partner, rubbing hands together, covering face with hands, hitting head with fist, placing palm on back of neck, holding chin in palm of hand while extending index finger along cheek with remaining fingers positioned below the mouth	having open hands, showing relaxed hands, touching one's heart with hand(s)
extending palms out, holding palms down	holding palms up
having a harsh and/or firm voice tone, accentuating vocal emphasis	having a warm and pleasant voice tone (soft volume, low pitch, slow speed)
frowning	smiling
demonstrating judgmental facial expressions (narrowing or closing eyes, drooping eyelids, squinting eyes, raising eyebrows, wrinkling or knitting eyebrows, tilting eyebrows downward, tightening jaw muscle, thrusting out chin, pursing lips, jutting jaw forward, turning up nose)	demonstrating facial expressions which indicate concern/acceptance/interest/involvement/responsiveness

Defensive Climates	Supportive Climates
using vocal characteristics and vocal segregates that indicate nonacceptance and/or disapproval (such as clicking the tongue/tsking, sighing deeply, gasping, emitting a deep breath/shhhing and harumphing, sneering and/or laughing at partner)	using vocal segregates that indicate support and concern (such as "uhhh" and "uh huh")[25]

Clearly, the way a listener responds verbally and nonverbally has a major impact on the success or failure of the therapeutic interaction. Paul Friedman summarizes well the difference between a therapeutic listening response conveying acceptance and one that conveys nonacceptance:

> An acceptant response imposes no judgment on the speaker. It is descriptive of what has been heard, not critical. Its intention is to comprehend or understand. It is problem-oriented rather than control-oriented, expressing a desire to collaborate in defining a mutual concern and seeking its solution, rather than trying to get the other person to see something the way we do. It is receptive, indicating a need for additional data and seeking clarification of a situation as the speaker views it, rather than having all the answers. It indicates respect for and supports the use of the speaker's own ability to think through and respond appropriately to what is bothering him or her.[26]

The listener who employs a verbal and nonverbal response of acceptance will be developing a supportive communication climate—a climate essential to effective therapeutic listening.

Listening with Empathy

Frequent references to therapeutic listening as empathic listening accentuate the importance of the listener developing empathy when he or she is listening to a troubled individual. In fact, empathy may be, as Robert Carkhuff believes, the basic dimension of helping: "Without an empathic understanding of the helpee's world and his difficulties as he sees them there is no basis for helping."[27] Indeed research by Raskin supports Carkhuff's view. After surveying practicing therapists to determine their perception of the factors that the ideal therapist must possess, he found that they ranked empathy as the most important factor.[28] To develop empathy, the listener must first understand what empathy is. Empathy is not apathy, which is an unfeeling attitude, nor is empathy sympathy, which is feeling *for* or *about* another person; rather, empathy is feeling and thinking *with* another person. To feel and think with another, the listener must recreate the other person's world by sensing that world as if it were his or her own world ("without ever losing the 'as if' quality"[29]); identify with the other's feelings and thoughts by entering the other's frame of reference (without losing his or her own identity); and replicate the other's feelings and thoughts by becoming a rational and emotional mirror. According to Milton Mayeroff, author of *On Caring*, the caring, empathic listener does not merely look at the sender "in a detached way from outside, as if he were a specimen," but rather the listener is "able to be *with* him in his world, 'going' into his world in order to sense from 'inside' what life is like for him, what he is striving to be, and what he requires to grow."[30] Truly, as an unknown writer has described, being empathic is being able "to see with the eyes of another, to hear with the ears of another, [and] to feel with the heart of another."[31]

A major problem in developing empathy is the personal factor. First, because of the many personal differences existing between the sender (or speaker) and listener, their shared perceptions and experiences are limited. For example, the listener may never have experienced the world of being handicapped, unemployed, divorced, a minority, a single parent, a prisoner-of-war, a widower, on welfare, in debt, on strike, etc., whereas the sender may have been a participant in such a world. Thus, separate worlds create separate perceptions, experiences, feelings, and thoughts, and thus prevent two people from ever sharing complete empathy. Second, there is considerable personal risk involved in entering another's world and sensing the way life appears to that person from his or her frame of reference; by truly identifying with and understanding the other person in his or her world, the listener risks being changed by this new understanding. Most listeners perceive being changed as a threat to be feared, for they are accustomed to and comfortable with their own selective way of seeing, hearing, and feeling. Indeed, most listeners are afraid to take the risk of empathically entering another's world, and as a result of this fear, feeling and thinking with another is rarely achieved.[32] With an interesting reference to the Japanese character for the word *listen,* Edgar Wycoff stresses that the listener must possess inner security in order to develop empathy with the sender:

> The Japanese character for "listen" is made up of the character for "ear" placed within the character for "gate." In effect, we enter into the other person's gate or world and we might sacrifice a bit of self to do so. A good deal of inner security is necessary to truly listen and to understand another person.[33]

Finally, the personal factor affects the listener's ability to empathize when he or she must hear what he or she does not want to hear. For example, when the sender discusses information which may be offensive to the listener or when the sender verbally attacks the listener, the listener is likely to allow emotions to interfere with his or her entering the sender's frame of reference and listening with understanding. Instead, the listener will tend to listen to what his or her own emotions are saying, "Defend yourself; retaliate." Rather than listening to his or her emotions during these times when empathy is most needed, the listener should, as Rogers and Farson suggest, listen to him or herself and share his or her feelings with the sender:

> To listen to oneself is a prerequisite to listening to others. . . . The ability to recognize and understand the meaning which a particular episode has for you, with all the feelings which it stimulates in you, and the ability to express this meaning when you find it getting in the way of active listening, will clear the air

and enable you once again to be free to listen. That is, if some person or situation touches off feelings within you which tend to block your attempts to listen with understanding, begin listening to yourself. . . . A person's listening ability is limited by his ability to listen to himself.[34]

Rogers and Farson suggest that it may be difficult to listen not only to these negative expressions but also to positive feelings. Emotional outbursts of praise and joy can be difficult for some persons to handle. Much of this problem, particularly in management, may stem from our social conditioning. As listeners, we may well hear negative complaints and criticism much more frequently than positive reinforcement. Indeed, persons of authority—managers, teachers—probably do not pay enough attention to communicating praise and reinforcement. Instead, many of us hear only negative messages from superiors.

Despite the personal factor, the listener *can* develop empathy. Essential to such development is learning about the other person. The more the listener knows about the sender's background and how this background affects his or her present perceptions, feelings, thoughts, and reactions, the better equipped is the listener to understand the sender's frame of reference. For the listener to gain this understanding, the sender must self-disclose. Realizing that self-disclosing makes one vulnerable and involves risk-taking—risking evaluation, ridicule, or rejection from the listener—the sender will more likely self-disclose if he or she feels "safe" from personal harm. To provide a safe world for the sender, the listener must develop a supportive communication climate and establish trust in the relationship. The listener's key to establishing a trusting rapport with the sender is to be trustworthy—to communicate to the sender that he or she will not take advantage of the sender's vulnerability in self-disclosing. David Johnson describes the communication of this trust:

[T]he expression of warmth towards the other person in a relationship builds a high level of interpersonal trust because it increases the other person's expectations that you will respond with acceptance and support when he self-discloses. In addition, the congruence of your verbal statements, nonverbal cues such as facial expression and tone of voice, and your behavior will affect the other person's perception of your trustworthiness.[35]

Thus, through providing an atmosphere of acceptance and establishing trust in the relationship, the listener encourages the sender to self-disclose; and as the sender discloses, the listener learns more about him or her and becomes, therefore, better equipped to enter the sender's world.

The development of empathy also is facilitated when the sender and listener have shared similar feelings. If the two have been in a similar situation or if they have been in two completely different situations but have experienced similar feelings, they can often achieve a high degree of empathy. For example, when members of groups such as Mothers Against Drunk Drivers and Parents Without Partners meet, there is frequently a high degree of empathy achieved since many members have shared/do share both similar experiences and similar feelings. However, as we have noted, all too often the listener and sender have not shared similar experiences. Still, not having shared similar experiences does not prevent the development of empathy *if* those who are interacting in the communication have shared *similar* feelings. To illustrate, suppose Gina, who has recently—and unexpectantly—been terminated from her job, needs a therapeutic listener and seeks out Bob. Now suppose that Bob has never been unemployed since he has been old enough to work. Although it might appear that Bob could easily feel *sympathy for* Gina by imagining how he would feel if he were fired, it might not appear that Bob could easily feel *empathy with* Gina since he has never shared a similar experience. However, Bob has, indeed, shared similar feelings. He has known the feelings of rejection, abandonment, exclusion, confusion, frustration, and hurt; these were the feelings he experienced when his wife suddenly left him. Although the experiences that led to Bob's feelings and to Gina's feelings are quite dissimilar, many of the feelings which Bob once experienced and Gina is now experiencing are quite similar; therefore, Bob can develop empathy with Gina. Just as Bob can develop empathy with his sender, most listeners can develop empathy by first understanding how the sender is feeling and then recalling a situation in which the listener him or herself experienced similar feelings.

Still another way in which one can achieve empathy is by actually entering into the world of another. In preparing for various roles, actors and actresses sometimes attempt to live the lives of those whom they are to portray on the screen or on the stage. Musicians, too, sometimes attempt to experience the type of life of those about whom they write, sing, and play. Perhaps the most poignant example of one who attempted to enter the world of others is John Howard Griffin, the white author of *Black like Me.* During 1959 and 1960, Griffin had his skin temporarily darkened by medical treatments and his hair shaved; then he traveled as a black man through the Deep South in order to truly understand the world of the American black in the southern states. Although it is rare for people to go to the extremes that Griffin did in order to achieve empathy, unfortunately it is also rare to find listeners who are truly empathic.[36]

Although empathic listeners may be rare, they do exist, and each sender may recognize them by the way they manifest their desire to understand the sender. To convey this desire to understand the sender—from the sender's frame of reference, each listener should have this desire from within. In *Listening As a Way of Becoming,* Earl Koile states that the listener can determine if he or she has this desire by checking his or her reactions to the sender's message:

> Are you saying to yourself: "Yes, I understand or I'm trying to understand your idea or how you feel." If your intent is to understand, if you want to hear, that attitude is likely to be conveyed. . . . As you listen, are you . . . saying to yourself in one form or another: "I agree." "I disagree." "You are right." "You are wrong." "You feel like I do." "You are different from me." If you are judgmental and listening critically, that attitude is likely to be conveyed.[37]

It should be noted here that the desire to understand (as well as the desire to judge) is conveyed not only verbally but also—and possibly with even more urgency—nonverbally. Research indicates that the "nonverbal systems of communication seem to be far more effective than the verbal in building empathy, respect, and a sense that the communicator is genuine."[38] Additionally, there is rather conclusive evidence that if the listener can convey an attitude of wanting to understand the sender, the intent to understand is likely to be perceived by the sender as meaning that the sender's thoughts and feelings are worth understanding; thus, conveying intent is of great importance in establishing perceived empathy.[39]

Having the desire to understand the sender, the effective empathic listener must then strive to turn this desire into actual understanding. Covertly asking the following questions can assist the listener in achieving this understanding:

What is the sender trying to tell me?

What does this mean to him or her?

How does the sender see this situation?[40]

What is the sender feeling right now?

How does the sender view this problem?

What does the sender see in his or her world?[41]

Answering these questions accurately—that is, truly understanding the sender—requires the therapeutic listener to enter the sender's world,"listen" with all sensory equipment, and convey this understanding by means of appropriate verbal and nonverbal responses. Without empathy, as Charles Kelly notes, the listener cannot truly understand: "[L]istening, by its very nature, *has* to be empathic; a person understands what he has heard, only to the extent that he can share in the meaning, spirit, or feeling of what the communicator has said."[42]

Responding Appropriately

Appropriate listener responses are crucial to effective therapeutic listening. Unfortunately, the listener's good intentions do not always result in helpful responses. In fact, many responses may have an adverse effect on the troubled sender; rather than encouraging the sender to continue exploring his or her problem, inappropriate responses may, indeed, inhibit further self-exploration as well as inhibit further sender-listener interaction.

Responding appropriately is a skill that the listener can learn first by understanding which responses *are not* conducive and which responses *are* conducive to further self-exploration by the sender. Then, the listener should practice these furthering responses. As fourteen of the most common responses are discussed in this section, the reader should analyze and assess the responses that he or she has made to the hypothetical messages presented in the beginning of this chapter. Although the authors will specifically discuss only the responses to the third hypothetical message, the reader should also utilize the information presented to analyze and assess his or her responses to the other two hypothetical messages.

I would interrupt him before he had finished his message. Although this way of responding may appear atypical and very few readers have checked that they would respond in this manner, interruptions by listeners are quite common. Among the many reasons that a listener might interrupt a sender are the following: the listener (1) may have been thinking of something he or she wanted to say to the sender prior to the sender's comment, and, thus, rather than attending to the sender's message, the listener states what he or she had been planning to say; (2) thinks he or she knows what the sender is going to say; (3) does not want to listen to what he or she thinks the sender is going to say; (4) cannot wait to make his or her point; (5) wants to assist the sender by filling in information or by correcting the sender; (6) wants to prevent the sender from saying too much; (7) may arbitrarily dismiss the sender's opinion prematurely; etc. In a revealing study conducted by West and Zimmerman, the researchers found that in conversations between males and females, men accounted for 96 percent of the interruptions, and in conversations between parents and children, parents accounted for 89 percent of the interruptions.[43] Regardless of what the reason is for the interruption or who the initiator of the interruption is, the act of interrupting is rude and goal-blocking, it conveys implicit disregard for and rejection of the sender and/or what the sender has to say, and it evokes interpersonal resentment.[44]

"Hey, what time are we scheduled to play racquetball this afternoon?" This is an unrelated response that the listener may give for many of the same reasons that are listed in the preceding paragraph. The first reason, which appears to be the only one that is not the result of intentional rudeness, may be prevented if the sender is certain that he or she has the listener's full attention before the sender conveys the message. Despite the listener's intention for giving the unrelated response, this kind of response—like the interruption—conveys rejection of and disregard for the sender and/or the sender's message.

"Promotions are a pain! I was in grade for what seemed like years! I didn't think I'd ever get my thirteen." This response is a tangential response in which the listener singles out a word or thought contained in the sender's message and then directs the conversation away from the sender's concern and toward the listener's concern as the listener focuses attention on him or herself. Often the listener engages in "one-upmanship" by attempting to share a larger and more serious problem that he or she has; for example, the listener may respond, "You think *you* have a problem? Why, *I*'ve been trying to get my grade thirteen for seven years now. *I*. . . ." The effective therapeutic listener must expend much effort to resist a temptation to share a similar problem, relate the sender's thoughts and feelings to his or her own life, and/or use the original sender as a "captive audience" to listen to his or her problem(s). The listener's attention and thoughts should be focused on the sender—not on self.

"Forget it. It's water over the dam now."/"Hey, cheer up. You'll get your promotion soon." Both of these responses discount the sender's feelings. They communicate that the listener does not accept the sender's feelings as being valid,

justified, or important. Although the listener does not have to approve of the sender's feelings, he or she should acknowledge that the sender does, indeed, have certain feelings and should encourage the sender to verbalize and explore them. Instead of acknowledging the sender's feelings, however, many listeners discount them. Some listeners ignore the sender's feelings by making responses such as, "That's life," "You can't win them all," "That's the way it is," "That's the way the cookie crumbles," etc.; such clichés show triteness and a lack of sensitivity. Other listeners attempt to encourage the sender to repress emotions by responding in some variation of "Don't feel that way; instead, feel another way.": "Cheer up," "Don't worry about it," "Don't cry; think of something pleasant," "Calm down. Getting angry isn't going to help; try to be reasonable," "You'd better not get too excited; you haven't been asked yet," etc. Still other listeners respond by denying the sender's feelings or encouraging the sender to deny his or her feelings: "You know you don't hate your boss," "You shouldn't feel unsure," "There's no reason for you to feel anxious about his visit," "Oh, you don't mean that," etc. However unpleasant the expressed feeling may be for the listener, however uncomfortable the listener may feel as the sender discusses these feelings, or however helpful the listener may think a discounting response may be, the listener should not ignore or deny the sender's feelings and/or encourage the sender to repress or deny those feelings. Discounting the sender's feelings will not minimize or change them, nor will it help the sender to identify them and deal with them in a constructive way. Rather, discounting the other person's feelings likely will inhibit further sender-listener interaction, lead to the sender suppressing feelings, and/or have negative effects (such as headaches, ulcers, and depression) on the sender's physical and psychological health. Truly, a troubled sender needs to express feelings in order to explore, clarify, and solve his or her problems. Therefore, an effective therapeutic listener should provide the sender with a supportive communication climate which encourages the sender's *expression* rather than *suppression* of feelings.

"Your problem is that you still think diligence pays off. Maybe it did in high school where you received a college scholarship. But, buddy, the reward system is different here. Those in power here are people-users, people-abusers, people-bruisers, and people-choosers. And you've just been used, abused, and bruised. But, you haven't been 'choosed' because you don't know how to play the game. The game of organizational politics consists of doing what you have to do to become the boss's chosen one." This statement is illustrative of the numerous listener responses which attempt to provide the sender with a lesson in psychology or philosophy. Such responses imply superiority (since the listener suggests that his or her "worldly wisdom" enables him or her to understand the sender's problem better than the sender understands his or her own problem), and such responses often create confusion, inaccuracies regarding the problem and the solution(s), and/or defensiveness in the sender.

"Well, I told you you'd better learn how to take constructive criticism without getting so defensive and hostile." The sender is likely to perceive this—the blaming or "I-told-you-so" response—as a personal attack or threat; thus, this response often leads to defensive behavior as the sender feels compelled to protect his or her self-image. To avoid further blaming responses, the sender also is apt to avoid sharing future problems with the accusing listener.

"You probably haven't demonstrated enough initiative on the job." This is an evaluative response which implies that the listener believes he or she is qualified to pass judgment on the sender's thoughts and/or behaviors. Carl Rogers has identified this natural tendency of the listener to evaluate the sender's message according to the listener's frame of reference—which is based on the listener's personal value system—as the greatest of all interpersonal listening barriers.[45] Indeed, it is an obstacle to effective therapeutic listening, and it becomes a greater impediment when the listener is emotionally involved in the communication situation; for the more deeply the listener is emotionally involved, the stronger the tendency to form evaluations from his or her own point of view.[46] These evaluations, phrased not only in statement form (such as "You shouldn't have gone to the beach for the weekend" or "You are just being inconsiderate of my feelings") but also in question form (such as "How could you possibly believe something as ridiculous as that?" or "Why do you always have to be so defensive?"), pose a threat to the sender's perception of self-worth. Feeling threatened, the sender tends to become defensive, suppress self-expression, and/or resist further interaction with the listener. Perhaps the following quotation by Samuel Johnson best explains why the evaluative retort is an inappropriate therapeutic response: "God himself, Sir, doesn't propose to judge a man until his life is over. Why should you and I?"[47]

"Why don't you discuss the issue with the inspector general?" With this response, the listener also uses questioning—not to evaluate but rather to direct the sender's thoughts toward a particular point of view, one that is held by the listener. This reply tends to be a controlling response which implies that the listener already knows how the sender should solve his or her problem. The inappropriateness of this type of response is discussed in the next paragraph.

"Well, I'll tell you what you should do. Transfer over to D-4, the new section that's being formed. Rumor has it that Collins, the woman who'll be the branch chief, really takes care of her own and is not afraid to speak up for her people in front of the promotion board. I realize that your experience is in system maintenance rather than in system design, but, heck, you could take a short course or two and pick up the needed knowledge quickly. Then, you'd fit right in and get your promotion fast. Plus, you'd be rid of Jones." In this as in the previous response, the listener is offering the sender advice on how to deal with his or her problem. Although some may view the previous reply as being merely a question of interest, it is advisory—just as this declarative response is. Both advisory responses illustrate a natural tendency in most listeners—the tendency to tell the sender how the listener would deal with the problem. The listener attempts to

try to change the sender's way of viewing the problem situation—to get the sender to view the situation through the listener's eyes—and to induce the sender to go in the direction the listener wants him or her to travel.[48] Indeed, as the reader may note when analyzing his or her responses to the three hypothetical senders' messages presented in the beginning of the chapter, listeners tend to give advice all too freely.

Although advisory responses are freely given, generally with the intention to be helpful, they are often inappropriate. There are many reasons why they are unsuitable:

1. Often the listener is in no position to give advice; that is, he or she does not have all of the information needed, is not a qualified/trained counselor or an expert in the area of the sender's concern (such as law, medicine, or education), and has only limited personal experiences upon which to base this advice.
2. A listener tends to ignore the individuality of the sender. Disregarding the fact that everyone is different and that a solution which is appropriate for one person may not be suitable for another, the listener suggests that the sender deal with the problem in the way the listener (or even a friend or an acquaintance) *has dealt* with a similar problem or in the manner in which the listener *would deal* with the problem.
3. Offering advice implies that the listener is not viewing the sender as an equal; rather, it indicates a superior-subordinate (such as parent-child, employer-employee, therapist-client, etc.) relationship.
4. Advising can result in the listener losing a friend if the listener's advice, adopted by the sender, proves to be harmful rather than helpful to the sender.
5. Offering advice is an obstacle to the sender's self-expression; the troubled sender needs to talk and listen to him or herself rather than to the dialogue partner.
6. Offering advice communicates a lack of trust in the sender's capacity to solve his or her own problems and thus can decrease the sender's feelings of adequacy/self-worth.
7. Offering advice reduces the sender's responsibility for clarifying the problem and exploring possible solutions. Indeed, some senders seek advice so that they can avoid responsibility for their own decisions; then, if the listener's suggested solution does not resolve the problem, the sender can always blame the listener for the failure. According to Mayeroff, the listener who denies the sender's "need to take responsibility for his own life" is "denying him as a person."[49]
8. Frequently, offering advice is proffering something which the sender does not want. For instance, in the three hypothetical messages presented in the beginning of this chapter, not one sender asks for advice. Yet how many readers offered advice? Even when the listener realizes that the sender has not asked for advice, this realization often does not prevent the listener from telling

the sender what to do: "I know you haven't asked, but I'd like to give you a piece of advice. What you should do is. . . ." Giving advice to someone who does not ask for it is giving someone something that he or she does not want. Many of those who are trained in counseling corroborate the inappropriateness of advice-giving. For example, clinical social worker, Jeffrey Moss, who conducts seminars on the unique challenge of two-career couples, cautions the partners not to give advice:

> There is a strong tendency to give advice, even when it is not asked for, and one of the things we have learned is that partners tend to resent advice on how to handle job-related issues. People prefer to direct their concerns to a good listener, an individual who will help him or her think through a problem rather than talk to a partner who will cloud the issue with a lot of advice.[50]

Additionally, the author of *Parent Effectiveness Training,* Thomas Gordon (a clinical psychologist), notes the potentially negative results of parental advisory responses:

> Such messages are often felt by the child as evidence that the parent does not have confidence in the child's judgment or ability to find his own solution. They may influence a child to become dependent on the parent and stop thinking for himself.[51]

Finally, psychologist Carl Rogers testifies how good one feels when the listener resists the desire to provide direction for the troubled sender: "I can testify that when you are in psychological distress and someone really hears you without passing judgment on you, without trying to take responsibility for you, without trying to mold you, it feels damn good."[52]

9. Offering advice to a sender, even when he or she asks for advice, is not giving the sender what he or she needs. This final reason for advising being an inappropriate therapeutic listener response is explained in the following discussion of appropriate therapeutic listener responses.

Rather than needing a listener who responds by interrupting, sending an unrelated message, focusing on him or herself, discounting the sender's feelings, philosophizing, blaming, evaluating, or advising, the troubled sender needs a listener who will serve as a "sounding board." This "sounding board" must be someone who truly listens and appropriately responds while providing the sender with the opportunity to unburden—to talk through his or her problem/concern in order to reach his or her own solution/decision. One who truly listens is one who, knowing the power of silence, listens much more than he or she talks; that is, he or she is a true "sounding board" rather than a "resounding board." Research findings in clinical psychology support the view that listening is more helpful to the troubled sender than is talking: patient improvement relates positively to patient talk time while it relates negatively to therapist talk time.[53]

Moreover, one who responds appropriately is one who, through his or her nonverbal attending behaviors and verbal responses, communicates to the sender the following message: "I genuinely care about your well-being and about you as you are rather than as I might want you to be, I sincerely desire to understand your feelings and thoughts, and I honestly believe that, as Ralph G. Nichols has said, 'The best way to understand people is to listen to them'[54]" Receiving a message such as this one, the troubled sender will probably experience what John Powell has experienced:

> [T]here . . . have been . . . moments when someone heard my secret and accepted my confidence in gentle hands. I . . . remember what he said to assure me, the compassion in his voice, the understanding look in his eyes. I remember what those eyes looked like. I remember how his hand took mine. I remember the gentle pressure that told me that I was understood. It was a great and liberating experience, and, in its wake, I felt so much more alive. An immense need had been answered in me to be really listened to, to be taken seriously, and to be understood.[55]

Indeed, for effective therapeutic listening to occur, the listener must possess the willingness to listen, the capacity to care, and the desire to understand.

An effective therapeutic listener must also possess four other personal traits. One of these is *discretion.* Rather than playing "amateur psychiatrist" with a sender whose problem is of a serious psychological nature, the listener should refer the troubled sender to a professional therapist.

Another trait is *honesty.* If the listener does not have a sincere interest in the sender, he or she should not try to pretend interest; instead, the listener should be honest with the sender and say, "I'm not the 'sounding board' you're looking for." Likewise, if the listener does not have time at the particular moment when therapeutic listening is required, he or she should honestly explain this lack of time to the sender and not enter into a rushed session. The task of talking through a problem cannot be hurried; it takes time for the sender to arrive at his or her own solution, and a sender may never arrive at a solution if he or she does not have ample time to analyze his or her problem. Thus, rather than rushing through a session, which would be neither productive to the sender nor satisfying for the listener, the listener should schedule a time—as soon as possible—to meet with the troubled sender. The listener should also be honest when he or she cannot listen effectively because of preoccupation with his or her own personal concerns. On such occasions, the listener has no room in his or her mind for the sender to enter, and the listener should share with the sender the reason for being unable to listen at that particular time.

A third trait, which is also time-related, is *patience,* a trait which the listener must possess in order to provide the sender with the time he or she needs to express him or herself adequately. Even though the listener may have a strong desire to say, "Please, get to the point," the listener must allow the sender "to digress and expand and elaborate and repeat . . . [for] there are times when listening well means listening long, means listening very . . . very . . . patiently."[56] In addition, it means listening a little longer when the listener thinks he or she is through listening; this extra silent time will give the sender a sense of not being rushed.

The last trait is *faith*—faith in the sender's ability to solve his or her own problem. That the sender can solve his or her own problem is a basic assumption which underlies the entire premise of therapeutic listening. Essentially, it is a valid assumption. Most people can solve their own problems if only they have the opportunity to talk them through. By verbalizing one's problem to a therapeutic listener, one is able to listen more clearly to one's self, see the problem in a better perspective, reduce the problem to a manageable size, and thus deal with his or her problem in a more psychologically healthy manner. However, should the problem be great enough to require clinical, professional assistance, the therapeutic listener, as we noted earlier, should not undertake to deal with it. A problem that requires psychological attention must be referred to the properly-trained therapist.

These personal traits are essential characteristics which the effective therapeutic listener must possess in order to respond in a way that will be helpful/productive to a troubled sender. It is the authors' belief that an understanding of these traits as well as an understanding of *in*appropriate responses will provide the reader with a greater understanding of the responses which *are* appropriate when one is serving in the role of therapeutic listener. Again, as these appropriate responses are discussed, the reader should analyze and assess the responses he or she has made to the hypothetical messages presented in the beginning of this chapter.

"What explanation did Jones give you for the turning down of your application for promotion?"/"You sound as if you really feel betrayed."/"You think Jones let you down, huh?"/"Am I correct in understanding that you feel betrayed because you think Jones has let you down?" These four responses are types of responses which the effective therapeutic listener should use. They are appropriate because they are furthering responses. Rather than inhibiting the sender's self-exploration (by disregarding the sender or the sender's message, shifting the focus of attention away from the sender, discounting the sender's feelings, philosophizing, blaming, evaluating, or advising), they encourage the sender to explore freely his or her feelings and thoughts on the problem and reach his or her own solution (by maintaining the focus of attention on the sender, conveying acceptance of the sender's feelings and thoughts, and expressing continued interest in the sender and the desire to understand the sender's feelings and thoughts). Unlike an inappropriate advisory retort, these responses also enhance the sender's skills in dealing with future problems. Heun and Heun illustrate this notion of enhancement well by relating it to the following adage: "If you give a man a fish, you feed him for a day; if you teach a man how to fish, he can feed himself for a lifetime."[57] Indeed, by advising the sender on how to solve his or her problem (giving a man a fish), the listener may *possibly* help the trou-

bled sender with his or her current problem (feed him for a day); however, if the listener—serving as a "sounding board" and responding appropriately—provides the sender with an opportunity to talk through the problem and reach his or her own solution (teaching a man how to fish for himself), the sender will learn how to cope effectively and independently with problems that he or she may encounter throughout his or her life (feeding him for a lifetime). Truly, what the sender needs, rather than advice, is the opportunity to develop those skills which will enable him or her to solve his or her own problems. As we examine closely each of these appropriate responses, we will see how each one provides the sender with this opportunity for further skill-development.

"What explanation did Jones give you for the turning down of your application for promotion?" This probing response is a furthering response which encourages the sender to continue. The listener's intent—in using the probing response—may be to seek additional information in order to learn more about the sender's feelings and thoughts, to assist the sender in expanding on a certain line of thought in order for the sender to gain a clearer perspective of that thought, to clarify a vague aspect of the sender's message in order for the listener to gain a better understanding of the sender's feelings and thoughts, to induce the sender to go beyond superficial statements, and/or to elicit further discussion between the dialogue partners. A probing response shows listener interest in the sender and the sender's message. It also demonstrates the listener's desire to understand. Furthermore, a probe can effectively temper or soften the "adult" image of the listener in certain interactions, such as encounters between parent-child, employer-employee, older sibling-younger sibling, etc. To achieve the desired results, the listener must carefully phrase the probing response. Two of the most effective ways to phrase it are (1) as an open-ended question—"Who exactly is saying this to you?" "How do they display their feelings?" "What do you mean by that word?" (rather than one that has an evaluative or advisory tone as *why* questions tend to have—"Why don't you . . . ?") and (2) as a restatement—in a form of a question—of a portion of the sender's message—"You really believe that the boss is after you?" "You're not going back to school?" "You don't want to see your parents again?" (rather than one that is, in reality, merely a statement of the listener's view). One last point regarding questioning responses is that the listener should avoid bombarding the sender with questions such as (in responding to the hypothetical message of the seventeen-year-old nephew), "What makes you think your parents are impossible? What do you actually mean by *impossible?* What do they do to suggest this idea? Do you have any specific examples that show them being impossible? What similarities and differences are there in your mother's and father's behaviors? When do they . . . ?" One questioning response at a time is generally enough!

Although the probing response is a furthering response, it does not show as much understanding as do the remaining three furthering responses. They show that the listener is truly striving to feel and/or think *with*—rather than *about*—the troubled sender.

"You sound as if you really feel betrayed." This is a feeling response that indicates the listener's sensitivity to the sender's feelings and the listener's desire to feel with the sender. To confirm that he or she is, indeed, feeling with the sender, the listener employs the perception-checking approach. This approach consists of the listener listening to the sender's total message to identify the sender's inner feeling(s) and then verbally reflecting (in a tentatively-phrased manner) his or her interpretation to the sender for confirmation, modification, clarification, and/or correction; in short, the listener asks the sender to verify the listener's perception of the sender's feelings. An effective perception check does not convey listener approval or disapproval of the sender's feelings, nor does it imply mind-reading by the listener (for example, "Why are you so discouraged [or frustrated, demoralized, fearful, etc.]?"); rather, it conveys this message: "I want to understand your feelings—is this the way you feel?"[58]

Although uncovering feelings is important both to the sender for self-exploration of the problem and to the listener for understanding the sender/sender's problem, it often is a formidable task. One reason for the difficulty in uncovering feelings is that the sender quite frequently does not verbalize his or her feelings explicitly and specifically. Perhaps others have so often discounted the sender's feelings in the past that he or she has not learned to identify his or her feelings clearly or has learned to hide his or her feelings by sealing them inside and, thus, has never had the practice needed to articulate his or her feelings. Or, perhaps the sender is a male, and the listener is a male to whom the sender prefers not to disclose his emotions. Experimental research by Shimanoff, for example, indicates that males express their emotions significantly more often to females than to males; this finding has led Shimanoff to suggest that there may be supportive behavioral differences between male and female listeners or that males may "feel safer in expressing their emotions to females, who are perceived to be more nurturing and supportive of disclosures of affect."[59] Also, if the sender is a male, he may be less expressive of his emotions nonverbally than a female is, for males generally have been conditioned to believe that it is not manly to display their emotions.[60] Still another possible reason is that the sender has an inadequate feeling vocabulary which prevents him or her from describing his or her feelings. Indeed, most people have deficient feeling vocabularies; too many people rely on general and vague terms, such as *good, bad, fine, okay, terrible, up, down,* etc., to describe their feelings rather than describing them by using some of the more specific feeling words listed below:[61]

Feelings of Anger

aggravated
angry
annoyed
belligerent
bitter
bugged
cool
hostile
intolerant
irritated
mad
mean
peeved
perturbed

Feelings of Anger

cruel
ennerved
enraged
furious
hateful
resentful
spiteful
vengeful
vindictive

Feelings of Sadness

abandoned
alienated
alone
ashamed
awful
blue
crushed
defeated
depressed
despondent
disappointed
down
forelorn
foresaken
grief
hopeless
humiliated
hurt
lonely
low
neglected
rejected
sad
small
sorrow
unhappy
unloved (able)
worthless

Feelings of Fear

afraid
alarmed
anxious
apprehensive
desperation
embarrassed
fearful
frightened
horrified
insecure
intimidated
nervous
overwhelmed
panicky
restless
scared
shy
tense
threatened
timid
uneasy
worried

Feelings of Inadequacy

broken
cowardly
crippled
deficient
demoralized
disabled
feeble
helpless
impotent
inadequate
incompetent
ineffective
inferior

paralyzed
powerless
small
useless
vulnerable
weak

Feelings of Stress

ambivalent
anxious
baffled
bewildered
bothered
caught
confused
conflicted
disgusted
dissatisfied
distressed
disturbed
doubtful
exposed
frustrated
futile
helpless
hopeless
nervous
overwhelmed
perplexed
puzzled
skeptical
trapped
uncomfortable
unsure
upset
vulnerable

Feelings of Happiness

aglow
calm
content
elated
enthused
excited
fantastic
gay
glad
good
great
happy
joyous
overjoyed
pleased
proud
satisfied
thrilled
wonderful

Feelings of Love, Caring

affable
affectionate
altruistic
amiable
caring
close
concerned
considerate
cooperative
devoted
empathic
forgiving
friendly
fulfilled
genuine
giving
humane
intimate
kind
love (able)
peaceful
sensitive
sympathy
tender
warm(th)
whole

Feelings of Adequacy

able
adequate
bold
brave
healthy
important
nervy
peerless

Feelings of Adequacy

capable
competent
confident
effective
fearless
powerful
robust
secure
self-assured
stable
strong

Another reason why uncovering feelings may be difficult is that the listener may not be skilled in listening for feelings. Perhaps this lack of competence is the result of previous interactions with senders who do not explicitly and specifically express that they are confused, depressed, anxious, etc., or interactions with senders who—not knowing how to express their feelings constructively—have expressed their feelings in a way which has created defensiveness in the listener (for example, "You make me so angry when you act so stupid!") and has led the listener to stop listening rather than attempt to understand the sender's feelings. Also, it could result from the listener's inadequate feeling vocabulary; deficiency in feeling words limits the listener's ability to recognize and verbally reflect specific feelings. It is the authors' contention, however, that the listener's difficulty in discerning feelings results, to a large extent, from the listener's inattention to and inexperience with "listening with the third ear." That is, the listener fails to "listen" to what is not spoken, or he or she fails to detect the contradiction(s) between what is spoken and what is unspoken. As an example, Shelia Pearce, a protective social worker for the elderly, frequently confronts contradictory messages:

> [I]n a crisis case an elderly patient may say he agrees and is willing to go to a nursing home, thus leading me to believe that he feels there is no problem with this decision. At the same time as he rubs his face and twists his hands or a tear appears in his eye, the client is nonverbally saying the opposite.[62]

Research documents the importance of nonverbal communication in the conveying of feelings;[63] yet, although the listener may note such obvious contradictory messages as exhibited in the situation cited above, he or she often does not attend to the more subtle messages such as the nervous fingers, strained vocal tone, downcast eyes, scarcely-heard sigh, tense body, penetrating silence, and the thousands of other unspoken messages that the sender conveys.

Fortunately, by employing perception-checking feeling responses, as well as by demonstrating appropriate attending behaviors, developing a supportive communication climate, and listening with empathy, the listener can assist the sender in expressing his or her feelings. Moreover, the listener can develop the skill of listening for feelings by engaging in therapeutic listening sessions in which he or she can practice helping the sender express his or her emotions, by learning how to prevent being controlled by emotions when confronted with a sender who creates a defensive communication climate, by enlarging one's feeling vocabulary, and by becoming more attentive to and adept at decoding the sender's nonverbal messages. Developing skills to assist the sender in expressing his or her feelings clearly and improving personal skills to listen for feelings will enable the listener to make effective feeling responses. Both the sender and the listener can benefit. Feeling responses will aid the sender in exploring further his or her feelings, recognizing previously denied or buried feelings, clarifying these feelings, and, thus, dealing with a problem more effectively. Likewise, it will aid the listener in acknowledging the sender's feelings, viewing them from the sender's frame of reference, and thus understanding the sender/sender's problem more accurately.

"You think Jones let you down, huh?" This is a thought response that indicates the listener's desire to understand the sender's thoughts and to think with the sender. To test his or her understanding, the listener uses the approach of paraphrasing, which was first noted in chapter 6 as a means of increasing understanding during comprehensive listening. Equally useful for increasing understanding during therapeutic listening, this approach is discussed in detail in the following paragraph.

"Am I correct in understanding that you feel betrayed because you think Jones has let you down?" This response is both a feeling *and* thought response. It indicates that the listener, having used all of his or her sensory equipment to listen to the sender's total message (which usually consists of both feelings and thoughts), desires to verify this understanding by using a paraphrase. In paraphrasing, the listener's goal is not to approve or disapprove, agree or disagree, praise or condemn; rather, it is to understand—to understand empathically the sender's feelings and thoughts from the sender's frame of reference. In essence, paraphrasing enables the listener to convey this message to the sender: "This is my understanding of how you are feeling and what you are thinking. Am I understanding you correctly?" Unfortunately, many listeners fail to test their understanding, and, as a result of individual differences in assigning meaning to verbal and nonverbal expressions, true understanding never develops. Too often, listeners respond by saying, "I understand what you mean" or "I understand how you feel," and senders accept such responses as indicators of understanding when, in fact, there has been no real understanding expressed. Rogers and Farson stress the importance of testing for understanding by encouraging communicators to practice this "rule of thumb": "[A]ssume that one never really understands until he can communicate this understanding to the other's satisfaction."[64]

To develop the skill of paraphrasing, the listener must recognize and practice proper phrasing and timing. Proper phrasing consists of the listener reflecting—in one's *own* words—his or her understanding of how the sender is feeling and what the sender is thinking. In selecting the appropriate words, the listener should strive to be *accurate* (by not adding new feelings/thoughts or deleting important feelings/thoughts), *concise* (by generally using fewer words than the sender has used to prevent unnecessary redundancy), and *perceptive* (by showing an understanding of what is felt and said rather than just repeating word for word). In addition, the listener should develop an adequate vocabulary of entry phrases

Paraphrasing speaker's messages enables us to communicate that we are listening attentively.

Photo by Robert Tocha.

such as, "If I understand you correctly, you're saying . . .", "Do you mean that . . . ?", "Let me tell you what I'm sensing. You . . .", "Let me repeat what I think you're saying. You . . .", "What I'm understanding you to say is . . .", "Let's make sure I'm clear on how you're feeling. You feel . . .", "Are you saying that . . . ?", etc. An entry phrase which the listener should avoid is the commonly-used, "Are you trying to say . . . ?" The word *trying* may be insulting to the sender, and it implies that the listener intends to supply thoughts which the sender may not be thinking; in other words, it conveys the notion that the listener is viewing the sender's thoughts from the listener's—rather than with the sender's—frame of reference. It should also be noted that an entry phrase is not always necessary (as the thought response—*"You think Jones let you down, huh?"*—shows). To further illustrate, if the sender were to say, "I don't know what to do. I want to continue working, but, then again, I would just love to be free to do what I want to do," the listener could—without an entry phrase—paraphrase by saying, "You're unsure about retiring, huh?"

Knowing *how* to paraphrase, the listener should also know *when* to paraphrase. The listener does not interrupt the sender to add his or her paraphrase; rather, he or she, recognizing the sender's regulatory cues, paraphrases at natural breaks in the interaction. Furthermore, he or she paraphrases when there is a meaningful purpose: to eliminate guesswork/speculation; to admit confusion; to ask for clarification; to encourage the sender to continue talking so as to clarify, modify, expand, repeat, etc., his or her feelings and thoughts; to initiate the exploration of important feelings and thoughts which are still unexplored; to assist the sender in listening to him or herself with more clarity and accuracy; to help the sender uncover layers of hidden thoughts and feelings so that he or she can then move beyond these formerly impeding thoughts and feelings; to provide a supportive climate in which the sender feels comfortable, safe, and free of evaluation; to develop empathy; to establish rapport (and develop or maintain a positive relationship with the sender); to indicate recognition of, interest in, and concern for the sender; or to implement any other intent that will increase the listener's accurate understanding of the sender's feelings and thoughts from the sender's frame of reference and which will enhance the sender's self-exploration of his or her problem and help the sender reach his or her own solution.

As we have just noted, paraphrasing is, indeed, a very useful therapeutic listening skill; however, it is not without what some consider to be negative aspects. Paraphrasing is both energy-consuming and time-consuming. For the listener to travel with the sender beneath the sender's surface feelings in order to uncover layer upon layer of hidden feelings as well as to identify the sender's thoughts—many of which are often disjointed and unclear—and then reflect understanding of the sender's feelings and thoughts for confirmation demand a great deal of listener time and effort. Without doubt, utilizing this skill can be exhausting and lengthy, but listening to understand—truly understand—often is such a task. Another negative aspect is that paraphrasing can be redundant and annoying if the listener does no more than exchange or trade words with the sender. For example, if a sender says, "I'm depressed because you're leaving," and the listener responds, "Are you saying you're depressed because I'm leaving?", the listener is going to ridiculous extremes in using the paraphrasing approach. Accordingly, the listener should use discretion in determining when paraphrasing is not and when it is necessary to insure understanding.

Yet another disadvantage is that the listener often finds the paraphrasing approach to be extremely artificial and mechanical when he or she first begins to use it. However, learning this skill is just like learning any other new skill (such as driving, skiing, or typing); the more one properly practices the skill, the more skillful one becomes and the more automatic is one's behaviors. By understanding the need for expending energy and time to achieve true understanding, by using discretion in applying paraphrasing, and by practicing properly the skill of paraphrasing, the effective therapeutic listener can minimize what could be potentially negative aspects of paraphrasing, which is a very useful therapeutic listening approach.

By serving as an effective therapeutic listener by focusing attention, demonstrating attending behaviors, developing a supportive communication climate, listening with empathy, and responding appropriately, the listener is investing a part of his or her life in the life of a troubled sender—one who needs a "sounding board" in order to talk through a problem and reach his or her own solution. Helping a distressed person establish communication with him or herself contributes to that person's individual strength and satisfaction; this is the real advantage of therapeutic listening. Although what we have described sounds clinical, and indeed the term "therapeutic" is clinical, we are really urging empathic, helpful listening practices. A desire to serve in such a capacity and the ability to be a true "sounding board" for the speaker can enable an individual listener to function effectively as a therapeutic listener.

> *We listen with our hearts.*
> When I listen with the heart
> I stop playing the game of non-listening.
> In other words,
> I step inside the other's skin;
> I walk in his shoes;
> I attempt to see things from his point-of-view;
> I establish eye contact;
> I give him conscious attention;
> I reflect my understanding of his words;
> I question;
> I attempt to clarify.
> Gently,
> I draw the other out
> as his lips stumble over words,
> as his face becomes flushed,
> as he turns his face aside.
> I make the other feel that
> I understand that he is important,
> that I am grateful that he trusts me enough
> to share deep, personal feelings with me.
> *I grant him worth.*[65]

SUMMARY

In this chapter, we have described five skills which the listener should practice when he or she is engaging in therapeutic listening—listening to provide a "sounding board" to allow a troubled sender to talk through a problem to his or her own solution. These five skills are *focusing attention, demonstrating attending behaviors, developing a supportive communication climate, listening with empathy,* and *responding appropriately.* Additionally, we have provided the reader with a means (1) to analyze and assess his or her present therapeutic listening responses by comparing them with those responses recognized as inhibiting self-exploration by the sender as well as with those responses recognized as furthering self-exploration by the sender and (2) to develop, if necessary, more appropriate personal responses.

While we recognize the great need for therapeutic listeners today, particularly as people need "someone to talk to," we have stressed the difficulty of this type of listening. The successful therapeutic listener must have the willingness to listen, the capacity to care, the desire to understand, honesty, and the patience to assume the role of "sounding board"; he or she also needs faith that the sender is, indeed, able to come to grips with his or her problem and derive his or her own solution to it. Finally, it is important for the listener to use discretion in determining when and when not to serve as a "sounding board." The therapeutic listener should not play "amateur psychiatrist"; rather, he or she should deal only with those problems which do not have serious psychological ramifications. The rewards for listening with empathy, however, can be great, especially as you contribute to the well-being and growth of another human being.

SUGGESTED ACTIVITIES

1. If you have a "Hot Line" telephone counseling referral service in your community, arrange to attend one of the training sessions where volunteers are trained in the principles of listening with empathy. What principles are stressed? What are the differences in listening with empathy over the telephone and listening with empathy to a person face-to-face?
2. Practice techniques of therapeutic listening. Permit a friend to talk with you about a problem (nothing of a serious psychological nature) related to his or her family, his or her school work, a friend, etc. Listen to the problem therapeutically, providing a "sounding board" for your friend's problem. Employ only appropriate responses. Provide time for your friend to present with his or her own solution. After the listening experience, ask your friend how he or she felt about your role as a therapeutic listener. Have him or her react before you disclose the techniques you attempted to utilize. How do *you* feel about the experience? Were you an effective therapeutic listener? Why or why not? What will you do differently the next time you attempt to function as a therapeutic listener?
3. Arrange to interview a professional counselor. Ask him or her about his or her therapeutic listening techniques. What types of responses does he or she most frequently use? How does he or she listen with empathy and yet maintain a professional "doctor-patient" detachment? Does he or she find that the development of therapeutic listening skills improves with time?
4. Practice listening with understanding in order to develop skill in empathic listening. As someone talks with you about a problem, listen for both feelings and thoughts. Reflect your understanding by applying the approaches of perception-checking and paraphrasing.
5. Turn to the list of feeling words in the chapter. Expand the list with as many words as you can add. Why is it so difficult to handle such words?
6. Roleplay communication problems that you have personally encountered recently. During the roleplaying, practice therapeutic listening. Following the roleplaying, discuss the important aspects and skills surrounding therapeutic listening.

7. To gain experience/practice in listening for feelings, ask a friend to discuss some event that happened to him or her in the distant or immediate past. As your friend discusses this event, listen—with all of your sensory equipment—for his or her *present* feelings. Reflect your understanding of his or her present feelings for confirmation/correction. How successful were you in identifying the other person's feelings?
8. What would you say to reflect the feelings and thoughts of a troubled sender who said, "I really don't know what to say"?

NOTES

1. Robert Wicks, television interview with The Christophers, New York City, quoted in "Listening: First Aid for the Troubled Mind," *Grit,* 25 May 1980, p. 27.
2. Ray Jones, "The Art of Listening," *Virginia Magazine,* July 24, 1983, p. 14.
3. Ernest G. Beier and Evans G. Valens, *People Reading* (New York: Stein and Day, 1975), p. 154.
4. Carol Krucoff, "Families: Listening to Teens," *The Washington Post* 17 June 1980, p. B-5.
5. Colleen Onnen, "Don't Try to Fix it . . . Just Listen," *Family Circle* 96 (July 12, 1983): 6.
6. Josephine Novak, "In Touch," *The Evening Sun,* 6 October 1980, p. C-2.
7. *Ibid.*
8. B. D. Sorrell, "Is Anybody Listening?" *Data Management* 13 (December 1975): 34.
9. John H. Meyer and Teresa C. Meyer, "The Supervisor As Counselor—How to Help the Distressed Employee," *Management Review,* April 1982, p. 44.
10. Lynette Long, *Listening/Responding* (Monterey, California: Brooks/Cole Publishing Company, 1978), p. 2.
11. Hans D. Strupp and Suzanne W. Hadley, "Specific vs. Nonspecific Factors in Psychotherapy," *Archives of General Psychiatry* 36 (September 1979): 1125.
12. Carl R. Rogers and Richard E. Farson, "Active Listening," in *Readings in Interpersonal and Organizational Communication,* 2nd ed., eds. Richard Huseman, Cal M. Logue, and Dwight I. Freshley (Boston: Holbrooks Publishing Company, 1973), p. 548.
13. F. D. Kelly, "Communicational Significance of Therapist Proxemic Cues, *Journal of Consulting and Clinical Psychology* 39 (October 1972): 345; John Powell Stokes, "Model Competencies for Attending Behavior," *Counselor Education and Supervision* 32 (September 1977): 23–27; R. F. Haase and D. T. Tepper, Jr., "Nonverbal Components of Empathic Communication," *Journal of Counseling Psychology* 19 (September 1972): 417–424.
14. Research shows that in a communication interaction between two Caucasions at a distance of six feet, the average amount of eye contact in which the communicators engage is as follows:

Individual gaze	60 percent
while listening	75 percent
while speaking	40 percent
length of gaze	3 seconds
Eye contact (mutual gaze)	30 percent
length of mutual gaze	1½ seconds

See Michael Argyle, *Bodily Communication* (New York: International Universities Press, 1975), p. 229.

This nearly 2:1 ratio of looking while listening to looking while speaking may differ with black communicators; LaFrance and Mayo have found that in black-black interactions, black speakers tend to engage in more looking time at the listener while black listeners tend to engage in more looking away while attending to the speaker. See M. LaFrance and C. Mayo, "Racial Differences in Gaze Behavior during Conversations: Two Systematic Observational Studies," *Journal of Personality and Social Psychology* 33 (May 1976): 547–552.

15. Connie Broughton, "When Mother's Intuition Isn't Enough," *Redbook* 159 (May 1982): 56.
16. Kelly, "Communicational Significance of Therapist Proxemic Cues"; Stokes, "Model Competencies for Attending Behavior"; Haase and Tepper, "Nonverbal Components of Empathic Communication"; F. F. Haase, "The Relationship of Sex and Instructional Set to the Regulation of Interpersonal Interaction Distance in a Counseling Analogue," *Journal of Counseling Psychology* 17 (May 1970): 233–236; Peter K. Hamilton and William A. Glasgow, "An Experimental Study of the Effect of Listening Behavior on Self-Disclosure and Interpersonal Trust" (Paper delivered at the Central States Speech Communication Association Conference, Lincoln, Nebraska, April, 1983).
17. A. R. D'Augelli, "Nonverbal Behavior of Helpers in Initial Helping Interactions," *Journal of Counseling Psychology* 21 (September 1974): 360–363; E. W. L. Smith, "Postural and Gestural Communication of A and B 'Therapist Types' during Dyadic Interviews," *Journal of Consulting and Clinical Psychology* 39 (August 1972): 29–36; H. Hackney, "Facial Gestures and Subject Expression of Feelings," *Journal of Counseling Psychology* 21 (May 1974): 173–178; Hamilton and Glasgow, "An Experimental Study of the Effect of Listening Behavior on Self-Disclosure and Interpersonal Trust."
18. S. D. Duncan, Jr., "On the Structure of Speaker-Auditor Interaction during Speaking Turns," *Language in Society* 2 (October 1974): 161–180; Hamilton and Glasgow, "An Experimental Study of the Effect of Listening Behavior on Self-Disclosure and Interpersonal Trust."
19. Stokes, "Model Competencies for Attending Behavior."
20. S. M. Jourard, *Disclosing Man to Himself* (Princeton, New Jersey: Van Nostrand Reinhold, 1968), p. 65; J. E. Pattison, "Effects of Touch on Self-Exploration and the Therapeutic Relationship," *Journal of Consulting and Clinical Psychology* 40 (April 1973): 170–175; Annie Gottlieb, "Touching and Being Touched," *Mademoiselle* 83 (January 1982): 80–81, 167, 174.
21. Theodor Reik, *Listening with the Third Ear* (New York: Pyramid Books, 1948), pp. 124, 126.
22. Thomas Gordon, *Parent Effectiveness Training* (New York: Peter H. Wyden, 1970), pp. 41–45; Thomas Gordon, *Leader Effectiveness Training* (New York: Peter H. Wyden, 1977), pp. 60–62.
23. The authors' descriptions of characteristics are adapted from Jack R. Gibb, "Defensive Communication," *Journal of Communication* 11 (September 1961): 142.
24. Carl R. Rogers, *On Becoming a Person* (Boston: Houghton Mifflin Company, 1961), p. 336.

25. Stokes, "Model Competencies for Attending Behavior"; Desmond Morris, *Manwatching* (New York: Harry N. Abrams, Inc., Publishers, 1977), pp. 133–135, 186–190; Albert Mehrabian, *Silent Messages* (Belmont, California: Wadsworth Publishing Company, 1971); S. M. Jourard, *Disclosing Man to Himself;* Albert E. Scheflen, *Body Language and the Social Order* (Englewood Cliffs, New Jersey: Prentice-Hall, 1972); Albert E. Scheflen, "The Significance of Posture in Communication Systems," *Psychiatry* 27 (November 1964): 326–329; M. Wiener et al., "Nonverbal Behavior and Nonverbal Communication," *Psychological Review* 79 (May 1972): 210–211; Gerald I. Nierenberg and Henry H. Calero, *How to Read a Person like a Book* (New York: Pocket Books, 1973); P. F. Ostwald, *Soundmaking: The Acoustic Communication of Emotion* (Springfield, Illinois: Charles C. Thomas, 1963), p. 25.
26. Paul G. Friedman, *Listening Processes: Attention, Understanding, Evaluation,* 2nd ed. (Washington, D.C.: National Education Association, 1983), p. 18.
27. Robert G. Carkhuff, *Helping and Human Relations, Volume I* (New York: Holt, Rinehart and Winston, 1969), p. 173.
28. N. Raskin, "Studies on Psychotherapeutic Orientation: Ideology in Practice" cited by Carl R. Rogers, "Empathic: An Unappreciated Way of Being," *The Counseling Psychologist* 5 (1975): 5.
29. Carl R. Rogers, "The Therapeutic Relationship: Recent Theory and Research," in *The Human Dialogue,* eds. Floyd W. Matson and Ashley Montague (New York: The Free Press, 1967), p. 250.
30. Milton Mayeroff, *On Caring* (New York: Harper and Row, 1971), p. 30.
31. Ronald B. Adler, Lawrence B. Rosenfeld, and Neil Towne, *Interplay* (New York: Holt, Rinehart and Winston, 1980), p. 161.
32. Rogers, *On Becoming a Person,* pp. 18, 333.
33. Edgar B. Wycoff, "Canons of Communication," *Personnel Journal* 60 (March 1981), pp. 211–212.
34. Rogers and Farson, "Active Listening," p. 553.
35. David Johnson, *Reaching Out* (Englewood Cliffs, New Jersey: Prentice-Hall, 1972), p. 47.
36. Rogers, *On Becoming a Person,* p. 18.
37. Earl Koile, *Listening As a Way of Becoming* (Waco, Texas: Calibre Books, 1977), p. 91.
38. Dale G. Leathers, *Nonverbal Communication Systems* (Boston: Allyn and Bacon, 1976), p. 236.
39. R. D. Quinn, "Psychotherapists' Expressions as an Index to the Quality of Early Therapeutic Relationships" (Ph.D. diss., University of Chicago, 1955).
40. Rogers and Farson, "Active Listening," p. 547.
41. Lawrence M. Brammer, *The Helping Relationship* (Englewood Cliffs, New Jersey: Prentice-Hall, 1979), pp. 36–38.
42. Charles M. Kelly, "Empathic Listening," in *Bridges not Walls,* 2nd ed., ed. John Stewart (Reading, Massachusetts: Addision-Wesley Publishing Company, 1977), p. 224.
43. Carol Lynn Mithers, "When You Talk, Does He Listen?" *Mademoiselle* 86 (March 1980): 201.
44. E. Sundstrom, "An Experimental Study of Crowding: Effect of Room Size, Intrusion, and Goal Blocking on Nonverbal Behavior, Self-Disclosure, and Self-Reported Stress," *Journal of Personality and Social Psychology* 32 (October 1975): 645–654.

45. Rogers, *On Becoming a Person,* pp. 330–331.
46. *Ibid.,* p. 331.
47. Alan Loy McGinnis, *The Friendship Factor* (Minneapolis: Augsburg Publishing House, 1979), p. 71.
48. Rogers and Farson, "Active Listening," p. 545.
49. Mayeroff, *On Caring,* p. 34.
50. Josephine Novak, "Separating Fantasy and Reality in Two-Career Households," *The Evening Sun,* 16 May 1983, p. B-2.
51. Gordon, *Parent Effectiveness Training,* p. 322.
52. Carl R. Rogers, *A Way of Being* (Boston: Houghton Mifflin Company, 1980), p. 12.
53. Fred R. Staples and R. Bruce Sloane, "Truax Variables, Speech Characteristics, and Therapeutic Outcome," *Journal of Nervous and Mental Disease* 163 (August 1976): 135–140.
54. Ralph G. Nichols, "The Struggle to Be Human" (Paper delivered at the First Annual Convention of the International Listening Association, Atlanta, Georgia, February 17, 1980), p. 7.
55. John Powell, "Reflections on 'Estrangement' and 'Encounter' " in *Bridges not Walls,* ed. John Stewart (Reading, Massachusetts: Addison-Wesley Publishing Company, 1973), p. 178.
56. Judith Voist, "May I Have Your Attention, Please?" *Redbook* 153 (September 1979): 52.
57. Linda R. Heun and Richard E. Heun, *Developing Skills for Human Interaction,* 2nd ed. (Columbus, Ohio: Charles E. Merrill Publishing Company, 1978), p. 119.
58. John L. Wallen, "Developing Effective Interpersonal Communication" in *Communicating Interpersonally,* eds. R. Wayne Pace, Brent D. Peterson, and Terrence R. Radcliffe (Columbus, Ohio: Charles E. Merrill Publishing Company, 1973), p. 231.
59. Susan B. Shimanoff, "The Role of Gender in Linguistic References to Emotive States," *Communication Quarterly* 30 (Spring 1983): 178.
60. *Ibid.*
61. From *Active Listening Skills for Staff Development: A Cognitive Viewpoint* (St. Paul: Minnesota Department of Education), pp. 8–9.
62. Sharon L. DuBose, "Interview with Shelia F. Pearce." Unpublished paper, College Park, Maryland: University of Maryland, 1983. Used by permission.
63. Ray L. Birdwhistell, as cited in Mark L. Knapp, *Nonverbal Communication in Human Interaction,* 2nd ed. (New York: Holt, Rinehart and Winston, 1978), p. 30; Mehrabian, *Silent Messages,* pp. 43–44.
64. Rogers and Farson, "Active Listening," p. 549.
65. Loretta Girzaitis, *Listening a Response Ability* (Winona, Minnesota: St. Mary's Press, 1972), p. 42. Reprinted with permission.

Concepts You Will Encounter

Critical Listening
Persuasion
Coercion
Motivated Sequence
Ethos/Source Credibility
Logos
Inductive Arguments
Deductive Arguments
Syllogisms
Enthymemes
Validity
Truth
Reasoning Fallacies
Hasty Generalizations
Causal Reasoning
Analogical Reasoning
Non Sequitur
Arguing in a Circle
Ignoring the Issue
Evidence
Testimonies
Facts/Opinions/Inferences
Rumors
Propaganda
Biases
Statistics
Pathos
Need Levels
Emotional Appeals
Emotive Language
Responsibilities

Skills You Should Develop

Identifying the Dimensions of Source Credibility
Recognizing the Influence of Source Credibility
Evaluating Inductive Arguments
Evaluating Deductive Arguments
Detecting and Evaluating Reasoning Fallacies
Evaluating Evidence
Recognizing Need Levels
Identifying Emotional Appeals
Dealing Effectively with Emotive Language

Critical Listening

8

The fourth purpose for listening goes beyond comprehensive listening and adds the dimension of judgment, for critical listening is listening to comprehend and *then* evaluate the message. The critical listener makes a decision to accept or reject a message on the basis of sound criteria. Listening should be critical especially when the listener is exposed to a persuasive message—a message designed to influence a change in the listener.

The Need for Critical Listeners

Now, as never before, we are confronted by speakers who want to change our attitudes and our behavior. Daily, we are flooded with persuasive messages—ranging from family members' pleas to buy that beach condominium or to vacation in Hawaii, campaign speeches, radio and television commercials, salespersons' pitches, and telephone solicitations to problem solving discussions, lobbyists' views, briefings advocating new procedures, and leaders' pleas. Hayakawa describes the unparalleled position in which we are currently living:

> The citizen of today, Christian or Jew or Mohammedan, financier or farmhand, stockbroker or stockboy, has to interpret more words a day than the citizen of any earlier time in world history. Literate or semi-literate, we are assailed by words all day long: news commentators, soap operas, campaign speechs, newspapers, the propaganda of pressure groups or governments—all of these trying to tell us something, to manipulate our beliefs, whether about the kind of toothpaste to use or the kind of economic system to support.[1]

Since freedom of speech ensures equal rights to both the honest and dishonest speaker, we must be effective critical listeners if we are to protect and control ourselves rather than allowing others to control us. Wendell Johnson has stressed the importance of our being critical listeners.

> As speakers, men have become schooled in the arts of persuasion, and without the counter-art of listening a man can be persuaded—even by his own words—to eat foods that ruin his liver, to abstain from killing flies, to vote away his right to vote, and to murder his fellows in the name of righteousness. The art of listening holds for us the desperate hope of withstanding the spreading ravages of commercial, nationalistic, and ideological persuasion.[2]

Our becoming schooled in the art of listening critically, then, as Gunn stated, "may mean not just being realistic and alert to the times in which we are alive, but quite literally it may mean being and staying alive."[3]

As we have previously stated, the critical listener's decision to accept or reject a message must be based on sound criteria. Understanding the process of persuasion as it applies to listeners will aid the listener in establishing these criteria and making careful judgments when he or she is listening not only to so-called "informative" messages which are mere rumors but also to persuasive messages.

The concept of influence may be viewed in terms of a continuum of influences. On the one end is persuasion, which has been defined by Goyer as "the process by means of which one party purposefully secures a voluntary change of behavior, mental and/or physical, on the part of another party by employing appeals to both feeling and intellect.[4] On the other hand, we have coercion in which the receiver is given no choice or a choice between highly undesirable alternatives.

If you are told to vote for Raymond Jones for city mayor because he can accomplish his campaign promises, you are given a *persuasive* choice to accept or reject the speaker's thesis. If you are told to stop smoking because you will die of lung cancer, you are presented with a more *coercive* message. The extreme of coercive influence is the use of force. A robber's message of "Hand over your money" at gunpoint is a graphic example of where you, the receiver, would be left with no choice or with a choice between highly undesirable alternatives.

Most messages do not fit neatly into the persuasive or coercive category but, instead, fall somewhere along the continuum between the two extremes. Thus, advertising, propaganda, political campaigns, religion, education, and most means of social influence will share elements of persuasion and coercion. It is to be hoped, however, that these messages will ultimately be persuasive and, thus, leave listeners with a choice. The receivers' not being presented with a choice is inconsistent with a basic objective of American democracy: freedom of choice.

The process of influence usually takes the form of a psychological sequence. This sequence was identified by Monroe and has been labeled the "motivated sequence." According to Monroe, to persuade or to be persuaded, the message must include five basic steps:

1. Attention—getting the attention of the listener.
2. Need—demonstrating the problem, the need for the proposal.
3. Satisfaction—presenting the proposal to satisfy the need.
4. Visualization—illustrating what will happen if the proposal is accepted or what will happen if it is rejected.
5. Action—issuing a challenge or an appeal to the listener.[5]

These basic steps describe what occurs as we attempt to influence. It is a system, but it should be viewed as more of a process than the listing might suggest. Actually, some of the steps may transpire simultaneously. The results may be visualized, for instance, while the solution/satisfaction step is presented. Any persuasive message, however, whether it be an ad, a speech, or a sale's pitch, can be seen to conform to this psychological sequence.

Effective persuasion usually does not result in a change of behavior in the receiver on the basis of one persuasive message. A sequence of messages is required to accomplish the task. Thus, most persuasive efforts take the form of a campaign—television commercials, political campaigns, a series of speeches on an issue. When you consider the amount of stimuli bombarding us as receivers, it is understandable why a concerted effort over an extended period of time is necessary for meaningful change to result.

The Coleco Industries provides an effective illustration of the power of the persuasive process. Early in the 1983 Christmas shopping season, the firm designed a series of televised and printed advertising messages to market their Cabbage Patch Doll line. The ads emphasized the human-like qualities of the dolls: no two dolls manufactured by the firm were identical, and each came with a set of "adoption papers" to make the doll even more personalized. The response by the American public was phenomenal. The entire stock of the dolls (which had been on the market for several years) was purchased weeks before Christmas, and the firm was unable to keep up with the demand. One man, charging Coleco Industries with false advertising of a product not even available, launched a lawsuit against the firm. The firm, however, noted that it had taken its commercials off the air because the doll had received so much "free publicity" through media accounts of the search for the doll. This search inspired those who had been successful in purchasing the dolls to put them up for sale at scalpers' prices and customers who found stores that were able to get some of the stock to engage in customer fights and wait in long lines in order to purchase the dolls. One radio announcer in Milwaukee jokingly told listeners that they should go to the Milwaukee stadium over which a plane with a load of dolls was going to fly and dump the stock from the sky. Listeners were so desperate to find a doll that some actually did line up outside the stadium to await the plane! By Christmas time, the public was clearly divided into those who could and those who could not put a Cabbage Patch doll under the Christmas tree. The persuasive appeal, assisted greatly by the media, was highly successful.

Skills Involved in Critical Listening

Because the persuasive sequence takes time and leaves the receiver with a voluntary choice, it is useful to consider the components of an effective persuasive effort. The classical Greek rhetorician, Aristotle, first described our system of persuasion in *The Rhetoric.* He determined that a persuasive message required three components: ethos, speaker credibility; logos, logical arguments; and pathos, psychological appeals. These three components must interact to be maximally effective in securing a voluntary change in the listener. As critical listeners, we need to be aware of how these components function to persuade us.

Though we can analyze a persuasive message according to these three components, we should note that listeners often are unable to distinguish the emotional from the logical components of a particular persuasive message. Some individuals may respond on an emotional level to a logical argument, while others may be more responsive on the cognitive level.[6] Individual listeners will respond differently to the same persuasive message.

Research on speaker credibility has been helpful in enabling us to identify some of the factors and dimensions of the concept. The three most freqently cited dimensions of source credibility are trustworthiness, expertness, and dynamism.[7] Most senders are perceived by listeners as possessing these dimensions in varying degrees; however, it certainly is possible for a sender to be perceived as having a high degree of all three of these relatively independent dimensions. The independent nature of these dimensions can be illustrated by the person who, while listening to a speaker, says to her friend, "He definitely doesn't know what he's talking about, nor does he look very honest, but he surely has charisma." Although there are probably additional factors that influence a listener's perception of a sender's credibility, current research indicates that trustworthiness, expertness, and dynamism are the three dimensions that are the most influential.

Skills Related to Ethos

Identifying the Dimensions of Source Credibility

It is difficult at this point to draw any hard and fast conclusions as to the extent to which a speaker's credibility can influence us persuasively. Each listener will respond differently to the message source—before, during, and after the message presentation. The research does support the idea that there is some impact from credibility. Andersen and Clevenger analyzed the data and drew these conclusions:

> The finding is almost universal that the ethos of the source is related in some way to the impact of the message. This generalization applies not only to political, social, religious, and economic issues but also to matters of aesthetic judgment and personal taste. Some evidence even shows that "prestige-suggestion" can affect the appetite for certain foods and can influence performance and psychomotor tasks. On the other hand, there is not enough evidence to suggest that the amount of information gained from exposure to a message is related to the ethos of the source—at least this lack of relationship seems to be true of college populations. . . .
>
> Some auditors appear to be more susceptible to ethical appeal than others; some may be contra-suggestible. However, there is no evidence to show that suggestibility to prestige correlates well with intelligence, education, speech training, subject-matter competence, age, or sex. The only variable which seems clearly related to differences in suggestibility to prestige is the initial attitude toward the topic or the purpose: consistently, those who are neutral initially shift more often than do those who are at one extreme or the other.[8]

Recognizing the Influence of Source Credibility

The ethos of the source, since it does have some impact on the listener, operates even before the message is presented. Speaker credibility can influence the listener initially if the speaker has prestige, authority, and reputation with the listener. The persuasiveness of initial credibility once was demonstrated by a professional actor who was introduced to three sophisticated audiences (composed of psychiatrists, psychologists, psychiatric social workers, educators, and administrators) as "Dr. Fox," the possessor of several impressive (though fictitious) degrees and author of several impressive (though fictitious) books. With the introduction of the speaker, the listeners were conditioned or influenced to perceive the speaker as a higly credible source of information. With each audience, the actor presented a lecture on "Mathetmatical Game Theory As Applied to Physician Education" and then conducted a question and answer period; both the lecture and discussion consisted of meaningless, irrelevant, and conflicting content. Not one of the listeners detected the hoax.[9] A highly-reputed or well-known authority in his or her field, therefore, will have considerable weight with the listeners even before the speaker begins to present his or her message. As listeners, we need to be aware of how we can be influenced by a person's past reputation or even by the person's reputation itself.

As listeners, we also are influenced by the profession of a speaker, so much so, in fact, that the initial credibility of a person may well be determined by what it is, professionally, that the individual represents. In a November 1983 Harris poll, interviewers found that North Americans had a great deal of confidence in higher educational institutions, medicine, the United States Supreme Court, and the military. Television news, the White House, and organized religion ranked next in the confidence "index," while law fims and organized labor received the lowest rankings.[10] Skillful speakers who recognize the unpopularity of what they represent will make efforts to counter these negative perceptions of listeners before they present substantive issues. Public utility officials, for instance, before they deal with messages about conservation, will make an effort to counter public perceptions that utility rates are skyrocketing out of control.

The speaker's credibility can be developed during the speech by what McCroskey has defined as "derived ethos." This credibility is enhanced through techniques the speaker utilizes to demonstrate his or her character, knowledge, and goodwill. Politicians citing biblical quotations, for example, illustrate the effort to demonstrate character. The speaker who discusses his or her own research and experiences with the topic will demonstrate the expertise of a credible speaker. The good will of a listener can be developed by the speaker demonstrating that he or she actually has the best interests of the listener in mind as the speaker advances his or her proposal.

A good speaker will attempt to incorporate these techniques subtly rather than directly asserting that he or she is a credible speaker. The principle that operates in the listening process, essentially, is one of trustworthiness and belief.

If we, as listeners, believe in the speaker, then it is easier for us to accept the speaker's message.

John F. Kennedy (and his presidential speechwriter, Theodore Sorenson) understood the power of credibility in developing a responsive bond with listeners. Kenendy projected a young, vigorous, dynamic image, an image that was well set in the perceptions of the American public through the televised Nixon-Kennedy debates of the 1960 campaign. As President, Kennedy was skillful in communicating with the media through press conferences and through speeches. He demonstrated a solid grasp of the issues and communicated considerable authority and competence in his presentations. Further, Kennedy made efforts to demonstrate trustworthiness by suggesting that he shared common interests with his audience. Thus, the press was presented with opportunities to photograph his young children and beautiful wife, and the President would make references to his listeners in his speeches. One famous example of his expressing commonality with his audience occurred in a speech he presented on June 26, 1963, commemorating the eighteenth anniversary of the Berlin Wall. Kennedy journeyed to West Berlin and told his listeners that "Today, in the world of freedom, the proudest boast is 'Ich bin ein Berliner.' "[11] Throughout the world, people responsed favorably to his effort to associate himself with his besieged Berlin audience. (Yet it is interesting to note that "Ich bin ein Berliner"—due to the inclusion of the indefinite article *ein*—translates literally as "I am a pastry," rather than "I am a Berliner", a point that Berliners still chuckle about today!). Throughout the world, speakers attempt to enhance their credibility by demonstrating their expertise and their trustworthiness to their listeners.

The extensive credibility crisis suffered by former President Richard M. Nixon represents the power of this component of persuasion. Ultimately, the American public, as receivers, was unable to accept any of his messages, so he found it necessary to step down from office. Jimmy Carter, campaigning for re-election as President in 1980, encountered similar credibility problems as Americans lost faith in his ability to control inflation or to deal effectively with the release of American hostages in Iran.

President Ronald Reagan experienced what was coined a "gender gap" when he was perceived to be not very sensitive to the needs of women. Despite these White House credibility crises, combined with reports of corruption in many segments of governmental and corporate conduct, North Americans maintain some sense of trust in their institutions, a confidence reflected in the Harris poll. Indeed, one analyst was led to conclude that "[w]hile we criticize leaders and authorities of all sorts, . . . Americans continue to express a basic trust in the people we deal with in everyday life."[12]

As a trusting public, we can run the danger of being too persuaded by the credibility components. Political communicators, concerned with the "image" developed and projected by candidates, recognize that often the image is what "sells" the candidate to the voting public. As a result, political consultants, serving as image advisers to candidates during election campaigns, make a fortune as they develop media strategies for "selling" the candidates to voters. Joe McGinniss's *The Selling of the President 1968* details such efforts to "package" Nixon for the voters. McGinniss cites a memo from one of Nixon's image makers, Raymond K. Price:

> . . . we take the time and the money to experiment, in a controlled manner, with film and television techniques, with particular emphasis on pinpointing those *controlled* uses of the television medium that can *best* convey the *image* we want to get across. . . .[13]

As critical listeners, we should be aware of the influence of the image and not make our decisions solely on this basis.

Skills Related to Logos

The critical listener also must carefully examine the second persuasive component, logos: well supported arguments that consist of both *true* propositions (or evidence) and *valid* relationships between all the evidence presented and all the conclusions reached. Although some research indicates that the listener may not be able to recall specific lines of argument from a presentation, logical arguments are prevalent in everyday discourse, serve as the foundation for technical briefings, and certainly appear in persuasive messages of all types.[14] Because the arguments are so inherent in these messages, the critical listener should be familiar with the argument structures in order to identify the communicator's persuasive strategies. Basically, there are two argument structures: the inductive argument as traditionally studied is concerned with truth, and the deductive argument as traditionally studied is concerned with validity.

Evaluating Inductive Arguments

The inductive argument is the process of reasoning by which one arrives at a conclusion or generalization through examining specific, factual data of the same kind or class; it is reasoning from the specific to the general. In this type of reasoning, the speaker compares a number of instances to conclude that all other instances are the same.

For example, a teacher, citing past and present students who have studied and done well, may conclude that students who study receive high grades. From this observation, the teacher may reason inductively that all students who want to pass must study.

To determine the truth of an inductive argument, critical listeners should ask and answer the following questions:

1. Are the validating data true?
2. Are enough cases cited?
3. Are the cited instances representative of the whole being considered? Are they typical or atypical?

4. Is the class of persons, events, or instances about which the induction is made reasonably comparable in all relevant aspects?
5. Are there exceptions which do not lead to the expected conclusions? Are these exceptions accounted for?

Using these questions to evaluate the previously cited inductive argument, we see that the conclusion drawn by the teacher is not true. We all know students who do well in courses and yet do not study. In this case, other variables may not be accounted for in the argument: intelligence, aptitude, prior training, vocabulary, personality. We realize, too, that the number of specific examples supporting the conclusion must be sufficiently large to offset the probability of chance or coincidence; the critical listener demands many representative, specific instances before he or she will grant a general rule.

Evaluating Deductive Arguments

The second argument structure, the deductive (or syllogistic) structure, is the process of reasoning from a systematic arrangement of arguments consisting of a proposition stating a generalization (referred to as the major premise), a proposition stating a specific instance related to the generalization (the minor premise), and a conclusion which necessarily must follow from the premises. Deductive reasoning is reasoning from the general to the specific, and it infers that what is *presumed* true of all members of a class is true of some members of that class. The teacher might want to present his or her same argument deductively:

All students who want to pass must study.
You are a student who wants to pass.
Therefore, you must study.

To determine the truth of a deductive argument, the critical listener must ask and answer the following questions:

1. Is the generalization (major premise) universally true?
2. Does the specific item really belong to the general class?
3. Or, does the specific item represent an exception to the cited general class?

Fortunately, most people do not talk in direct syllogisms. As listeners, we are confronted with truncated deductive arguments that Aristotle identified as enthymemes. Enthymemes are actually modified forms of syllogisms that have one or more of their premises or their conclusions omitted. They can operate effectively only if speaker and listener can share, mentally, the premise(s) or conclusion which the speaker does not state. If we are alert to their utilization, we can better analyze the speaker's argument for its validity.

The teacher, for example, who *assumes* that those in the class want to pass most likely would use an enthymeme rather than a direct syllogism. The teacher might say, "You'd better study for the exam." If the students (here the listeners) mentally share with the teacher (the speaker) the omitted premises that all students who want to pass must study and that they are students who want to pass, the enthymeme can operate effectively.

Figure 8.1.
Diagram of a valid enthymeme.

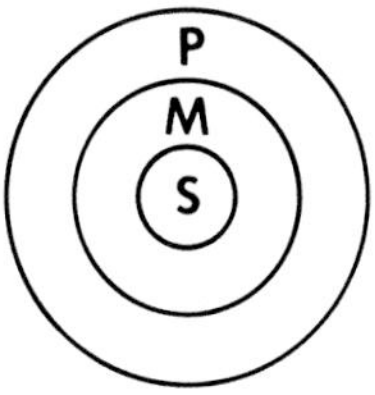

When analyzing the validity of an enthymeme, the critical listener should first set up the enthymeme in the formal arrangement of a syllogism. For example, if a speaker states this enthymeme, "Mr. Jones voted for Jane Baker; he must be a proponent of the E.R.A.," the listener should immediately set up this syllogism:

Major Premise: All who voted for Jane Baker are proponents of the E.R.A.
Minor Premise: Mr. Jones voted for Jane Baker.
Conclusion: Therefore, Mr. Jones is a proponent of the E.R.A.

To help us visualize a syllogism, we can put the relationships into symbols:

Middle term=M
Subject of conclusion=S
Predicate of conclusion=P
All M (people who voted for Jane Baker) are P (proponents of the E.R.A.)
S (Mr. Jones) is an M (voter for Jane Baker)
S (Mr. Jones) is a P (proponent of E.R.A.)

We can also diagram the relationship between the propositions of a syllogism by using circles to represent the classes involved. The premises give us the directions for the construction of the circles. In a valid argument, the directions compel the circles to show that the *conclusion is inescapable.* Let us examine the validity of the enthymeme above. The circles show that the conclusion is inescapable; thus, this enthymeme is valid (fig. 8.1).

At this point, we must more clearly differentiate between validity and truth. Validity reflects the nature of the relationships between propositions rather than the truth of the propositions. We can tell by the construction of the syllogism whether the argument is valid in itself. If the conclusion is forced by the premises, the argument is valid; if the conclusion does not necessarily follow, the argument is not valid. We test the validity of an argument by *assuming* the premises true for the sake of argument and then observe if the conclusion must follow. Can a syllogism be valid while the premises are not true? Yes. If an argument is valid and the premises are true, is the conclusion true? Yes. We must be careful not to confuse validity with truth. People too frequently are convinced of the truth

Figure 8.2.
Diagram of a valid syllogism.

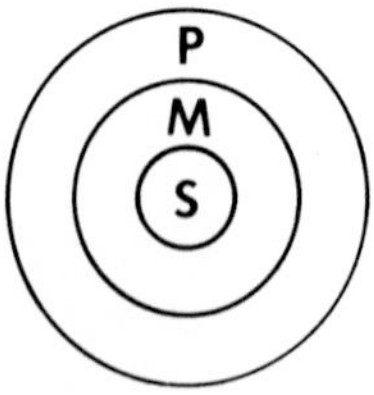

of a proposition because they can see that it logically follows from certain premises, while they fail to notice that the premises are not true. A sound argument, to repeat, depends on both *truth* and *validity.*

Previously, we evaluated the truthfulness of the teacher's syllogism, and we assessed it as being false, but let us see if it is valid.

Major Premise: All students who want to pass must study.
Minor Premise: You are a student who wants to pass.
Conclusion: Therefore, you must study.

Symbolically, it would be as follows:

All M (students who want to pass) are P (students who must study).
S (You) are an M (student who wants to pass).
S (You) are a P (student who must study).

Yes, the syllogism is valid (fig. 8.2); however, because the argument does not have both validity and truth, it is not sound.

To analyze more critically the validity of a syllogism, you must know what conditions a valid syllogism must meet. The most important conditions are the following:

1. There must be three terms, no more and no less.
2. Every term must be used twice, no more and no less.
3. A term must be used only once in every premise.
4. The middle term which *does not* appear in the conclusion must be *distributed* at least once. A term is distributed if the pattern of the statement indicates that the term refers to *all* (used in universal sense) the members of a class designated by it; it is undistributed if the pattern does not indicate that the term refers to *all* (or *every* or *none*) but instead uses terms such as *some* or *most.* We must be cautious of omitted qualifiers where *all* is assumed (for instance, "rock stars use hard drugs.")
5. Any term that is distributed in the conclusion must be distributed at least once in the premises.
6. At least one of the premises must be affirmative. Only one negative premise may occur in any given syllogism.

Figure 8.3.
Diagram of two valid syllogisms.

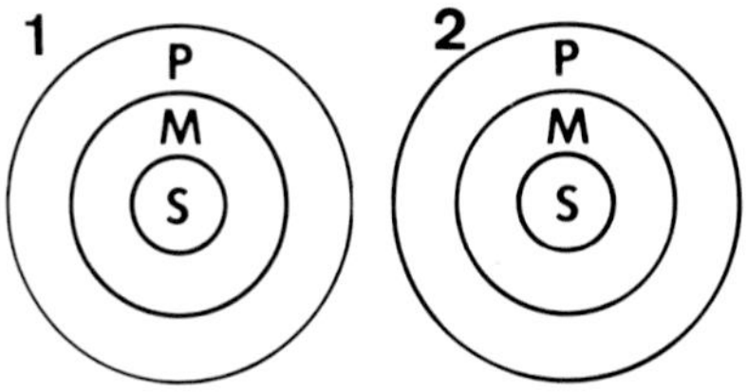

7. At least one premise must be universal (distributed); only one particular *(some, most)* premise can occur in a given syllogism.
8. If one premise is negative, the conclusion must be negative.
9. If one of the premises is particular, the conclusion must be particular.
10. A particular subject (minor premise) may not be distributed (universal) in the conclusion.

Often, the use of the enthymeme will involve more than one formal syllogism; it may be polysyllogistic: "Any drug that can lead to addiction is evil, and, therefore, codeine should be made illegal." This enthymeme, put in the formal and symbolic pattern of two categorical syllogisms, would be as follows:

All M are P	1. Drugs that can lead to addiction are evil.
S is an M	Codeine is a drug that can lead to addiction.
S is P	Therefore, codeine is evil.
All M are P	2. That which is evil should be made illegal.
S is an M	Codeine is evil.
S is P	Therefore, codeine should be made illegal.

This is a valid argument (fig. 8.3).

As you have studied this material, you have probably wondered how you as a listener can possibly mentally convert enthymemes into formal syllogisms, draw cirlces, ask and answer the crucial questions, and determine the validity as well as the truth of the speaker's argument while the speaker continues to speak. Michael Scriven offers some guidance in his seven steps of argument analysis; he recommends that we analyze arguments by

1. Clarifying the meaning of the terms and other elements of the argument.
2. Identifying the stated and unstated conclusions.
3. Portraying the structure (the relationships between the conclusions and the premises) of the argument.
4. Formulating the unstated assumptions of the argument.
5. Criticizing the stated and unstated premises and inferences.
6. Introducing other relevant arguments.
7. Evaluating the overall argument as a result of the first six steps in the analysis.[15]

We admit that these acts may be difficult to perform in the beginning, but developing an understanding of how to analyze logical arguments, concentrating intently, exerting physical and mental energy, capitalizing on the difference between speech speed and thought speed, asking questions whenever possible, and practicing will make you more effective critical listeners.

Detecting and Evaluating Reasoning Fallacies

As listeners, we cannot assume that all speakers present sound arguments. Too frequently, the speaker may use faulty reasoning—fallacious reasoning that allows a listener to draw from evidence a claim that is not justified. Yet sound arguments should be the only arguments acceptable to us as listeners. "The most basic demand that receivers should make of argumentation," stresses Richard Crable, "is the demand to be presented with good reasons for claims."[16] We must have the ability to recognize fallacies in reasoning so that we can reject the false claims advanced by some speakers.

Hasty Generalizations. We may be exposed more to the hasty generalization than to any other fallacy in oral discourse. This fallacy consists of the speaker drawing unwarranted, general conclusions from an insufficient number of cases (instances). A principal whose school has been vandalized by *some* long-haired youths might fall prey to the hasty generalization; at the next P.T.A. meeting, the principal may then condemn *all* long-haired youths as vandals and urge parents to restore law and order in the home. Such a hasty generalization , or stereotyping, is based on too few instances and does not account for many of the other variables which could be involved. In order to evaluate the hasty generalization, the critical listener should use the following questions:

1. Is there a sufficient number of cases cited to warrant the conclusion?
2. Is the generalization consistent with all known facts?
3. Is there an exception to the generalization?
4. Have negative instances been accounted for?
5. Are qualifiers (*some, few,* etc.) used?
6. Are the instances cited representative of the entire class? Have the instances been selected entirely at random?

Carefully evaluating the hasty generalizations will prevent the critical listener from falling prey to the speakers who use them.

Faulty Causal Reasoning. Another fallacy involving generalizing is the faulty causal generalization. Some speakers, recognizing that other factors do contribute to the effect, speak of one event being *the cause* of another because it is the important difference; they mean it is the cause with a high degree of probability. Unfortunately, other speakers do not recognize that there are other contributing factors, and they argue that what *usually* (or *sometimes* or even *often*) happens *always* happens; instead of indicating that they recognize other contributing factors by saying "a common cause," "a frequent cause," "a prominent cause," "one cause," or "a probable cause," they use "the cause" without qualification, and, as a result, they make a faulty causal generalization. For example, Betty may say, "My allergy disappeared the day after I took Clogless. I certainly recommend the use of that medicine!" The speaker is alleging that Clogless was the *cause* of the disappearance of her allergy (effect).

Another type of faulty causal reasoning is *post hoc, ergo propter hoc* ("after this, therefore, because of this") reasoning. *Post hoc* reasoning is used by the speaker, who—without proof—supposes that because one event follows another event, the first is the cause of the second. An effect, granted, must follow a cause, but a prior event does not necessarily cause the event that follows. Craig, for instance, is using *post hoc* reasoning when he remarks, "I didn't make that big sale this afternoon because I walked under a ladder right before I met with Mr. Gwynn."

The critical listener, when listening to such faulty causal reasoning, should use the following questions in order to evaluate the reasoning:

1. What is the alleged cause?
2. What is the alleged effect?
3. Is the cause really capable of producing the effect?
4. Is the effect the result of a sequence of events or a coincidence of events?
5. Are there possibly other intervening causes?
6. Was the cause really operating? Have the alleged facts been verified?
7. When past experience is involved, has the alleged effect *always* followed the observed cause?
8. Does the alleged cause precede the alleged effect?

These questions—asked mentally or orally—can greatly assist the critical listener in uncovering faulty causal reasoning.

Faulty Analogical Reasoning. In addition to using faulty causal reasoning, speakers frequently use faulty analogical reasoning. An analogy is the assertion that cases which resemble each other in some respects will resemble each other in some other respects. Every analogy must break down at some point since no cases are identical. Speakers use faulty analogies when they assume (1) that shared properties will continue indefinitely and/or (2) that shared properties are similar in all aspects relevant to the issue being discussed, when in truth they are not. For example, Mary Beth tells her friend, "Leving Motors fixed my Chevy really well; it hasn't needed any additional repair work for three years. I bet Leving mechanics can correct the problems with your Mercedes just as well." Here the speaker is assuming that the shared properties (two cars and each—at one time—in need of repair) will continue indefinitely and that the shared properties are similar in all relevant aspects. The critical listener should immediately ask several questions. Does Leving Motors still exist? Does Leving Motors specialize only in repairing Chevrolets? Does Leving Motors also repair Mercedes Benzes? Is the repair work at Levings as good now as it was three years ago? Are the mechanics who repaired the Chevy still working at Leving Motors? Are the present mechanics equally qualified to repair both Chevrolets and Mercedes Benzes? Are parts as easily accessible for the Mercedes as for the Chevy? Is the type of repair work that the Mercedes needs the same as that which the Chevy once needed? The answers to these questions may indeed illustrate that the compared cases are not alike in all essential aspects.

To detect the faulty analogical reasoning of examples such as this one, the critical listener should ask and answer the following questions:

1. Are there significant points of similarity?
2. Are there enough resemblances to warrant a comparison?
3. Are the compared cases alike in all essential aspects?
4. Does the comparison overlook fundamental differences? Are the points of difference critical? Noncritical?
5. Is the analogous situation representative?
6. Do the points brought out really exist?
7. Are only literal analogies used as logical proof?

By using these questions when confronted with analogical reasoning, the critical listener will have one more means of controlling his or her own decision making.

Three of the many other common types of reasoning fallacies are *non sequitur,* arguing in a circle, and ducking or ignoring the issue. These, too, can be deceiving to the listener.

Non Sequitur. Translated literally, *non sequitur* means "it does not necessarily follow," and it is a general name for all irrelevancies. Although it is involved in all invalid syllogisms since they claim that a conclusion follows when it does not, the term is generally used to refer to the widely irrelevant conclusion.

A graphic example of the *non sequitur* is the argument critics advanced against the National Aeronautics and Space Administration's Apollo moon missions. Opponents of the program argued that the money spent on the missions should be spent on earth for domestic needs. Such an argument did not follow because it assumed that the small N.A.S.A. budget would be reallocated to meaningful "earthly" causes while it overlooked the spin-off benefits of the space program to technology, medicine, and science throughout the world. And this *non sequitur* persists today as people complain about the costs of the space shuttle program.

Arguing in a Circle. Another common fallacy is arguing in a circle. When using this fallacy, the speaker tries to prove a given statement with another statement that depends for its proof upon the first statement. The speaker who argues that the promises of Iran's Ayatollah Ruhollah Khomeini cannot be trusted because Khomeini does not keep his word is arguing in a circle; the "reason" that follows the word *because* is the same assertion that precedes *because.* Arguing in a circle can be seen in its height of absurdity in the following example: Living together without benefit of marriage is justified because living together without benefit of marriage is justified.

Ignoring the Issue. The third common reasoning fallacy is ducking or ignoring the issue. The speaker who uses this type of fallacy uses irrelevant arguments to cloud the real issue or argument. One of these irrelevant arguments is the *ad hominem* argument—attacking the personal character of the source of the statement rather than focusing on the content of the issue itself. Presidential candidate George McGovern's first running mate in 1972, Senator Thomas Eagleton of Missouri, was the victim of this fallacy—character assassination. Rather than focusing on his political record and proposals as a prospective vice-president, critics forced his resignation by concentrating on his former psychiatric record.

A second irrelevant argument is the *ad populum* argument—appealing to the people in terms of their prejudices and passions rather than focusing on the issues at hand. An example of this argument is the following: A woman is running for mayor of Laurel, Maryland; her opponent has been a resident of the city for only five years. In one of her campaign speeches, she states, "I was born in Laurel, and I have been a Laurelite all my life. I attended Laurel Elementary School, Laurel Junior High School, and Laurel Senior High School. Many of you were there when I missed that final desperation shot and our girls' basketball team lost that heartbreaking final game at the state tournament. And, many of you were there to share my happiness when I was crowned Laurel's Junior Miss. . . ."

The final form of ignoring the issue is the *ad ignoratiam* argument. The speaker who uses this argument attempts to prove that a statement is true (or false) because it cannot be disproved (or proved). Not being able to disprove a point is not the same as proving it; only concrete evidence can prove or disprove a statement. An example of this fallacy is the following: Since the opponents of the discipline policy cannot prove that detention has not improved discipline in the school, it follows that detention is an effective disciplinary measure.

These are just a few of the numerous fallacies which speakers intentionally and nonintentionally use. It is vital that critical listeners be aware of these fallacies as well as others if they wish to become more adept in evaluating speaker's arguments.

Evaluating Evidence

The effective critical listener will analyze the soundness of not only the speaker's argument but also the speaker's support—the evidence.[17] A speaker can support his or her assertions with any of a variety of types of evidence, including testimonies, facts, opinions, inferences, and statistics.

Regardless of the type of evidence the speaker uses, the listener can apply some tests to the evidence in order to assess its soundness. The listener should seek to determine the *clarity* of the evidence (how clear and intelligible it is), the *accuracy* of the evidence (how true, precise, and correct it is), and the *reliability* of the evidence (how dependable, trustworthy, and credible it is).

This determination may be made through the application of some basic questions to the evidence:

1. Is the evidence clear?
2. Is the evidence consistent with other known evidence?
3. Is the evidence consistent with the speaker?
4. Is the evidence timely?
5. Is the evidence applicable to the argument?
6. Is the evidence pertinent to the argument?
7. Is the source of the evidence reliable?
8. Is the source of the evidence competent in the area in which he or she is being quoted?
9. Is the source of the evidence free to report all of his or her findings?
10. Is the source of the evidence suppressing or distorting facts in order to prove his or her point?
11. Is the source of the evidence sincere?

Detecting Fallacious Testimonies. Most of us are quite aware of the fallacious testimonies with which the advertising industry bombards us. Testimonies from famous models, movie stars, and sports stars endorsing products appeal to our sense of imitation, even though experts in the field would be in a better position to offer sound support. Thus, a carpet manufacturer will call on a glamorous model rather than a Ph.D. in textiles to sell the company's product. And we are all most likely familiar with Joe Namath, the famous football hero who endorses items from popcorn poppers to panty hose. Unfortunately, many listeners pay no more attention to evaluating the credibility of the source when they are listening to messages of grave concern than they do when they are listening to commercials.

Distinguishing among Facts, Opinions, and Inferences In addition to evaluating testimonies, the critical listener must distinguish between statements of fact and statements of opinion. Although many of us believe that a fact is a fact and that there is nothing else to say about facts, too frequently speakers pass opinions off as facts (often introduced by words such as "It is said that . . . ," "They say that . . . ," "I heard that . . . ," "It is a fact that . . . ," "We all know that . . . ," "Obviously, . . . ," "It is reported that . . . ," "There can be no doubt that . . . ," "As a matter of fact, . . . ," "Of course, . . ."—a phrase that seems to be becoming as popular as the filler "you know," etc.). It is apparent that often listeners do not challenge the accuracy and reliability of the speakers' so-called "facts." Whether or not speakers use facts or opinions to "prove" their assertions should be a crucial question for the critical listener, or he or she may become, as Windes and Hastings believe, what the American audience has become:

> . . . the American audience has become so accustomed to hidden persuasion, so victimized by the engineers of consent that it will accept the truth of assertions with virtually no proof except the authority of the advocate, whether . . . a news commentator, politician, or public figure, or . . . a commercial announcer.[18]

Facts are truths known to exist. They can be determined by direct observation and/or they can be verified by a reliable source. When we cannot directly observe facts we can investigate through reliable sources "as to what the facts probably were, are, and will be."[19] Facts are open to anyone who wishes to investigate them, and they can stand independent of the sources who report them. However, since few of us—as listeners—can actually investigate the majority of the facts we listen to, it is increasingly essential that we consider the credibility of the speakers who present them.

Opinions, on the other hand, are statements of personal judgments and preferences. Though open to dispute, opinions cannot be positively and objectively proved or disproved because they are expressions of their possessors' own perceptions. Although opinions cannot be tested for proof, they can be evaluated, and the critical listener should carefully examine whether or not the stated opinions are made by reliable sources who are speaking in their areas of competency and whether or not the sources have any factual data upon which to base their opinions.

In assessing the factual basis of speakers' message content, the critical listener must not accept inferential statements as statements of facts. Inferences are statements of interpretation, which, limited only to the speaker's imagination, can be made by anyone (including the incompetent speaker) anytime. Sometimes directly stated and at other times merely implied, inferences are speakers' guesses or conclusions about what is not known, made on the basis of what is known; the "known" may be an observation/series of observations or an inference/series of inferences. Frequently, a speaker's inferences are in the form of predictions, as is the one that follows: "If merit pay for public school teachers were instituted, students' SAT scores would improve." Speakers may not, knowingly or unknowingly, identify their material, so what is presented from their inferences may appear to be facts.

William V. Haney's famous uncritical inference test illustrates the inability of most of us to distinguish what is presented to us as fact, inference, or judgment (opinion). Haney states that we have difficulty but that ". . . one can learn to make this distinction habitually and thus markedly increase his 'inference-awareness.' "[20]

Diplomats become adept at recognizing facts, opinions, and inferences. A political officer assigned to an embassy overseas, for example, spends a great deal of time interviewing officials in the host country in order to obtain a fair assessment of the conditions in the country to report back to the United States Department of State. It is necessary for this officer to recognize what is being reported by the sources as factual and what is actually representative of the sources' editorial interpretation of the country's conditions. Like diplomats, we as critical listeners must learn these distinctions and then base our acceptance or rejection of inferences on the basis of evidence used to support them as well as on the credibility of the source. We recommend that the critical listener use the following questions as guides in evaluating inferences:

1. Is the inference based on observations? How many observations? How many individuals made the observation(s)?
2. Is the inference based on another inference or a series of inferences? What is/are the other inference(s)?
3. Do past experiences support/dispute the inferences being made?
4. Is the source of the inference competent/incompetent? Honest/deceitful? Biased/objective? Trustworthy/not trustworthy?

Detecting Rumors. Another type of biased communication that can be especially troublesome to the uncritical listener is the rumor. In the classic study of rumor, Allport and Postman defined rumor as "a specific (or topical) proposition for belief, passed along from person to person, usually by word of mouth, without secure standards of evidence being presented."[21] The rumor frequently represents a magnified inference which becomes more distorted as it is transmitted from person to person. It may not be used on any factual data at all.

North Americans have experienced several examples of costly rumors in recent years. The hydrogen leak at the nuclear power plant at Three Mile Island near Harrisburg, Pennsylvania, precipitated a major rumor throughout the region that the plant was about to explode, even though Nuclear Regulatory Commission officials assured residents—by way of televised newscasts—that the rumor was not true. McDonald's fast food chain also faced a major rumor that customers had found worms in their hamburgers; this rumor required the company officials to embark on a major advertising campaign to assure customers that only 100 percent ground beef was used in their products. Another rumor—perpetuated by young people—was that eating Pop Rocks candy while drinking soda would cause a person's stomach to explode! In New York, Robert Entenmann, the head of Entenmann's Bakery, had difficulty countering the rumor that his bakery was owned by the Reverend Sun Myung Moon's Unification Church. Entenmann had to send letters to New England churches to assure customers that the "Moonies" had not taken over the bakery, and the company resorted to putting the logo of the Warner-Lambert Company (the parent company of the bakery firm) on their boxes. The logo of Procter & Gamble inspired a rumor that the corporation was somehow connected to a mystical cult, primarily because of the figures embedded in the printed symbol. On a December morning in 1981, a dramatic rumor reached Wall Street: the rumor was that President Ronald Reagan had suffered a heart attack; by midafternoon, it was rumored that he had died. The rumor's impact on the stock market was strong: the price of gold soared $15.50 an ounce, and the commodities market came alive. Clearly, rumors can be costly.

Because rumors can be so disruptive, not only to the economy but also to the general welfare of the American public (as were both the Tylenol scare of tampering with pharmaceutical products and the A.I.D.S. scare about blood transfusions), some organizations have set up rumor control centers to help individuals separate factual information from gossip and exaggeration. The city of Baltimore, for instance, has established a Rumor Control Center, serviced by a community relations representative, in order to provide information to citizens concerned about rumors. One rumor specialist, Ralph Rosnow, asserts that persistent rumors, such as the recurring sightings of U.F.O.'s, fulfill a very human need to "understand the human condition and a hunger for the supernatural."[22] Rosnow also believes that "rumors persist because they touch on the real anxieties and uncertainties of the times.[23] The critical listener should work to avoid being part of the "rumor mill" which can perpetuate costly, injurious mis-information. The critical listener should seek the evidence, verify the sources, and sort out the biases in the communication so that rumors are not allowed to continue.

Detecting Propaganda. Still another type of biased communication which the critical listener must be able to recognize is propaganda. According to Miller, propaganda is an "expression of opinion, or fact or alleged fact, or it is action—calculated to influence the opinions and actions of groups and individuals, with reference to some predetermined end."[24] If you are thinking that this definition is a definition of persuasion, you are correct, for, simply speaking, propaganda is persuasion. As a form of persuasion, it involves conflict or "sides," and it is consciously designed to influence the listener(s) to accept or reject some cause, view, action, person, etc. Although we usually view the word *propaganda* as a negative term describing an undesirable persuasive attempt, propaganda can be positive or desirable when, for example, the propagandist (or persuader) attacks racial discrimination, unequal housing standards, unfair labor practices, or air and water pollution.

If propaganda can be positive, then, why does it have such a derogatory or pejorative connotation? The blame lies with both the unscrupulous sender of propaganda and the uncritical listener of propaganda. However, your authors believe that the uncritical listener bears a greater share of the blame. Why? There undoubtedly will be speakers who use propaganda as long as there are listeners who are *not* skilled in *detecting* (1) emotional appeals (upon which the propagandist relies almost exclusively), (2) the speaker's purpose (which, for the propagandist, is primarily to benefit personally), (3) the speaker's evidence (which may consist only of the propagandist's biases and opinions as well as distorted or alleged "facts"), (4) propaganda techniques (which the propagandist regularly uses), and (5) the speaker's underlying and/or hidden motives/intent (which, for the propagandist, may not be readily apparent but can be held suspect if he/she heavily utilizes the propagandistic characteristics enumerated in this sentence). Likewise, there undoubtedly will be speakers who use propaganda as long as there are listeners who are *not* skilled in *rationally evaluating* the propagandistic characteristics which they do, indeed, detect. In other words, critical listeners, skilled in detecting and analyzing propaganda, can eliminate unscrupulous senders of propaganda.

Again, according to Miller, the capacity to analyze propaganda "depends upon one's familiarity with relevant facts, together with one's capacity for testing the propaganda in the light of the facts. That capacity, in turn, depends upon one's education, upon the conditioning of his mind, upon what he has been trained to consider 'good' or 'bad'."[25] To assist you in developing the capacity to analyze propaganda, the authors encourage you to (1) familiarize yourself with the facts relevant to any issue with which you are involved; (2) utilize the suggested guidelines for evaluating reasoning and evidence; and (3) recognize how your own emotions and frames of reference affect your listening behavior and attempt to control their influences when you listen to propagandistic messages. In addition, you should understand the propaganda techniques which are commonly used so that you can detect them and then analyze them.

Among a number of devices recognized by The Institute for Propaganda Analysis as propaganda techiques are the following: (1) *name-calling*—attaching an objectionable/unfavorable/undesirable label to a person, object, event, cause, etc., to encourage disapproval/rejection/condemnation of a person, etc. *(radical, traitor, the establishment, loser);* (2) *glittering generality*—attaching a vague but virtuous-sounding label to a person, object, event, cause, etc., to encourage automatic approval/acceptance of a person, etc. *(dedicated to equality, strong proponent of justice, earmarked for success);* (3) *transfer*—associating positive qualities of a respected/revered person, group, party, object, cause, etc., with the person, object, event, cause, etc., expounded by the propagandist ("We Democrats, the party of FDR. . . .", the American flag, Puritan work ethic, "as American as baseball and hot dogs"); (4) *plain folks appeal*—attempting to identify with the audience (whom the propagandist hopes to persuade) by adopting the language, dress, behavior, etc., of the listeners; (5) *card-stacking*—manipulating (by withholding, ingoring, adding, over- or under-emphasizing) evidence and giving only the evidence that supports the propagandist's cause, proposition, etc.; (6) *half truths*—deliberately suppressing basic elements of the argument/story, of which the propagandist has knowledge, and telling only one part—the part he/she favors—of the argument/story ("Merit pay for teachers will improve the quality and motivation of teachers and the learning of students." Are there other sides to the issue?); and (7) *bandwagon*—using phrases and sentences to create the impression of universal approval and ignoring individuality ("All my friends are. . . .", "Millions of people can't be wrong.", "Vote a straight Republican ticket."). Two other commonly-used propaganda devices are *hasty generalizations* (discussed under "Detecting and Evaluating Reasoning Fallacies" in this chapter) and *testimonials* (discussed previously in this section). Knowing the characteristics of propaganda, being able to detect common propaganda devices, and developing your capacity to analyze propaganda will enable you to escape from the control of propagandists as well as to contribute to the elimination of unscrupulous propagandists.

Detecting Biases of Chief Information Sources. A revealing discussion of biases of our chief sources of information—the press, the government, pressure groups, and professional scholars—is found in Newman and Newman's book,

Evidence.[26] Newman and Newman stress that all sources of information have limits and that these limitations affect the evidence we draw from our sources. It is essential to remember that since individuals have differing perceptual capacities to observe and transmit information, distortion of evidence results: "Ideology, national or other group interest, individual self-interest, career involvement, unconscious partisanship, exile mentality, reaction against one's past, and desire for power are some of the biases which distort perception."[27] The critical listener would do well to assess the biases of the sources of information in order to determine the acceptability of the evidence from those sources.

Analyzing Statistical Data. The discerning listener also should read Huff's delightful *How to Lie with Statistics,* an eye-opening exposé of the misuses of statistical data.[28] Huff, a statistician, illustrates many distortions from statistical evidence and recommends that individuals ask five questions to test statistical evidence: Who says so? How does he know? What's missing? Did somebody change the subject? Does it make sense?[29] We suggest that the critical listener also use the following questions as guides in evaluating statistical evidence:

1. Who wants to prove what?
2. Do the statistics come from reliable and objective sources?
3. How were the statistics gathered?
4. Are the statistics based on an adequate and representative sample?
5. Do the statistics cover a sufficient period of time?
6. Are the units being compared actually comparable?
7. Are the statistics the most current available?
8. How were the data treated statistically?
9. What conclusion do the statistics support?
10. How relevant to the issue are the statistics?
11. Can the results be verified?
12. Are the statistics supported by other findings and other sources?

Obtaining the answers to these and other questions relevant to assessing statistical evidence will help the critical listener, as Huff suggests, "avoid learning a remarkable lot that isn't so."[30]

Skills Related to Pathos

Recognizing Need Levels

In addition to ethos and logos, the third key component of persuasion is pathos, the psychological appeals used by the speaker to gain emotional response from the listener. As humans, we respond at various need levels. Maslow proposes that we have five such levels.[31] At the first, most basic level are physiological needs—food, sleep, sex, drink, shelter. These needs must be satisfied before an individual can be motivated at a second level—the safety needs. Safety needs such as security, stability, protection, and strength are important motivators when any sort of threat to these needs might be present. The third level consists of the belongingness and love needs, our social motivators. Americans are highly motivated by this need to belong, as evidenced by our affiliations with many groups. The fourth need level is identified by Maslow as the esteem needs. These needs represent both self-esteem, our desire for achievement and mastery, and esteem of others, our desire for reputation and prestige. These needs spring from our belongingness needs and represent a further stage in accomplishing our goals. Finally, at the fifth level in the hierarchy, Maslow identifies the need for self-actualization, our desire for self-fulfillment. Maslow suggests that we may be striving for this if other needs have been met, but the self-actualized person probably does not exist.

The need levels are reflected in the American value system, or what people in the United States want most in their lives. In a revealing survey, William Watts identified Americans' hopes and fears, hopes and fears which illustrate those values which most powerfully motivate us to respond. Watt's survey identified the following major values.

Personal Hopes	**Personal Fears**
Better or decent standard of living	Lower standard of living
Good health for self	Ill health for self
Economic stability in general	War
Happy family life	Economic instability in general
Peace of mind; emotional maturity	Unemployment
Hopes for the Nation	**Fears for the Nation**
Economic stability; no inflation	War
Peace	Economic instability
Employment	Unemployment
Improved standard of living in general	Lack of law and order
Law and order	Threat of communism[32]

While this survey was conducted in 1981, it represents an updating of previous studies conducted by Watts' researchers in 1964 and 1974. The hopes and fears revealed in the survey represent some of the major motivators which we as Americans carry with us.

Communicators on Madison Avenue and in the political arena understand these motivators and need levels, and thus they target message appeals to best fill the needs that we have as listeners. Skillful persuaders who wish to secure a change in our mental or physical behavior regarding some person, some belief, some product, some act, some policy, some philosphy can—by employing appeals to our needs—motivate us to respond to our feelings rather than to our reasoning.

Identifying Emotional Appeals

If we, as critical listeners, know the appeals which are commonly used and can identify them as emotional appeals, we will be able to participate in communicative acts in a more rational manner. One method which can aid us in maintaining our rationality and objectivity is the following visual technique. As a speaker presents a persuasive message, we can observe his or her emotional and logical content by visually placing the two types of content (E-E for emotional and L-L for logical) in two continua which *intersect* at some point between the two extremes. Thus, we will have a visual means to assist us in determining whether the message content is balanced, high in emotional content, or high in logical content. (See figure 8.4.) When we conclude that there is an excess of emotional appeal, we will become more aware of how we are being persuaded. Furthermore, to assist us in maintaining our rationality and objectivity, we should ask ourselves these questions when we are confronted with emotional appeals:

1. What is the speaker's intent?
2. Is the speaker attempting to manipulate me?
3. Does the speaker have honest motives?
4. Is the speaker making promises that he or she cannot fulfill?
5. Who will benefit if the speaker's intent is achieved?
6. Does the speaker combine emotional appeal with reasoning (evidence)?
7. How am I responding?
8. Am I responding on a purely emotional level?
9. Am I allowing my emotional weaknesses to be exploited?

Utilizing these questions will assist us in understanding our responses to the numerous psychological appeals we receive. Among the emotional appeals that speakers employ are the following eighteen which Monroe has identified.[33]

Acquisition and Savings. The speaker might appeal to our need for acquisition and saving by stressing how the proposal can save us money. Generally, everyone likes a bargain, especially in inflationary times, so a considerable amount of product advertising is based on this appeal.[34]

Adventure. A second appeal is the appeal to adventure. The listener's desire to explore new worlds, see exciting things, and participate in different events is often stressed. Amusement and theme parks and travel agencies are two industries which rely heavily on our desire for adventure.

Companionship. A third appeal, companionship, arouses in us the desire to be with other people. Have you ever noticed how advertisers seldom associate a product with just one person? Since we are motivated by companionship, motivational researchers have concluded that it would not be wise to associate products with loneliness. Appeals by organizations for membership will frequently stress the benefits of companionship with the organization.

Creativity. The appeal to creativity may be another motivator. Most of us enjoy expressing ourselves through some creative means such as decorating our

Figure 8.4. Diagrams of perceived message content: balanced, high logical, and high emotional.

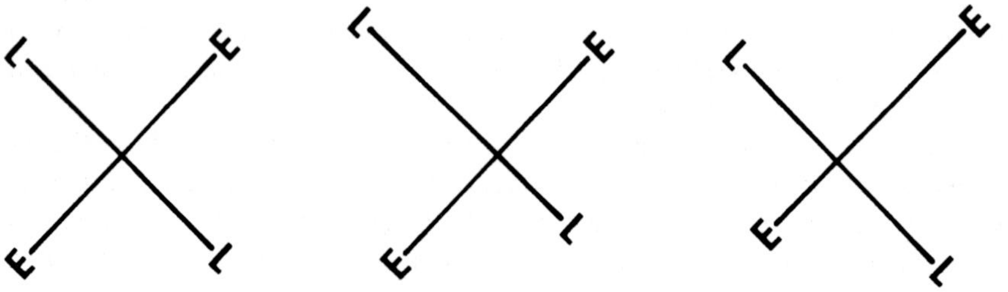

homes, designing innovative products, or satisfying our artistic drives. The influence of this motivational force can be demonstrated by the numerous arts and crafts shows and kits as well as the do-it-yourself manuals that are currently so popular.

Curiosity. An additional appeal is the appeal to curiosity. When our curiosity is aroused, we often respond by seeking answers to the *whys, whens, wheres, whos, whats,* and *hows* which we wish to investigate. Besides capitalizing on our desire to know, the appeal to curiosity frequently operates with our desire for adventure, particularly if we are motivated to travel or explore new territory.

Destruction. Some speakers may attempt to use the appeal to destroy. This appeal calls for destruction of an existing rule, institution, etc. If the existing factor is made to appear as a real problem, a desire to overthrow it can be aroused. It is a difficult appeal to handle because it can be so destructive. The critical listener should be certain that the speaker has an alternative to replace what is to be destroyed. In the late 1960s, many students—as well as non-students—were vehemently calling for the overthrow of the entire institution of higher learning. What was missing in so many of the appeals to destruction, however, was any attempt to offer real alternatives to the existing structure of higher education.

Fear. The fear appeal, presenting a sense of threat to the receiver, attempts to motivate the receiver to act. Research in the fear appeal indicates that it may be possible for the speaker to overdo a fear appeal so that the listener may be even further strengthened in opposition to the threat. This strengthening of the opposing view is known as the "boomerang effect" and has been identified in several studies of the appeal. After reviewing research studies of the use of the fear appeal, Colburn recognized that it is difficult to generalize as to the effectiveness of the appeal since it will affect each individual receiver differently. He noted, however, that "when fear-arousing appeals are used, speakers and writers will be more likely to gain acceptance of their recommendations if the strength of those appeals is proportionate to the importance of the issue in listeners' minds."[35]

Fighting. Closely allied to the appeal to destruction is the appeal to fighting. Prior to utilizing the destruction appeal, a speaker often employs the appeal to fighting by arousing the anger of his or her listeners. The appeal to fighting probably has more effect if it is used with a group of listeners rather than with one individual in an isolated setting. The speaker who asks, "Are you happy with your tax bills? Do you feel we've had enough?" is tapping the sense of anger in his or her taxpaying listeners.

Imitation. A less hostile appeal is that of imitation. This strongly motivates Americans, as indicated by advertising appeals aimed at us to purchase cosmetics endorsed by famous Hollywood stars or shaving equipment used by great sports figures. In our attempts to "keep up with the Joneses," we demonstrate our drive to emulate others.

Independence. While our desire to emulate others is strong, a conflicting motivation may be our sense of independence. Some product advertisers have attempted to use this appeal to associate certain brands of cigarettes, for instance, with the independent cowboy alone on his horse or the liberated woman. Independence lies at the heart of our constitutional democracy, and therefore it is inherent in American value systems. Wartime speakers, too, made considerable use of this appeal to mobilize public support for the war effort.

Loyalty. Keeping America independent also represents an appeal to loyalty. Loyalty to our nation, our friends and family, and our organizations is an important characteristic. Loyalty to the nation, for example, represents patriotic appeals which continue to change. The "America—love it or leave it" movement polarized Americans so that some Americans no longer will respond to flag-waving patriotic appeals.

Personal Enjoyment. We are all highly motivated by personal enjoyment. Advertisers—recognizing that we long to fulfill our sensory and psychic desires for pleasures such as comfort, luxury, security, contentment, beauty, recreation, freedom, space, and sensory satisfaction—employ appeals to our experiences of present pleasures, our memories of past pleasures, and our anticipation of future pleasures. These appeals indicte how we are capable of responding on a higher order of Maslow's hierarchy. Thus, if our basic needs are met, we can turn to fulfilling needs of enjoyment and aesthetics.

Power and Authority. There are times when the speaker may wish to appeal to the listener's sense of power and authority. Such a motivator could be appropriate in developing more responsibility in a group of administrators. It is an appeal used in the auto industry to persuade buyers to purchase large engines. The appeal to power is also a strong motivator to a mobilize a nation to wage war.[36]

Pride. Another powerful emotional incentive is the appeal to our sense of pride. Recognizing the motivational force of individual self-esteem, speakers frequently strive to develop a positive self-concept in their listeners. Managers have relied on an appeal to pride in work well done in industry in order to motivate workers to accomplish rigorous production schedules. Motivational research reveals that job satsifaction frequently stems from factors intrinsic within the job itself.[37]

Reverence. Still another appeal is the appeal to reverence or worship. This can be seen through manifestations of hero worship—having deep admiration, for example, for sports stars, entertainers, or historical figures—or in religious behaviors.

Revulsion. A motivator which is inherent in all of us is revulsion. As a specific type of fear, this appeal can be effective. A speaker illustrating the effects of water pollution, for example, may show photographs and cite statistics on the effects so as to motivate receivers to support legislation for clean water. Such an appeal, if not overdone, can accomplish an initial arousal to action.

Sexual Attraction. Found in a great deal of advertising is a more pleasant appeal: sexual attraction. This associates the beautiful young woman with the automobile commercial or the handsome young man with hair care products. While it is a motivator, it can be overdrawn if the appeal does not relate to the product or the issue under consideration.

Sympathy. A potent appeal is the appeal to sympathy. A speaker who depicts homeless children, mistreated elderly, or forgotten veterans can motivate us to give our time, money, and talents. Political speakers like to use this appeal to gain support for their causes and for their own elections.

Since we are motivated by such appeals, it helps listeners to know why they are responding as they are if they can identify the specific type of appeal which the speaker is using for psychological effect. At the extreme, the speaker will use only emotional appeals as a persuasive device. Such an attempt may succeed in persuading listeners at the moment. Over a period of time, however, we tend to forget the impact of such appeals and are left with only the core of the argument from the message. If there is no valid logical argument, then the message probably will not have a long-lasting effect.

Dealing Effectively with Emotive Language

In addition to using emotional appeals to arouse the listeners, persuaders frequently employ emotive language—often in the forms of name-calling and labeling. Using terms intended to degrade the object referred to (whether it be a person, issue, party, event, etc.) and stereotyping a person, party, issue, or event on the basis of limited knowledge are methods speakers use to influence listeners to accept their views. An opponent of a certain candidate, for example, uses name-calling when he or she remarks to a voter. "Don't vote for Menard; she's a radical," and a person who may have seen a long-haired male arrested on television uses labeling when he or she says to a neighbor, "You'd be insane to hire that Colson boy; he's just one of those long-haired freaks who only cause trouble." "Hate" rhetoric, designed to arouse listeners' emotions, often utilizes highly

Daily, we are flooded with emotional appeals—appeals made on the telephone, the radio, the television. . . .
Photo by Robert Tocha.

emotional language to characterize the particular racial, ethnic, or religious group which might be the particular target of the speaker.

As listeners, we tend to react in two ways to language that triggers emotional reactions in us. If the views expressed are congruent with our point of view, we accept—without question—what is said and are ruled by our feelings rather than by our minds. On the other hand, if the views expressed are incongruent with our point of view, we immediately reject what is said and exercise emotional censorship; we become "deaf" to what we do not want to hear and again are ruled by our feelings. Both responses are reactions which the critical listener should disclaim.

Critical listeners should attempt to reduce the impact which certain emotionally "loaded" words have on them. They should first recognize their own biases toward certain emotive words, analyze why these words affect them as they do, and then attempt to perceive the words rationally. With this new awareness, listeners will be better able to deal with such words when they meet them in communicative situations. Dealing with them effectively consists of recognizing them for what they are—emotive words, maintaining self-control while listening to the remainder of the speaker's message, examining the speaker's message for evidence to prove or disprove the speaker's claim, asking the speaker to provide evidence to support his or her claim if the evidence has not been presented, and then accepting or rejecting the speaker's view on the basis of having made a rational rather than an emotional decision.

Responsibilities of the Critical Listener

Critical listeners respond to persuasive messages designed to change attitudes and actions voluntarily. Understanding how these messages incorporate speaker credibility, arguments, and emotional appeals can enable listeners to more systematically and soundly evaluate those messages in order to decide whether to accept or reject the speaker's proposal. According to Charles Larson, the critical listener has two major responsibilities.

> First, he must watch himself as he is persuaded or as he is subject to persuasive appeals; second, he must find some way to systematize his awareness by applying carefully considered criteria to the appeals he processes, judging their relevance, their truth, and their applicability to him.[38]

Accepting these responsibilities may make the difference between our being uncritical listeners controlled by others or being critical listeners controlled by ourselves.

SUMMARY

In this chapter, we have examined the need for critical listening—listening to comprehend and *then* evaluate—as it applies primarily to messages that are persuasive in intent. To assist the critical listener in understanding the process of persuasion and establising criteria to be used as a basis for the listener's decision to accept or to reject a persuasive message, we have presented (1) a definition of persuasion, (2) a psychological sequence that the process of influence usually follows, and (3) a detailed explanation of how the three components of persuasion—ethos, logos, and pathos—function in the persuasive effort. We also have provided lists of questions which the critical listener should ask and answer when evaluating various aspects of these three components. Finally, we have discussed the following critical listening skills that the critical listener must develop in order for him or her to more systematically and soundly evaluate persuasive messages: identifying the dimensions of source credibility; recognizing the possible influence which source credibility may have on the listener; analyzing inductive and deductive argument structures to determine their truth and validity; detecting and evaluating reasoning fallacies; judging the clarity, accuracy, and reliability of evidence; recognizing need levels; and identifying psychological appeals and emotive language and recognizing their effects on the listener. The critical listener who develops these skills will have a sound basis upon which to evaluate persuasive messages and hence should have control over his or her decision.

SUGGESTED ACTIVITIES

1. Identify at least three radio and television commercials which follow Monroe's Motivated Sequence. Then, present a detailed description (orally or in writing) of how each commercial uses each of the five basic steps.

2. Create your own examples of inductive arguments and read them to the class; the class will assess the truthfulness of the arguments.
3. Create your own enthymemes, put the relationships into symbols, diagram the relationships by using circles, read the enthymemes to the other members of the class, and have the class determine the validity and truth of the enthymemes.
4. Identify other conjunctions besides *because* that imply causal relationships. Examine your own written papers to determine what causal terms you have used and whether your causal reasoning is sound.
5. Bring in examples of logical fallacies found in various forms of communication (speeches, commercials, editorials, etc.). Share the examples with the class.
6. Identify five radio or television commercials which utilize fallacious testimonies. Then, describe orally each product being endorsed, the person doing the endorsing, and the name, title, or field of a person who would present a credible testimony.
7. Compile a list of special interest groups (religious, racial, political, professional, sexual, economic, etc.). Then, locate three or four statements of fact, opinion, and inference in articles that express the views of special interest groups. Each student will read each of his or her statements, and students will determine what type of statement (fact, opinion, or inference) is being used. When an opinion is stated, students will try to determine why that opinion is held by a particular special interest group.
8. Carefully note several opinions that your other instructors state. Then, privately meet with one instructor and find out why the instructor holds a particular opinion.
9. Find examples of statistics in the various medias and share the examples with the class. Students will evaluate critically the soundness of the examples.
10. Identify words or phrases that emotionally upset you. Then, share these words with the class, analyze why these words have such emotional impact, and try to eliminate your conditioned reactions to these words.
11. List examples of emotional appeals and emotive words with which you are confronted over the next few days. Do not rely heavily on commercials. Then, share these examples with the class at the next class session.
12. Compile a list of biases and stereotypes you possess. Then, consider how and why you have developed them, how they affect your listening behavior, and how you could minimize or eliminate them from your listening and thinking.
13. List all of the examples of bias and stereotyping that you hear in speeches, lectures, conversations, on television, on radio, etc., during a week. Compare your examples with those of other students. What examples are most frequently listed? Why do you think these particular biases and stereotypes exist? How did these examples affect you and your listening behavior when

you first heard them stated? How did they affect other students and their listening behavior?

14. List all of the loaded words and phrases that you hear in speeches, lectures, conversations, on television, on radio, etc., during a week. Place each word in one of two columns labeled "positive" and "negative." Compare your list with other students' lists. Which words are most frequently listed? What connotative meanings do the words have? What makes these words "positive" or "negative"?
15. Make a copy of an article or speech that contains highly emotional words. Rewrite the message by replacing the emotional words with neutral words. Examine the revised material to determine the validity of the claim(s) being made.

NOTES

1. S. I. Hayakawa, "The Task of the Listener," *ETC* 7 (Autumn 1949): 9–10.
2. Wendell Johnson, "Do We Know How to Listen?" *ETC* 7 (Autumn 1949): 3.
3. M. Agnella Gunn, "Background Preparation for the Role of Today's Teacher of English," paper presented at the Annual Convention of the National Council of Teachers of English, Chicago, Illinois, 1960.
4. Robert Goyer, class notes, Purdue University, 1965.
5. Douglas Ehninger, Bruce E. Gronbeck, and Alan H. Monroe, *Principles and Types of Speech Communication,* 8th brief ed. (Glenview, Illinois: Scott Foresman and Company, 1980), pp. 245–252.
6. See, for example, Stanley F. Paulson, "Social Values and Experimental Research in Speech," *Western Speech Communication* 26 (Summer 1962): 133–139.
7. For a discussion of the dimensions of source credibility, see James C. McCroskey, *An Introduction to Rhetorical Communication* (Englewood Cliffs, New Jersey: Prentice-Hall, Inc., 1972), chapter 4. See also James C. McCroskey and Thomas J. Young, "Ethos and Credibility: The Construct and Its Measurement after Three Decades," *Central States Speech Journal* 32 (Spring 1981): 24–34, for McCroskey's critique of the research on the construct of source credibility and his conclusion that source credibility must be considered as part of a broader construct of person perception.
8. Kenneth E. Andersen and Theodore Clevenger, Jr., "A Summary of Experimenal Research in Ethos," *Speech Monographs* 30 (June 1963): 77.
9. Donald H. Naftulin, John E. Ware, Jr., and Frank A. Donnelly, "The Doctor Fox Lecture: A Paradigm of Educational Seduction," *Journal of Medical Education* 48 (July 1973): 630–635.
10. Louis Harris, "Confidence in Institutions Rises Slightly," New York: The Harris Survey, November 17, 1983, pp. 2–3.
11. John F. Kennedy, "Ich Bin Ein Berliner," *Public Papers of the Presidents: John F. Kennedy, 1963* (Washington, D.C.: United States Government Printing Office, 1964), p. 525.
12. Philip Shaver, "The Public Distrust," *Psychology Today* 14 (October 1980): 44.
13. Joe McGinniss, *The Selling of the President 1968* (New York: Trident Books, 1969), p. 38.

14. Sandra L. Marcus, "Recall of Logical Argument Lines," *Journal of Verbal Learning and Verbal Behavior* 21 (October 1982): 549.
15. Michael Scriven, *Reasoning* (New York: McGraw-Hill, 1976), pp. 39–45.
16. Richard E. Crable, *Argumentation as Communication* (Columbus, Ohio: Charles E. Merrill, 1976), p. 215.
17. The real impact of evidence in persuasive discourse may be disputed. After analyzing experimental research studies on the use of evidence, McCroskey drew conclusions which suggest that listeners may not be responsive to a speaker's evidence:
    1. Including good evidence has little, if any, impact on immediate audience attitude change or source credibility if the source of the message is initially perceived to be high-credible.
    2. Including good evidence has little, if any, impact on immediate audience attitude change if the message is delivered poorly.
    3. Including good evidence has little, if any, impact on immediate audience attitude change or source credibility if the audience is familiar with the evidence prior to exposure to the source's message.
    4. Including good evidence may significantly increase immediate audience attitude change and source credibility when the source is initially perceived to be moderate-to-low credible, when the message is well delivered, and when the audience has little or no prior familiarity with the evidence included or similar evidence.
    5. Including good evidence may significantly increase sustained audience attitude change regardless of the source's initial credibility, the quality of the delivery of the message, or the medium by which the message is transmitted.
    6. The medium of transmission of a message has little, if any, effect on the functioning of evidence in persuasive communication.

    See James C. McCroskey, "A Summary of Experimental Research on the Effects of Evidence in Persuasive Communication," *The Quarterly Journal of Speech* 55 (April 1969): 169–176.
18. Russel R. Windes and Arthur Hastings, *Argumentation and Advocacy* (New York: Random House, 1965), p. 96.
19. *Ibid.,* p. 99.
20. William V. Haney, *Communication Patterns and Incidents* (Homewood, Illinois: Richard D. Irwin, Inc., 1960), p. 21.
21. Gordon Allport and Leon Postman, *The Psychology of Rumor* (New York: Holt, Rinehart and Winston, Inc., 1947), p. ix.
22. Ralph L. Rosnow and Allan J. Kimmel, "Lives of a Rumor," *Psychology Today* 13 (June 1979): 91.
23. *Ibid.*
24. Clyde R. Miller, "Detection and Analysis of Propaganda," *Public Opinion Quarterly* 5 (Winter 1941): 662.
25. *Ibid.*
26. Robert P. Newman and Dale G. Newman, *Evidence* (Boston: Houghton Mifflin Company, 1969).
27. *Ibid.,* p. 72.
28. Darrell Huff, *How to Lie with Statistics* (New York: W. W. Norton and Company, 1954).
29. *Ibid.,* pp. 122–142.

30. *Ibid.*, p. 122.
31. Abraham Maslow, *Motivation and Personality* (New York: Harper and Row, Publishers, 1970), pp. 35–38.
32. William Watts, "The Future Can Fend for Itself," *Psychology Today* 15 (September 1981): 36–48.
33. Alan H. Monroe and Douglas Ehninger, *Principles and Types of Speech,* 7th ed. (Glenview, Illinois: Scott Foresman and Company, 1974), pp. 270–282.
34. For a scholarly treatment of motivational research and its application in the advertising industry, see James F. Engel, David T. Kollat, and Roger D. Blackwell, *Consumer Behavior* (New York: Holt, Rinehart and Winston, 1973).
35. C. William Colburn, "Fear-Arousing Appeals," in *Speech Communication Analysis and Readings,* eds. Howard H. Martin and Kenneth E. Andersen (Boston: Allyn and Bacon, 1968), pp. 214–223.
36. For a current discussion of this appeal, see David C. McClelland, "Love and Power: The Psychological Signals of War," *Psychology Today* 8 (January 1975): 44–48.
37. For a review of the research, see T. O. Jacobs, *Leadership and Exchange in Formal Organizations* (Alexandria, Virginia: Human Resources Research Organization, 1971), pp. 122–154.
38. Charles U. Larson, *Persuasion: Reception and Responsibility* (Belmont, California: Wadsworth Publishing Company, 1973), p. 13.

Concepts You Will Encounter

Appreciation
Sensory Stimulation
Enjoyment
Aesthetic Experience
Music
Speech Style
Oral Reading
Theatre
Mass Media
Experience
Willingness
Attention

Skills You Should Develop

Gaining Experience in Appreciative Listening
Developing a Willingness to Listen Appreciatively
Concentrating Attention

Appreciative Listening

9

Appreciative listening is the highly individualized process of listening in order to obtain sensory stimulation or enjoyment through the works and experiences of others. The process is highly individualized—perhaps even more individualized than other purposes of listening—because it incorporates so many of a person's sensitivities in order to derive impressions and/or pleasure from the stimulus. As such, appreciative listening may represent a basically emotional response. A person may listen appreciatively, for example, to a television movie. If the movie is a romantic comedy, the experience may be pleasurable. As a listener, then, the appreciation may be that of enjoyment. If the television movie is a horror story, on the other hand, the response may not be so pleasurable. The listener certainly will gain images and heightened emotions while feeling considerable tension at the horror depicted on the screen.

The Process of Listening Appreciatively

Since appreciative listening is highly individualized, there are no criteria by which to draw up a formula for the appreciation of anything for all people. However, an understanding of ours and others' views regarding appreciative listening may help you to develop your personal formula.

A controversy exists in many of the fine arts fields (art, music, dance, theatre) as to how to develop appreciation. Some scholars in these fields would encourage specific training in the components which make up the artistic expression (the elements of a symphony, for example). The stress here is on understanding the individual parts which make up the whole creative product. Others would claim, however, that such specific training can interfere with true appreciation—that such training builds critical facility.

Paul Friedman, writing about training people as appreciative listeners, notes that listeners can recognize "subtle musical nuances that otherwise might go unnoticed" through knowledge of the composition of a musical piece.[1] Friedman recognizes, however, that overemphasis on understanding the intricacies of music may work against the appreciative listener: "If the listener becomes too concerned with the principles of musical form and structure, his or her enjoyment of the pure musical experiences may be diminished."[2]

It is not our purpose here to take sides in the controversy. We have known theatre people, for instance, who could not enjoy a theatre production because they were trained to study every element of the production. Other theatre friends who have had similar backgrounds are able to set aside critical perspectives and truly appreciate a production. It would seem, therefore, that such differences reflect our point: appreciative listening is an individual process. What some listeners may appreciate, others may not.

The individualized process of appreciative listening involves interpreting spoken, nonverbal, or musical language and relating that language to past experiences. A listener's perception, experience, background, mental set, understanding of the presentation, expectations, motivation, interest, and previous knowledge brought to the appreciative experience combine with the quality of the presentation to determine one's appreciative levels.

Opportunities for Appreciative Listening

Essentially, appreciative listening can include listening to music, the oral style of a speaker, environmental sounds, oral interpretation of literature, theatre, or radio, television, and film. It is not so much the source of the appreciative listening act as it is the individual response to it.

The appreciative listener listens for the power and beauty of well-chosen words or music which describe people, places, things, qualities, and abstractions. The color and mood of languages or music and the rhythm of language and music symbols are immeasurable except in an appreciative context. As the listener listens appreciatively to the reading of literature, or a theatre production, or a piece of music, or a speaker's rhetorical style, or environmental sounds, he or she will be listening to appreciate the works of others, to identify with their experiences, and to establish an emotional bond with them.

In order for listeners to develop this emotional bond when listening to music, music educators have stressed that our responses to music should fall in the fluid categories of sensual, emotional, and intellectual. Training in music appreciation is designed to combine these levels so that the listener can derive ultimate appreciation from the sound itself.

Machlis has identified the role of the appreciative listener in music:

> The enjoyment of music depends upon perceptive listening, and perceptive listening (like perceptive anything) is something that we achieve gradually, with practice and some effort. By acquiring a knowledge of the circumstances out of which a musical work issued, we prepare ourselves for its multiple meanings; we lay ourselves open to that exercise of mind and heart, sensibility and imagination that makes listening to music so unique an experience. But in the building up of our musical perceptions—that is, of our listening enjoyment—let us always remember that the ultimate wisdom resides neither in dates nor in facts. It is to be found in one place only—the sounds themselves.[3]

Another specialist in music appreciation, Charles Hoffer, suggests that there are three interrelated types of listening which can lead to enjoyment of music. One type of listening, "sensuous," refers to the physical effect of the music on the listener. A second type of listening involves the feeling or mood evoked by the music itself for the expressive meaning. The third type of music listening requires concentration on what happens in the music in order to appreciate the sounds and their manipulation.[4]

A more complex level of appreciative listening is listening to the oral style of a speaker. It is a difficult form of appreciative listening because, to be truly appreciative, the listener must filter out his or her responses to the speaker's content and concentrate on the speaker's rhetorical style. Jane Blankenship, in a popular book on speech style, has defined style as an individual's "characteristic way of using the resources of the English language."[5] These resources include the selection of words (word choice) and their combination (syntax) to achieve desired effects.

Several authors on speech style have characterized effective speech style. Wilson and Arnold provide us with one such set of characteristics which can be utilized as listening guidelines:

Accuracy—the precision by which ideas are expressed.

Clarity—ease of language.

Propriety—the appropriateness of the style to the speaker, the audience, and the occasion.

Economy—conciseness of langauge.

Force—vigor, power in language.

Strikingly quality—the vividness of the style.

Liveliness—the energy and movement of the language.[6]

These characteristics of style can be applied to the appreciation of the beauty and the power of the rhetorical language of effective public speakers. Contemporary speakers such as Martin Luther King, Jr., and John F. Kennedy were noted for their speech style. Consider the emotional impact of King's "I Have a Dream" speech presented in Washington, D.C., in August 1963, before a huge crowd at the Lincoln Memorial: "With this faith we will be able to work together, to pray together, to struggle together, to go to jail together, to stand up for freedom together, knowing that we will be free one day."[7] And we are all familiar with the emotional impact of Kennedy's conclusion to his January 1961, inaugural address: "And so, my fellow Americans: Ask not what your country can do for you—ask what you can do for your country. My fellow citizens of the world: Ask not what America will do for you, but what together we can do for the freedom of man."[8]

A unique appreciative listening experience is to listen to environmental sounds around us. A walk through a wooded parkland in the spring can provide the listener with a symphony of birds. The wind gently rustling the trees is another appreciative level provided by nature. Novelist-essayist Alice Walker notes that "if you are quiet enough you hear incredible things. . . . You begin to realize that you are everyone and everyone is you."[9] Finding inspiration in nature's sounds as she engages in the creative process of developing her artistic works, she encourages us to go out into the country "to listen to what the earth is saying and hear better our own thoughts."[10] Even the hectic pace of an urban environment can provide us with appreciative listening to people, traffic, and construction crews. And contemporary advocates of meditation reflect on the value of "listening" to silence.

Illustrating the joys of listening to sounds around us, Olive Ghiselin wrote an extensive description of the sounds of Europe. Some of the vivid sound images which she recalls are fascinating to anyone who has traveled to Europe:

> I remembered the splash of fountains in the Alhambra gardens, and the great fall of water at the Fountain of Vaucluse. . . . I recall the booming and churning of a wild surf at Lequeitio. . . . And the gratified groaning of wooden carts loaded with the grapes of Bordeaux. The pursuing screams of beggar children at Naples. . . . Outside, above the Atlantic, the winds of Normandy wailed. I contrasted this lusty sizzling in Nice, as a waiter prepared crepes in a silver pan. . . .[11]

Portable cassette audio recorders enable all of us to capture sounds on vacation if, indeed, we do not have the words and phrases to recapture such sounds as vividly as Ghiselin is able to do.

We also create environments through sound. In the 1940s, media specialist Tony Schwarz developed a series of records believed to be the first to capture sound that was part of everyday life. Known as the New York 19 project, the record enabled the listeners to experience actual sounds. Today, Schwartz (famous for his television "Daisy" commercial for Lyndon Johnson's presidential campaign against Barry Goldwater) argues that we create much of our environment through sounds—electronically mediated and amplified:

> This has radically affected the structure of sound for listeners and created a new relation between sound and space. Sound need no longer be contained within a physical environment that defines boundaries for the sound. Amplification of sound . . . is so overwhelming that it creates its own walls . . . that *contain* a listener.[12]

Listening to the oral interpretation of literature affords a further opportunity for appreciative listening. In the reading of literature, the reader serves to bring to life the author's material—prose, poetry, and drama—for the listener, providing sufficient interpretation to allow "mental pictures" to form in the mind of the listener. Oral interpretation can take several forms, from an individual reader presenting a program to the currently popular readers theatre medium.

A new industry is bringing to the sighted an oral interpretation experience that the blind have known for years: cassette-recorded books. Describing the popularity of taped books, Alice Digilio notes that "the habit of listening to books read aloud, an activity replaced a long time ago by the habit of watching television, appears to be making a comeback."[13] And, indeed it is as customers can now rent or buy tape-recorded books from numerous companies—companies which offer a wide variety of current as well as classic literary selections ranging from J. R. R. Tolkien's *The Hobbit* (read by Tolkien) to Dylan Thomas's poetry (read by Thomas) to *Hamlet* (performed by such recognized actors as Paul Scofield).[14] Found particularly enjoyable by commuters and joggers (who listen to literature on their automobile and portable tape units), this commercially-available form of appreciative listening is gaining many avid listeners who also listen on their home tape units. One such avid listener is columnist George F. Will, who has found listening to books on tape to be a satisfying experience:

> The pleasure is not just in the particular books. It is also in learning to listen. I now know that I was not very good at something that I wrongly thought was as natural and easy as breathing.
>
> It is well known that reading is something that can be done with widely varying degrees of efficiency. So is listening. . . .
>
> Listening to a book—not just following the plot but following the syntax of 19th-century sentences rich in semicolons and parenthetical clauses—requires a special kind of concentration, and it exercises segments of my brain that have been unexercised since my father read me the exploits of Horatio Hornblower.[15]

Americans love to listen to stories. While the popularity of commercial tapes of books illustrates our love affair with storytelling, so, too, does the growth of the National Storytelling Festival reveal our appreciative listening. For three days, storytellers and listeners come together in Jonesborough, Tennessee, to share stories. Many of the storytellers are professionals, though often the listeners come to swap tales of their own. Among the appreciative listeners are children: "Children sit entranced for long hours. Their parents remember when radio did this to them—or better, when grandmother rocked and told tales."[16] Describing the process, storyteller Jack Torrence says, "We've been living off other people's imaginations for so long. If you can go to the mountain with Jack and ride the unicorn, holding on by a strap, you have forgotten you've got to pay bills."[17] And Jonesborough Mayor Jimmy Neil Smith works to "preserve the intimacy between teller and listener,"[18] even though the attendance at the festival grows every year.

Coger and White, in writing about the readers theatre medium, note that audience members can derive substantial benefits from their participation in the activity:

> For them, it provides the opportunity to explore the wide horizons of literature—great novels, memorable short stories, stirring poetry, and distinguished plays seldom produced in the theatre—and it challenges them to participate in the literary experience.[19]

In readers theatre, a group of interpreters presents the material to a live audience. While readers theatre depends on the interpreters to create the mental

Figure 9.1. Through listening appreciatively to the reading of oral literature, we can climb mountains, visit lions, touch stars. . . . Photo by Robert Tocha

pictures, theatre as a medium provides yet another level of appreciative listening. The form differs from readers theatre in that it can be more explicit—scenery, lighting, costuming, and makeup combine with the actors to create an illusion for the listener.

Effective theatre calls on the listener to bring to play his or her imagination in creating the illusion. Recent theories of theatre have emphasized the need to involve the audiences as much as possible in the theatrical activity, viewing the listener as fifty percent of the total creative event. Consequently, much of the revolutionary theatre, for instance, is designed to elicit overt responses from the listeners. A recent Broadway production of *Candide* exemplifies this involvement: the orchestra and playing spaces were located throughout the audience areas, so the listeners were totally surrounded by the production. The popular *Cats* puts the audience into a junkyard scene.

On a different level, mass media offers appreciative listening through radio, television, and film. The listener's involvement in the medium has been theorized by Marshall McLuhan and Quentin Fiore. They suggest that the electronic media has shaped our lives, both personally and socially:

> Societies have always been shaped more by the nature of the media by which men communicate than by the content of the communication. The alphabet, for instance, is a technology that is absorbed by the very young child in a completely unconscious manner, by osmosis so to speak. Words and the meaning of words predispose the child to think and act automatically in certain ways. The alphabet and print technology fostered and encouraged a fragmenting process, a process of specialism and of detachment. Electric technology fosters and encourages unification and involvement. It is impossible to understand social and cultural changes without a knowledge of the workings of media.[20]

The popularity of the medium is obvious in this mass media society. While television and film are perennial favorites of the majority of Americans, radio has its devotees, too. Those who enjoy listening to music, talk shows, and non-stop news often prefer the radio medium. Another group of radio followers is baseball fans, who enjoy following along and visualizing the plays as play-by-play announcers describe the action of the game. Phil Jackman, sports writer for the Baltimore *Evening Sun,* suggests a reason for this preference: "Baseball is radio's game, a joy to have as a companion on a warm summer evening, during a long auto trip or most any time. What makes it so is that it gives our often dormant imaginations something to play with."[21] Moreover, radio is becoming a favorite for many listeners as it appears to be making a "comeback" with a revival of popular radio dramas. At the University of Wisconsin, for instance, a series of radio plays, "EARPLAY," are produced for the Corporation for Public Broadcasting and distributed to the public radio stations of National Public Radio. Radio stations in metropolitan centers are rerunning such popular series as "Stella Dallas," "The Great Gildersleeve," and "The Green Hornet." Cassette tape companies are distributing copies of many of the shows from the "Golden Age" of radio for persons who collect these broadcasts. Indeed, the famous Orson Welles's "The Shadow" broadcasts have repopularized the opening question, "Who knows what evil lurks in the hearts of men?"

Even copy writers for ads encourage us to listen appreciatively. Ads for Sir Walter Raleigh steak and salad restaurants in the Washington, D.C., area, for example, encourage people to come to "Listen to the Crackling Fire" of the open grill and of the fireplace in the dining room. And, Ruth Chris's Steak House urges customers to "Listen to the sizzle of the steak" itself. Another ad, one for "Miracle Ear" hearing aids, phrased the appreciative listening experience descriptively: "LISTEN TO LIFE. There is a world of beauty surrounding you . . . the vibrant world of sound . . . the privacy of a whisper, the beautiful sounds of music, the joys of conversation. . . ."[22]

The variety of media for appreciative listening provides the listener with a number of experiences from which he or she can choose. Despite the type of experience, it may be assumed that exposure to the stimulus, motivation, and attention enable the listener to gain from the experience what will be his or her own individual appreciation. From this appreciation, greater understanding and experience may result, providing the listener with a heightening of his or her appreciative capacities.

How to Improve Appreciative Listening

Although appreciative listening is a highly individualized level of response, some techniques for improving appreciative listening skills have been found to be useful.

Larry Barker offers the listener five suggestions for improving appreciative listening in social or informal situations. He recommends that the listeners determine what they enjoy listening to most and then analyze why they enjoy these listening settings. Listeners are wise, then, to compare their likes and dislikes in listening with those of others and develop a strong sense of curiosity in approaching any appreciative listening setting. Further, Barker observes, it is helpful to read and consult to learn more about the areas in which listeners do find enjoyment.[23]

Charles Hoffer, the specialist in music appreciation, recommends that the listener increase listening ability through (1) improving your memory for music; (2) concentrating on main themes and the important musical ideas; (3) hearing as much detail as possible; (4) encouraging your reactions to music; (5) avoiding the visualization of specific scenes; (6) applying knowledge to your listening; and (7) following a listening skills development program.[24] Ultimately, Hoffer suggests, the improvement of appreciative listening rests with the development of a positive attitude for creating an increased understanding: "Learning to listen is more accurately a matter of wanting to understand the music than it is of the techniques for understanding music."[25] This understanding, indeed, applies to the appreciation of all the art forms to which we attend as listeners. And through this appreciation we can expand and develop our experiences as human beings.

Describing the influences of the audience on the theatre, Cameron and Gillespie believe that a person should prepare for participating as an audience member by understanding the theatre as an art form and by developing a sympathy for the work to be presented. A good audience participates, they stress, by "making its imagination work when that imagination is stirred by the performance . . . and by remaining open to new ways of being moved, entertained, and excited. . . ."[26]

Thomas R. Lewis and Ralph G. Nichols have identified five steps that listeners can take to enhance the ability to listen appreciatively. These steps include the identification of the things we like most, the verification of why we like these things, and the observation of how these things we like most affect others.[27] In addition to dealing with the familiar things we like most, Lewis and Nichols recommend that we broaden our horizons in the search for new aesthetic expression. After the new aesthetic experience, it is helpful to study the art form, discuss it with others, and return to it for new insights.[28] "Appreciative listening, then, depends chiefly upon our willingness to learn."[29]

Gaining Experience in Appreciative Listening

The major step in improving one's appeciative listening abilities is to gain experience as an appreciative listener. The more practice you have in responding to appeciative material, either for pleasure or for impression, the more likely you will be to understand your responses and appreciate them.

It would seem to be helpful to gain experience in many different types of appreciative listening areas. The person who attends just rock music concerts, for instance, is deprived of the opportunity to respond to classical symphony concerts. A live theatre experience enthusiast could try opera or ballet productions. Broadening the range of appreciative listening can lead to understanding your responses and perhaps contrasting those responses with other forms. You may come to recognize why you prefer films over stage shows, for instance, and, consequently, establish firmer standards for your appreciative responses. Also, the more frequently you select listening experiences of high quality, the more likely you will be to refine your listening appreciation.

Developing a Willingness to Listen Appreciatively

In addition to gaining experience as an appreciative listener, it is useful to take advantage of the appreciative experiences and allow the material to elicit an aesthetic response from you as a listener. Friedman suggests that "simply being open to the impact that music can have on us, just allowing it to work its magic on our sensory organs, rather than analyzing its contents or feelings, can be a major part of the listening response."[30] Writer Tom Donnelly makes this suggestion in his "Sounds" column: "Listen to that music which speaks to your secret heart. You don't need someone who's a 'critic' to tell you what touches your secret heart. . . . Take some chances. Music can bring you back to your center. Listen with an open mind, ear and heart, and when you find something that touches you, bind it close and never let it go."[31] According to Charles Price, the response can be heightened when you are listening to an orchestra if you are willing to not "even listen to the orchestra, strange as it may seem to say. Listen, rather, to the music *through* the orchestra. . . . The musical play's the thing, not the actors. Any orchestra worth listening to should have this transparency about it."[32] Comparing bluegrass music to an orchestra, Rhonda Strickland encourages listeners of bluegrass music to listen at several levels:

> Listen to what each instrument is doing and you'll discover bluegrass is as complex as a classical musical orchestra.
> Listen to the voices and the vocal arrangements.
> Listen to the lyrics.
> Be entertained.[33]

Strickland further urges bluegrass listeners to become immersed in the listening experience: "Listening with your heart as well as your mind will open up whole new channels of feelings and new ways of expressing those feelings."[34] Edgar Dale also calls attention to the importance of our being willing to listen appreciatively. Describing film appreciation, he emphasizes that appreciation is "to enjoy with understanding."[35] To understand, he argues, you must have a standard by which to measure the value of the experience: "Growth in appreciation comes through a willingness to try out the standards which others have found effective."[36] Your willingness to listen appreciatively—to let the material have the impact it is designed to have—can enhance your abilities as an appreciative listener.

Concentrating Attention

In addition to gaining experience as an appreciative listener and developing a willingness to listen appreciatively, you can improve at this level of listening through careful attention to the aesthetic stimulus so that you can get the entire emotional impact of it. A person listening to the song of a cardinal or a mockingbird, for example, should concentrate his or her attention so as to appreciate the subtle nuances in the song. Machlis points out that true aesthetic listening requires more than the hearing of sounds: "To listen perceptively requires that we fasten our whole attention upon the sounds as they come floating through the air; that we observe the patterns' key form, and respond to the thought and feeling out of which those patterns have emerged."[37]

Dave Kopp, a professional organist, describes how he came to understand the importance of concentrated listening as he listened to other organists—not for the musical whole but for specific musical elements. He offers the following advice to other organists: (1) listen to the whole song; (2) play the song through; (3) listen for the organ registration; (4) listen for single note and harmonic treatment of the melody; (5) listen for the left hand and pedal techniques; (6) listen for introductions and endings in the arrangement; (7) listen for key changes; and (8) imitate techniques. To be an effective organist, stresses the successful artist, the organist must "know how to listen."[38]

The broadening of your appreciative listening experiences can increase your enjoyment of life, provide you with a means of relieving daily tensions and releasing pent-up emotions, and offer you the enrichment of expanding your aesthetic horizons and discovering new art forms. At the same time, it can help you discover new dimensions of yourself.

SUMMARY

In this chapter, we have presented some ideas about appreciative listening—the highly individualized process of listening for sensory stimulation or enjoyment. This type of listening encompasses such experiences as listening to music, the oral style of a speaker, environmental sounds, oral interpretation of literature,

Being willing to let the material work its magic on us can enhance our abilities as appreciative listeners.

Photo by Robert Tocha.

theatre, television, film, and radio. Some appreciative listeners let the material "happen" to them, and thus they gain appreciation from the total sensory impact of the experience. Other appreciative listeners gain greater appreciation through information and even technical insight into the material and the presentation techniques. It is recommended that you acquire experience as an appreciative listener, develop a willingness to listen appreciatively, and concentrate your attention to aesthetic stimuli in order to become more effective appreciative listeners.

SUGGESTED ACTIVITIES

1. Attend a musical presentation (opera, concert, etc.). Listen attentively to the material. What sensory impressions did you get from the material? Did you enjoy the material? What factors combined to enhance your appreciation of it? Would you want to repeat the experience? What have you learned about your own appreciation of music from this experience?
2. Some early morning, go out into your neighborhood and listen to the environmental sounds around you. Do you hear city traffic sounds? Country/woods' sounds? As you listen attentively, can you appreciate what you hear? Do the sounds create any poetic or musical images for you?
3. Attend an oral interpretation reading hour or a readers theatre performance. These presentations are designed to get you, the listener, totally involved through your own creative imagination. Did you visualize the scenes and the characters as you listened to the material? What did the readers do to enhance your involvement in the material?
4. Attend a theatre performance. Listen attentively to the material. What sensory impressions did you get from the material? Did you enjoy the material? What factors combined to enhance your appreciation of it? Would you want to repeat the experience? What have you learned about your own appreciation of theatre from this experience?
5. Some radio stations broadcast "reruns" of the old radio drama shows that were so popular. ("The Shadow," for instance). If you can locate such a broadcast in your area, listen carefully to the presentation. What is done to enhance the material to create vivid images in the listeners' minds? Why do you think this type of presentation was so popular during the "Golden Age" of radio?
6. Attend a *new* appreciative listening event, something (a concert, a ballet, an opera, etc.) that you have not experienced before. Allow yourself to become involved in the material. After the event, reflect on your appreciation of it. Did you enjoy the experience? Why or why not? Would you like to repeat the experience? Would you like to learn more about this particular art form?
7. What pleasant sounds do you recall from your early childhood? What pleasant sounds do you most enjoy today? Discuss these sounds with the class.
8. Make an audio tape recording of something you listen to appreciatively (music, sounds, reading, etc.); share your tape with the class. Describe what it is that you particularly appreciate in the material.

NOTES

1. Paul G. Friedman, *Listening Processes: Attention, Understanding, Evaluation* (Washington, D.C.: National Education Association, 1978), p. 26.
2. *Ibid.*
3. Joseph Machlis, *The Enjoyment of Music* (New York: W. W. Norton and Company, Inc., 1957), p. 423.

4. Charles R. Hoffer, *A Concise Introduction to Music Listening* (Belmont, California: Wadsworth Publishing Company, 1974), pp. 10–11.
5. Jane Blankenship. *A Sense of Style: An Introduction to Style for the Public Speaker* (Belmont, California: Dickenson Publishing Company, 1968), p. 2.
6. John F. Wilson and Carroll C. Arnold, *Public Speaking As a Liberal Art* (Boston: Allyn and Bacon, Inc., 1974), pp. 215–225.
7. Martin Luther King, "I Have a Dream," reprinted in *Contemporary American Speeches,* eds. Wil A. Linkugel, R. R. Allen, and Richard L. Johannesen (Dubuque, Iowa: Kendall/Hunt Publishing Company, 1978), p. 365.
8. John F. Kennedy, "Inaugural Address," *Ibid.* p. 369.
9. Ellen Foley, "Writer Walker Says We Can Learn by 'Listening' to Trees," *Minneapolis Star and Tribune,* 3 March 1983, p. 1C.
10. *Ibid.*
11. Olive Ghiselin, "Europe by Ear: Sounds without Score," *Travel and Leisure,* October 1975, p. 11.
12. Tony Schwartz, *The Responsive Chord* (New York: Anchor Books, 1974), p. 47.
13. Alice Digilio, "The Best Books You've Ever Heard," Book World Section, *The Washington Post,* 20 February 1983, p. 4.
14. Among the companies that sell and/or rent cassette-recorded books are the following: Audio Books, 223 Katonah Avenue, Katonah, New York 10536 (914) 232–3814; Books on Tape, P.O. Box 7900, Newport Beach, California 92660 (800) 854–4139; Caedmon, 1995 Broadway, New York, New York 10023 (800) 223–0420; Listen for Pleasure Ltd., 417 Center Street, Lewiston, New York 14092 (716) 754–8750; Recorded Books, 6306 Aaron Lane, Clinton, Maryland 20735 (800) 638–1304; Spoken Arts, Inc., Dept. R., P.O. Box 289, New Rochelle, New York 10802 (914) 636–5482; Tape-Worm Inc., P.O. Box 5524, Rockville, Maryland 20855 (800) 638–8798; The Mind's Eye, P.O. Box 6726, San Francisco, California 94101 (800) 227–2020.
15. George F. Will, "Heard Any Good Books Lately?" *The Washington Post,* 12 December 1982, p. C-7.
16. Mark Childress, "A Time for the Magic of Stories," *Southern Living,* 18 (Septemer 1983): 166.
17. *Ibid.*
18. *Ibid.*
19. Leslie Irene Coger and Melvin R. White, *Readers Theatre Handbook* (Glenview, Illinois: Scott, Foresman, 1967), p. 7.
20. From *The Medium Is the Massage* by Marshall McLuhan and Quentin Fiore. Coordinated by Jerome Agel. Copyright © 1967 by Bantam Books, Inc. Reprinted by permission of the publisher. All rights reserved.
21. Phil Jackman, "Oriole Fans Blessed When It's Miller Time on Radio," *The Evening Sun,* 23 June 1983, p. C-4.
22. Direct mail ad from Miracle-Ear, Minneapolis, Minnesota.
23. Larry L. Barker, *Listening Behavior* (Englewood Cliffs, New Jersey: Prentice-Hall, Inc., 1971), pp. 81–82.
24. Hoffer, *A Concise Introduction to Music Listening,* pp. 11–12.
25. *Ibid.,* p. 10.
26. Kenneth M. Cameron and Patti P. Gillespie, *The Enjoyment of the Theatre* (New York: Macmillan Publishing Company, 1980), pp. 42–43.

27. Thomas R. Lewis and Ralph G. Nichols, *Speaking and Listening* (Dubuque, Iowa: Wm. C. Brown Company Publishers, 1965), p. 192.
28. *Ibid.*
29. *Ibid.*, p. 193.
30. Friedman, *Listening Processes: Attention, Understanding, Evaluation,* p. 23.
31. Tom Donnelly, "Listening with an Open Mind, Ear and Heart," *Montgomery Journal,* 30 January 1981, p. B2.
32. Charles Price, "Listening to an Orchestra," *Southern World* 2 (December 1980): 36.
33. Rhonda Strickland, "Listening to Bluegrass Requires 'Opening Your Heart'," *Montgomery Journal,* 10 August 1983, pp. B1, B8.
34. *Ibid.*, p. B1.
35. Edgar Dale, *How to Appreciate Motion Pictures* (New York: Arno Press, 1970), p. 6.
36. *Ibid.*, p. 7.
37. Machlis, *The Enjoyment of Music,* p. 3.
38. Dave Kopp, "Stop, Listen, and Learn!" *Sheet Music Magazine,* August/September 1983, pp. 38–39.

Concepts You Will Encounter

Intrapersonal Listening
Listening to Self
Recoding
"Inner Speech"
Interpersonal Listening
EgoSpeak
Interview Question Schedules
Small Group Maintenance and
Task Functions
Hidden Agenda
Decision-Making Agenda
Teleconferences
Public Listening
Social Facilitation
Polarization
Circular Response
Pedestrian, Passive, Selected,
Concerted, and Organized
Audiences
Audience Analysis Profile
Listening Grid
Caring

The Listener's Communication Roles 10

Thus far in this book we have analyzed the process of listening as it constitutes an important part of the human communication function. We have looked at listening as communication and have identified it as an equal partner with speaking in the transaction. Further, we have analyzed the listening process, which includes the sequence of receiving, attending to, and assigning meaning to the verbal and nonverbal stimuli. In this process the listener has been perceived as having the responsibility in the communication transaction to respond to the message by providing feedback for the source (and thereby becoming the sender of the feedback message and thus going beyond the technical parameters of listening per se). This complex interchange functions, then, within specific listening purposes, purposes which serve to define what it is that the listener is attempting to gain from the transaction. While not discrete categories, the listening purposes are useful in establishing a taxonomy for the listener's development of skills in discriminative, comprehensive, therapeutic, critical, and appreciative listening.

Completing this analysis of the functions of the effective listener requires that we consider how the listener functions at the various communication levels: intrapersonal, interpersonal, and public. As listeners, we function in different roles, depending upon the setting and upon the situation in which we are placed. We listen intrapersonally when we make a conscious effort to listen to ourselves. We listen interpersonally in informal conversation, in formal interviews, and in small group discussions, and in teleconferences. At the public level, we attend the theatre, listen to speeches, and listen to radio and television. The levels of communication are formal or informal, depending upon the structure of the communication context itself.

Intrapersonal Listening

Listening to the Self

The effective listening communicator is one who, first of all, comes to an understanding of his or her self. It is necessary to be able to recognize one's own frame of reference in order to understand why one is responding in a particular way to a particular verbal or nonverbal message. The beliefs, attitudes, and values which a listener holds play a major role in shaping the frame of reference, and this frame of reference, in turn, greatly influences how a listener deals with and interprets a communication message in order to derive some meaning from the information that is presented.

While self-disclosure represents an important means for understanding the self and why we respond as we do, a good listener ought to consider making a conscious effort to listen to his or her self. Listening researchers Paulin and Canonie have devised a S.E.L.F. (Self Evaluation Listening Form) based on the premise that "there is a definite need to know more about ourselves, to listen to who we are, to accept what we discover, and to act on that information."[1] Listening to the self, then, can be helpful in achieving an understanding of one's self-concept as it affects communication behaviors.

Listening to the self also is important in that some part of the assignment of meaning may well require a process of "inner speech" in which the listener repeats the verbal message. Lundsteen describes this aspect of meaning assignment as "recoding," in which listeners repeat the words in a message. This process of inner speech results in the recoding of the spoken symbols "by noting changes in sound and in the order in which they occur. As they [listeners] regroup the sounds, they may translate them into images while they rehearse the sounds to themselves."[2] This effort to recode the spoken message may well assist the listener in attempts to interpret the message as accurately as possible and thus to bring the listener closer to the intended meaning of the speaker.

If recoding is to function effectively, it is evident that the listener should make an effort to monitor this process. A good listener should strive to listen to how he or she is recoding the message or, in essence, listen to the "inner speech" while interpreting the spoken message. This strategy may well lead to greater accuracy in the entire decoding of the communication transaction. Such monitoring requires motivation to attend consciously to one's own inner process, a complicated sequence at best. Listening to the self, however, enables the listener to become cognizant of his or her own responses as a communicator.

Listening to the self, therefore, is a process of intrapersonal communication. And the process of listening, being intrapersonal in nature, utilizes the individual's *internal* channels of communication to process the stimuli and to make it more meaningful in the transaction. As Goss notes, "[L]istening is an intrapersonal process that makes possible all kinds of communication. . . . Listening is best understood from an information processing point of view."[3]

Interpersonal Communication

Conversation

The person who can listen to his or her own self probably functions more effectively when listening to others. A solid understanding of the self and why one is responding as one does respond ought to enable the listener better to understand and regulate responses while in communication transactions with other persons. One of the greatest challenges we have in this regard is that of effective listening in casual conversation. Listening in casual conversation requires attention, concentration, and—perhaps most important—a willingness to listen.

Research on conversational listening reveals that the comprehension of these informal messages is limited and, thus, reflects the casual approach that most of us take to these interactions. Communication in conversation is conducted with minimal effort, so the listening is not very systematic. Reviewing the research on listening in conversation, Goss concludes that "unless the situation calls for precise recollection of the utterances, people in everyday conversations comprehend the gist of the conversation more than the exact words spoken."[4]

Frequently, conversation patterns for most of us can be characterized as *non*-listening. These characteristics, while important to casual listening, unfortunately may not be all that representative of our behaviors in most conversations. Instead of listening, many of us anticipate what the person will say and just eagerly await our "turn" to chime in with our own tale.

Janet: "And then she said she was sure I had strep throat and that I'd better. . . ."
Mary: "Oh yes, I had strep throat once. I was put on penicillin, and it cleared up very fast. But I certainly was sick until. . . ."
Janet: "Yes, it certainly is miserable. I remember looking at the little white spots in my throat and wondering. . . ."
Mary: "Well, my throat was very red, and all my muscles ached, and I. . . ."
Janet: "I heard that Larry went to Denver yesterday. . . ."

And on it goes. We need to be careful not to fall into this conversation trap of not listening. In a very interesting book entitled *Egospeak,* Addeo and Burger describe this problem of not listening in conversations:

> The reason that no one listens, usually, is that our egos get in the way, in the sense that we're mentally formulating what *we're* going to say when the other person gets through speaking. Instead of digesting the other person's information, we are most often busy thinking only of how best we can *impress* him with our next statement. The result is what we call *EgoSpeak*.[5]

This interruptive behavior in conversation does not lead to a very satisfying communication for either person. Steiner suggests that much of this interruption stems from our desire to control the conversation, but the interruption can leave a lasting negative effect on the other person: "Sometimes when I am interrupted in the middle of a sentence, I feel like a bird shot out of the sky. . . . My feelings are a combination of rage and hopelessness."[6] To prevent your fellow communicator from leaving with rage or hopelessness, you should, as Steiner advocates, listen "to understand how the other person is experiencing the situation. Not necessarily to agree with it, but to become fully aware of how that other person sees whatever it is that she is talking about."[7]

Listening in interpersonal interactions may, like credibility, be a matter of perception. It seems essential that the other communicator in a conversation perceive the listener as an active participant in the transaction. "Actual listening may matter little in the maintenance of most interpersonal interactions," suggests Daly, who goes on to say, "No matter how effective, skilled, or competent an individual is in listening, unless he or she is perceived as listening by the other interactants, little may be accomplished."[8]

Some people who are recognized as great conversationalists may not be as talkative as the image suggests. Indeed, they may be attentive listeners who really say very little in a conversation. Persons in international affairs, for example, often note the differences between British and American conversation patterns. Britons, who are noted throughout the world as conversationalists, offer verbal responses to their conversation patterns. Americans, on the other hand, tend to rely on "uh huh" and nodding the head responses. Partners of attentive, responsive listeners tend to leave the conversation feeling good about the experience and grateful for the opportunity to have had someone with whom to converse.

Interviews

On a more formal level, we listen in interviews. An interview may be characterized as conversation with purpose. The purpose may be to gather information, to advocate a position, to determine a policy, to solve a problem, or to provide a therapeutic experience. Professional interviewers recognize the value of careful listening in their work. Individuals who conduct employment interviewing for companies must listen to the responses in order to make decisions as to the potential of a particular applicant. Performance appraisal interviewers must be able to listen with considerable empathy to an employee's description of any qualities or circumstances which he or she perceives may affect the job performance under review. Counseling interviewers naturally must listen with empathy in order to provide the necessary "sounding board" for the client to begin to understand and to deal with his or her own problem. And medical intake interviewers must listen with comprehension in order to understand the exact nature of the patient's distress before sending the patient to a particular physician specialist in a clinic.

To achieve its purpose, a good interview is carefully structured with an opening designed to establish rapport between the interviewer and the interviewee and to clarify the purpose of the interview. This step is necessary to develop an open communication climate, one in which both individuals feel comfortable as communicators.

The body of the interview, then, consists of the questions and responses, the heart of the interview itself. The questions, selected as to the purpose of the interview, may be as follows:

open, designed for permitting a variety of responses ("Could you tell me how you happened to become interested in a career in broadcasting?")
closed, designed to focus a particular response ("Do you feel that the present American foreign policy needs reassessment?")

probe, designed to explore in greater depth ("You indicate that you feel we need to establish more substantial energy conservation measures. Could you tell me why you feel that way?")

mirroring, designed to reflect back what the person has said in order to get him or her to continue talking. This is particularly useful in therapeutic listening. ("You don't feel your study habits are working very well?")

leading, designed to specify a response, usually the response you want to hear. This form can be manipulative, particularly if it becomes a "loaded" question. ("You don't really want to continue this process, do you?")

A good interviewer uses a variety of these question types and prepares a short "schedule" of questions in advance so that the interview will acquire some focus and thus allow the interviewer and interviewee to accomplish their objectives within the specified time frame. A schedule of questions might take the form of a "funnel" going from more general questions to more specific ones. This form may be particularly helpful in information gathering interviews where you want to explore any of a number of directions in getting the information. An "inverted funnel" schedule, on the other hand, leads from specific to more general questions. It is useful in a problem-solving interview, for instance, where you might initially identify the specific problem and then pursue various, generalized solutions to that problem.

Whatever the schedule, the interviewer should recognize that it is designed to serve just as a *general* guide for the interview. The good interviewer will *adapt* to the interviewee and, if necessary, follow the interviewee's direction of thought in an interview if that train of thought will serve to accomplish the intended purpose just as well as the original plan. The interviewee should listen carefully to the questions asked and respond appropriately. As a general rule, it is most effective to stay within the line of questioning offered by the interviewer. If you have additional information, however, or if you feel that a different direction may more efficiently accomplish the objective of the interview, you might try moving beyond the schedule of questions that the interviewer has prepared. Some of the most effective interviews are those which are spontaneous, offering a true give and take between the two interview communicators.

In the closing of the interview, it is appropriate to use time to explore any further concerns, unclarified points, or questions the interviewee may have. Also, it is wise to sum up what has been accomplished in the interview and, if needed, specify the next step to be taken, so that both the interviewer and the interviewee know what to expect as an outcome of the communication.

While attention and responsiveness are keys to effective listening in an interview, there are barriers to listening effectiveness for which the interview listener should be on the lookout. Downs, Smeyak, and Martin identify these barriers as the tendency to evaluate, the tendency to be impulsive, the tendency to never respond, the tendency to use irritating nonverbal habits (e.g., avoiding eye contact, looking at your watch, doodling), and the tendency to allow interruption (either in person or by telephone).[9]

To overcome such barriers, Stewart and Cash recommend that interviewers and interviewees accept critical listening responsibilities. The interviewer, they recommend, must (1) listen carefully to the full response of the interviewee; (2) look at the interviewee while he or she is responding; (3) keep the evaluative criteria in mind; (4) avoid making evaluations too quickly; (5) probe for complete answers; (6) compare verbal responses with nonverbal behavior and any other evidence; (7) take detailed notes; and (8) withhold a final evaluation until the interview is completed.[10] These interviewing experts also characterize the interviewee's listening responsibilities: (1) listen fully to the entire question before responding; (2) observe the nonverbal cues and behavior which accompany each question; (3) ask for clarification as necessary; (4) counter-question if one needs time to think or if one feels trapped; (5) take sufficient time to ask questions; and (6) obtain details and take notes if possible.[11]

The key to effective listening in interviewing, then, is to listen carefully. Concentrate on what the other person is saying and, then adapt your responses accordingly. The interviewer must listen in order to pursue the train of thought with meaningful questions. And the interviewee must listen in order to understand the questions and provide the appropriate responses. Since both persons must adapt to each other, listening becomes the central core of communication in an interview.

Small Group Discussions

Many of the principles of effective listening in the interview apply as well to listening in small group discussions. People may spend a great deal of time at work in small group discussions at all levels of an organization. Business meetings, seminars, staff sessions, quality circles, and customer meetings all require the application of effective listening skills in small groups. The small group process applies to communication outside of the workplace as well. We engage in small group discussions at the family dinner table, in social and civic organizations to which we belong, and even in more unstructured social settings with friends. Skill in listening when more than one other communicator is involved requires special strategies because the communication process becomes so much more complex with the addition of other communicators to the transaction.

Since a small group discussion typically involves five to seven people, each individual will spend the majority of his or her time engaged in listening. S. I. Hayakawa notes the importance of listening in discussions and conferences: "If a conference is to result in the exchange of ideas, we need to pay particular heed to our listening habits."[12] It is a process of careful listening and then adapting remarks to the general thrust of the content of the discussion. Brack urges that greater attention be placed on listening in the small group communication process. Poor listening, he says, can be a serious problem in the small group because it (1) disrupts the process and misdirects the flow of thought; (2) weakens one's input because responses are not appropriate; (3) dampens enthusiasm for others to contribute; and (4) undermines the basic assumption of small group communication, that each person contributes.[13]

Group discussions are characterized by maintenance and task functions. Individuals in groups perform these functions through the roles that they assume during the course of the group deliberation.

Maintenance functions refer to the interpersonal needs of the group—the human interaction itself. A group proceeds through the stages much like two people in an interpersonal relationship, and it is helpful to recognize these stages and listen to (and be sensitive to) the interpersonal needs of the group members during these stages.

The formation stage involves the building of rapport and opening of the channels of communication through careful listening among the members of the group. Once the group has come together and established a communication base, it frequently is necessary to break down conflicts that may occur among members. Various people in a group may clash on issues or even procedures, so many conflicts must be resolved before members will feel comfortable communicating with each other.

Resolution of conflict in a group may extend to the breaking down of "hidden agenda"—individual objectives which may not necessarily be compatible with the overall purpose of the group. A person may enter a group, for instance, to build a power base in order to assume a position of dominance. If assuming power is the true, but hidden, purpose of this individual, such an objective may work at cross purposes with the needs of the group. All persons must listen carefully in order to recognize areas of conflict and work to overcome them.

Once a communication bond has been established, however, a group will build cohesion, insuring that individuals do feel a sense of commitment to the group and to each other as members of that group. The development of cohesion—a sense of belonging—in a group can be implemented through reinforcement. A group member who does actively participate as a listener as well as a speaker in the group and who is reinforced for that participation will feel good about belonging to the group. Throughout the discussion, sensitivity to the maintenance needs of the individual members and of the group as a whole requires each person to listen and to respond appropriately.

In addition to these maintenance functions, the sensitive discussion participant will be an active listener in order to accomplish the task functions of the group. The task functions—getting the job done—will depend upon the purpose of the group discussion.

The group may come together for social purposes, in which case participants probably will engage in general conversation and thus participate as active informal listeners. As we have noted, effective listening in conversations requires attention, concentration, and a willingness to listen.

A group may have a therapeutic purpose, in which case the objective of the group is to afford each person an opportunity to express his or her feelings, frustrations, concerns. A successful therapeutic group depends very much on a warm, supportive climate. Each participant, therefore, should apply the principles of therapeutic listening and build an atmosphere of trust so that individuals can express themselves with minimum risk.

A third discussion purpose is that of information sharing. Like information-sharing interviews, these discussions should be characterized by careful distinction between facts and opinions so that the information presented will be accurate and authoritative. All members of the group should research thoroughly in preparation for participation in the discussion. This research base is essential to the thorough understanding of the information presented by the various group members. Through active listening, the participant can adapt remarks to those made by previous participants and also gain a complete perspective on the information presented.

A decision-making discussion, on the other hand, requires participants to listen with understanding to the information presented and then to evaluate the ideas in order to arrive at a satisfactory solution. Most decision-making groups structure their agenda to follow a series of problem-solving steps similar to those suggested by John Dewey in *How We Think:*

1. Locating and defining the problem.
2. Exploring the problem.
3. Suggesting solutions.
4. Evaluating the solutions.
5. Choosing the best solutions.[14]

The key to effective implementation of Dewey's format is to explore the causes and effects of the problem thoroughly (essentially an information-sharing discussion) before moving on to the deliberations of how to solve the problem. Again, careful listening and adaptation are the keys to this process. Although participants will have their own ideas about how to solve the problem, it is imperative that participants be willing to listen to other points of view and to accept different points of view if they are valid.

Bormann and Bormann note that effective listening in task-oriented groups requires that you be willing to be a message receiver when it is appropriate to listen, to know the basic skills of listening as communication, and to practice and apply effective feedback techniques.[15]

In one of the few works written specifically about listening in group discussions, Kelly argues that we tend to think we should listen critically to messages in group discussion. He suggests that this tendency to critical listening interferes with understanding the message and that we should concentrate on listening empathetically in discussions. Kelly makes these recommendations for the discussion listener:

Remember the characteristics of the poor listener.
Make a firm initial commitment to listen.
Get physically and mentally ready to listen.

As participants in group discussions, we must be message receivers when it is appropriate to listen.

Photo by Robert Tocha.

Concentrate on the other person as a communicator.
Give the person a full hearing.
Use analytical skills as supplements to, not instead of, listening.[16]

It should be evident that the accomplishment of the task and maintenance functions in a group discussion depend, to a very great extent, upon the listening skills of all of the participants. These listening skills may extend to the assumption of leadership roles as well. A person may assume a position of leadership in a group at a particular time in order to facilitate task and/or maintenance needs of the group. In some groups, one individual will maintain the role of leader throughout a discussion, but more typically, two or three people may share leadership functions. One person, for instance, may work to keep the group organized—on the agenda—while another person may work to bring the group members to closure in their discussion of various issues. Just as individual participants, then, must be careful listeners in a discussion, so too should those individuals who assume roles of leadership listen actively. Since small group discussions involve a number of people, the greater part of each person's time will be spent in active listening. The accomplishment of the group's objectives will depend, then, on each person assuming the listening roles seriously.

Teleconferences

A special type of group discussion that has become increasingly popular as a cost-effective process is the teleconference: a conference through electronic media (usually the telephone) among persons who are physically separated. Though many of the characteristics of face-to-face group discussions likewise are descriptive of teleconferences, listeners should recognize that the developing technology may lead to special considerations for effective listening in these electronic transactions.

There are many types of teleconferencing. Among these are (1) *audio* (transmitting voice via telephone and allowing participants at all sites to interact orally); (2) *audiographic* or audio-plus (transmitting voice and transmitting graphics or any other written materials via facsimile or telecopier through telephone facilities and allowing participants at all sites to interact orally and share the visuals); (3) *captured frame video,* which is also called slow scan or freeze frame video (transmitting voice and still pictures via television equipment through telephone lines and allowing participants at all sites to interact orally); (4) *computer conferencing* (transmitting only written messages by linking computer terminals through telephone lines, permitting only written interaction between/among participants); and (5) *full motion video* (transmitting voice and motion pictures from a full motion-video conferencing room—in the business establishment itself, a local television station, or other facility with uplink, or transmitting, equipment—via satellite if the distance warrants it or via conventional methods for short distances and allowing participants at all sites to interact orally and visually).[17] The capabilities of these types of teleconferencing range from one-way audio only to the ultimate two-way audio and two-way video.

Presently, many businesses, organizations, and institutions are offering teleconferencing capabilities and are utilizing the teleconferencing system. Businesses, especially hotels (Holiday Inn, Marriott, and Inter-Continental—to name a few), are providing teleconferencing capabilities by installing permanent dishes (earth stations that furnish access to a variety of satellites) and other necessary equipment and facilities, while many other organizations (such as Bank of America, Pan American World Airlines, Hewlett-Packard, Aetna Life and Casualty, Baskin-Robbins, National Education Association, Republican National Committee, United Steelworkers of America, and many universities) are holding teleconferences in either their own facilities (where they have installed permanent dishes or are utilizing portable dishes) or other facilities equipped for teleconferencing. Among the many ways that teleconferencing is being employed are the following: conferences, seminars, business meetings, strategy sessions, workshops, symposiums, training sessions, employee orientations, project planning sessions, engineering design reviews, policy reviews/decision-making, new product introductions, continuing education, sales incentive meetings, and press conferences. As they hold teleconferences for various reasons, teleconferencing users are discovering that this communication system, in addition to being cost-effective, provides many benefits, including increasing the frequency of communication, meeting the needs for communication immediacy, conducting more structured meetings (due primarily to improved pre-planning of meetings), providing more people with opportunities to make policy decisions, and obtaining more points of view/opinions from those tied in through the teleconferencing.

As we can see, listening plays a vital role in all types of teleconferencing (with perhaps the exception of computer teleconferencing), in all of the stated ways in which teleconferencing is being employed, and in all of the stated benefits of teleconferencing. The importance of listening is directly related to one of teleconferencing's major advantages as a communication system: interactivity between/among participants. According to James Black, executive vice-president of VideoStar Connections (a prominent supplier of satellite communication services), interactivity is of prime importance in teleconferencing: "The most important thing is to have two-way audio communication so that the audience can interact with the speaker. Only about three to four percent of our teleconference business opts for two-way video conferencing."[18]

The interactive nature of the teleconference process creates some unique communication constraints for listeners. For example, it is necessary for the participants conferring by telephone to identify who they are as they begin to speak so that all parties on the telephone line recognize the speaker. (Video conferencing may eliminate this need, but presently the capabilities for video conferencing are quite limited compared to those for audio conferencing.) Also, the conversation among the participants tends to be much more structured, and the discussion moderator must play a key role in providing internal summaries throughout the conference. Since telephone time is expensive, it becomes necessary for the discussion to move forward with efficiency; thus, there is little time for handling any interpersonal maintenance functions. Researchers at John Hopkins have discovered that communicators in teleconferences are much less interruptive and that such communicators present different messages when they do interrupt: "When communicators have the freedom to interrupt, they exchange more messages, messages are shorter, and messages are exchanged faster. . . ."[19] At the present time, however, research on teleconferencing is in its infancy. The Johns Hopkins researchers conclude that "largely unexplored are the effects such systems might have on the people using them."[20]

To predict the far-reaching effects that teleconferencing will have in the world is impossible; however, by basing our predictions on the use of teleconferencing in its infant stage, we can conjecture, as has Joseph Smith, senior vice president of marketing for Inter-Continental Hotels (which provides international teleconferencing): "Teleconferencing is going to have an important place in the communciations spectrum—somewhere between face-to-face meetings and telephone calls."[21] And complementing teleconferencing's important place, we will find listening's important role.

Public Audiences

Just as active listening is essential in conversations, interviews, group discussions, and teleconferences, it is crucial to effectiveness in public listening. As listeners, we participate in all sorts of public audiences. On the one hand, we become part of theatre audiences for live stage productions and/or motion picture screenings. We attend concerts and other types of musical performances. We witness ceremonies and participate in religious services. Also, as listeners, we attend speeches of all types from after-dinner presentations at organizational meetings to political rallies to technical briefings at work to formal lectures sponsored by a local historical society. Participation as a public listener necessitates understanding how we become part of this public audience and applying techniques to derive the most from our public listening experiences.

The process of becoming a listener in a public event is not accidental. The process is designed to help you get involved in the event. One element in this carefully-constructed process is what is known as "social facilitation." You are seated next to other people so that their responses (laughter, applause, silence) can affect—facilitate—how you will respond. You lose some of your self-identity and become part of the audience, perhaps laughing at a speaker's joke which, at home alone with the television set or radio, you would not find funny at all.

Another dimension of the audience process is known as polarization. The lights go down, and all attention is focused on the actors on the stage. You cease your interaction with those next to you (unless you continue to chat during the overture or have to get up for latecomers). This polarizing of attention enhances your willingness to "let go" and to concentrate on the production while you lose some of your own concerns and attitudes in the transformation.

An audience also functions through the process of a "circular response." The responses you give to speakers, actors, musicians (through your applause, laughter, even coughing and distractions) communicate to them. They, in turn, work to project the ideas, emotions, dialogue, lyrics, or dances to you and adapt as necessary to the response levels of the people in the audience. The response you give to a production ultimately takes you back to your individuality. *Your* standards and values will structure your responses, so your reactions may differ from those of other people in the same audience. The more homogeneous (sharing similar backgrounds, purpose) the audience is, the more likely the response of the listeners will be similar and predictable.

Herbert Kupferberg, writing about the concert audience, notes that audience behavior often offers "perplexities and paradoxes." Concert season subscribers loyally pass down their tickets from generation to generation within a family; yet, they will complain loudly about an orchestra's programs or policies. Leopold Stokowski, the famous conductor, was noted for his scoldings of Friday matinee subscription holders, "especially when they coughed, sneezed or rustled during his performance."[22]

While Stokowski's matinee audiences may not be typical, Hollingworth (in a classic study on the audience) identified five types of audiences that speakers may confront.[23] The pedestrian, casual, audience reflects the least amount of attention. Shoppers who stop to watch a demonstration of omelet making in a shopping center, for instance, would be a pedestrian audience. A passive audience, on the other hand, typically consists of captive listeners, much like those found in a classroom of students required to take a course. A more specific type of audience is the selected group consisting of individuals who have come together for a unified purpose (attending a civic association meeting on neighborhood safety, for example). The concerted audience is even more organized in its purpose, as the individuals probably have some direct "stake" in the outcome. The audience at a political rally, for instance, would be a concerted audience. At the most organized level, then, is the organized audience with total orientation to the speaker. A military drill team, for example, would be an organized audience, completely controlled by the speaker.

Regardless of the orientation, effective communicators are prepared to anticipate the responses of the listeners in a public audience and to deal with those responses effectively. Paul Holtzman, for example, has drawn up a checklist of forty-four audience/listener factors which a speaker should analyze in preparation for communicating with a group. The checklist is an extensive enumeration of the factors which make up a profile of the listeners in a speaker's audience:

Speaker-Image Factors

Perceived friendship
Perceived common ground
Perceived authority
Perceived trustworthiness
Motivational expectancies
Ability expectancies
Language expectancies

Motivational Factors

Expressive needs: general
Expressive needs: self-esteem
Commitments
Values
Values: priorities
Values: the common premise
Personality: authoritarianism
Personality: open-mindedness
Personality: need for self-esteem
Personality: need for cognitive clarity
Personality: cognitive style

Environmental Factors

Physical surroundings
Social context: predispositions
Social context: self-selection
Social context: sense of fitness
Listener to listener: conformity influence
Listener to listener: factors for polarization

Group-Membership Factors

Ages
Sexes
Races
Educational levels
Occupations
Avocational interests
Socioeconomic levels
Political affiliations
Social organizations
Religious affiliations
Cultural backgrounds
Geographical backgrounds
Information channels
Group norms
Extent of commitment

Cognitive Factors

Listener experiences
Listener knowledge
Listener beliefs
Latitudes of acceptance
Latitudes of rejection[24]

From his research on public listening, Holtzman was led to conclude that "[l]istener 'set' is different in private and public communication . . . different enough to warrant close attention in any audience analysis."[25]

An audience analysis profile, therefore, can assist a speaker in making decisions about how best to adapt his or her message to the listener. The listener who conforms to the factors anticipated by means of such a profile, consequently, will be responsive both to the communication and to his/her function as a communicator in the transaction, according to the objectives established by the speaker and by the listener him/herself. Some writers who have described the effective public listener have stressed this need for establishing objectives in the public communication.

One informative exposition of the listener's public performance is offered by management specialist John E. Baird, Jr. Baird advises participants who attend management seminars to develop listening skills in order to benefit from the presentations by speakers in the seminars. Baird encourages seminar participants—the listeners—to begin by establishing objectives for attending the seminar, establishing one's overall goal and subgoals in order to focus subsequent listening. Then the seminar listener should take stock of what he or she already knows about the topic of the seminar and, equally important, what attitudes and beliefs he or she holds about the subject. Such self-analysis can lead to developing priorities for acquiring knowledge or for modifying behaviors relevant to the seminar topic. Further, the seminar participants—while in the seminar—should utilize listening stragtegies (focusing on the content, maintaining objectivity, capitalizing on "thought speed," taking notes, asking questions) in order to derive the most from the seminar itself. "Efficient listening," concludes Baird, "means identifying things to listen for so that it becomes easier to note what is important and to sort out those ideas from others that are of secondary concern."[26]

Echoing Baird's advice for listening in management seminars, Andrews recommends that the "public listener," the individual listening to a public speaker, must incorporate seven tactics for actively listening in the public communication transaction. "Since a piece of communication is designed to get a response from you," says Andrews, "you ought to ask yourself what it is doing to and for you as you listen."[27] The tactics which Andrews recommends are good suggestions for listeners in any public communication:

1. Think about your own identity.
2. Listen with a purpose.
3. Understand the setting.
4. Try to understand to whom the speaker is talking.
5. Examine your assessment of and knowledge about the speaker.
6. Consider the speaker's purpose.
7. Listen defensively.[28]

In other words, the "defensive" public listener is one who understands his or her own response to the public communication and seeks actively to adapt that response to the appropriate objective of the communication. Thus, the individual who joins an audience to listen to a public speech should be able to concentrate all of his or her time, energy, and attention on the speech itself. Much of Ralph Nichols's research on listening comprehension deals with listening to lectures and speeches, so his advice to concentrate is especially useful. The principles of listening comprehension are pertinent if the speech is informative or inspirational. If the speaker is attempting to persuade the audience, then critical listening techniques will also be necessary. These techniques have been detailed in previous chapters. The theatre/concert listener, on the other hand, usually is listening for appreciation. Consequently, our suggestions for gaining greater appreciation from a listening experience may be helpful.

Whether one is a public listener to a speech or at a theatrical/musical event, it is helpful to recognize that we become part of an audience through a rather systematic process. This process plays a significant role in shaping our responses as listeners and in developing the public in the public communication transaction.

Radio-Television

In addition to listening in the theatre and to live public speakers, we listen to the public communication media. The popularity of mass media today means that we spend a great deal of our waking time as listeners—attending to radio and television broadcasts. In their infancy, both radio and television were much more oriented to larger audiences. Because only a few people could afford receivers, entire extended families or even communities would come together in the home of the fortunate radio or television set owner for an evening of listening. Indeed, in some less-developed countries, these gatherings are still common. Preparing television commercials for South American television, for instance, requires a "broader" approach, aimed to larger audiences in homes.

In the United States, however, we usually are "isolated" listeners, so that radio and television have become very intimate media. Going to and from work, we listen to the radio in our cars on the expressway. Frequently, we have more than one television set in a home, so we are the sole viewers. Thus, to create more of a sense of public communication, producers will tape shows before a live studio audience or incorporate a "laugh track" to help "cue" the listener at home to respond as if he or she were in a larger audience.

Radio, of course, relies solely on sound to project images. Thus, we let radio listening "happen" to us through our auditory channels. In its heyday of popularity, radio became a very creative instrument for American culture and entertainment. Such popular shows as "The Shadow" and "Amos and Andy" reflected the effort by broadcasters to develop the medium in order to spark the imagination of the listener. Through vocal inflections and through sound effects, the listener was involved in the experience and, with concentration, could become a true participant in the event.

Radio today provides listeners with opportunities to become more active participants *on the air.* Listeners participate not only in call-in contests (in which they can win prizes and money) but also in call-in talk shows. Many radio stations feature talk shows with controversial hosts who invite listeners to talk with them via telephone. In some cities, the host—who becomes almost abusive to the caller—generates a strong "drive time" following in a highly competitive audience market. Some radio analysts believe that these talk shows serve an important need for people who are desperate to have someone listen to them—so desperate that they are willing to endure verbal abuse on the air just to have a chance to speak out on some issue.

Contemporary radio reflects some effort to return to its creative roots. Certain stations are willing to do more than broadcast the "Top 40" records and commercials with, perhaps, five minutes of news every hour. Radio drama has been revived, and even commercials have become more creative. Commercials for Blue Nun wine, for instance, feature clever scenarios by comics Anne Meara and Jerry Stiller. Radio advertising is especially suited for adaptation to the particular demographics of an audience in a particular locality. Spending for radio ads grew 12 percent to 1.3 billion dollars in 1983, and analysts predict continued increases into 1990.[29]

Radio commercials represent a unique problem to advertising specialists and illustrate the complexity of a medium aimed at the listening ear. Since visual images are not possible in radio commercials, the audio images must be highly compelling. This need becomes even more significant when one realizes that most radio serves as background accompaniment to what individuals are doing: driving, doing household chores, typing, completing homework, etc. Consequently, radio "listening is almost always accompanied by simultaneous activity that places widely varying demands on the individual's attention process."[30] One result is what some researchers have called the "NOLAD level"—the *non-listening attention demand*.[31] Interestingly, little is known in the industry about how best to solve some of these problems inherent in radio advertising in order to reach the potential listeners, listeners who are relying solely on the auditory channel for communication.

Television, on the other hand, is designed to be more of a video medium. We look at the screen and watch the action. Tony Schwartz, the famous media specialist, argues, however, that television is more auditory than we think. He recommends an experiment—turn out the picture and listen to the sound. He suggests that we would be impressed with how much, like radio, the television audio portion does involve us as listeners.[32] As television listeners, most of us have regular access to television sets. As we have seen, some 83.3 million North American households owned at least one set as of January 1983.[33] And the medium grows increasingly more dominant in these households. Video-tape recorders have been marketed extensively, so much so that entire retail stores have been established just to handle the demand for videotape recorders, tapes, and supplies. Moreover, pay cable television outlets have increased as more communities offer hook-ups for subscribers. Viewing of cable programming increased 42 percent from 1981 to 1982.[34]

In its infancy in the 1940s and 1950s, television relied on live productions in which anything could—and did—happen. Viewing television as an entertainment medium, producers attempted to offer live theatre (such as *Studio One* and *Philco Playhouse*) on a regular, consistent schedule. Shortly thereafter, television began to assume its role as an information medium that is unsurpassed in the world. As viewers, we have been taken to the moon with NASA's astronauts; we have been united in grief through the coverage of President John F. Kennedy's assassination and funeral; we have been taken under the sea with Jacques Cousteau and into the heart of Africa's jungles with *National Geographic;* and we have all been brought closer together as citizens of the world as we have shared information and experiences that have helped us better understand one another and our world. From the most rural areas of South America to the most urban sections of Paris, people have become much more homophilous through this powerful medium. Indeed, television's value as an information medium is powerful, but, unfortunately, today's commercial television industry is very much geared to the presentation of lightweight situation comedies, soap operas, adventure shows, and news shows. Public television has attempted to compensate for some of the deficiencies of such programming by offering such outstanding children's shows as *Sesame Street* as well as a wide array of educational and public affairs programs.

Despite some advances in educational television, one major concern about American television viewing habits is the effect that television portrayal has on us as individual viewers. The Federal Communication Commission and the Federal Trade Commission have studied the effects of advertising on children, and several agencies are concerned about the impact of televised violence on both children and adults. This impact was dramatized in August 1977, when a 15-year-old, Ronald Zamora, and a 14-year-old, Darrell Agrella, of Miami, Florida, were accused of fatally wounding an elderly neighbor with her gun while stealing $415 and her car. Zamora's attorney claimed that his continuous diet of violent crime shows on television was responsible for his behavior. Indeed, Zamora told the court that he had been influenced by a *Kojak* television program in designing his crime. He was convicted of murder and sentenced to life imprisonment.

George Gerbner and his colleagues at the Annenberg School of Communications in Philadelphia have conducted studies of violence on television and have devised "Violence Profiles" to demonstrate the amount of violence depicted on television. The 1979 study revealed that "in prime time, 70 percent of all programs still contained violence."[35] Gerbner and his colleagues stress that television has become a powerful medium, dominating our lives from infancy on:

> The television set has become a key member of the family, the one who tells most of the stories most of the time. Its massive flow of stories showing what things are, how things work, and what to do about them has become the common socializer of our times. These stories form a coherent if mythical "world" in every home.[36]

As television shapes our perceptions of the world, it is interesting to note that the stories presented on television shows primarily are written and produced in Los Angeles. In an interesting book analyzing the influence of Los Angeles on television, Ben Stein argues that the view of society depicted on these adventure shows and on situation comedies is distorted. What we see is perhaps not representative of the other geographical regions of the United States.[37]

One prominent distortion in prime time programming is the vast amount of criminal activity depicted in television shows. Analysts Lichter and Lichter conclude their study of crime on television by noting that there is no real "crime problem" on these shows: "In the fantasy world of TV entertainment (unlike the real world) most lawbreakers are thwarted and crime is punished—yet ordinary law enforcement officials are presented as highly fallible. More often than not, they either fail to catch the crook or they play supporting roles for the heroic private eyes who are television's real crime stoppers."[38] Another distortion perpetuated by television may be the image of American businessmen. The Media Institute analyzed 200 prime-time episodes on all three major networks and discovered that two of three businessmen are depicted as foolish, greedy, or criminal; furthermore, they noted that almost half of all work activities performed by these businessmen involved illegal acts.[39] While businessmen are involved in illegal acts, workers on television are seldom depicted as working! Edward Cornish, President of the World Future Society, reviewed such popular shows as "Dallas," "Newhart," and "Love Boat" and concluded that "nobody works on television. . . . Television does not show people doing real work; it shows them doing pretend work—loafing at their jobs."[40] Cornish suggests that this distortion has upset the American work ethic.

In addition to distorted television programming, viewers are influenced by television news. Americans, placing a great deal of faith in television news, turn to television news shows as the major source of news information.[41] Indeed, some pollsters used to rate Walter Cronkite, former CBS anchor, as the most credible person in the United States! It should be recognized, however, that television news has inherent editorial bias much like that which one would find in newspaper organizations. Consequently, editing decisions will affect very much what becomes part of the news broadcast; because the news broadcast must operate in a very short time frame, what is presented to the viewer is greatly compressed and limited. Many of the more recent court cases concerning unfair treatment in broadcasts of such shows as CBS's "Sixty Minutes" and ABC's "20/20" reflect an increased recognition that what is edited in and out of an interview may present an unfair perception of the subject under scrutiny in the broadcast. Jamieson and Campbell remind viewers that "[a] story is more likely to be aired on television if there is footage available in the archive, if the event is visual, if the item concerns newsworthy people, if it is inoffensive to audience tastes, and if there is little chance that the sheer fact of coverage itself will become newsworthy."[42] And journalism professor James Carey reminds us that television news is journalism: "All journalism, including objective reporting, is a creative and imaginative work, a symbolic strategy; journalism sizes up situations, names their elements, structure, and outstanding ingredients, and names them in a way that contains an attitude toward them."[43]

Even though Americans rely heavily on television for news and for entertainment, how efficient are we as television listeners? In a recent study conducted by Jacob Jacoby, a consumer psychologist, 2700 viewers in 12 geographic areas were asked questions about televised segments that they were shown. It is significant to note that the vast majority of the viewers in this study—more than 90 percent—misunderstood some part of what they saw. The range of misunderstanding was between one-fourth and one-third of any type of broadcast, though viewers were less likely to misunderstand commercials than entertainment or news programs. Jacoby argues, however, that the television listener brings to each viewing his or her past experiences and mental frame of reference as a means of interpreting and misinterpreting the messages. "Given that it is not possible to eradicate either the influence of past experience or the individual's current mental set, it may well be impossible to eradicate miscomprehension."[44]

In spite of the misinterpretations which viewers bring to their television listening, research examining the influences of television on North Americans of all ages has led federal researchers to conclude: "In the 1980's, television will no doubt continue to be pervasive and ubiquitous in American life. Information about its role and its effects will be needed by all those who will help to shape television's future and to make decisions about it."[45] In recognition of the profound effects that television does have on American viewers, many television researchers consider that teaching about television in order to create a more critical viewing public is an important priority for the 1980's. One curriculum for training individuals to be more critical television viewers identifies six objectives:

1. Ability to describe own television-viewing habits.
2. Ability to describe why a program is selected.
3. Ability to identify the role of television in personal life amid the activities it competes with.
4. Ability to describe the consequences of viewing and the other activities with which television competes.
5. Ability to identify program-content characteristics.
6. Ability to identify uses of different programs.[46]

Understanding how television works to shape perceptions, then, can be an important step for becoming discerning, effective media listeners.

The Listening Grid

Listeners function in a variety of listening roles in intrapersonal, interpersonal, and public communication. We listen for different purposes, purposes which have been categorized as discriminative, comprehensive, therapeutic, critical, and appreciative. As effective listeners, we also may need to establish distinct listening objectives for different listening situations, overlaying our objectives on the listening roles that we have selected. This concept might be illustrated by a listener's grid (fig 10.1).

This grid illustrates the interactive nature of our purposes and our roles as listeners. It should be recognized that these are by no means discrete categories; for example, an individual may select a discriminative purpose but also find himself or herself listening therapeutically once the communication transaction gets underway. The listener's grid can further illustrate the concept with the addition of key variables to it. (See fig 10.2.)

Figure 10.1.

	Self	Conversation	Interview	Small Group	Tele-conference	Public Speech	Theatre/Concert	Radio/Television
Appreciative								
Discriminative								
Comprehensive								
Therapeutic								
Critical								

Figure 10.2.

Wolvin-Coakley Listening Grid

	Self	Conversation	Interview	Small Group	Teleconference	Public Speech	Theatre/ Concert	Radio/ Television
Appreciative	Attention Concentration Sensitivity	Attention Concentration Sensitivity	Attention Concentration Sensitivity	Attention Concentration Sensitivity	Attention Concentration Sensitivity	Attention Concentration Sensitivity	Attention Concentration Sensitivity	Attention Concentration Sensitivity
Discriminative	Attention Concentration Sensory Acuity	Attention Concentration Sensory Acuity	Attention Concentration Sensory Acuity	Attention Concentration Sensory Acuity	Attention Concentration Sensory Acuity	Attention Concentration Sensory Acuity	Attention Concentration Sensory Acuity	Attention Concentration Sensory Acuity
Comprehensive	Attention Concentration Understanding	Attention Concentration Understanding	Attention Concentration Understanding	Attention Concentration Understanding	Attention Concentration Understanding	Attention Concentration Understanding	Attention Concentration Understanding	Attention Concentration Understanding
Therapeutic	Attention Concentration Understanding Empathy	Attention Concentration Understanding Empathy	Attention Concentration Understanding Empathy	Attention Concentration Understanding Empathy	Attention Concentration Understanding Empathy	Attention Concentration Understanding Empathy	Attention Concentration Understanding Empathy	Attention Concentration Understanding Empathy
Critical	Attention Concentration Understanding Evaluation	Attention Concentration Understanding Evaluation	Attention Concentration Understanding Evaluation	Attention Concentration Understanding Evaluation	Attention Concentration Understanding Evaluation	Attention Concentration Understanding Evaluation	Attention Concentration Understanding Evaluation	Attention Concentration Understanding Evaluation

As this grid emphasizes, it is apparent that attention and concentration represent keys to effective listening in all of these listening modes. Depending upon the role that he or she is to assume and the purpose that the listener (and the other communicator) wishes to achieve, the good listener will establish objectives and utilize his or her listening resources.

Listening Commitment

The way we listen and the responses we give, thus, become major tasks for the listener who wishes to be an effective communicator. The listener who assumes responsibility for the communication transaction cannot be a passive, non-involved participant in the process. Rather, effective listening requires commitment and the acceptance of our obligation to give the speaker a fair hearing. Ross describes the importance of this commitment to a fair hearing: "We should show *tolerance* and work at understanding intent. Fair hearing replaces force in a free society."[47] Maintaining a free society, therefore, requires that we develop the necessary listening skills and attitudes in order to offer a fair hearing in all of our communication transactions.

Each semester, as a project in our listening course, we ask our students to interview a person whose livelihood depends to a great extent on effective listening. Students interview a variety of professionals—psychiatrists, counselors, physicians, attorneys, customer service representatives, ministers, diplomats, account clerks. The interviews yield interesting information about how these listeners do listen and what techniques and training they feel are important. Much of the information parallels what we have covered in this book, but there is a further dimension to effective listening which professional listeners almost always cite—*care.* They stress that all the techniques and theory prove to be meaningless unless listeners assume responsibility for the process by genuinely caring about how their listening behavior will affect them as well as the others in the communication.

Taking the time and the trouble to listen well is rewarding. If you care about yourself as a listener and if you care about the other person as a human being, you both will feel enriched for the experience. And that intangible reward may be the greatest payoff we have in human relationships at home, at work, and in the world at large.

SUMMARY

In this chapter, we have examined the roles which a listener assumes. We function intrapersonally when we listen to ourselves. In addition, we assume interpersonal listening roles when we participate in conversations, interviews, group discussions, and teleconferences. And we play different roles as members of public audiences (speeches, theatre, radio-television).

By accepting the responsibility of genuinely *caring* about how our listening behavior affects us as well as others, we become "people hearing *with* listening."
Photo by Robert Tocha.

The objectives we set for our listening behavior within these roles will depend, to a great extent, upon what we want to derive from the listening experience and upon what the source of the message wants us to derive from it. Consequently, attention and concentration are keys to effective listening in all situations; but other factors may vary, depending upon our listening goals and the particular demands of the role we must assume.

SUGGESTED ACTIVITIES

1. Consciously attempt to listen to yourself. Concentrate on this when you are alone, processing your own thoughts. And concentrate on this when you are in communication with someone else. Listen to your self as you speak with this other person; monitor what you are saying and why you are saying it. What are you discovering about your self as a communicator?
2. Arrange to interview a specialist in your major field of study. Ask this person about the role that listening plays in your field. What is the importance of listening in your field? What different types of listening are required at various levels within the field? Ask the specialist to suggest any articles in your field which discuss the role of listening. Compose a short paper summarizing the role of listening in your field.

3. Arrange to conduct an interview as the interviewer; draw up a schedule to give you some general guidelines as you ask the questions. Do not take notes, but arrange to close with a summary of the information you have gained. After the interview, analyze your listening behavior. Were you able to comprehend the interviewee's responses and to adapt your questions to these responses? What were your listening objectives? Did you achieve them? Do you feel that that you were an effective listener? Do you feel that the interviewee perceived you as an effective listener? Why or why not?
4. Arrange to participate in a group discussion. In addition to offering meaningful comments, strive to be an attentive, comprehensive listener throughout the discussion. As you listen, try to adapt your responses to meet task or maintenance needs of the group as the needs arise. At the end of the discussion, summarize for the group what has been accomplished. After the discussion, analyze your listening behavior. Did you accomplish your objectives as a listener? Were you effective as a listener in the group discussion? Why or why not?
5. Attend a "live" public speech and endeavor to be a comprehensive listener. Observe the other listeners around you. After the speech, try to participate in the question-answer session to clarify any points you may have had difficulty following. Summarize the content of the speech by identifying the central point and the main points of the speech. Was the speech clearly organized? Was it effectively developed and presented? What efforts were made to develop and maintain the group as an audience? Did you note efforts at social facilitation? Polarization? Speaker adaptation to audience feedback? Were you an effective public listener?
6. Attend a "live" theatre production and observe the audience. What efforts were made to develop social facilitation? Polarization? Do you feel that the actors were responsive to the audience? Was there supportive feedback at the curtain call?
7. Contact the Customer Service Division of your local telephone company and arrange to talk with an individual who has responsibility for setting up teleconferences for customers. What insights can this individual give you about the unique features of participating in a teleconference? What facilities are available in your area for setting up teleconferences?
8. Listen attentively to a radio broadcast of a radio drama. What efforts are made to communicate the characters and the setting? What efforts were made to create tone and mood? Note vocal work by actors and the sound effects.
9. Watch a television broadcast of a situation comedy taped before a live studio audience. What effect does the audience response have on your responses at home? Do you feel that the presence of audience laughter, applause, etc., causes you to respond at home to situations that you might not find funny if you did not hear the audience response?

NOTES

1. Kenneth Paulin and P. J. Canonie, "It's Time to Listen to Ourselves," *Effective Listening Quarterly* 3 (December 1983): 1.
2. Sara W. Lundsteen, *Listening: Its Impact on Reading and the Other Language Arts* (Urbana, Illinois: ERIC Clearinghouse on Reading and Communication Skills, 1979), p. 391.
3. Blaine Goss, "A Cognitive Look at Intrapersonal Communication" (Paper presented at the Speech Communication Association Convention, Washington, D.C., November 1983), p. 15.
4. *Ibid.*, p. 15.
5. Edmond G. Addeo and Robert E. Burger, *EgoSpeak* (Radnor, Pennsylvania: Chilton Book Company, 1973), p. xii.
6. Claude M. Steiner, *The Other Side of Power* (New York: Grove Press, 1981), p. 182.
7. *Ibid.*, p. 183.
8. John Daly, "Listening and Interpersonal Evaluations" (Paper presented at the Central States Speech Convention, Kansas City, Missouri, March 1975), pp. 1–2.
9. Cal W. Downs, Paul Smeyak, and Ernest Martin, *Professional Interviewing* (New York: Harper and Row, 1980), pp. 79–80.
10. Charles J. Stewart and William B. Cash, *Interviewing* manuscript for 4th ed. (Dubuque, Iowa: Wm. C. Brown Company Publishers).
11. *Ibid.*
12. S. I. Hayakawa, "How to Attend a Conference," *ETC* 3 (Autumn 1955): 5.
13. Harold A. Brack, "Listening—A New Priority in Small Group Process" (Urbana, Illinois: ERIC Clearinghouse on Reading and Communication Skills), p. 4.
14. Adapted from John Dewey, *How We Think* (Boston: D.C. Heath Company, 1910), pp. 68–78.
15. Ernest B. Bormann and Nancy C. Bormann, *Effective Small Group Communication* (Minneapolis: Burgess Publishing Company, 1976), pp. 27–28.
16. Charles Kelly, "Empathic Listening," in *Small Group Communication: A Reader,* eds. Robert S. Cathcart and Larry S. Samovar (Dubuque, Iowa: William C. Brown Company Publishers, 1970), pp. 257–258.
17. "The ABC's of Audio-Video Teleconferencing: Coming to Terms with 'Satellite Speak,' " *Meeting News,* December 1982, pp. 44, 45, 61.
18. Susan Crystal, "Marriott Hooks Up 15–City Teleconferencing Network," *Meeting News,* September 1982, p. 5.
19. Alphone Chapanis and C. M. Overbey, "Studies in Interactive Communication: III. Effects of Similar and Dissimilar Communication Channels and Two Interchange Options on Team Problem Solving," *Perceptual and Motor Skills* (Monograph Supplement 2–V38, 1974), p. 373.
20. Peter D. Pagerey and Alphone Chapanis, "Communication Control and Leadership in Telecommunications by Small Groups," *Behaviour and Information Technology,* 2 (1983), p. 180.
21. Mona Bergen, "Hotel Chains Dish out Satellite Services with More Frequency," *Meeting News,* December 1982, p. 61.
22. Herbert Kupferberg, "The Audience," *Stagebill,* July 1980, p. 20.
23. H. L. Hollingworth, *The Psychology of the Audience* (New York: American Book Company, 1935), pp. 19–35.

24. Paul D. Holtzman, *The Psychology of Speakers' Audiences* (Glenview, Illinois: Scott Foresman, 1970), pp. 118–119.
25. *Ibid.*, p. 25.
26. John E. Baird, Jr., "Getting the Most Out of Seminars: Listening by Objectives," *IEEE Transactions on Professional Communication,* PC-24 (December 1981): 190.
27. James R. Andrews, *Essentials of Public Communication* (New York: John Wiley and Sons, 1979), p. 34.
28. *Ibid.*, pp. 34–36.
29. Christy Marshall, "Ad Spending Seen Climbing 13.8%," *Advertising Age,* December 19, 1983, pp. 3, 56.
30. Robert C. Gross, Wallace H. Wallace, and Wayne G. Robertshaw, "The 'NOLAD' Concept," *Journal of Advertising Research* 23 (February/March 1983): 47.
31. *Ibid.*
32. Tony Schwartz, "Listen," *TV Guide,* February 24, 1979, pp. 5–7.
33. A. C. Nielson Company, *1983 Nielson Report on Television* (New York: A. C. Nielson Company, 1983), p. 3.
34. *Ibid.*, p. 15.
35. George Gerbner et al., "The 'Mainstreaming' of America: Violence Profile No. 11," *Journal of Communication* 30 (Summer 1980): 13.
36. *Ibid.* p. 14.
37. Ben Stein, *The View from Sunset Boulevard* (New York: Basic Books, 1979).
38. Linda S. Lichter and S. Robert Lichter, *Prime Time Crime* (Washington, D.C.: The Media Institute, 1983), p. 60.
39. *Crooks, Conmen and Clowns: Businessmen in TV Entertainment* (Washington D.C.: The Media Institute, 1981).
40. Edward Cornish, "Do We Need a Department of Play?" (Speech presented at the World Future Society Conference on Working Now and in the Future, July, 1983), reprinted in *Vital Speeches of the Day* 49 (September 15, 1983): 725.
41. Louis Harris, "Confidence in Institutions Rises Slightly," (New York: The Harris Survey, 1983), p. 2.
42. Kathleen Hall Jamieson and Karlyn Kohrs Campbell, *The Interplay of Influence* (Belmont, California: Wadsworth, 1983), pp. 34–35.
43. James W. Carey, "The Communications Revolution and the Professional Communicator," in *The Sociology of Mass Media Communicators, The Sociological Review Monograph,* no. 13, ed, Paul Halmos (University of Keele, January 1969), p. 32.
44. "The Miscomprehension of Televised Communications" (Report by the Educational Foundation of the American Association of Advertising Agencies, New York, May 1980), p. 7.
45. "Television and Behavior" (Washington, D.C.: National Institute of Mental Health, 1982), vol. 1, p. 87.
46. J. A. Anderson and M. E. Ploghoft, *The Way We See It: A Handbook for Teacher Instruction in Critical Receivership* (Salt Lake City: Media Research Center, 1978).
47. Raymond S. Ross, *Speech Communication Fundamentals and Practice,* 6th ed. (Englewood Cliffs, New Jersey: Prentice-Hall, 1983), p. 22.

Afterword

At the outset of this book, we expressed our concern that the United States is a nation of non-listeners. This book, then, is an attempt to resolve what we perceive to be some of the problems which result from so little attention being devoted to listening skills in our communication transactions. It has been our purpose to provide the listener with a solid understanding of how he or she functions in the listening process. We have identified the major purposes of listening and the key factors which influence the way we listen. Furthermore, we have offered the listener a perspective on how we function in a variety of communication roles. Throughout our discussion, we have stressed that the listener must understand what he or she is doing in the process and that the listener must make intelligent decisions as to which listening strategies will facilitate effective listening at any given time within the communication transaction.

It should be evident at this point, then, that listening—like all of human communication—is a highly complex process, a process that requires a lifetime commitment to improving skills, attitudes, and behaviors on the part of the listening communicator. One unit on listening in a communication course, or even one complete semester in a listening course, cannot begin to provide the listener with all that is needed in order to be truly effective in the process. Rather, what we hope to provide is a solid foundation for the serious listener to develop an understanding of the process and a thorough awareness of how he or she does function as a listener. This understanding and awareness, combined with a sincere motivation to improve, should be a strong basis for making plans for continuing improvement.

But how does the listener know that he or she is charting the right course for listening improvement? We have provided you with extensive strategies for increasing your skill as a listener. And your listening instructor will have given you ample opportunity to practice these skills. In addition, standardized tests are available for follow-up assessment. Our students also find it useful to maintain journals in which they record listening experiences and chart their listening growth and development. Such a journal can be an effective vehicle for a comprehensive self-assessment of one's own listening growth at the end of formal listening instruction.

In a summary essay, one of our students concluded her journal by assessing her own strengths as a listener, identifying areas which she felt she still needed to improve, and highlighting what she still intended to do to build that improvement. The essay is illustrative of what you, as a listener, can do to formulate your own self-assessment.

One of the real benefits from this course for me has been the opportunity to examine and anaylyze my listening behaviors, which has added a dimension to my personal awareness. The knowledge that I have been utilizing some listening skills appropriately has been gratifying, while on the other hand, I see challenges ahead as I continue to learn and improve upon others. The opportunities for me to practice and apply these skills are endless—not only can I pursue them in my personal life, but also I foresee the personal benefits of this pursuit in my working relationships.

My immediate plans are to concentrate on my weakest listening behaviors, integrating the necessary skills/attitudes/habits into my daily interactions, so that I can become more accomplished.

Learning to ask clarifying questions is one particular area that I plan to improve upon. This is going to require a real effort on my part because I've always had a tendency to withhold questions for fear of appearing incompetent. However, since I've recently changed to a new career field, I find myself constantly in situations where I need to ask clarifying questions regarding my work. I see an opportunity here to begin work immediately on changing my old image of myself as incompetent to one of a sensible person utilizing questions to take care of my communication needs of the moment.

Putting a real effort into listening to the speaker rather than using my time to formulate my response is another specific area I am working on. Reaching the point of becoming more accepting of myself, I find the need to "impress" people has lessened for me somewhat, and I feel more free to let go of this behavior. My plans are to remain on guard for any recurrence of this and to keep my focus and mind on the speaker/speaker's message. I have an excellent opportunity to practice what I'm preaching in my work situation with my supervisor. Since I've received my promotion, I'm feeling a little less confident about my abilities to handle my new job, and I constantly find myself needing to impress my boss with all the right answers, worded in just the right way. Therefore, in my daily contacts with him, I plan to spend my thinking time reviewing his ideas and thoughts rather than planning my repsonse to him—I have a feeling that he'll appreciate it also!

Seeking out opportunities to gain experience in appreciative listening is another area which I plan to pursue. My excuse has always been that I never have the time, but now I want to make the time to enrich my life. I've observed the benefits derived from appreciative listening and have become more willing to let myself relax and enjoy. My plans for the future are to spend more time taking nature walks and listening to the sounds around me, attending concerts, continuing to sing in my church choir, and taking advantage of any new opportunities that will widen my listening experiences.

Finally, I've made a conscious decision to be on guard against falling back into some of my old inconsiderate listening behaviors at all listening levels—the discriminative, comprehensive, therapeutic, critical, and appreciative levels. I believe my consideration for others will always be the basis for my effectiveness as a listener. Along this same line, I plan to try and communicate to others the impact effective listening attitudes, skills, and behaviors has upon personal relationships. I may not be able to prevent any wars, but perhaps I can help mend a broken relationship or two![1]

Such self-assessment should characterize our listening behavior as communicators not only at the end of formal listening instruction but also throughout our lifetimes as listeners. As we continue to function as listeners, we should continue to grow and increase effectiveness in our communication transactions. This realization of our abilities as total communicators can help us to overcome our failure to listen and, hopefully, enable us to begin to achieve greater social priority for effective listening. Perhaps then we can be a nation of "people hearing *with* listening. . . ."

NOTES

1. Jeanne L. Rector, "Plans for Future Listening Improvement." Unpublished paper, College Park, Maryland: University of Maryland, 1981. Used by permission.

Bibliography

Anastasi, Thomas E., Jr. *Listen! Techniques for Improving Communication Skills*. Massachusetts: CBI Publishing Company, 1982.

Anastasi, Thomas E., Jr., and Dimond, Sidney A. *Listening on the Job*. Reading, Massachusetts: Addison-Wesley Publishing Company, 1972.

Banville, Thomas. *How to Listen, How to Be Heard*. Chicago: Nelson-Hall, 1978.

Barbara, Dominick. *The Art of Listening*. Springfield, Illinois: Charles C. Thomas, 1968.

———. *How to Make People Listen to You*. Springfield, Illinois: Charles C. Thomas, 1971.

Barker, Larry. *Listening Behavior*. Englewood Cliffs, New Jersey: Prentice-Hall, 1971.

Brammer, Lawrence M. *The Helping Relationship*. 2d rev. ed. Englewood Cliffs, New Jersey: Prentice-Hall, 1979.

Colburn, C. William, and Sanford B. Weinberg. *An Orientation to Listening and Audience Analysis*. Chicago: Science Research Associates, 1981.

Crable, Richard E. *Argumentation As Communication: Reasoning with Receivers*. Columbus, Ohio: Charles E. Merrill Company, 1976.

Duker, Sam. *Listening: Readings*. New York: The Scarecrow Press, 1966.

———. *Listening Bibliography*. Metuchen, New Jersey: The Scarecrow Press, 1968.

———. *Listening: Readings II*. Metuchen, New Jersey: The Scarecrow Press, 1971.

———. *Time-Compressed Speech: An Anthology and Bibliography in Three Volumes*. Metuchen, New Jersey: The Scarecrow Press, 1974.

Erway, Ella. *Listening: A Programmed Approach*. New York: McGraw-Hill, 1978.

Faber, Carl A. *On Listening*. California: Perseus Press, 1978.

Floyd, James J. *Listening A Practical Approach*. Glenview, Illinois: Scott, Foresman and Company, 1985.

Friedman, Paul G. *Listening Processes: Attention, Understanding, Evaluation*. 2d rev. ed. Washington, D.C.: National Education Association, 1983.

Gigous, Goldie M. *Improving Listening Skills*. Dansville, New York: Owen Publishing Corporation, 1967.

Girzaitis, Loretta. *Listening a Response Ability*. Winona, Minnesota: St. Mary's College Press, 1972.

Glatthorn, Allan A., and Adams, Herbert R. *Listening Your Way to Management Success*. Glenview, Illinois: Scott, Foresman, 1983.

Goss, Blaine. *Processing Communication*. Belmont, California: Wadsworth Publishing Company, 1982.

Hirsch, Robert O. *Listening: A Way to Process Information Aurally*. Dubuque, Iowa: Gorsuch Scarisbrick Publishers, 1979.

Howell, William S. *The Empathic Communicator*. Belmont, California: Wadsworth Publishing Company, 1982.

Jamieson, Kathleen Hall, and Campbell, Karlyn Kohrs. *The Interplay of Influence*. Belmont, California: Wadsworth Publishing Company, 1983.

Johnson, Wendell. *Your Most Enchanted Listener*. New York: Harper & Row, 1956.

Kerman, Joseph. *Listen.* 3d rev. ed. New York: Worth Publishing Company, 1980.
Koile, Earl. *Listening As a Way of Becoming.* Waco, Texas: Calibre Books, 1977.
Larson, Charles U. *Persuasion: Reception and Responsibility.* Belmont, California: Wadsworth Publishing Company, 1983.
Long, Lynette. *Listening/Responding.* Monterey, California: Brooks/Cole Publishing Company, 1978.
Lorayne, Harry, and Lucas, Jerry. *The Memory Book.* New York: Ballantine Books, 1974.
Lundsteen, Sara W. *Listening: Its Impact on Reading and the Other Language Arts.* Urbana, Illinois: ERIC Clearinghouse on the Teaching of English, 1979.
Maidment, Robert. *Tuning In.* Gretna, Louisiana: Pelican Publishing Company, 1984.
Mills, Ernest Parker. *Listening: Key to Communication.* New York: Petrocelli Books, 1974.
Montgomery, Robert L. *Listening Made Easy.* New York: AMACOM, 1981.
Moray, Neville. *Attention and Listening.* Baltimore: Penguin Books, 1969.
Morris, Jud. *The Art of Listening.* New York: Industrial Education Institute, 1968.
Newman, Robert P., and Newman, Dale R. *Evidence.* Boston: Houghton Mifflin Company, 1969.
Nichols, Ralph G., and Stevens, Leonard A. *Are You Listening?* New York: McGraw-Hill Book Company, 1957.
Reik, Theodor. *Listening with the Third Ear.* New York: Pyramid Books, 1948.
Schwartz, Tony. *Media: The Second God.* New York: Random Books, 1981.
———. *The Responsive Chord.* New York: Anchor Books, 1974.
Spearritt, Donald. *Listening Comprehension—A Factorial Analysis.* Melbourne, Australia: G.W. Green & Sons, 1962.
Steil, Lyman; Barker, Larry L.; and Watson, Kittie W. *Effective Listening Key to Your Success.* Reading, Massachusetts: Addison-Wesley Publishing Company, 1983.
Taylor, Stanford E. *Listening: What Research Says to the Teacher.* Washington, D.C.: National Education Association, 1973.
Weaver, Carl H. *Human Listening.* New York: Bobbs-Merrill Company, 1972.
Wolff, Florence I.; Marsnik, Nadine C.; Tacey, William S.; and Nichols, Ralph G. *Perceptive Listening.* New York: Holt, Rinehart and Winston, 1983.
Wolvin, Andrew D., and Coakley, Carolyn Gwynn. *Listening Instruction.* Urbana, Illinois: ERIC Clearinghouse on Reading and Communication Skills, 1979.

Index